A battle with

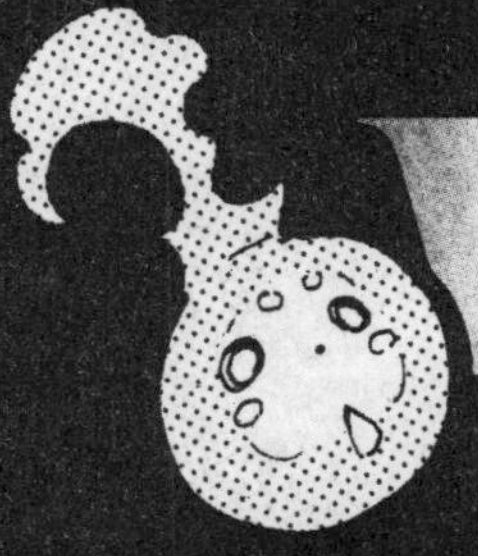

with

FIRE FORCE

FIRE FORCE 31

CONTENTS

CHAPTER CCLXVIII:
THE KNIGHT KING'S BATTLE ACCOUTERMENTS

Arthur equips the Star Ring.

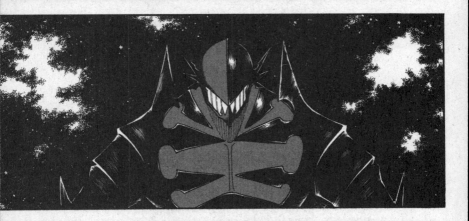

A Dragon appears!

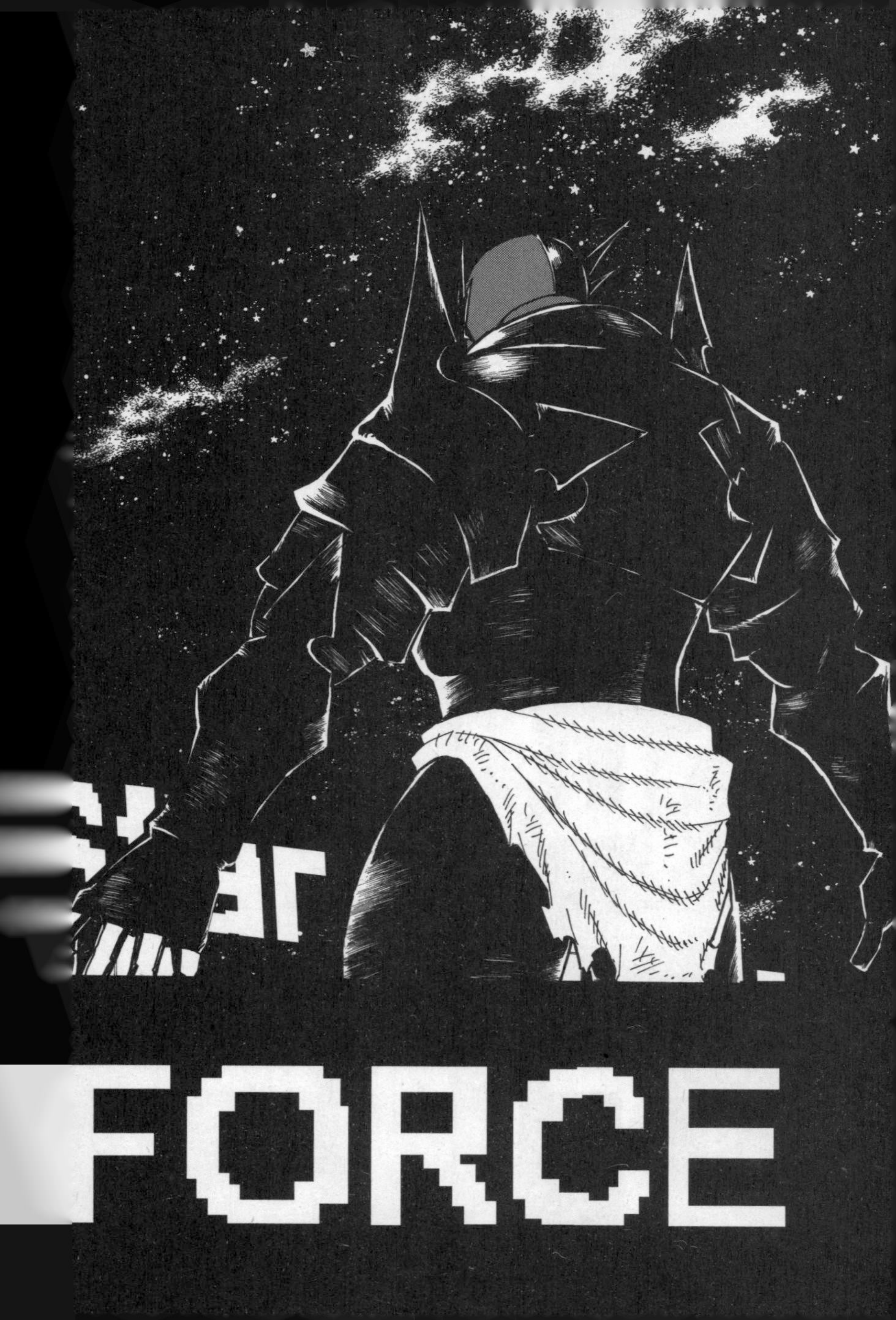
FORCE

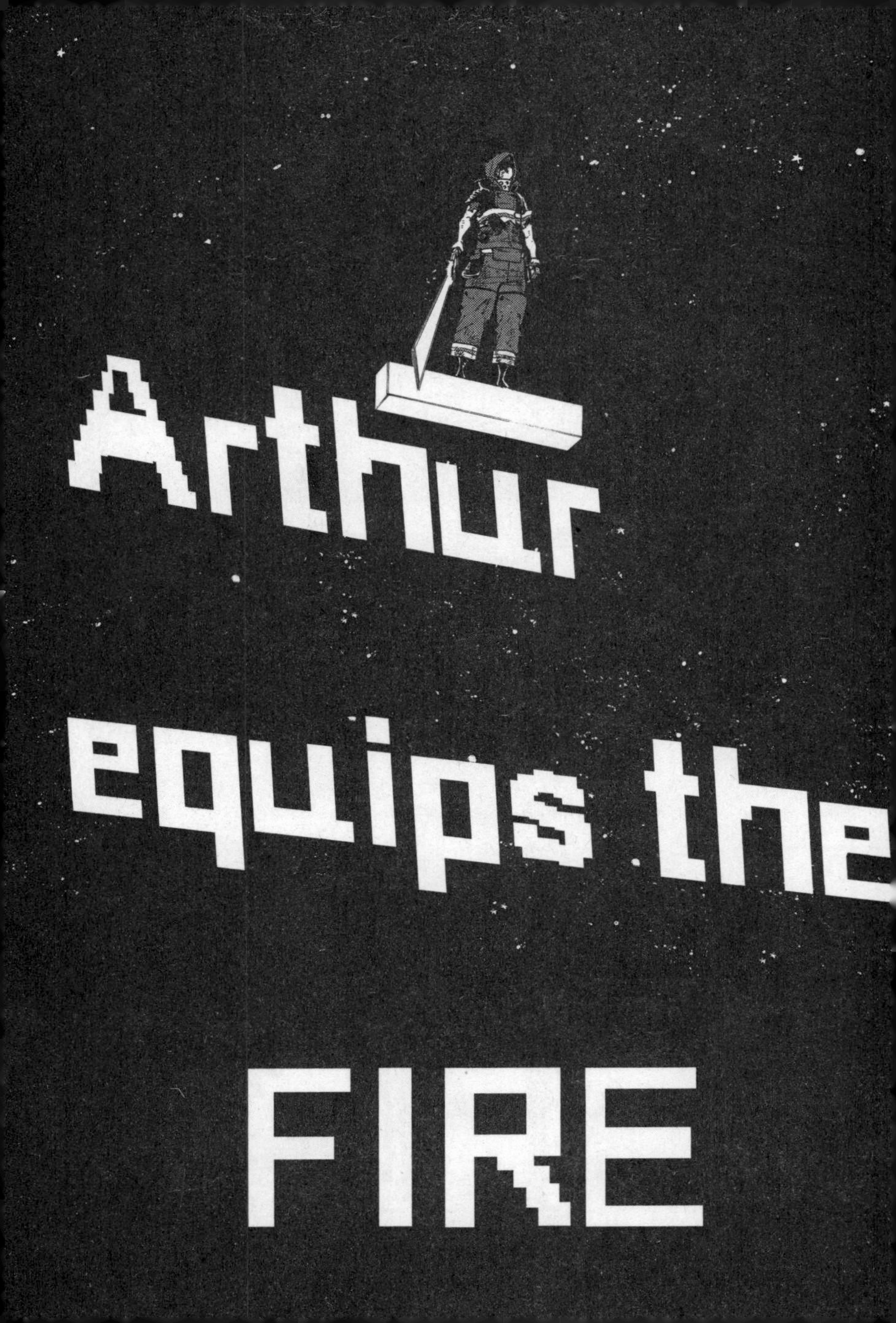
Arthur
equips the
FIRE

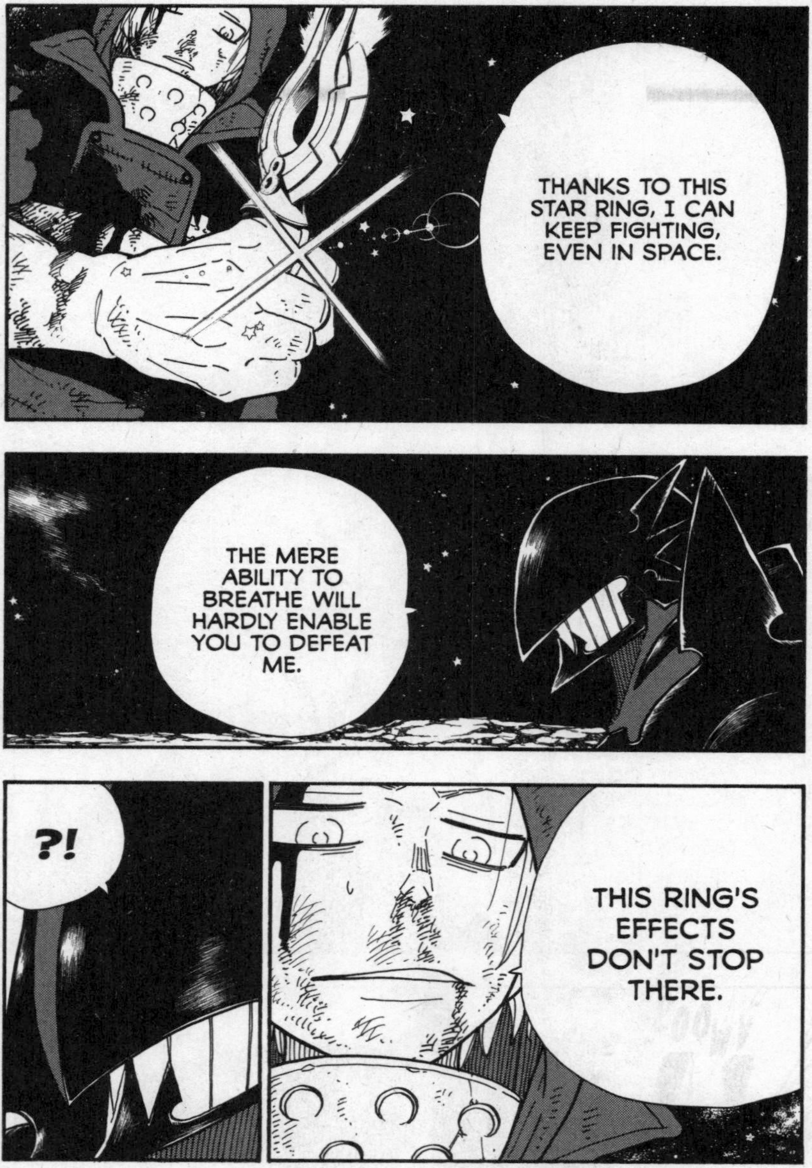
THANKS TO THIS STAR RING, I CAN KEEP FIGHTING, EVEN IN SPACE.
THE MERE ABILITY TO BREATHE WILL HARDLY ENABLE YOU TO DEFEAT ME.
THIS RING'S EFFECTS DON'T STOP THERE.
?!

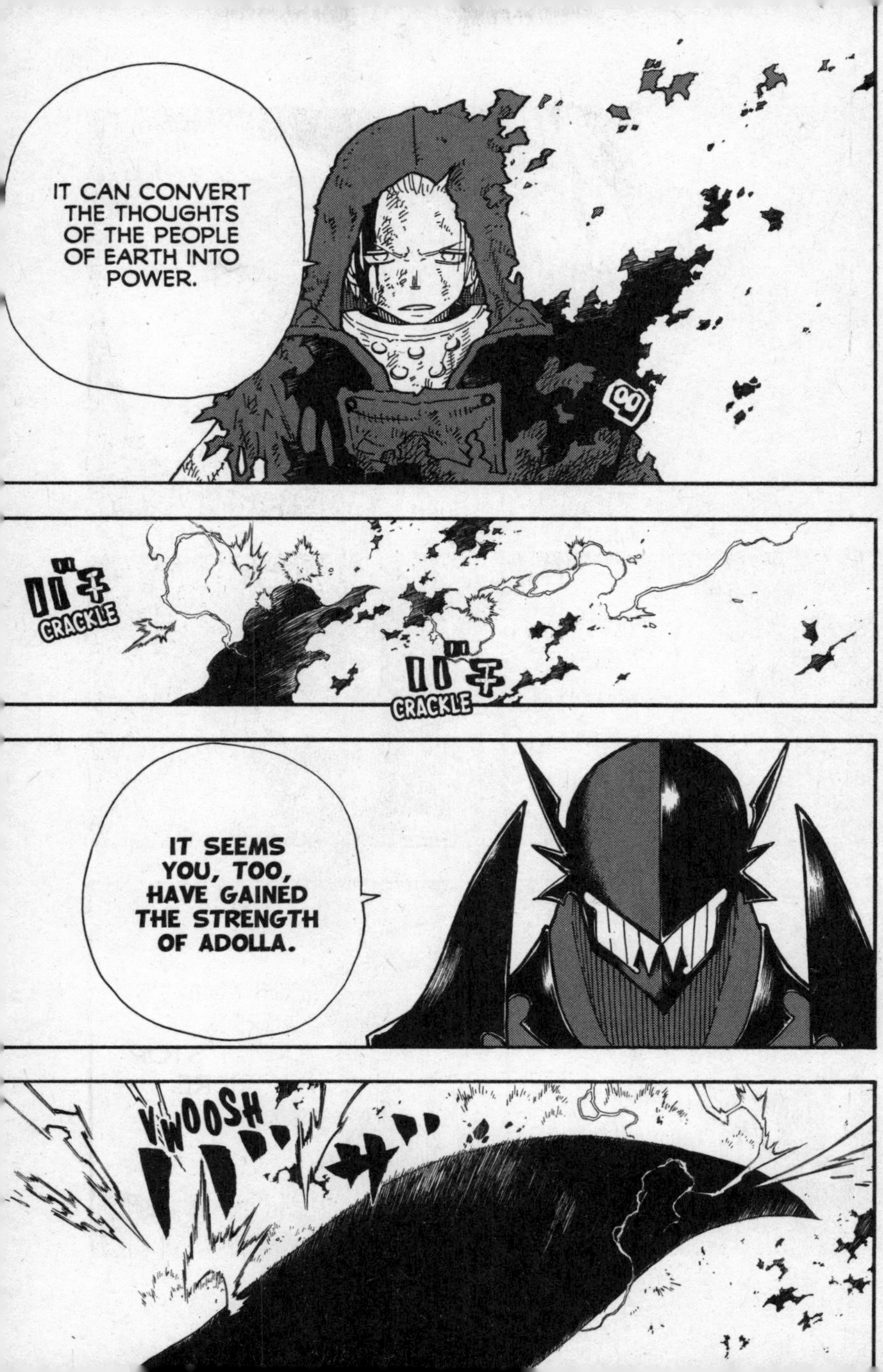
IT CAN CONVERT THE THOUGHTS OF THE PEOPLE OF EARTH INTO POWER.
CRACKLE
CRACKLE
IT SEEMS YOU, TOO, HAVE GAINED THE STRENGTH OF ADOLLA.
VWOOSH

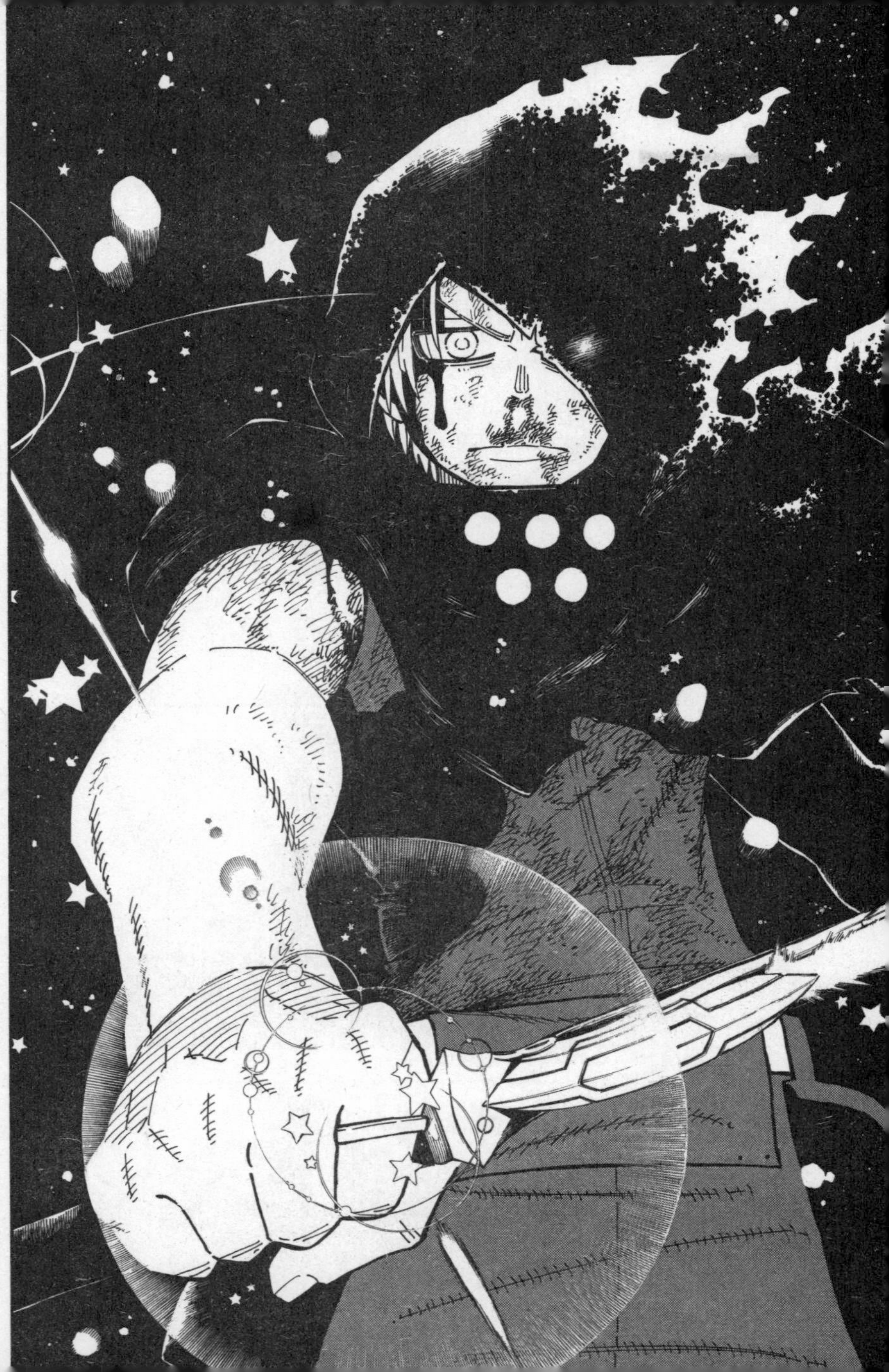

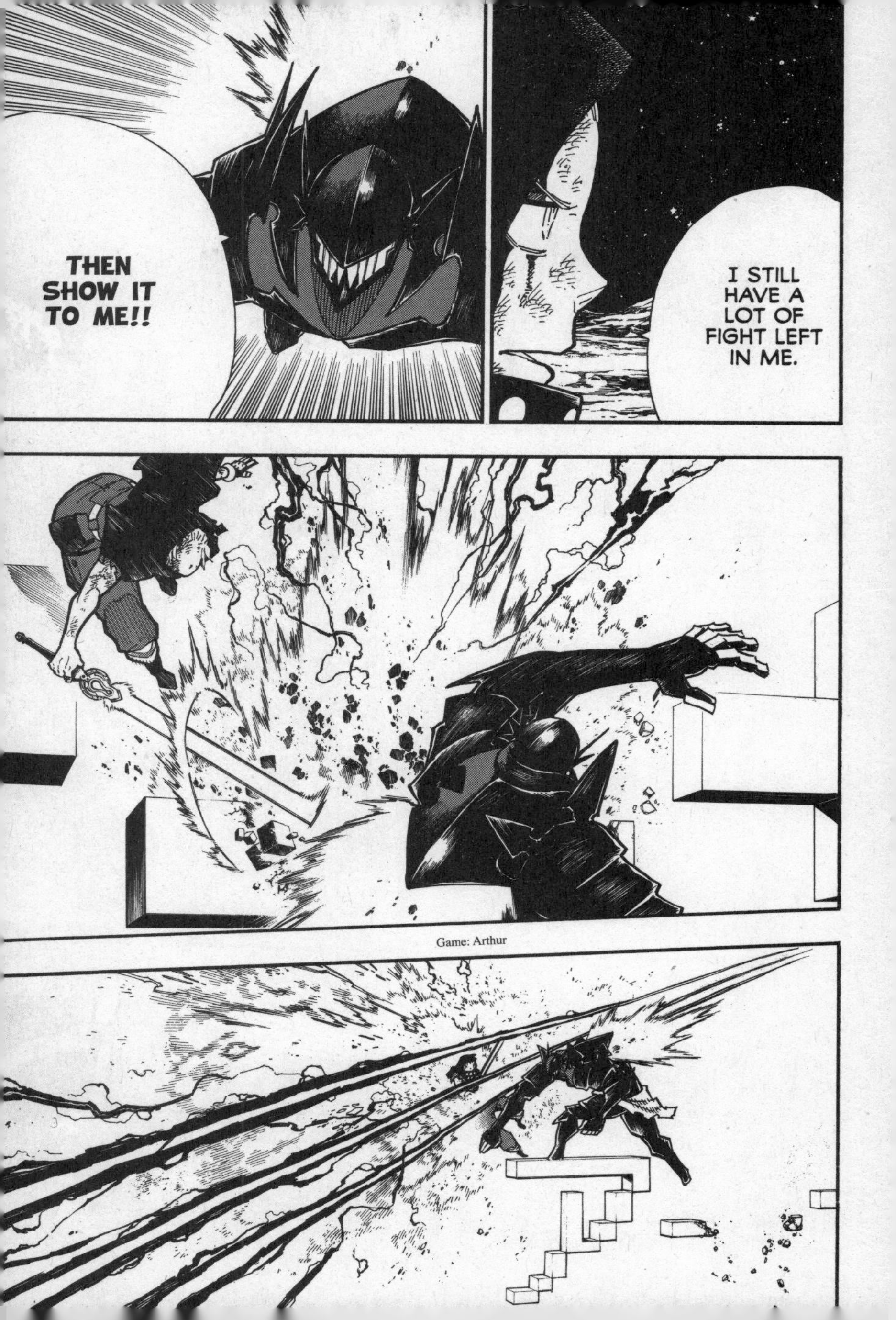
I STILL HAVE A LOT OF FIGHT LEFT IN ME.
THEN SHOW IT TO ME!!
Game: Arthur

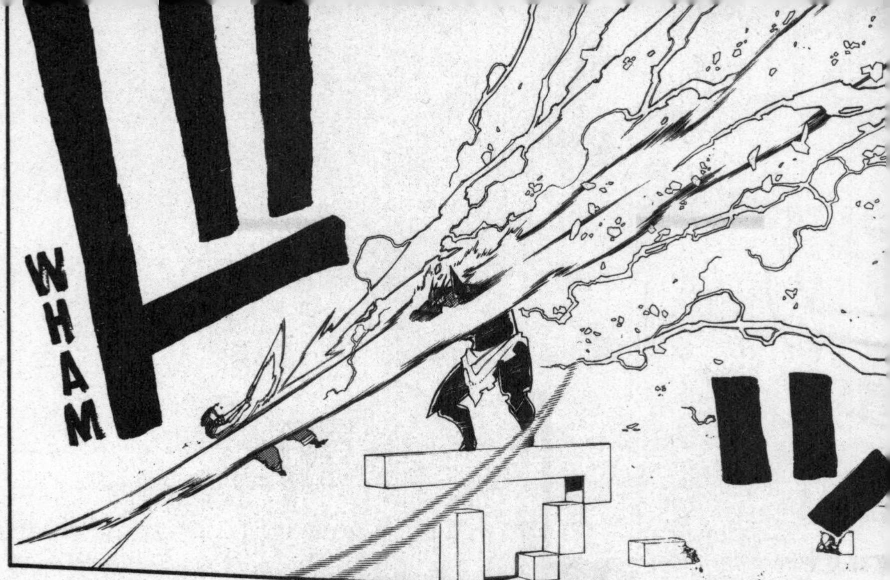
WHAM

Game: Arthur

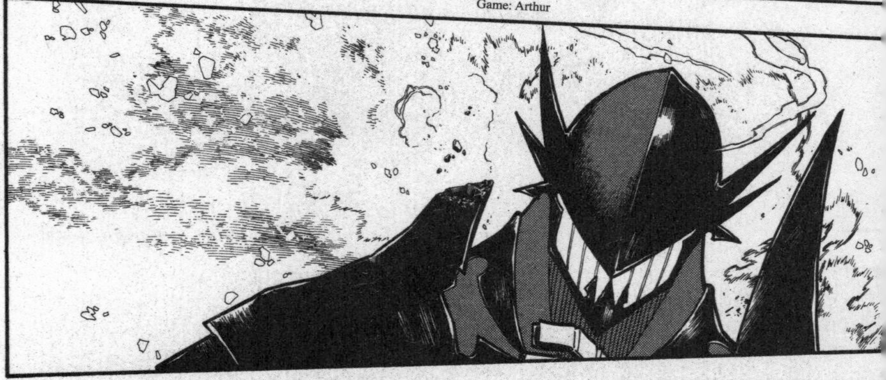

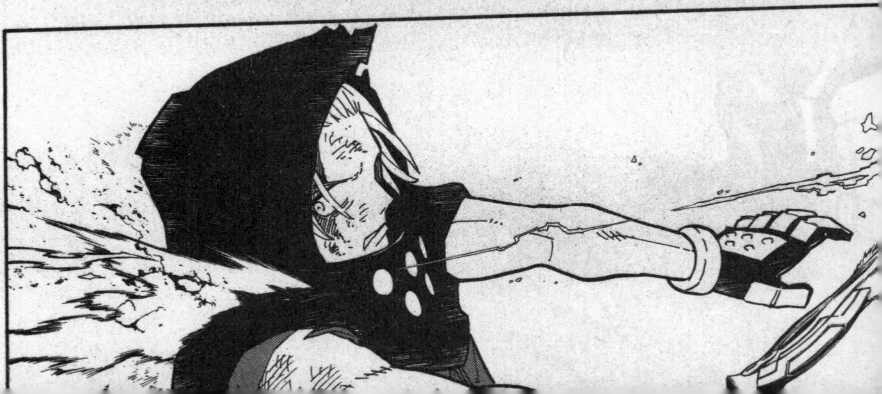

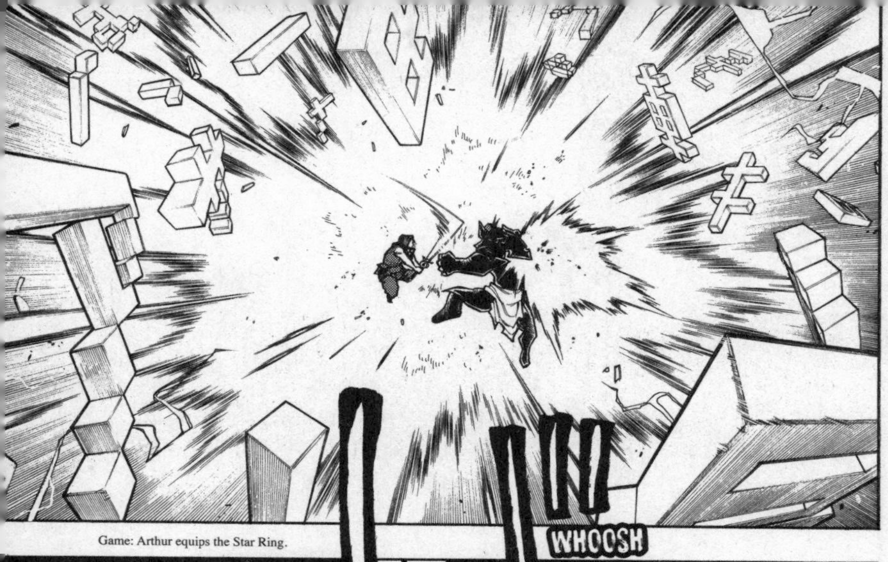
WHOOSH
Game: Arthur equips the Star Ring.

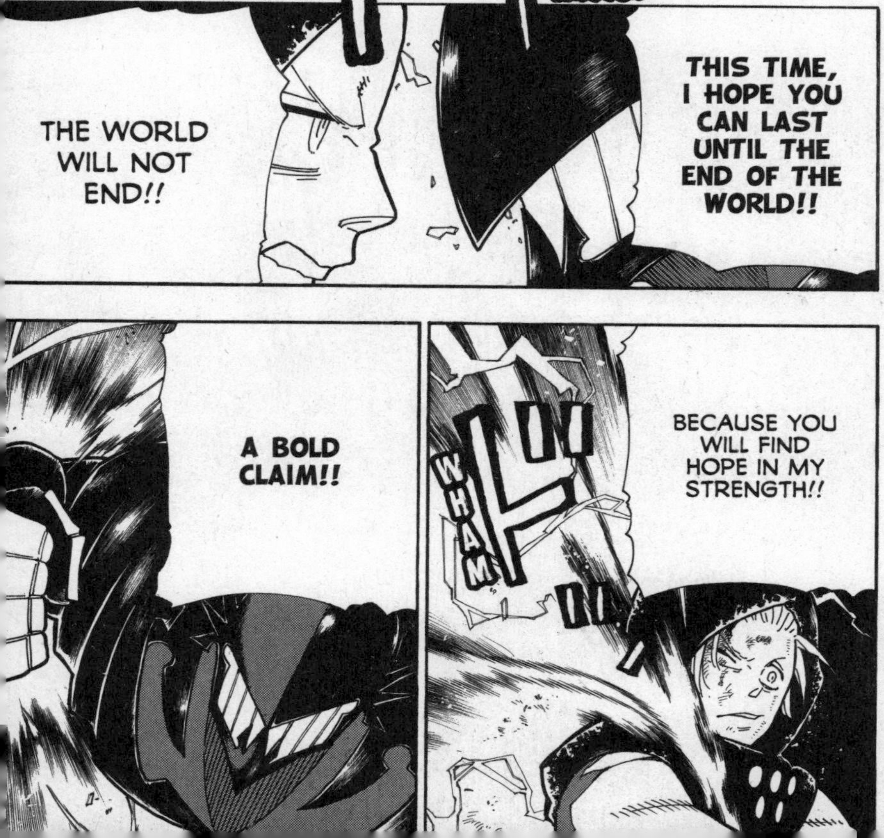
THIS TIME, I HOPE YOU CAN LAST UNTIL THE END OF THE WORLD!!
THE WORLD WILL NOT END!!
WHAM
BECAUSE YOU WILL FIND HOPE IN MY STRENGTH!!
A BOLD CLAIM!!

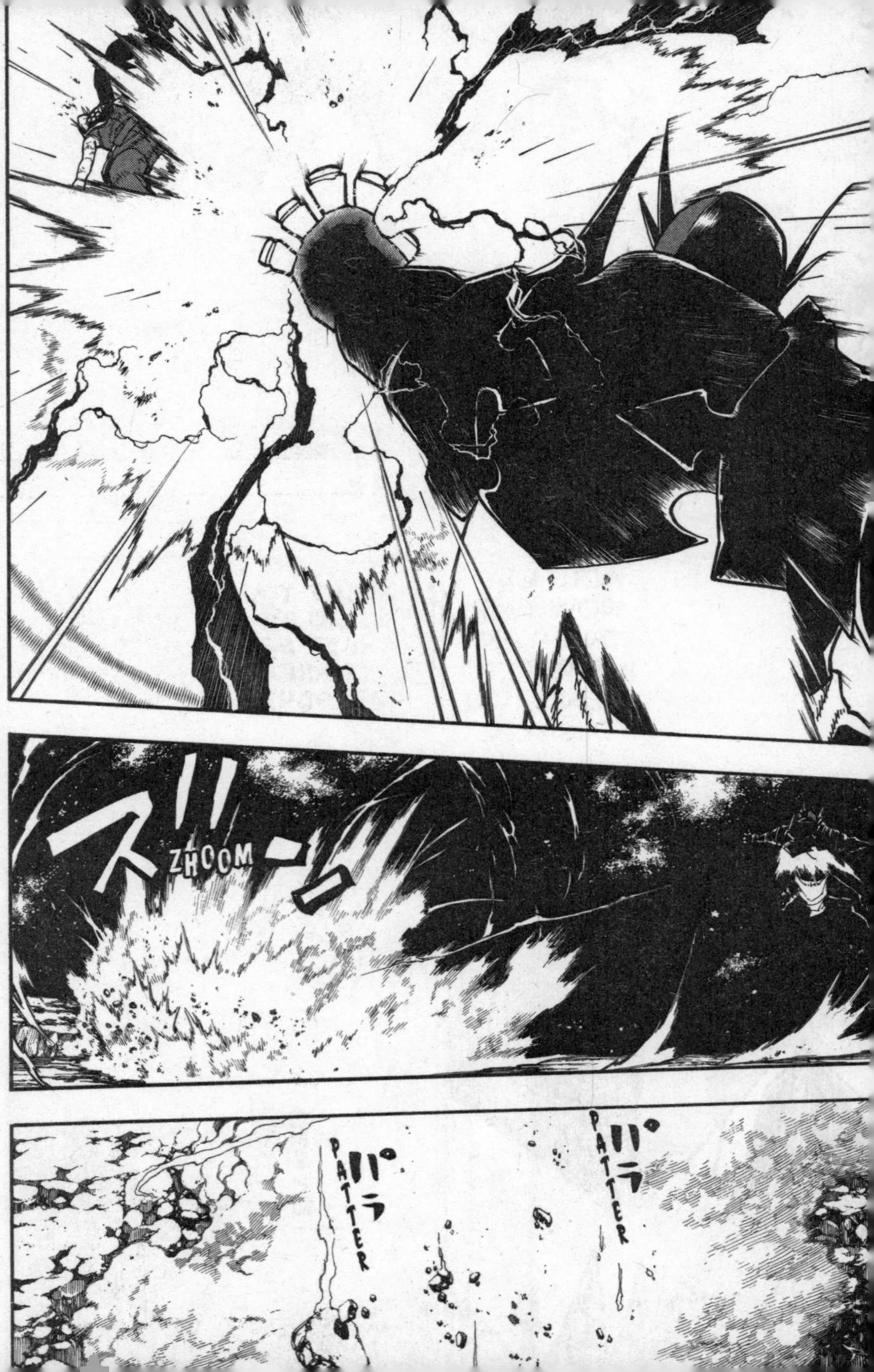
ZHOOM
パラ
PATTER
パラ
PATTER

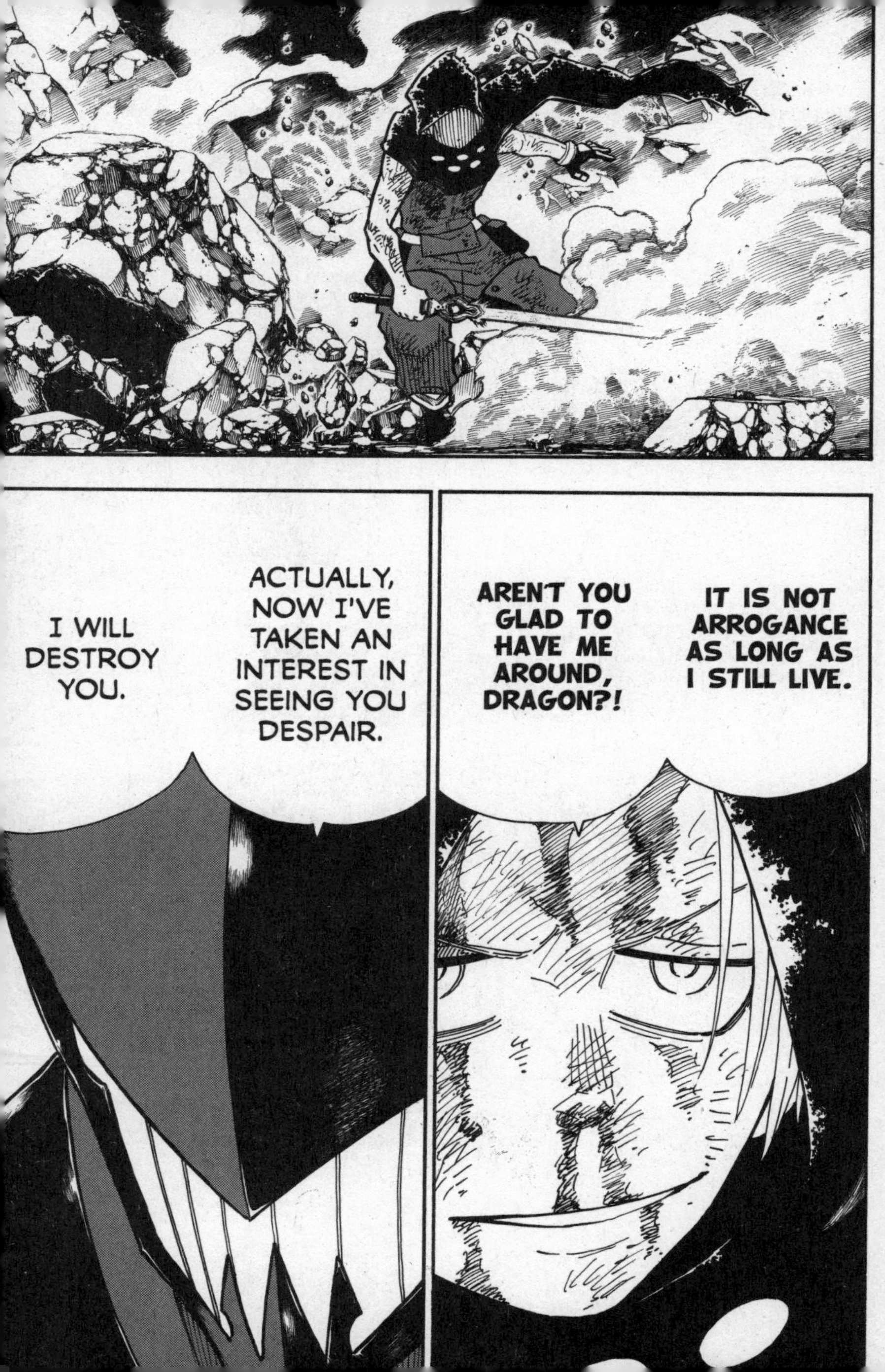
IT IS NOT ARROGANCE AS LONG AS I STILL LIVE.
AREN'T YOU GLAD TO HAVE ME AROUND, DRAGON?!
ACTUALLY, NOW I'VE TAKEN AN INTEREST IN SEEING YOU DESPAIR.
I WILL DESTROY YOU.

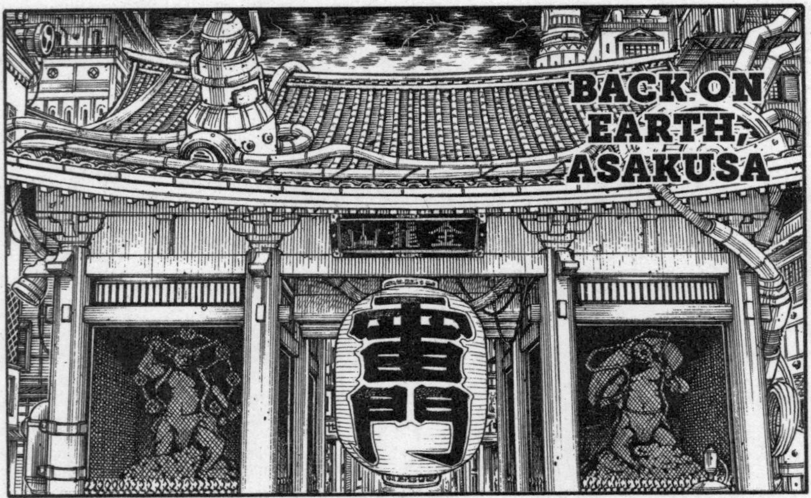
BACK ON EARTH, ASAKUSA

Temple: Kinryūzan
Lantern: Kaminarimon

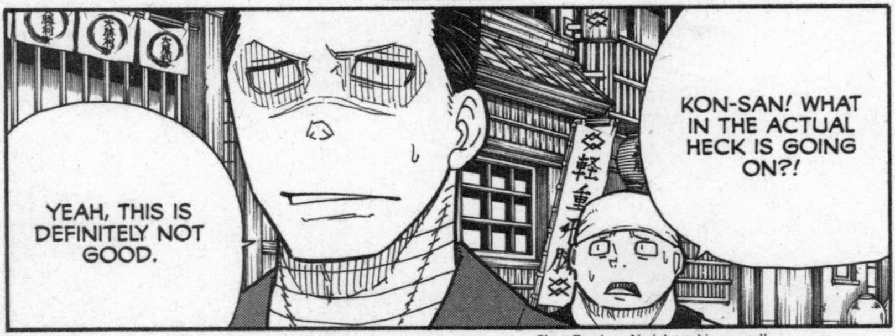
KON-SAN! WHAT IN THE ACTUAL HECK IS GOING ON?!
YEAH, THIS IS DEFINITELY NOT GOOD.

Sign: Courier—No job too big or small

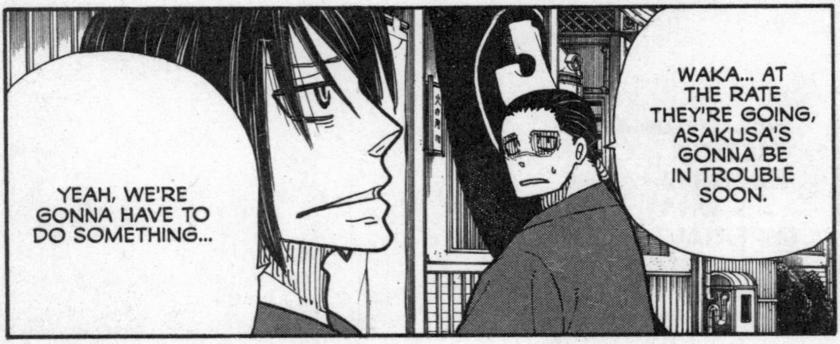
WAKA... AT THE RATE THEY'RE GOING, ASAKUSA'S GONNA BE IN TROUBLE SOON.
YEAH, WE'RE GONNA HAVE TO DO SOMETHING...

I HEARD THOSE "DOPPELGANGERS" ARE POPPING UP OUTSIDE OF ASAKUSA.
SO WHAT HAPPENED WITH THE OLD BOSS IS HAPPENING EVERYWHERE.
LUCKY FOR US, THERE AREN'T ANY IN ASAKUSA. WONDER WHY THAT IS...
...
BECAUSE WHAT ASAKUSANS SEE WHEN THEY PICTURE DEATH ISN'T THE SAME AS WHAT THE IMPERIALS SEE...

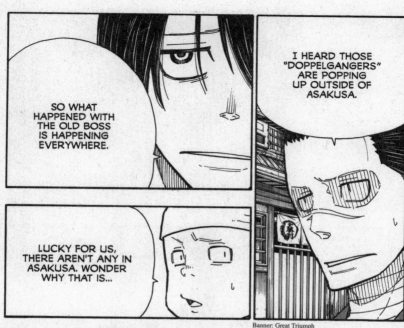

Banner: Great Triumph

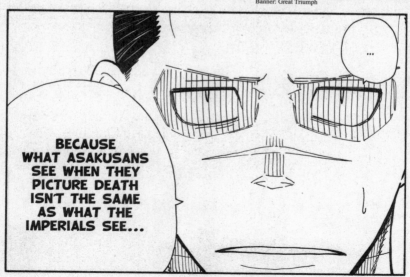

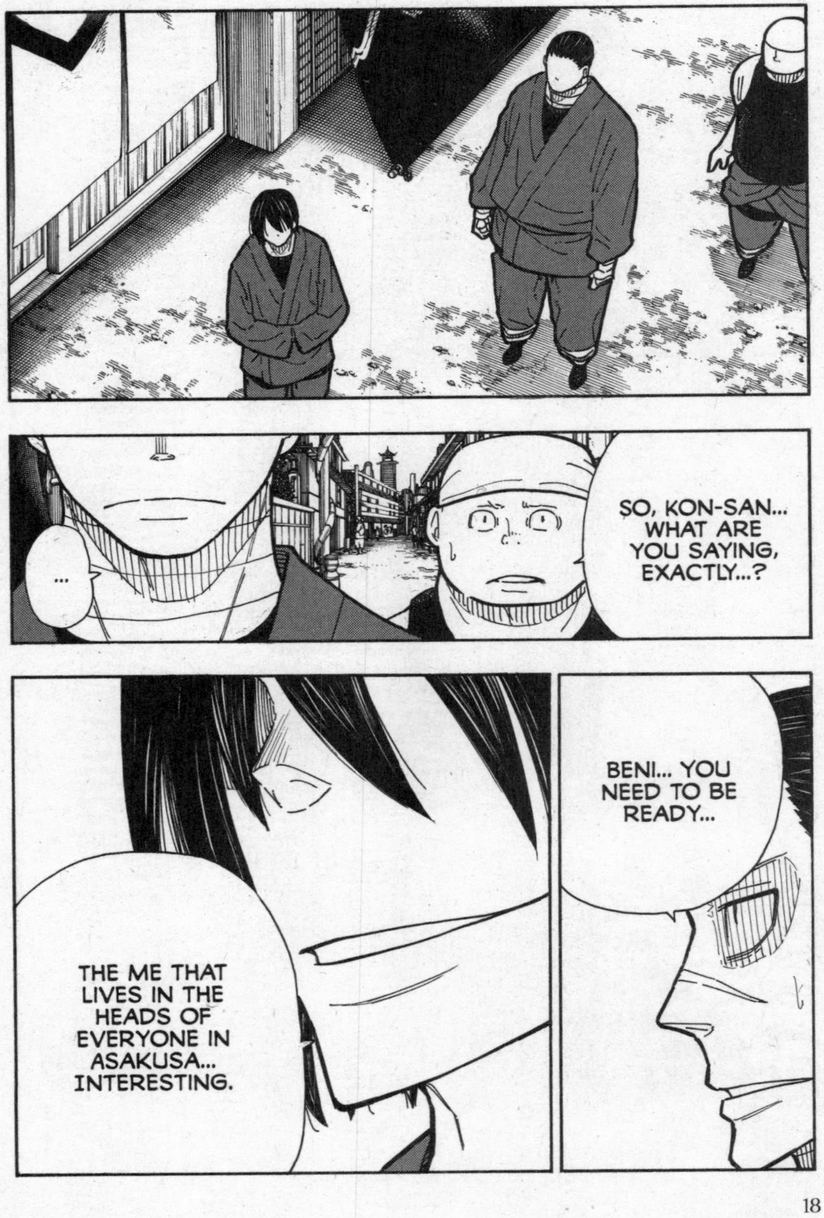
SO, KON-SAN... WHAT ARE YOU SAYING, EXACTLY...?
...
BENI... YOU NEED TO BE READY...
THE ME THAT LIVES IN THE HEADS OF EVERYONE IN ASAKUSA... INTERESTING.

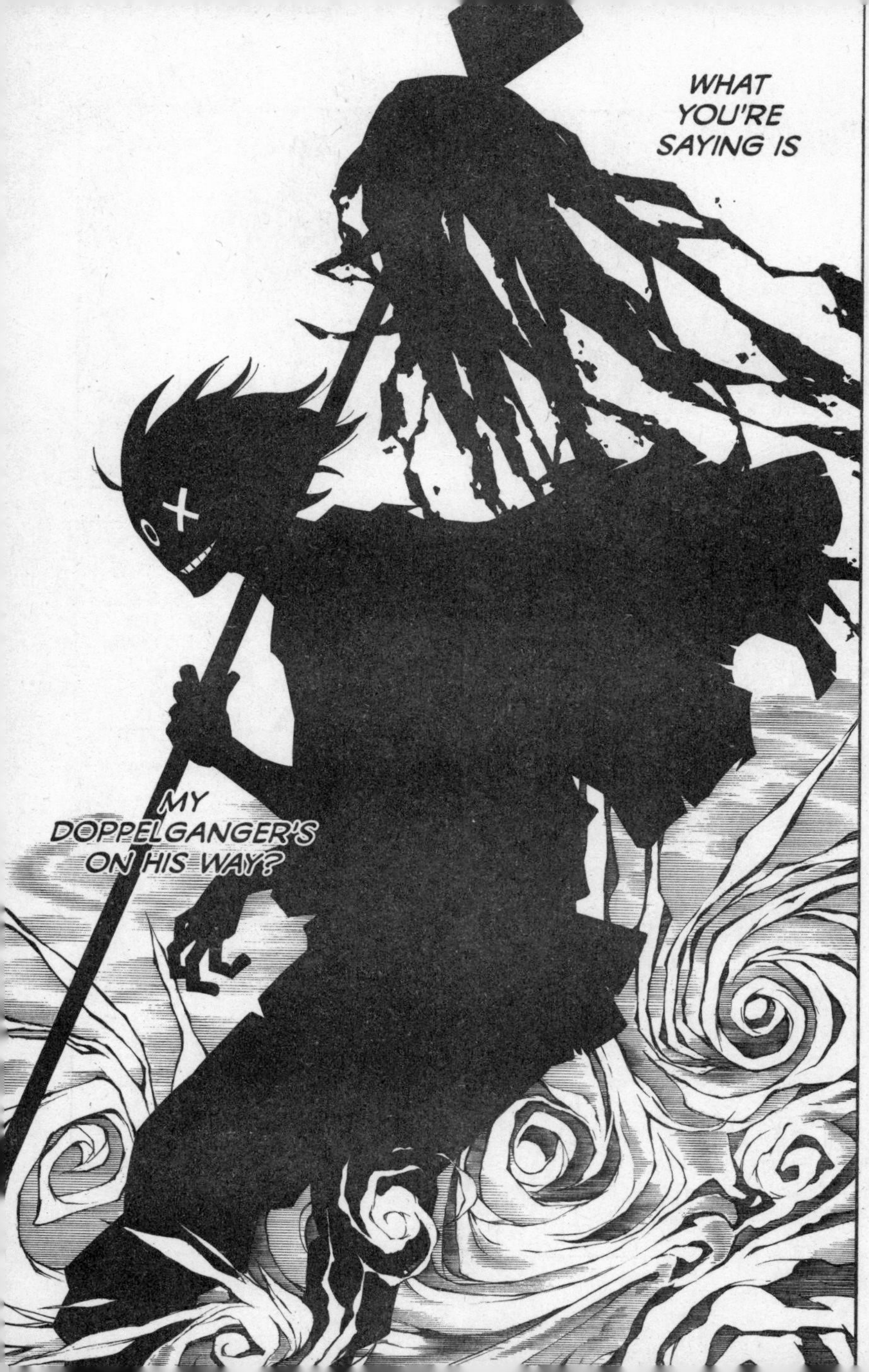
WHAT YOU'RE SAYING IS
MY DOPPELGANGER'S ON HIS WAY?

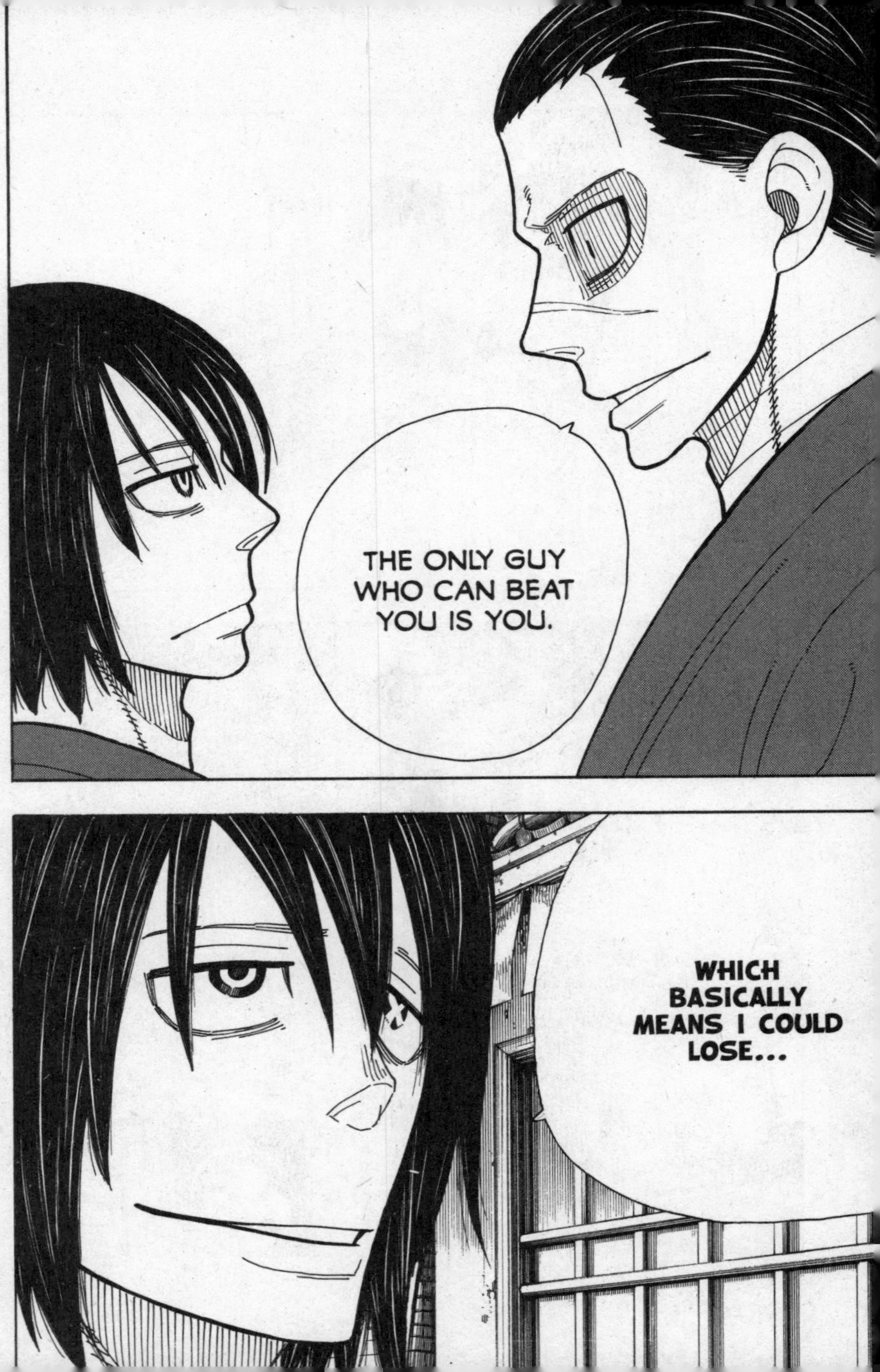
THE ONLY GUY WHO CAN BEAT YOU IS YOU.
WHICH BASICALLY MEANS I COULD LOSE...

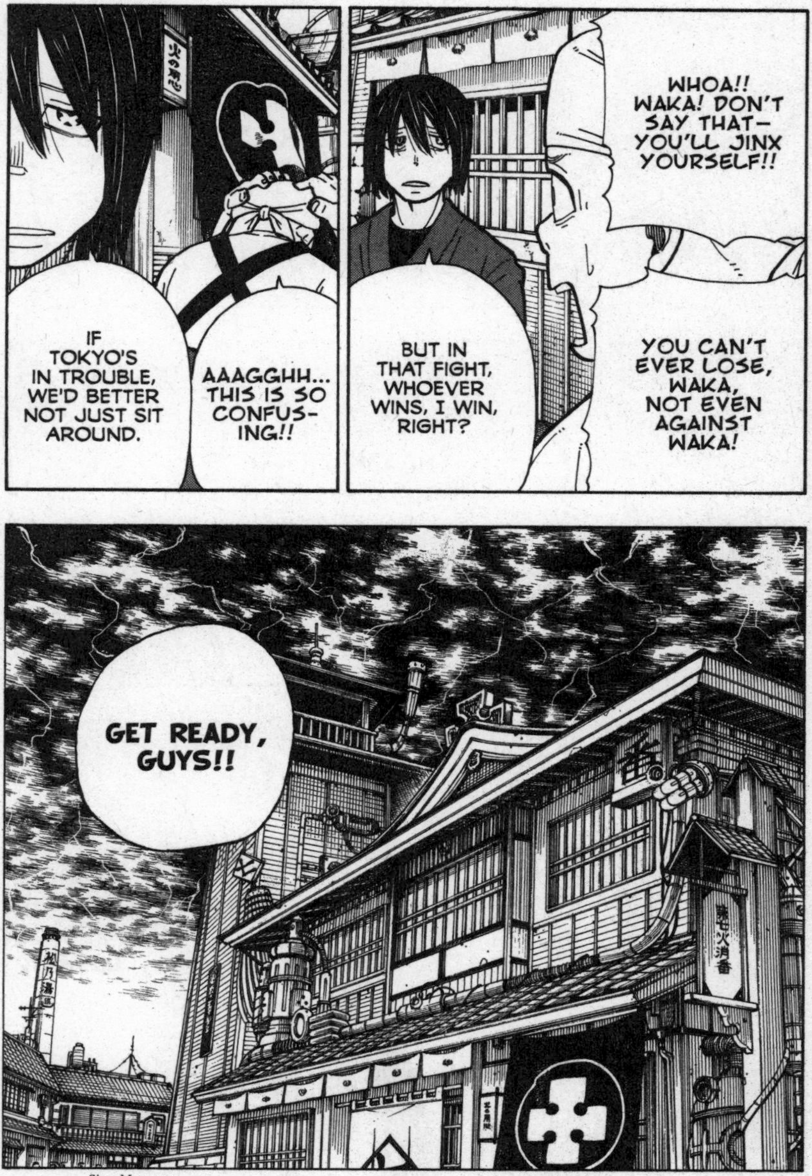
BUT IN THAT FIGHT, WHOEVER WINS, I WIN, RIGHT?
WHOA!! WAKA! DON'T SAY THAT— YOU'LL JINX YOURSELF!!
YOU CAN'T EVER LOSE, WAKA, NOT EVEN AGAINST WAKA!
AAAGGHH... THIS IS SO CONFUS-ING!!
IF TOKYO'S IN TROUBLE, WE'D BETTER NOT JUST SIT AROUND.
GET READY, GUYS!!

Sign: Guardhouse
Sign: Special Fire Guardhouse 7
Sign: Practice Fire Safety

Sign: Matsunoyu
Sign: 7

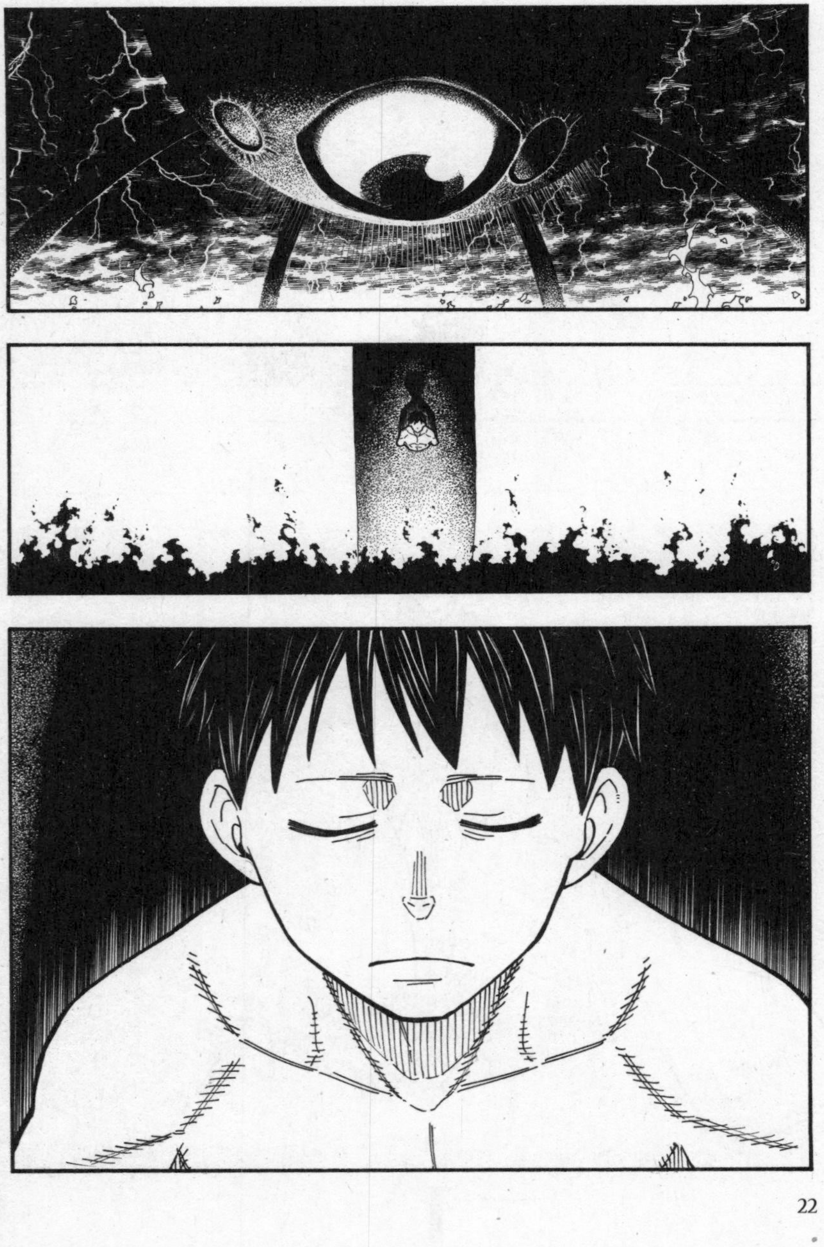

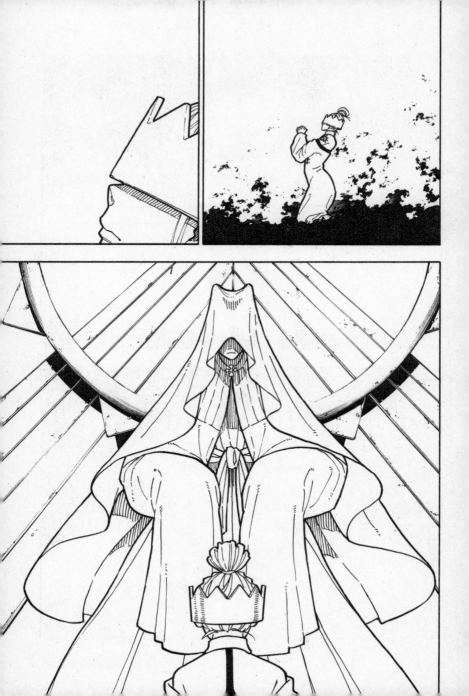

FIRE FORCE

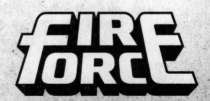

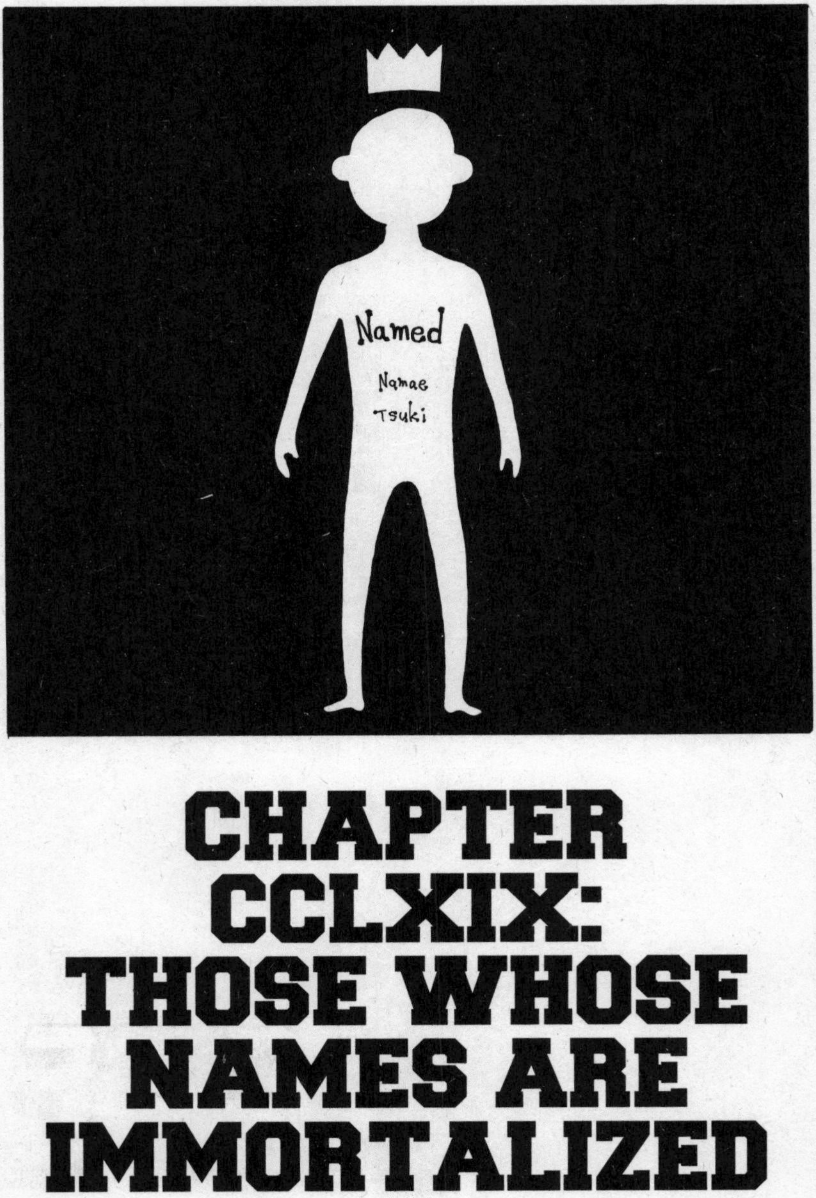
Named
Namae
Tsuki

CHAPTER CCLXIX: THOSE WHOSE NAMES ARE IMMORTALIZED

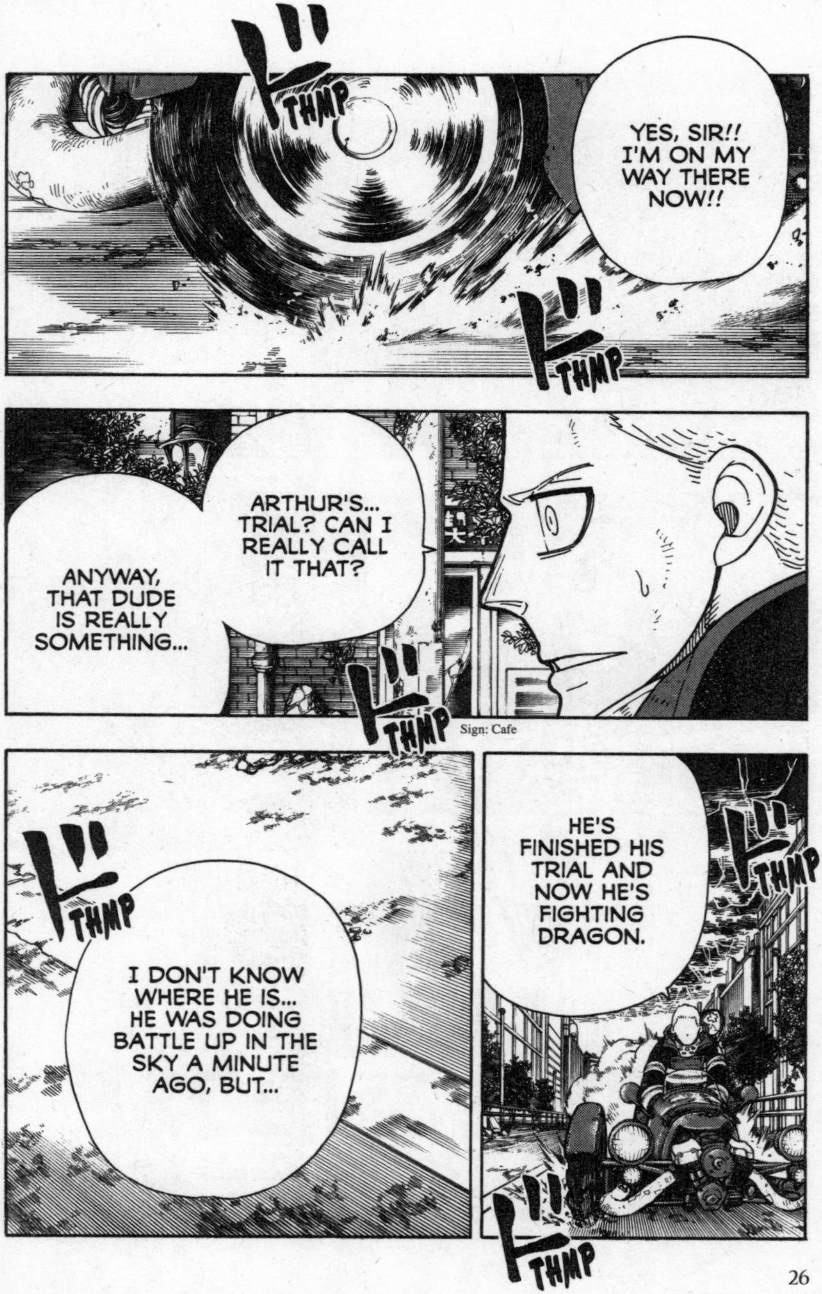
THMP
YES, SIR!! I'M ON MY WAY THERE NOW!!
THMP
ARTHUR'S... TRIAL? CAN I REALLY CALL IT THAT?
ANYWAY, THAT DUDE IS REALLY SOMETHING...
THMP
HE'S FINISHED HIS TRIAL AND NOW HE'S FIGHTING DRAGON.
THMP
THMP
I DON'T KNOW WHERE HE IS... HE WAS DOING BATTLE UP IN THE SKY A MINUTE AGO, BUT...
THMP
Sign: Cafe

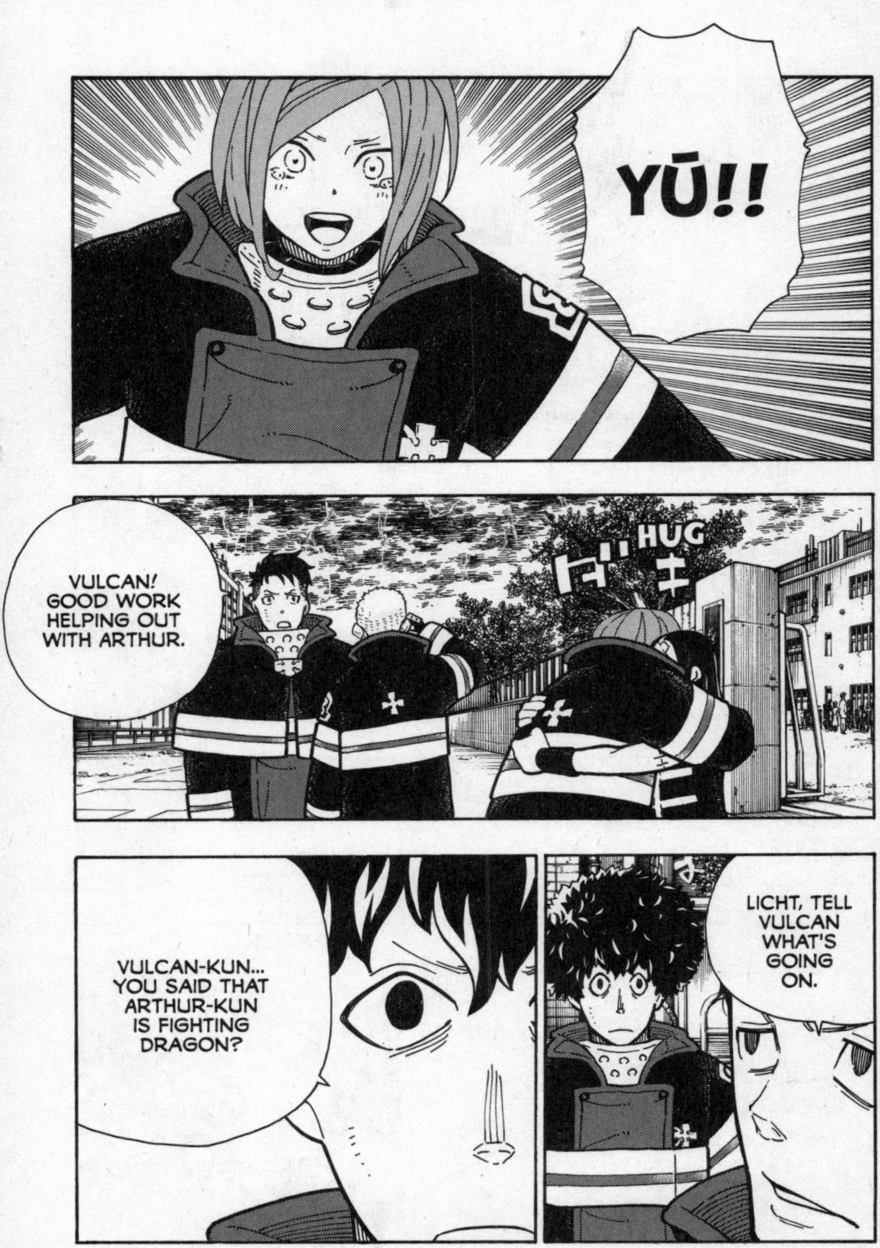
YŪ!!
HUG
VULCAN! GOOD WORK HELPING OUT WITH ARTHUR.
LICHT, TELL VULCAN WHAT'S GOING ON.
VULCAN-KUN... YOU SAID THAT ARTHUR-KUN IS FIGHTING DRAGON?

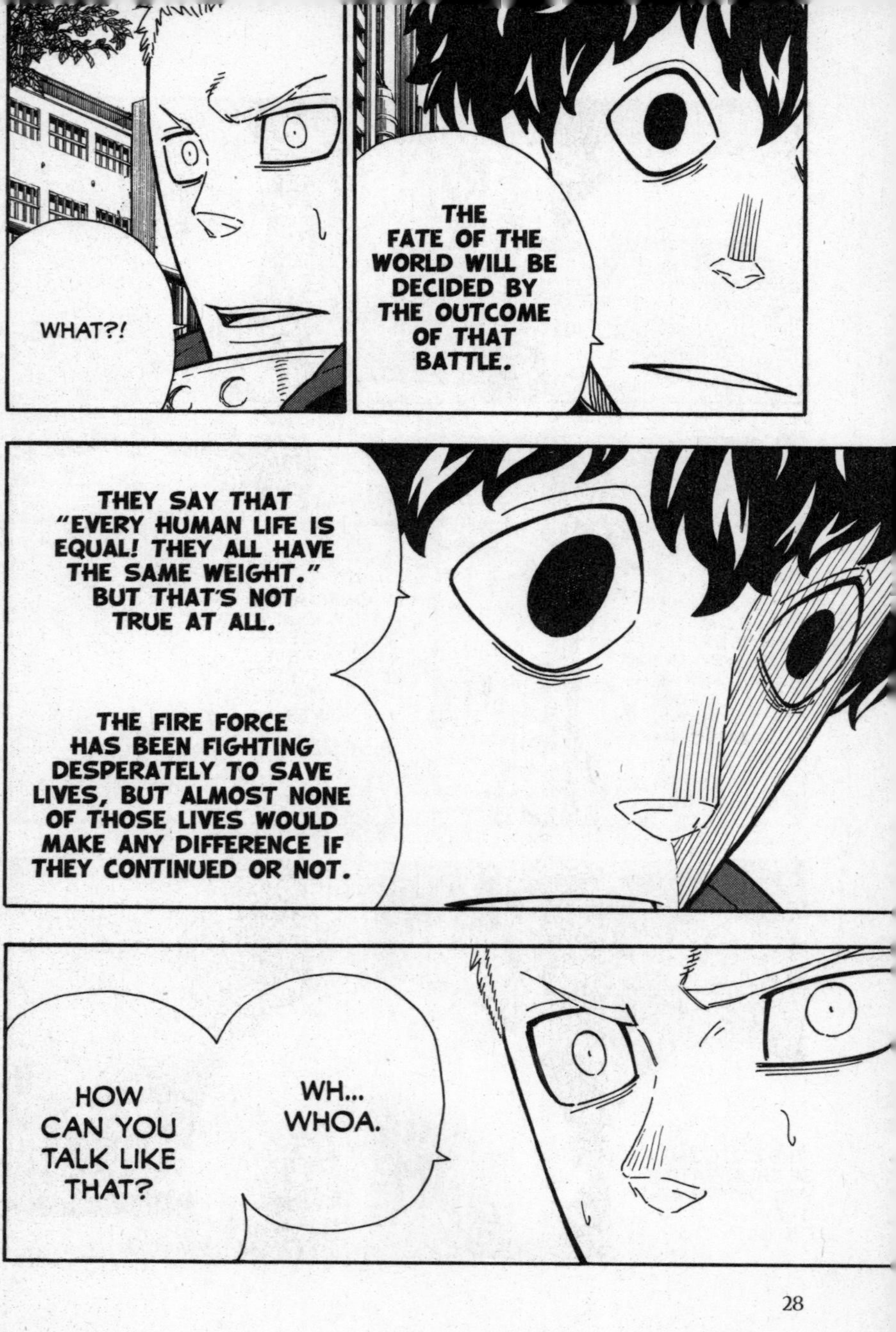
THE FATE OF THE WORLD WILL BE DECIDED BY THE OUTCOME OF THAT BATTLE.
WHAT?!
THEY SAY THAT "EVERY HUMAN LIFE IS EQUAL! THEY ALL HAVE THE SAME WEIGHT." BUT THAT'S NOT TRUE AT ALL.
THE FIRE FORCE HAS BEEN FIGHTING DESPERATELY TO SAVE LIVES, BUT ALMOST NONE OF THOSE LIVES WOULD MAKE ANY DIFFERENCE IF THEY CONTINUED OR NOT.
WH... WHOA.
HOW CAN YOU TALK LIKE THAT?

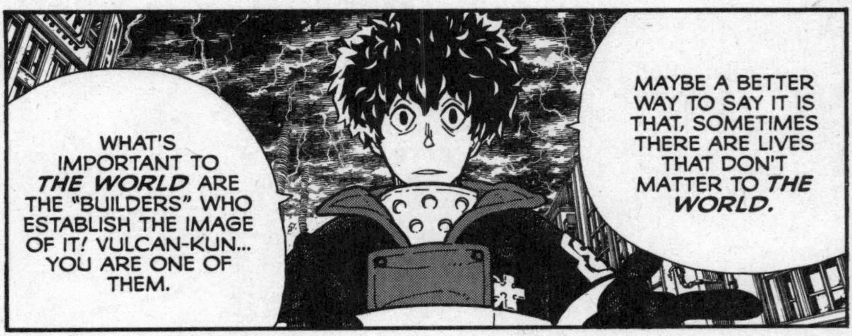
MAYBE A BETTER WAY TO SAY IT IS THAT, SOMETIMES THERE ARE LIVES THAT DON'T MATTER TO *THE WORLD.*
WHAT'S IMPORTANT TO *THE WORLD* ARE THE "BUILDERS" WHO ESTABLISH THE IMAGE OF IT! VULCAN-KUN... YOU ARE ONE OF THEM.

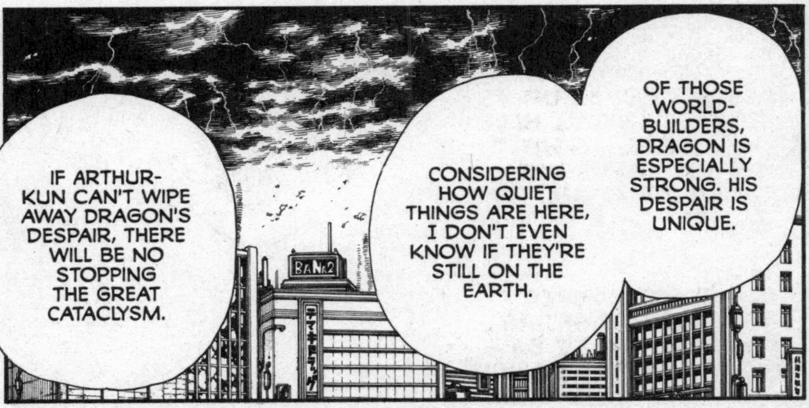
OF THOSE WORLD-BUILDERS, DRAGON IS ESPECIALLY STRONG. HIS DESPAIR IS UNIQUE.
CONSIDERING HOW QUIET THINGS ARE HERE, I DON'T EVEN KNOW IF THEY'RE STILL ON THE EARTH.
IF ARTHUR-KUN CAN'T WIPE AWAY DRAGON'S DESPAIR, THERE WILL BE NO STOPPING THE GREAT CATACLYSM.

Sign: Temaki Drugstore

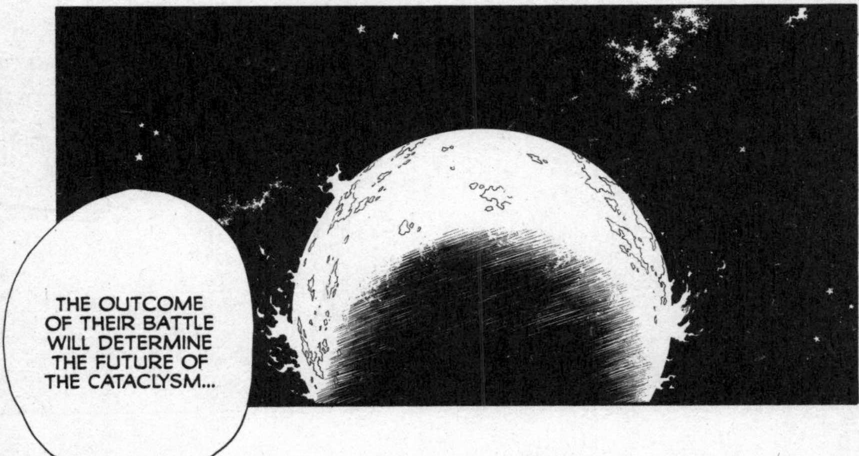
THE OUTCOME OF THEIR BATTLE WILL DETERMINE THE FUTURE OF THE CATACLYSM...

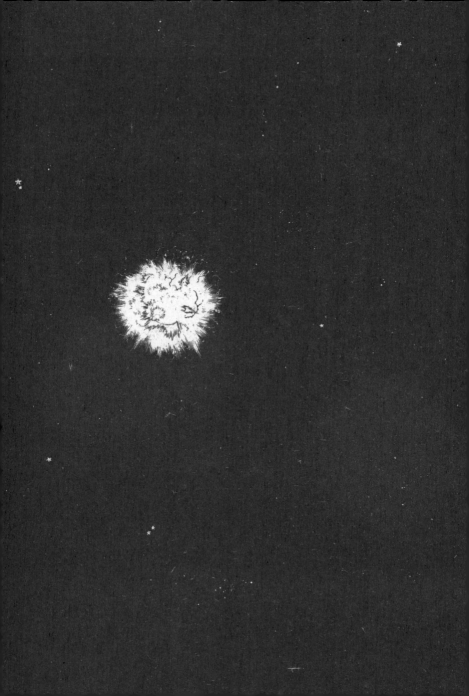

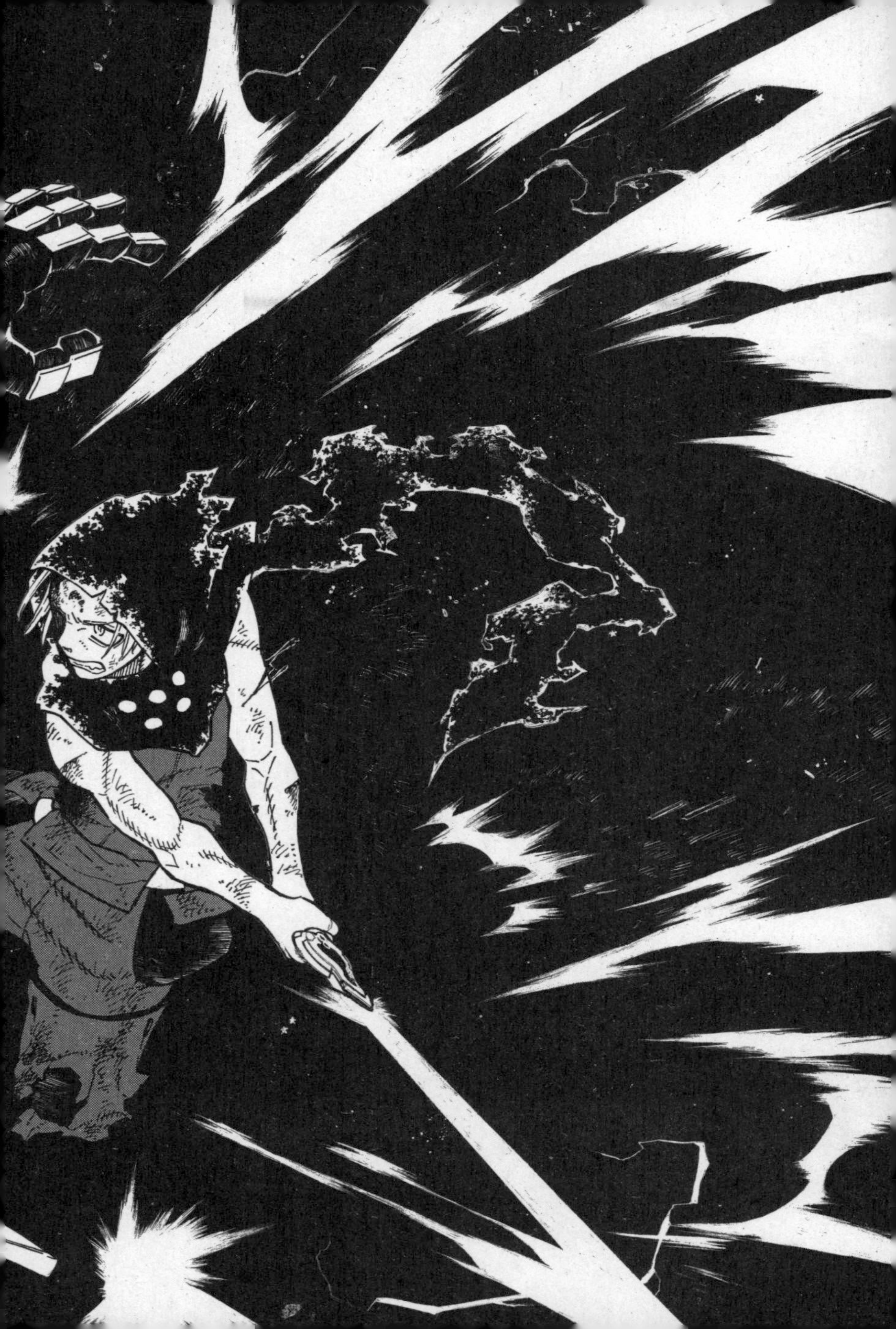

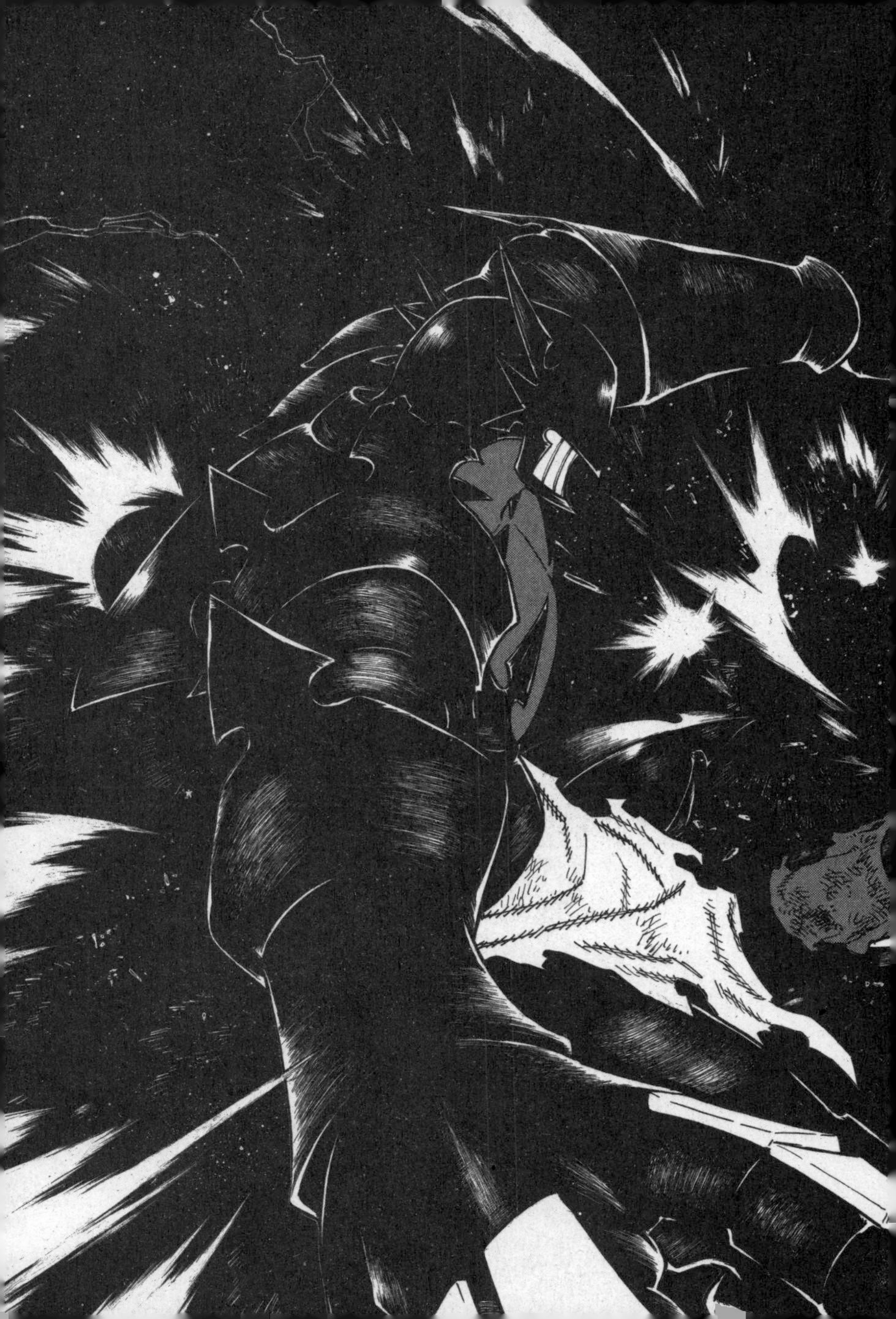

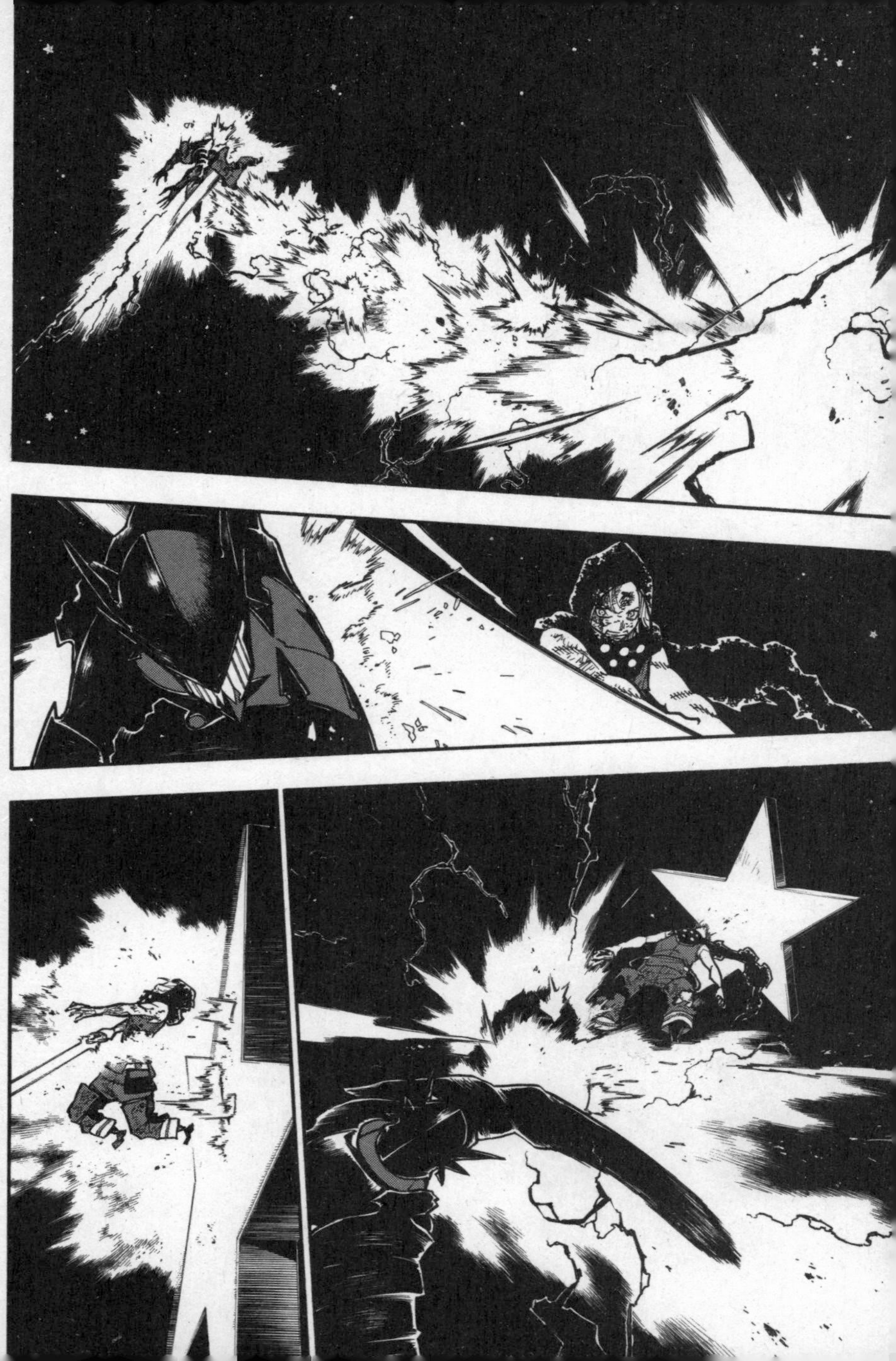

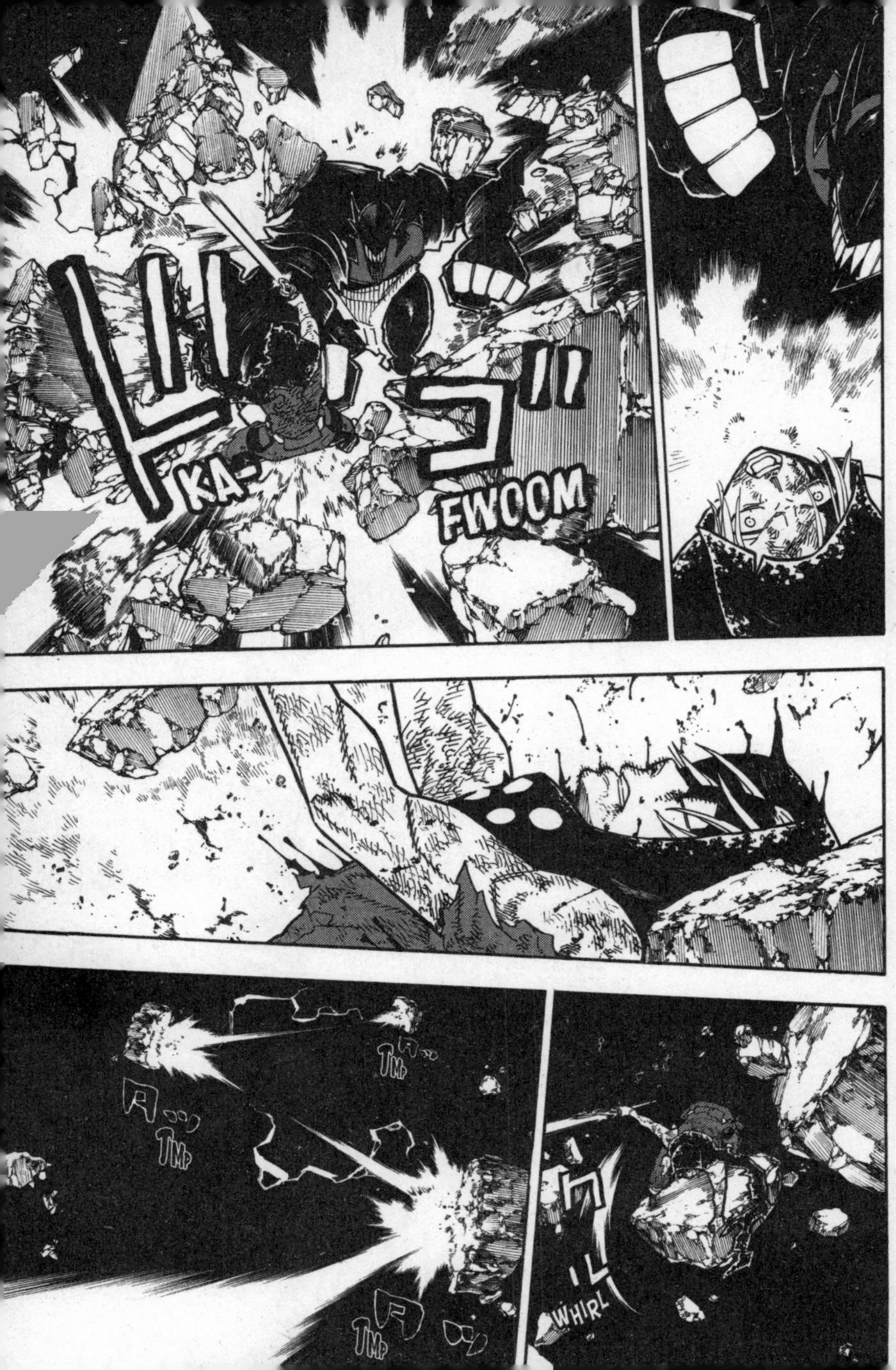
KA-
FWOOM
WHIRL
TMP
TMP
TMP

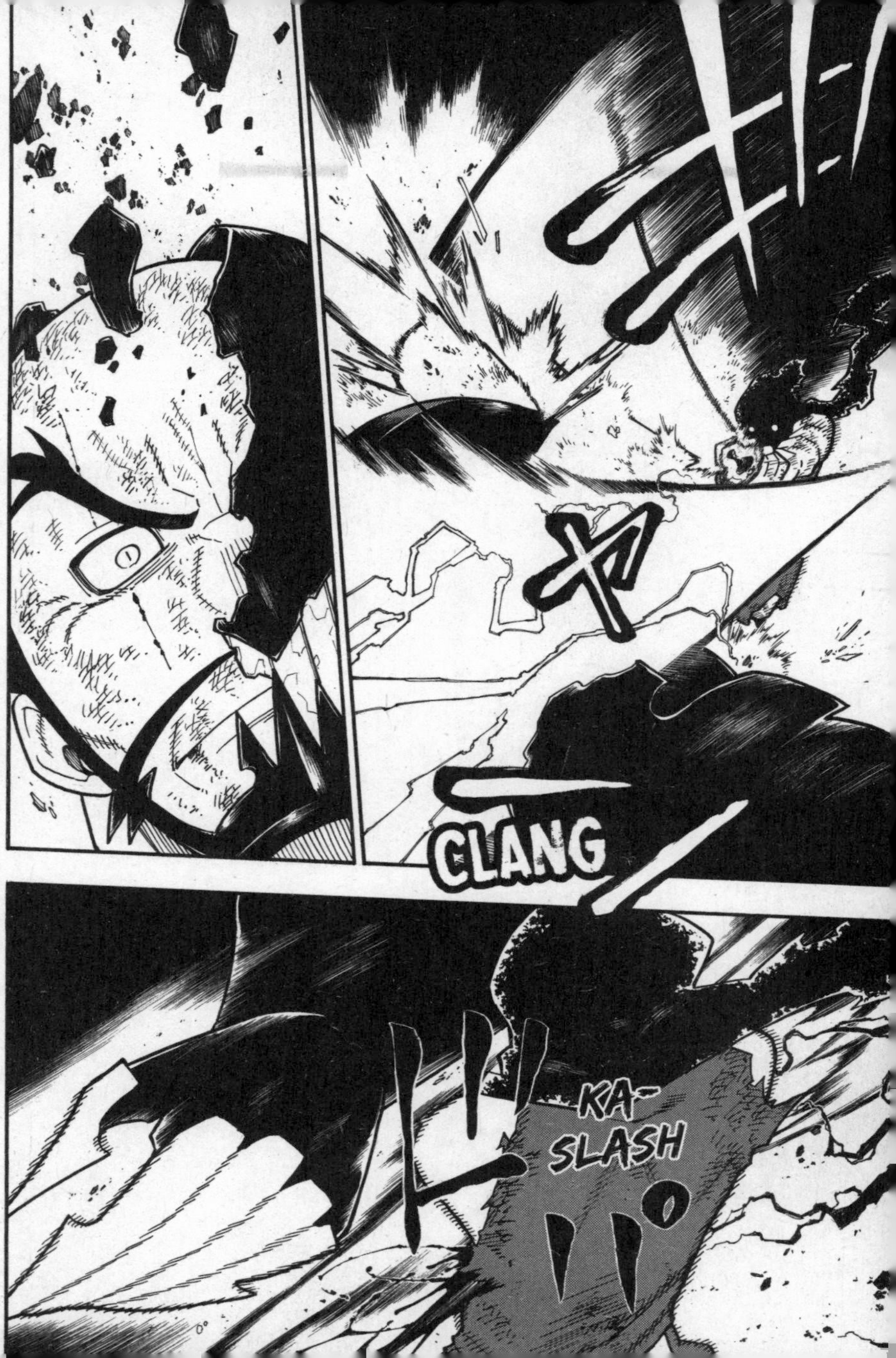
CLANG
KA-
SLASH

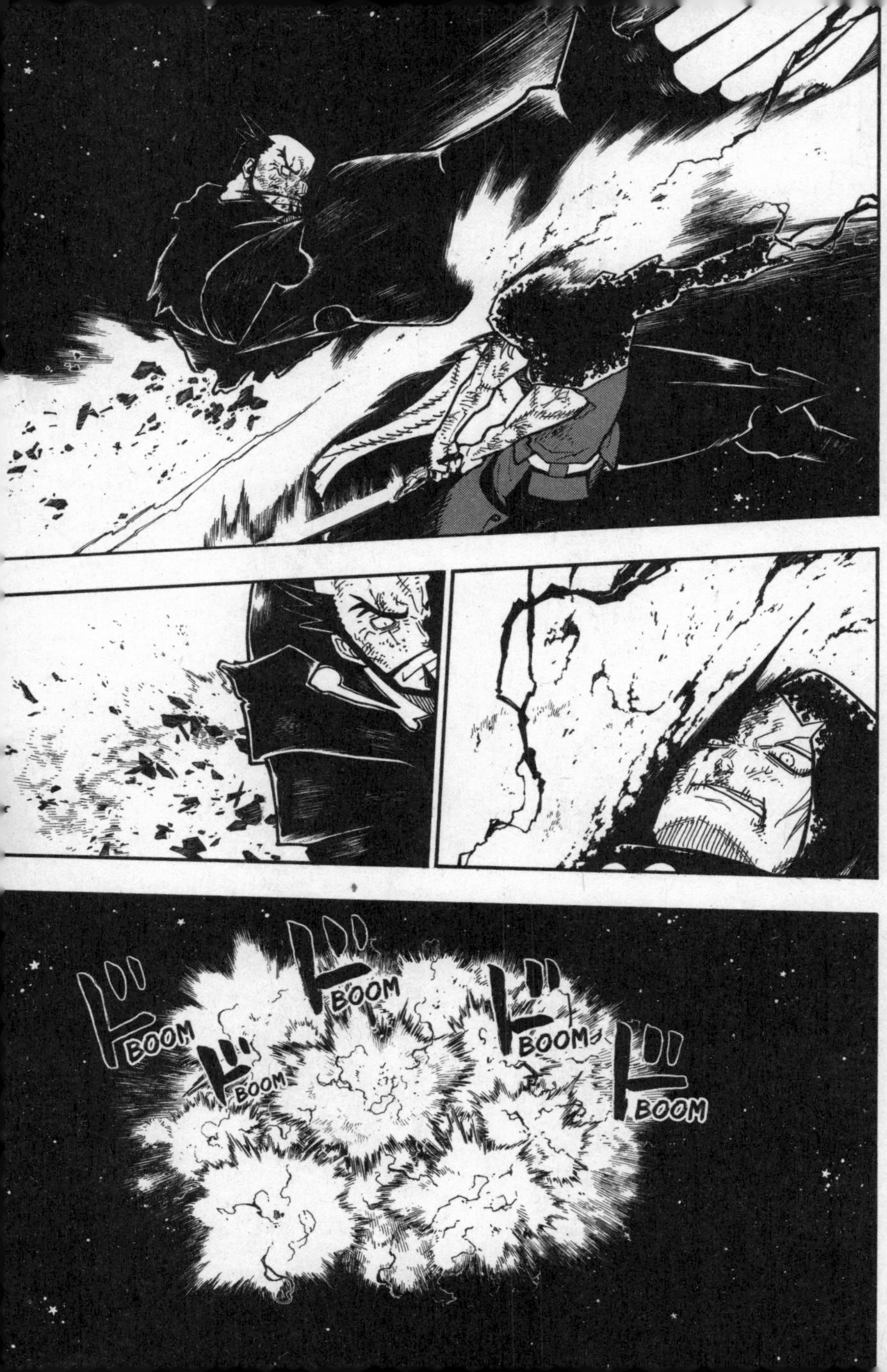
ド BOOM
ド BOOM
ド BOOM
ド BOOM
ド BOOM

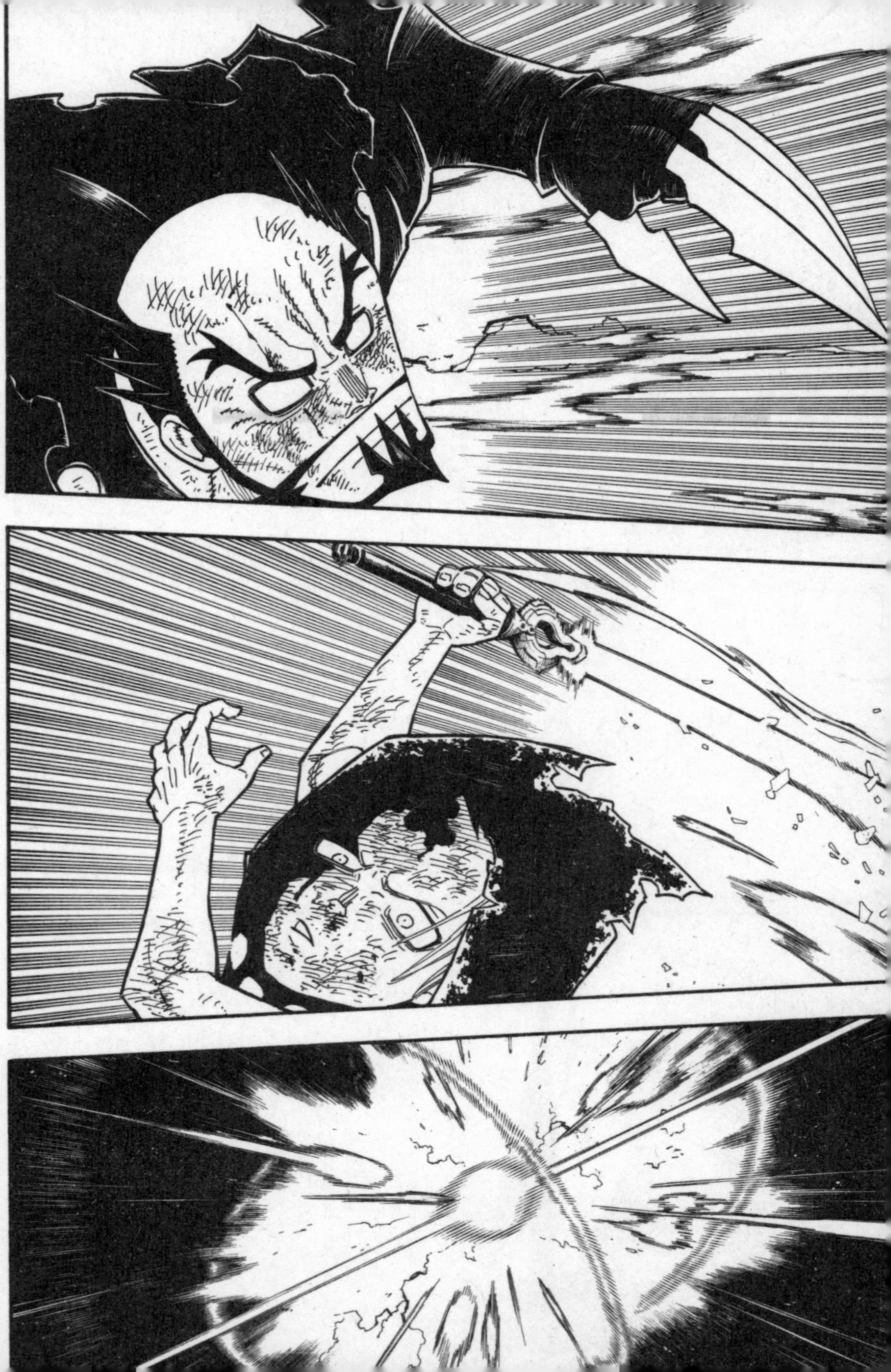

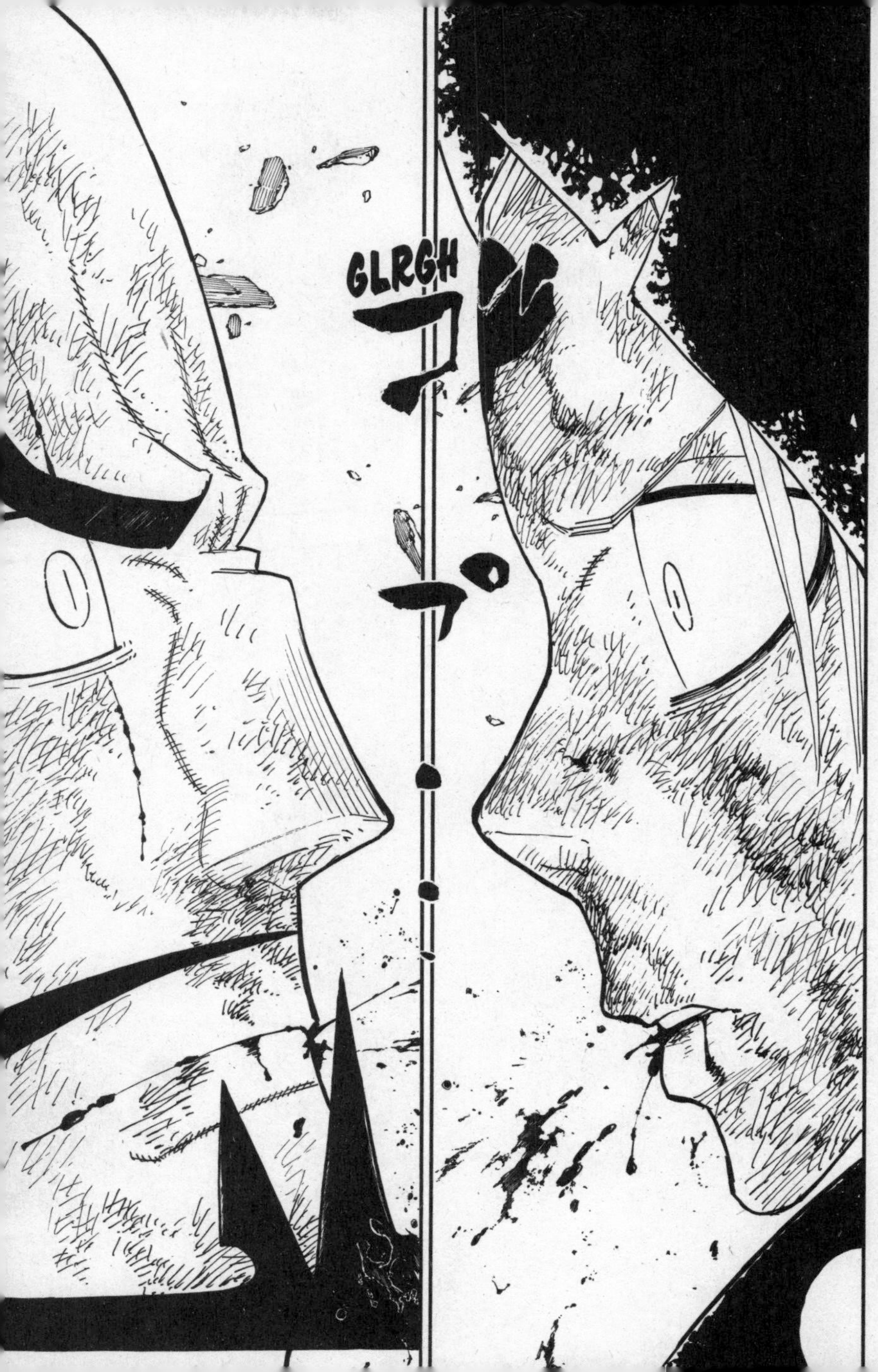
GLRGH

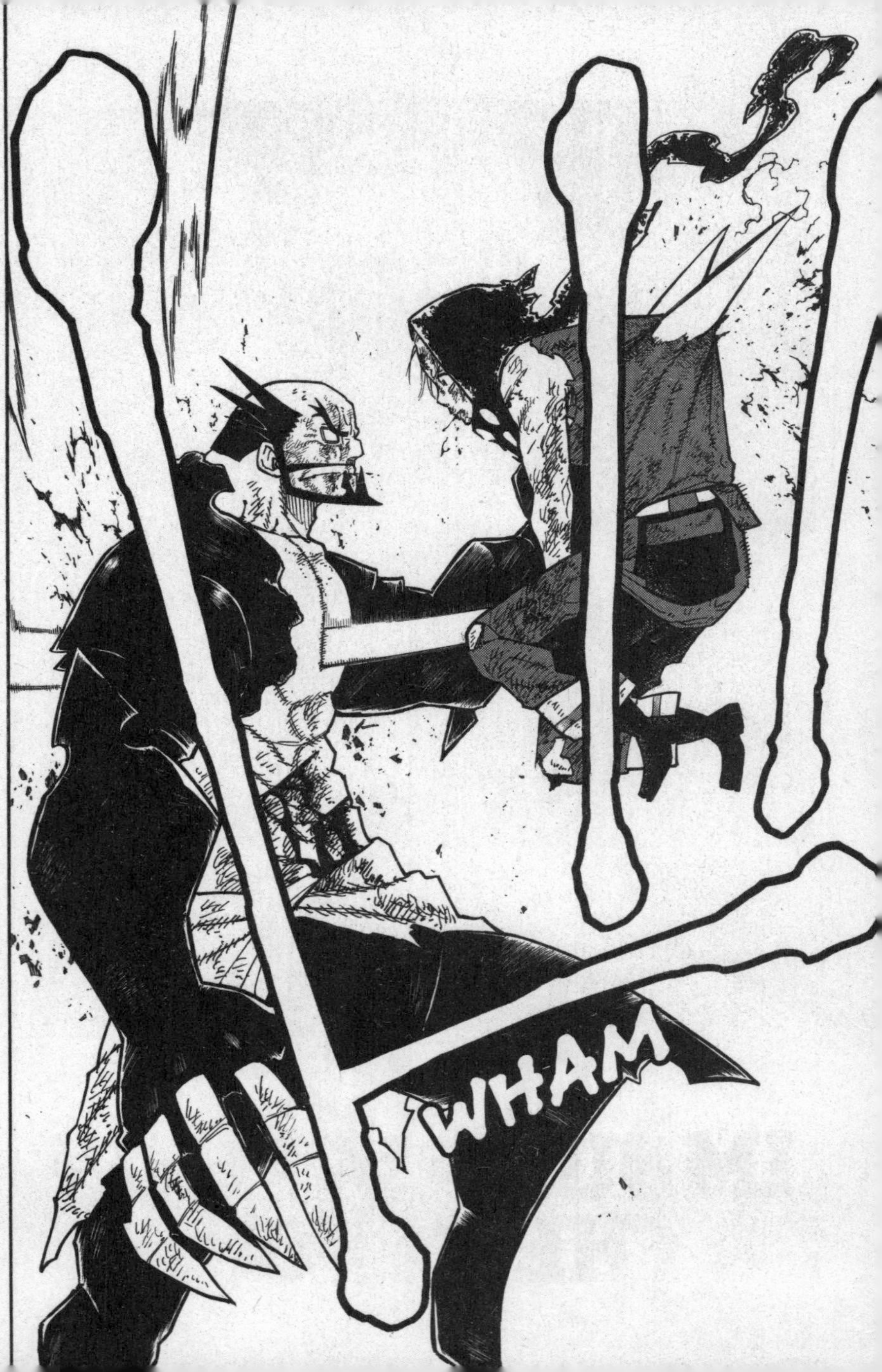
WHAM

CHAPTER CCLXX: IMBUED WITHIN THE SWORD

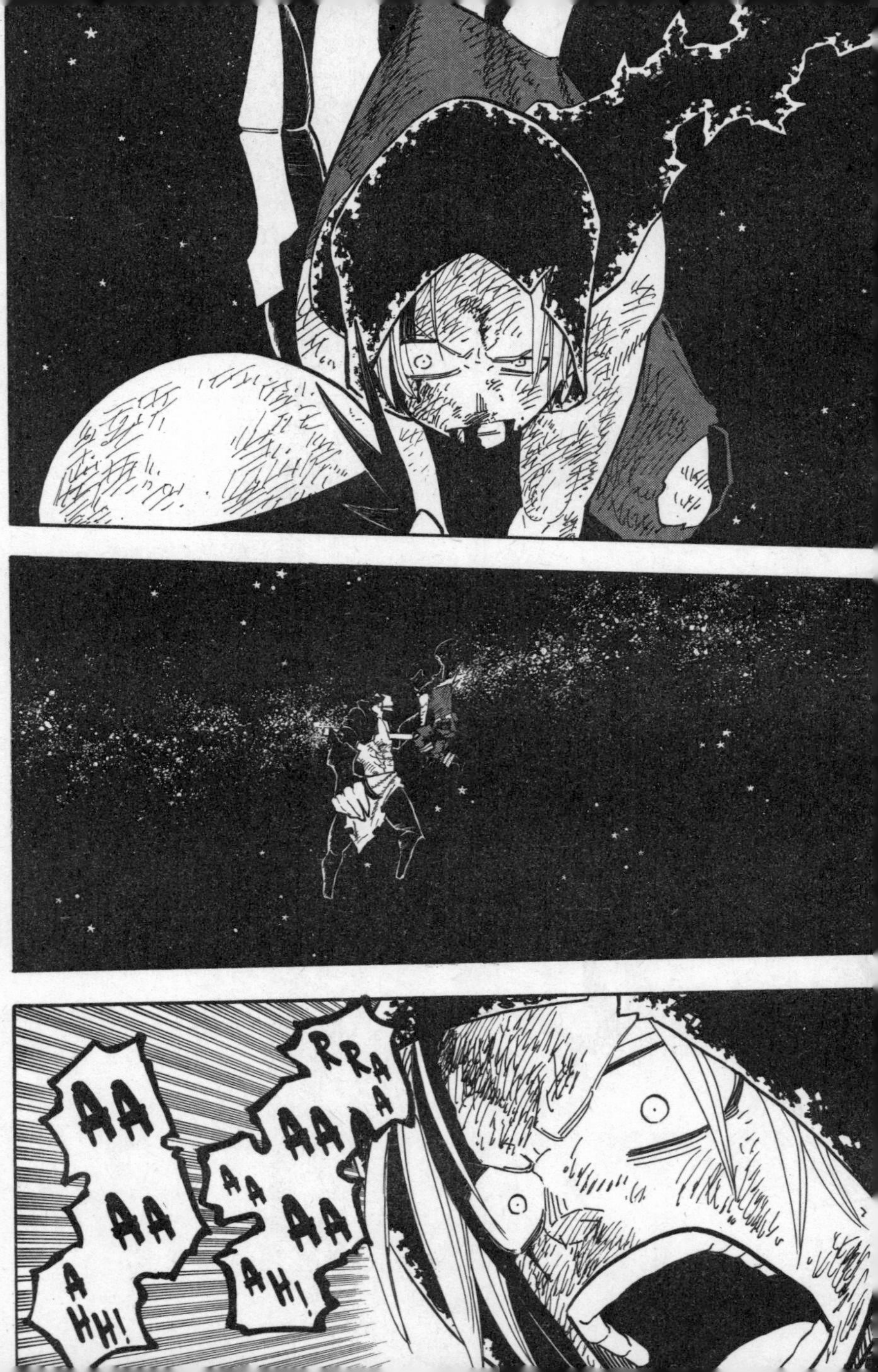
RRAAAAAAAAAAAH!
AAAAAHH!

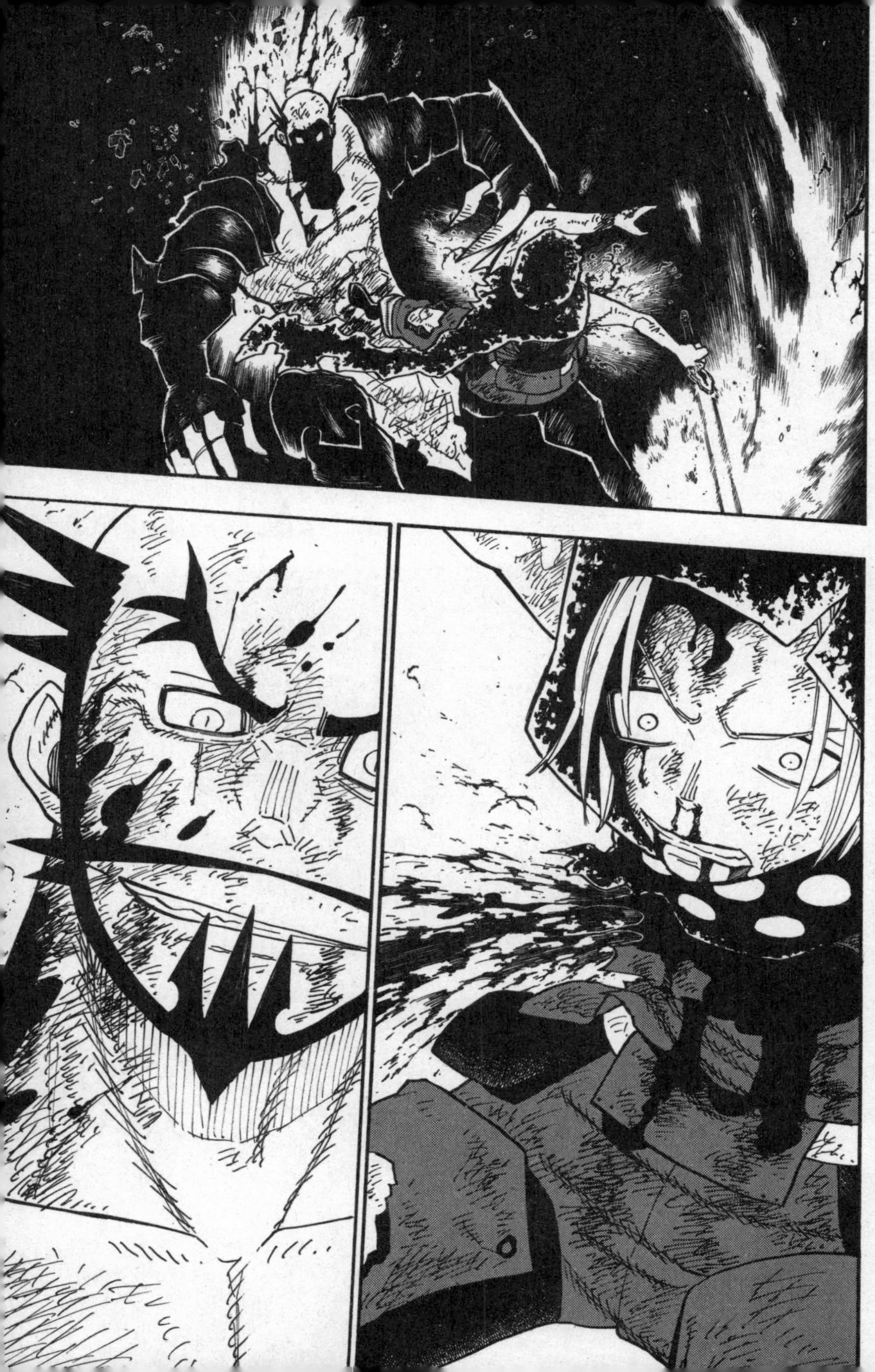

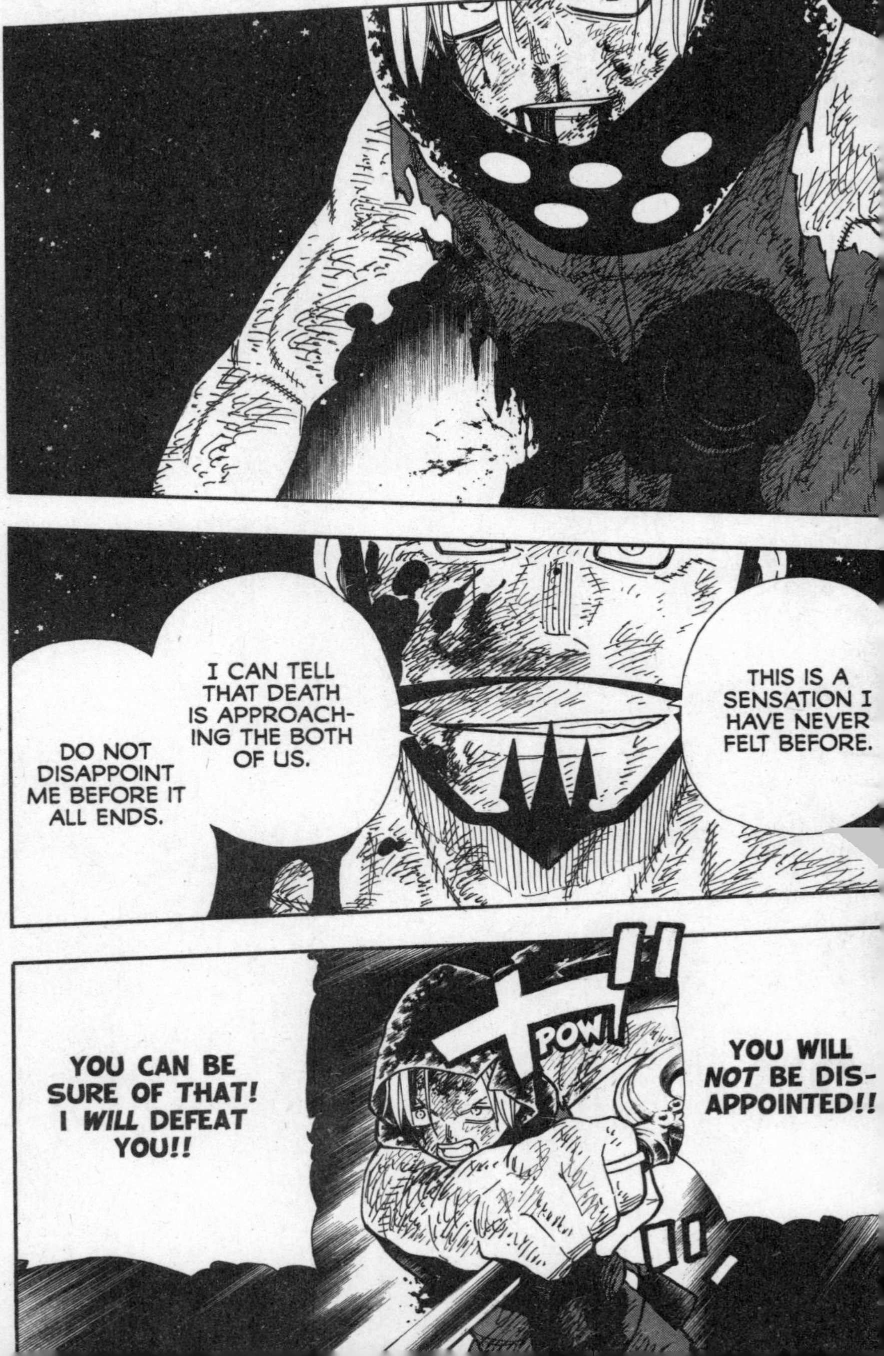
THIS IS A SENSATION I HAVE NEVER FELT BEFORE.
I CAN TELL THAT DEATH IS APPROACH-ING THE BOTH OF US.
DO NOT DISAPPOINT ME BEFORE IT ALL ENDS.
POW
YOU WILL *NOT* BE DIS-APPOINTED!!
YOU CAN BE SURE OF THAT! I *WILL* DEFEAT YOU!!

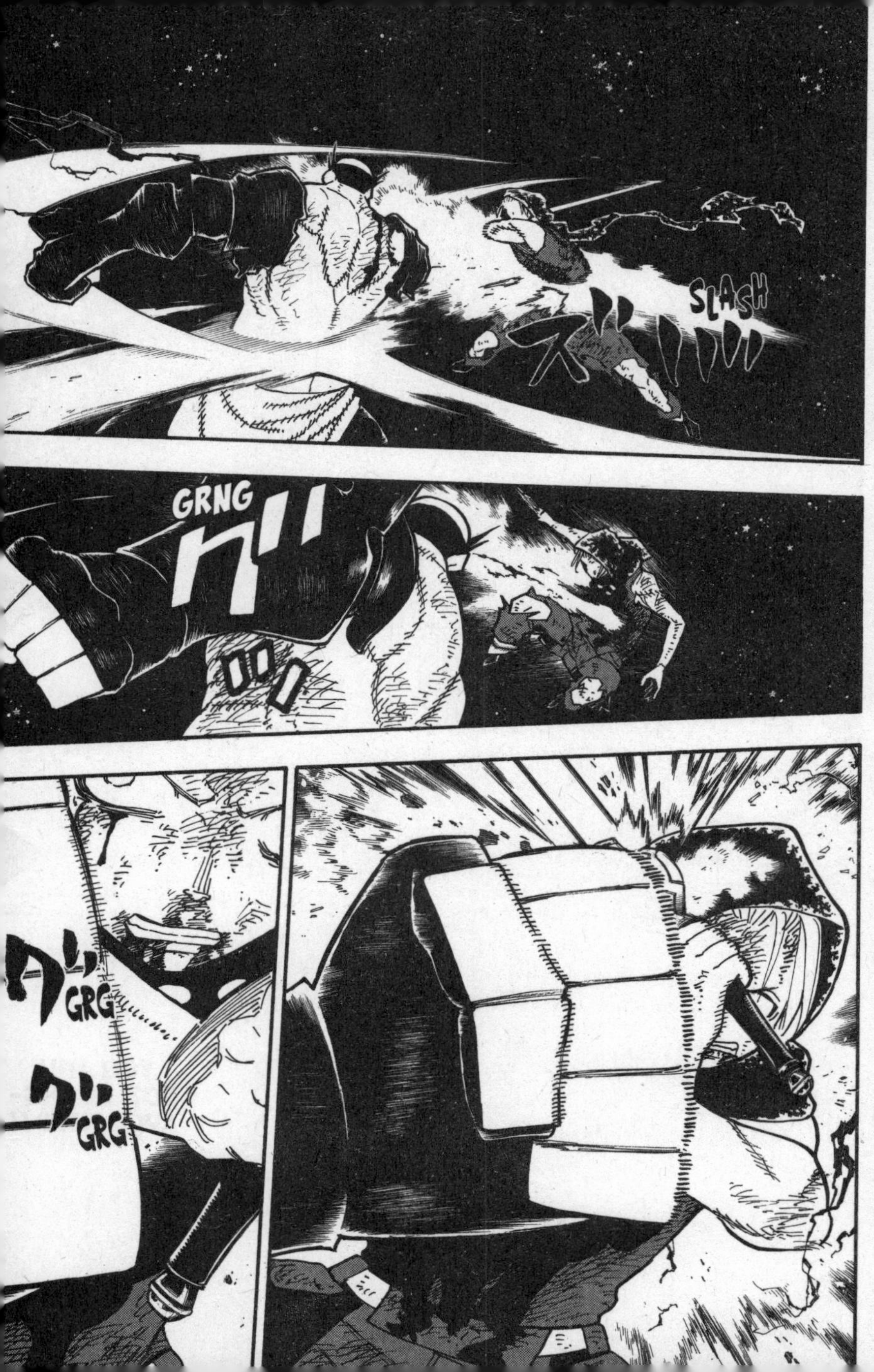
SLASH
GRNG
GRG
GRG

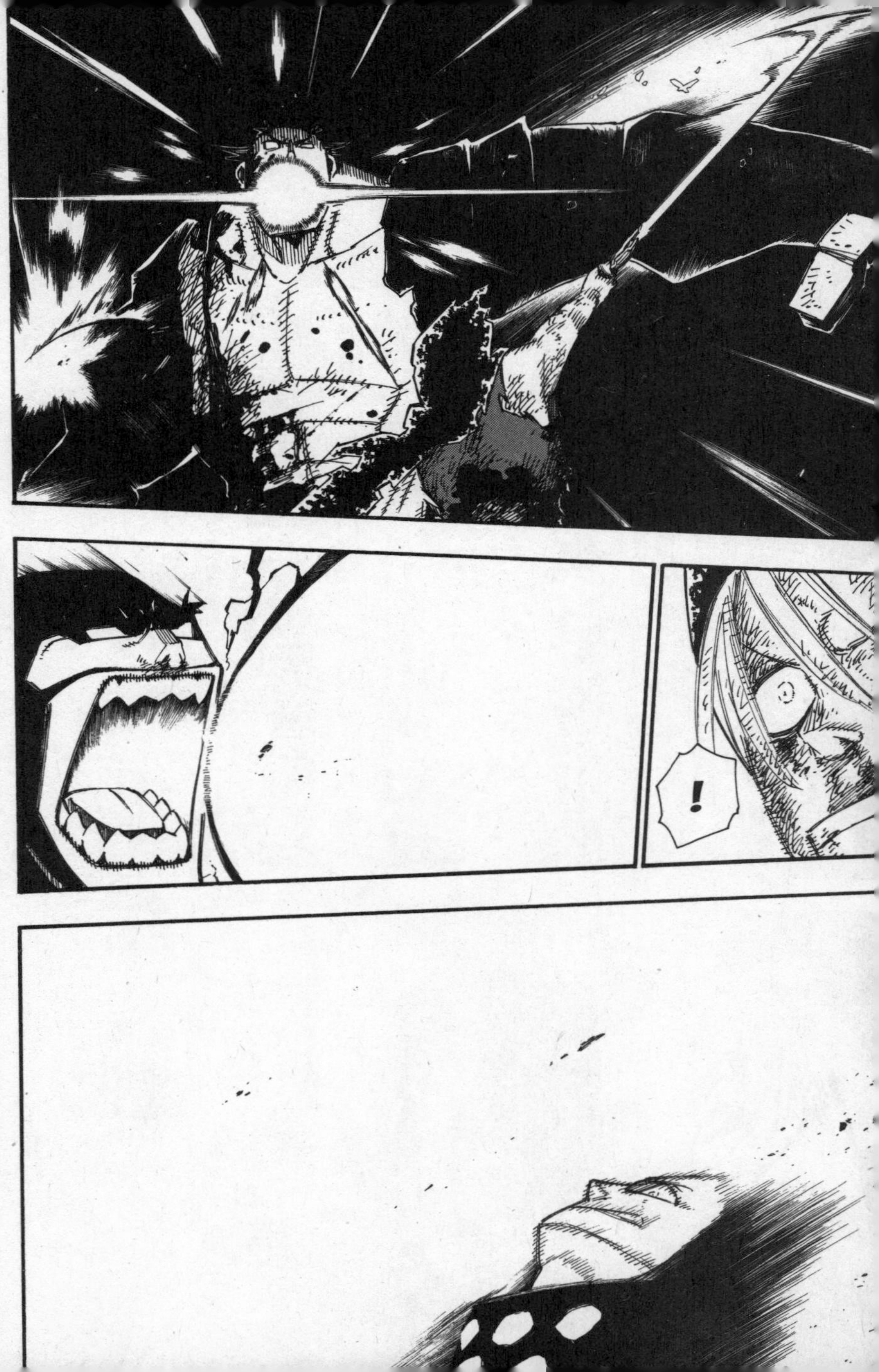
!

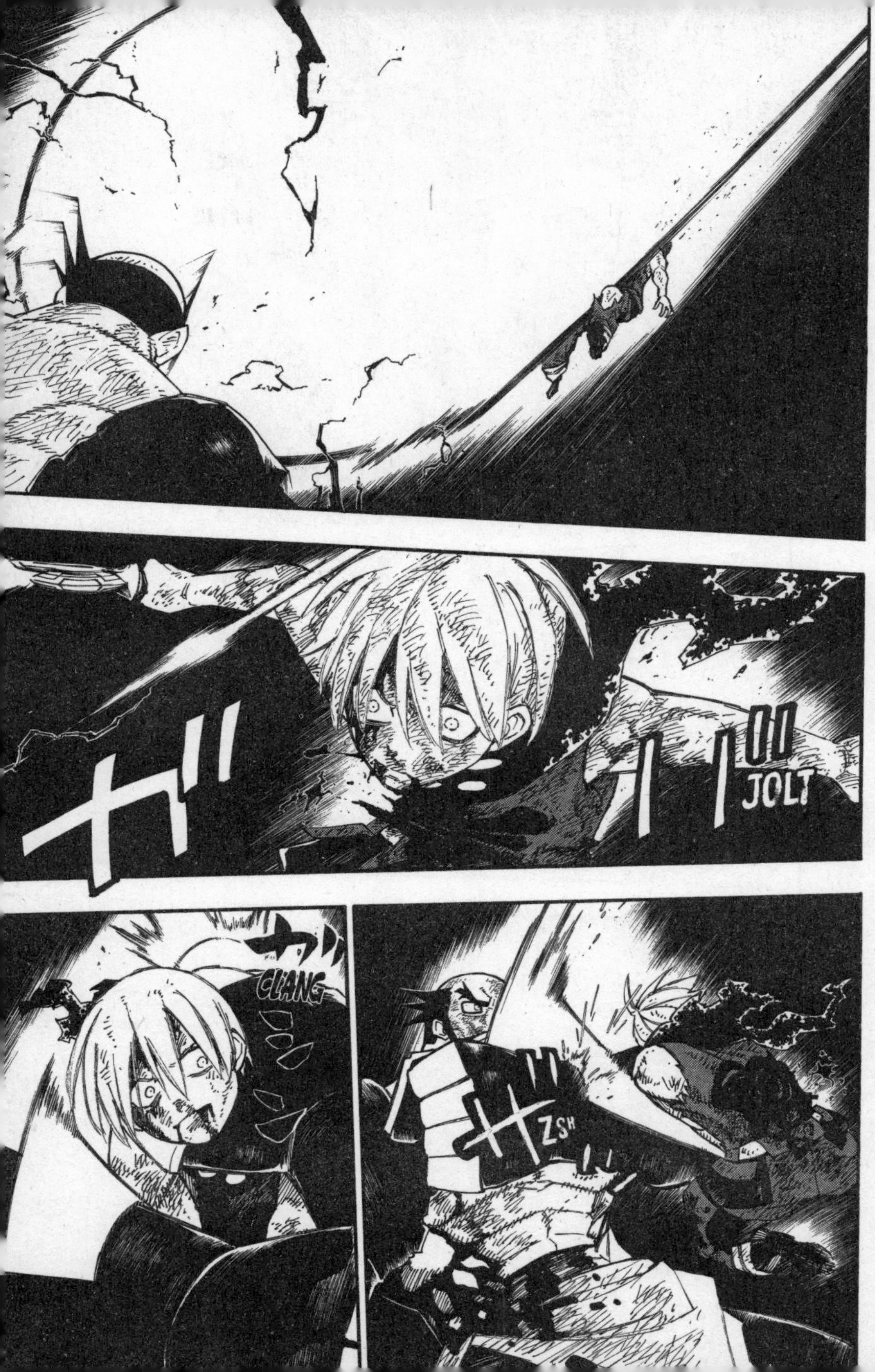
JOLT
ZSH
CLANG

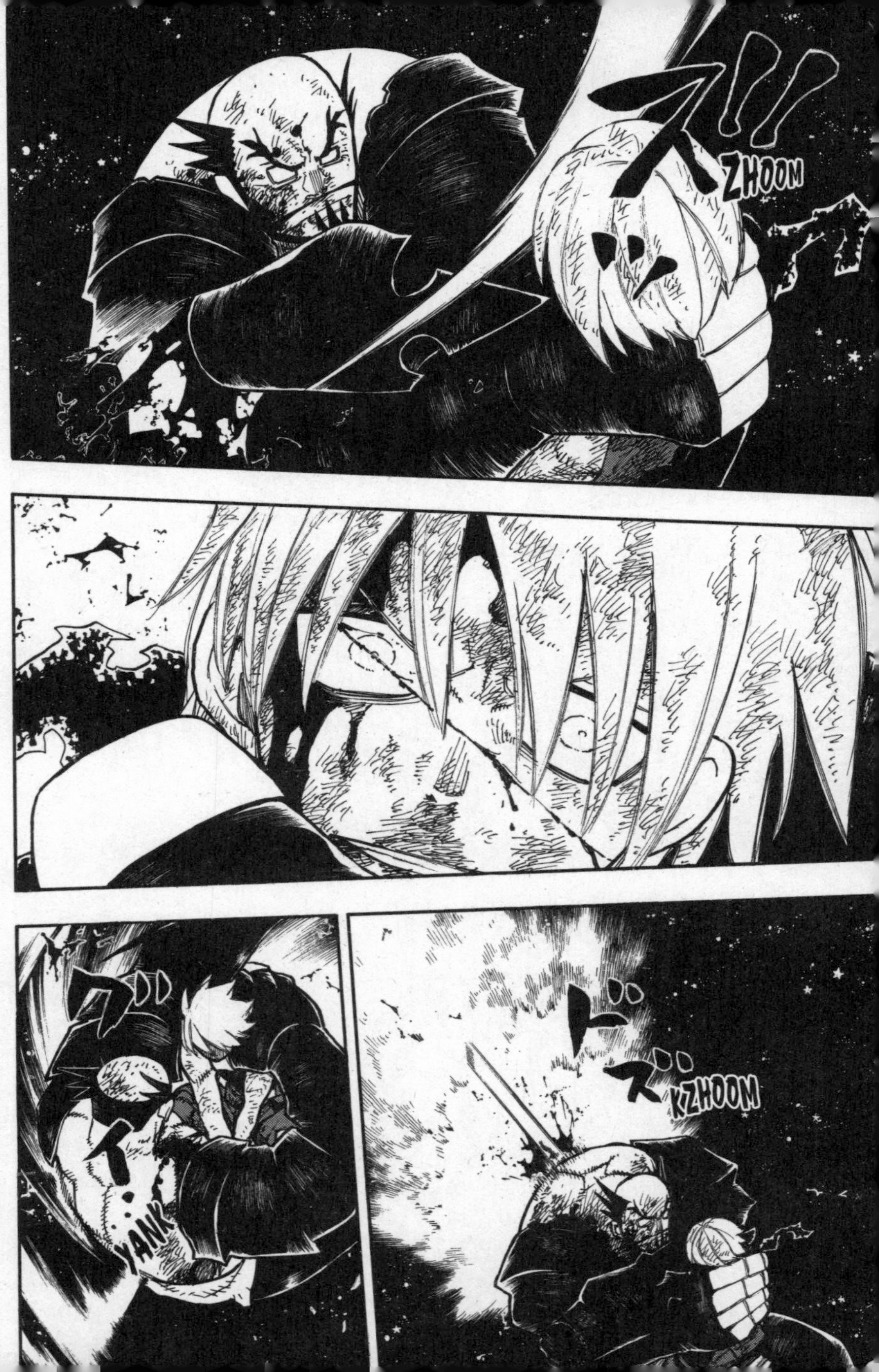
ZHOOM
KZHOOM
YANK

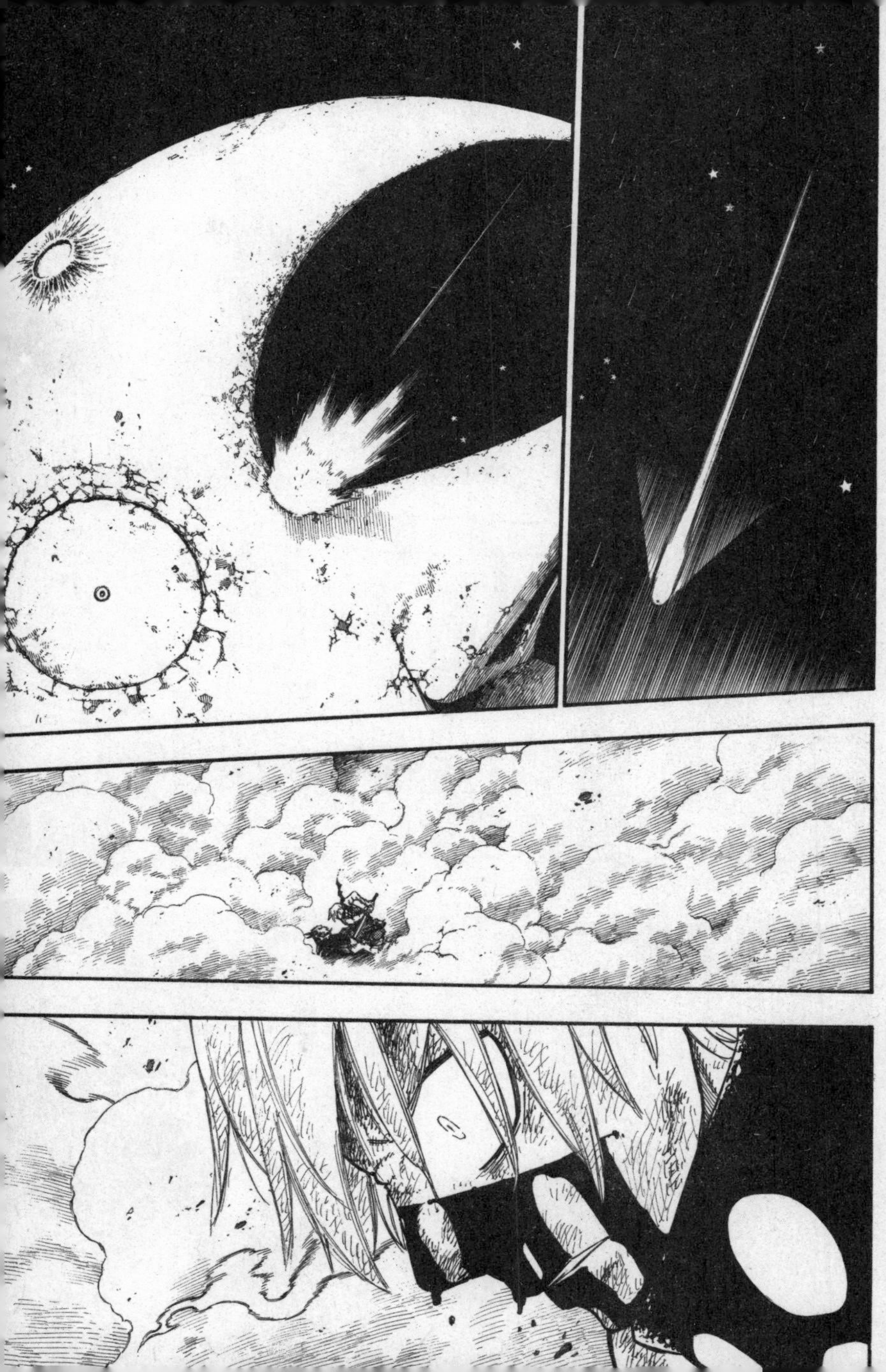

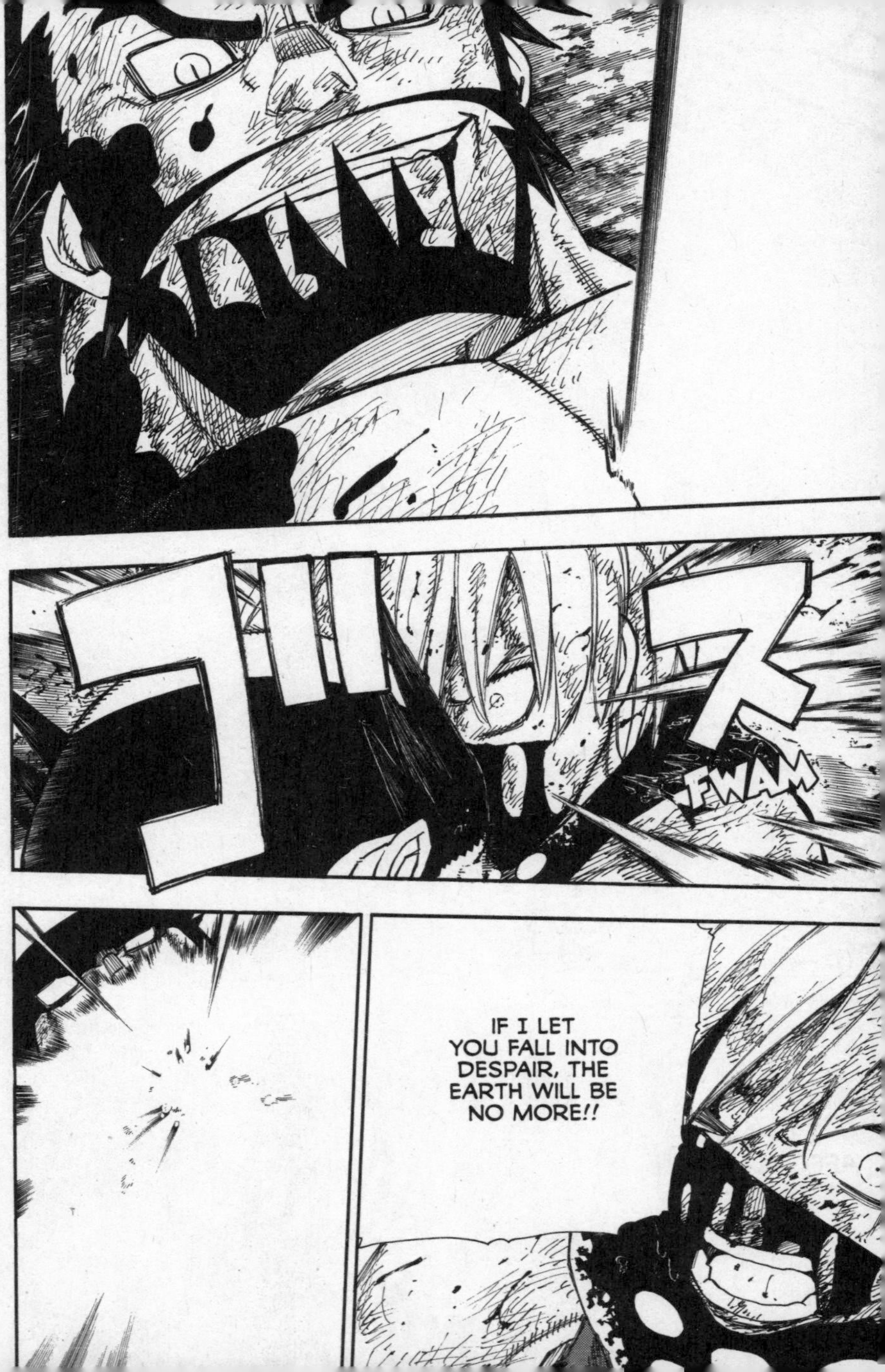
FWAM
IF I LET YOU FALL INTO DESPAIR, THE EARTH WILL BE NO MORE!!

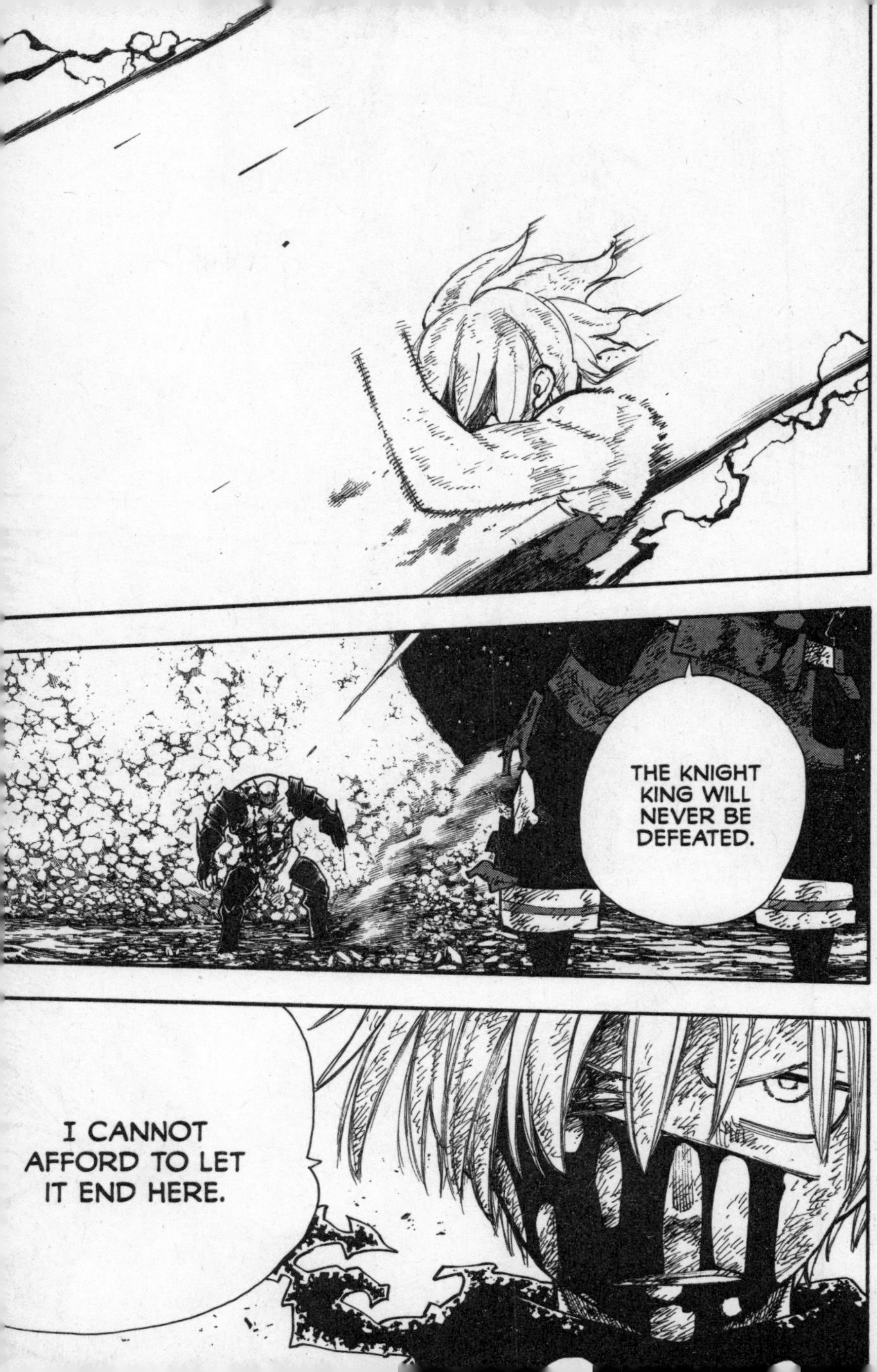
THE KNIGHT KING WILL NEVER BE DEFEATED.
I CANNOT AFFORD TO LET IT END HERE.

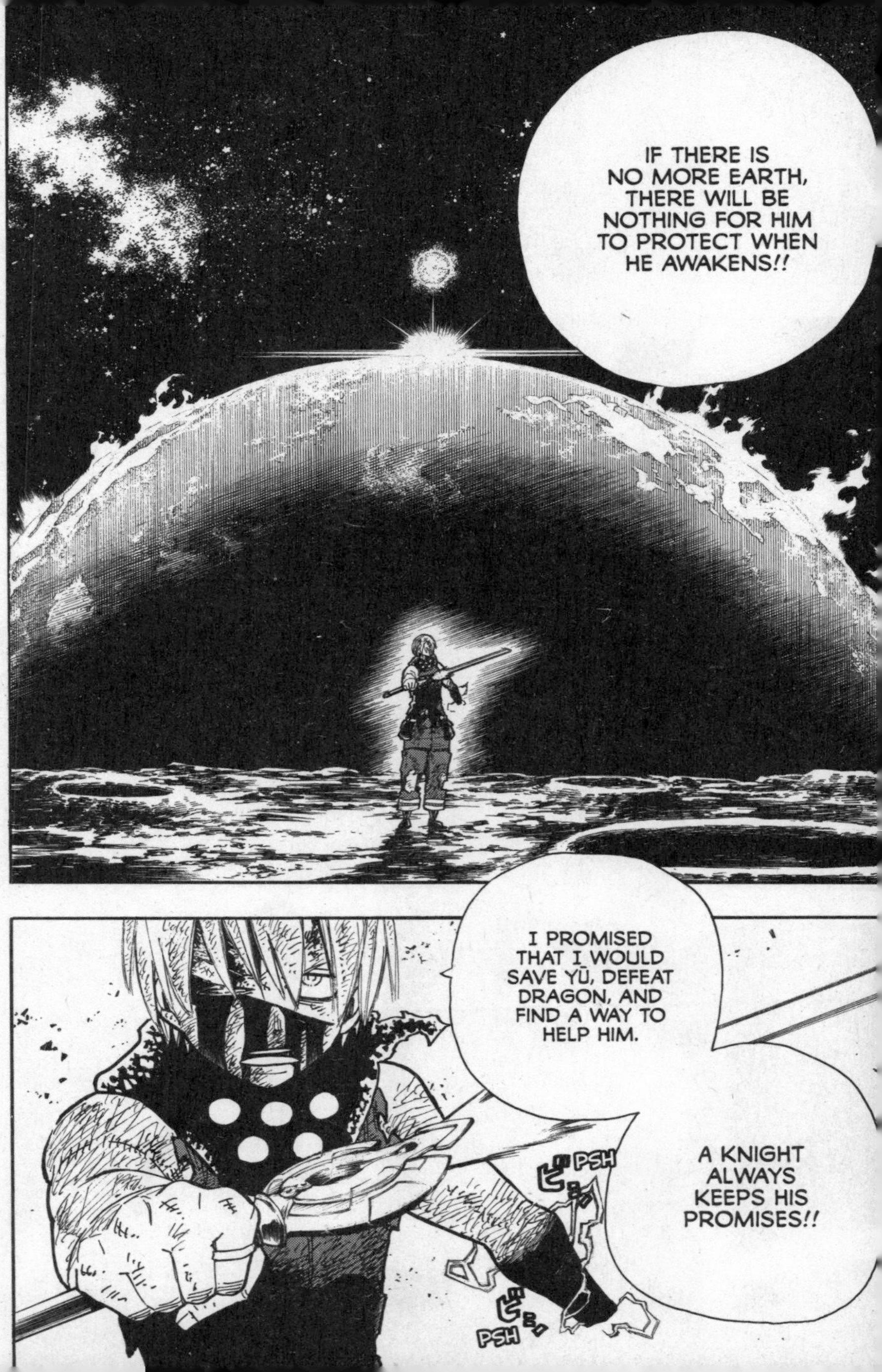
IF THERE IS NO MORE EARTH, THERE WILL BE NOTHING FOR HIM TO PROTECT WHEN HE AWAKENS!!
I PROMISED THAT I WOULD SAVE YŪ, DEFEAT DRAGON, AND FIND A WAY TO HELP HIM.
A KNIGHT ALWAYS KEEPS HIS PROMISES!!
PSH
PSH

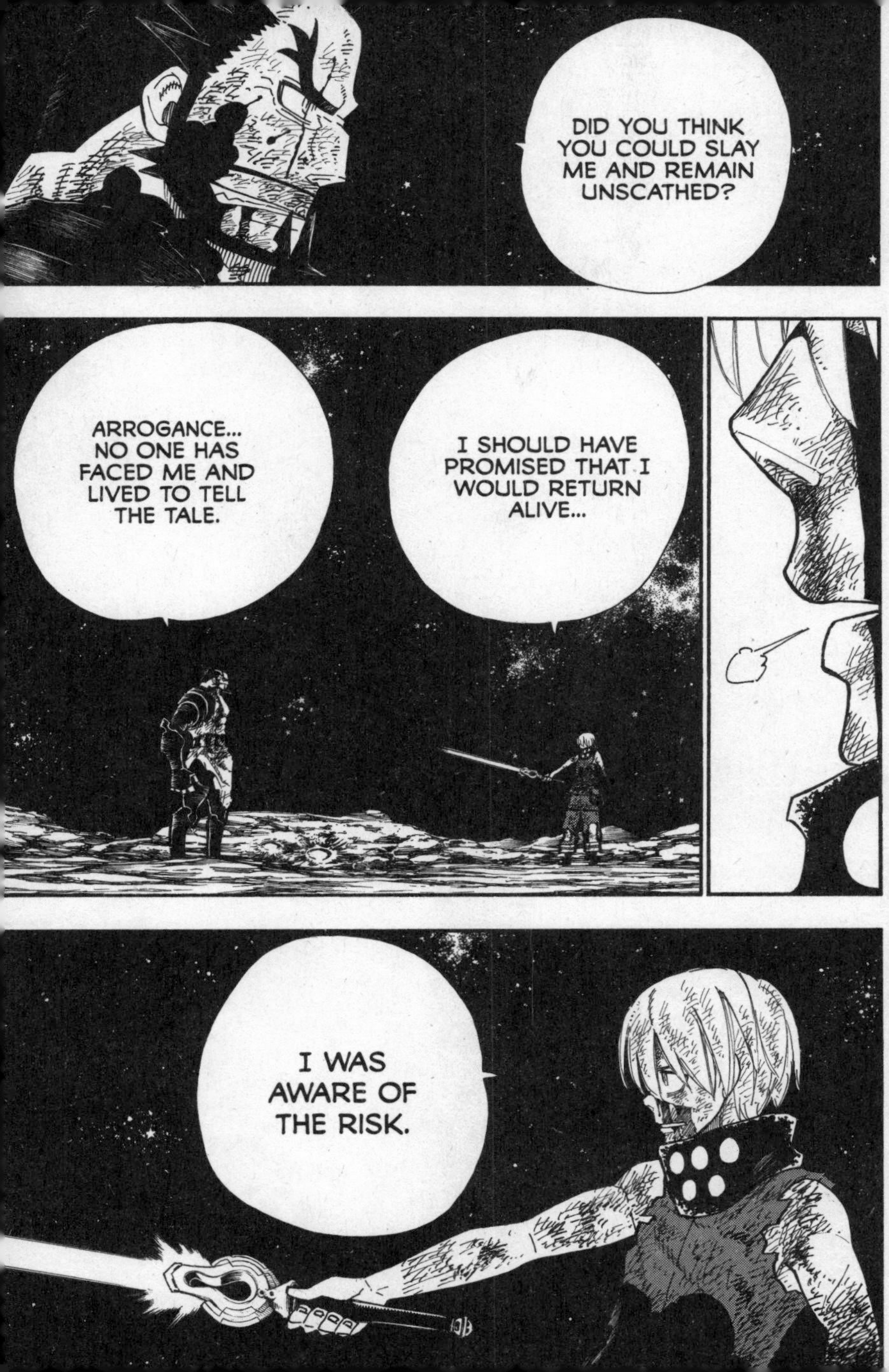
DID YOU THINK YOU COULD SLAY ME AND REMAIN UNSCATHED?
I SHOULD HAVE PROMISED THAT I WOULD RETURN ALIVE...
ARROGANCE... NO ONE HAS FACED ME AND LIVED TO TELL THE TALE.
I WAS AWARE OF THE RISK.

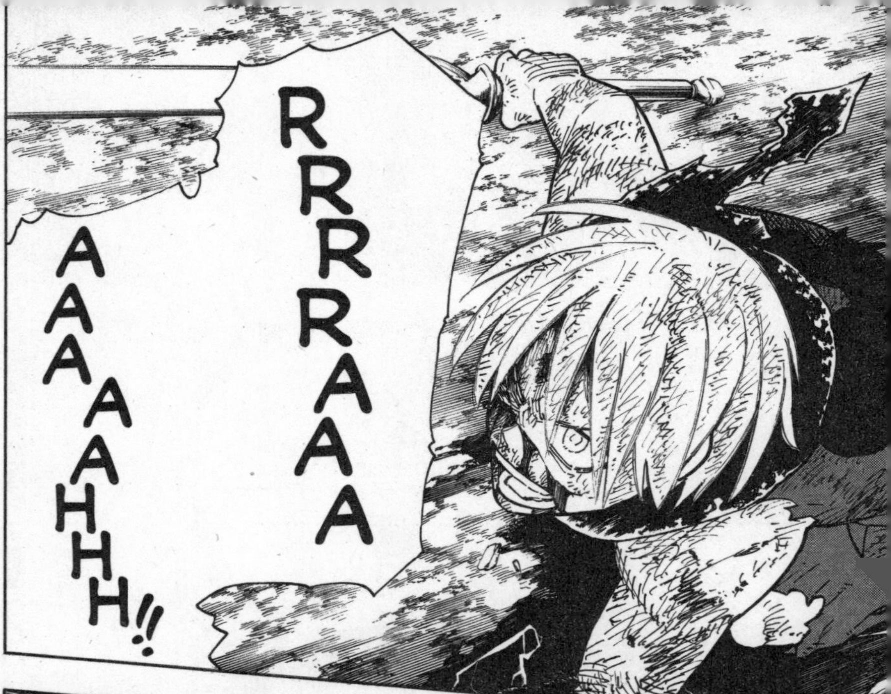
RRRRAAA
AAAAAHHH!!
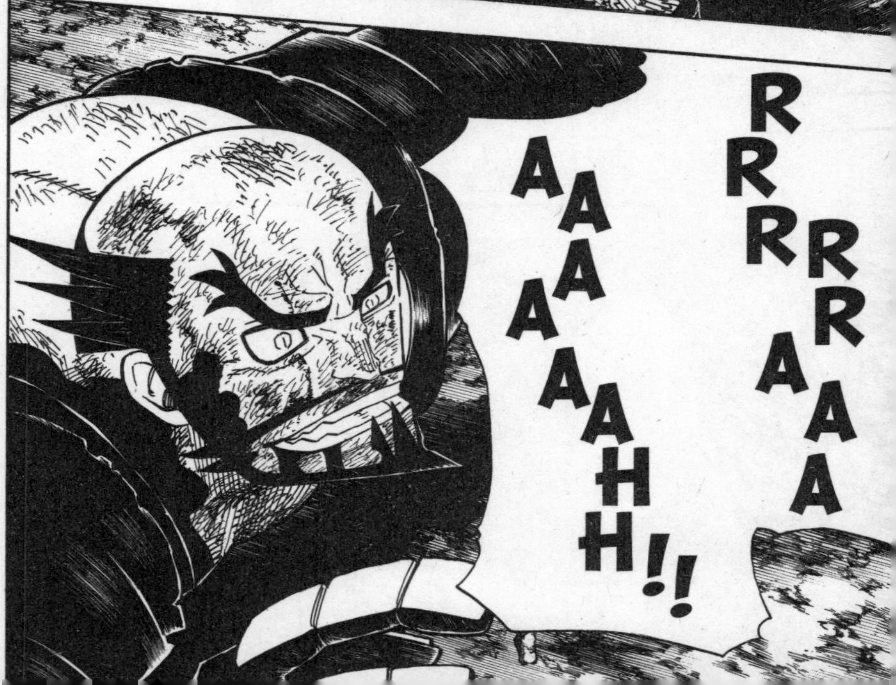
RRRRRAAA
AAAAAAAHH!!

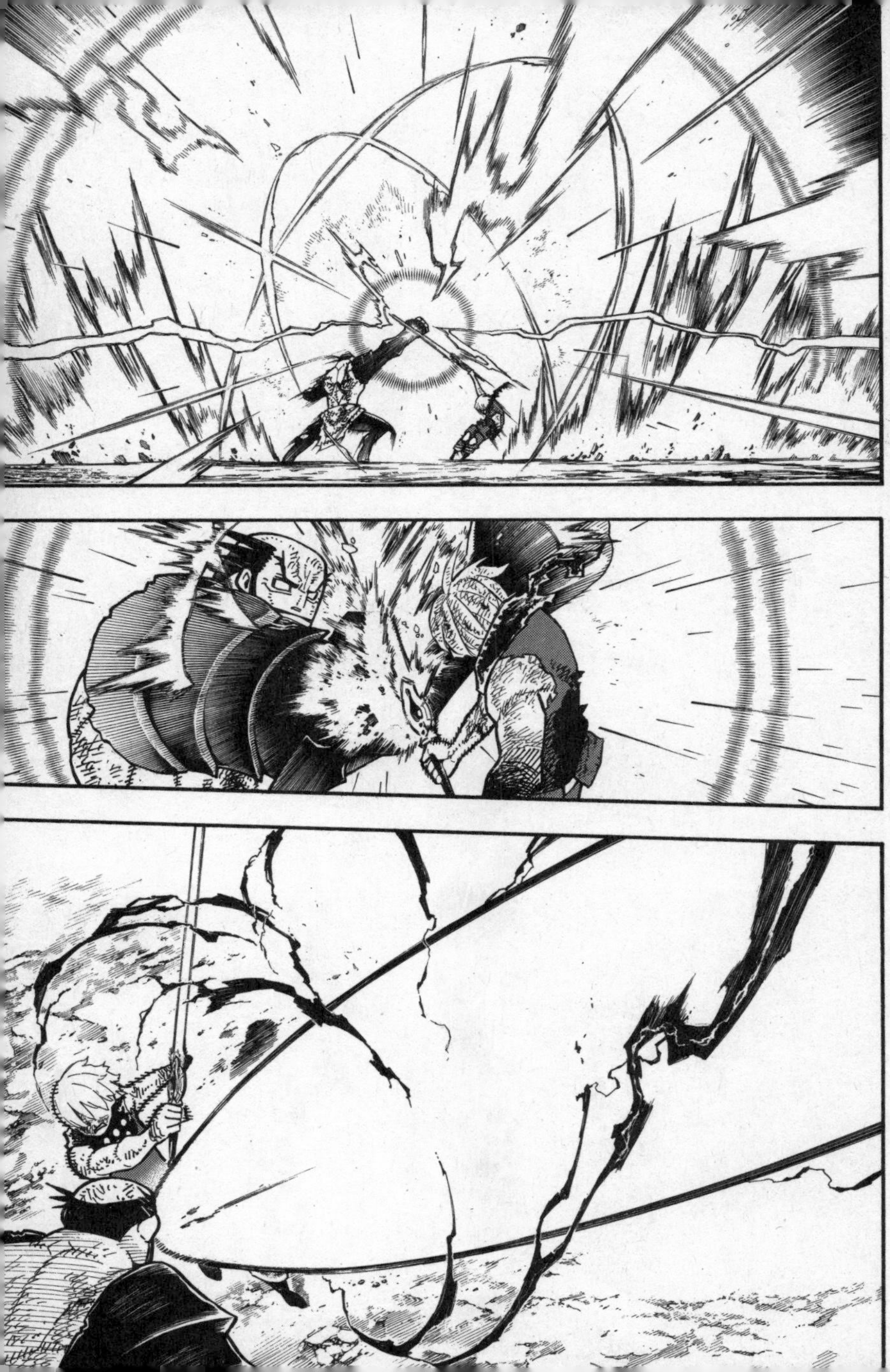

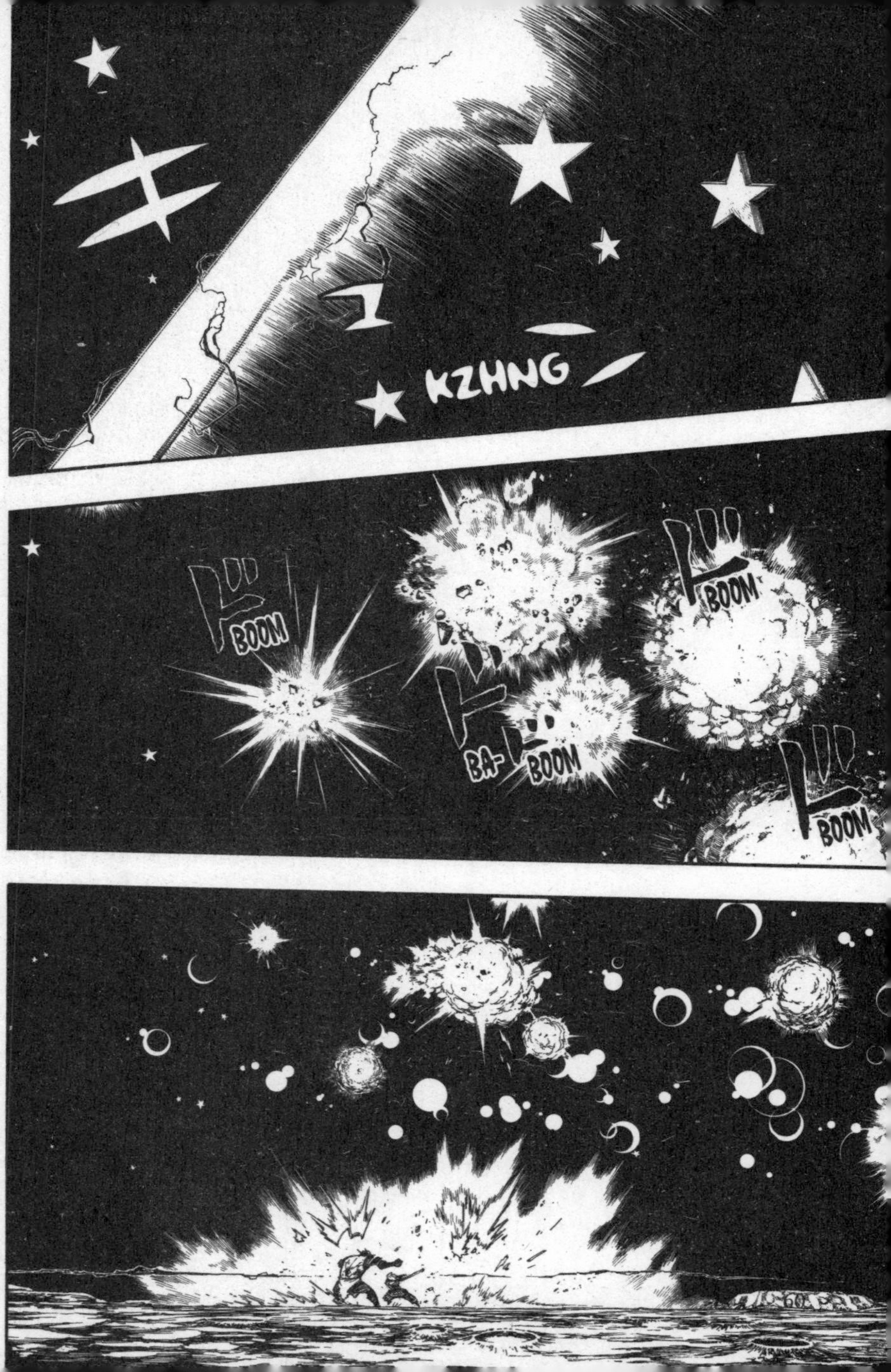
KZHNG
BOOM
BOOM
BA-BOOM
BOOM

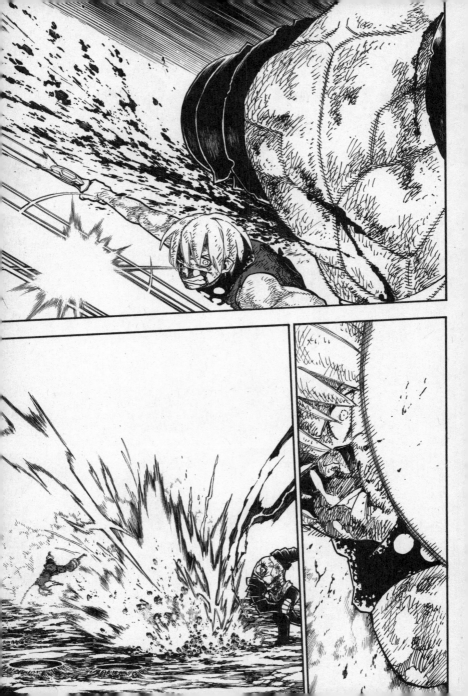

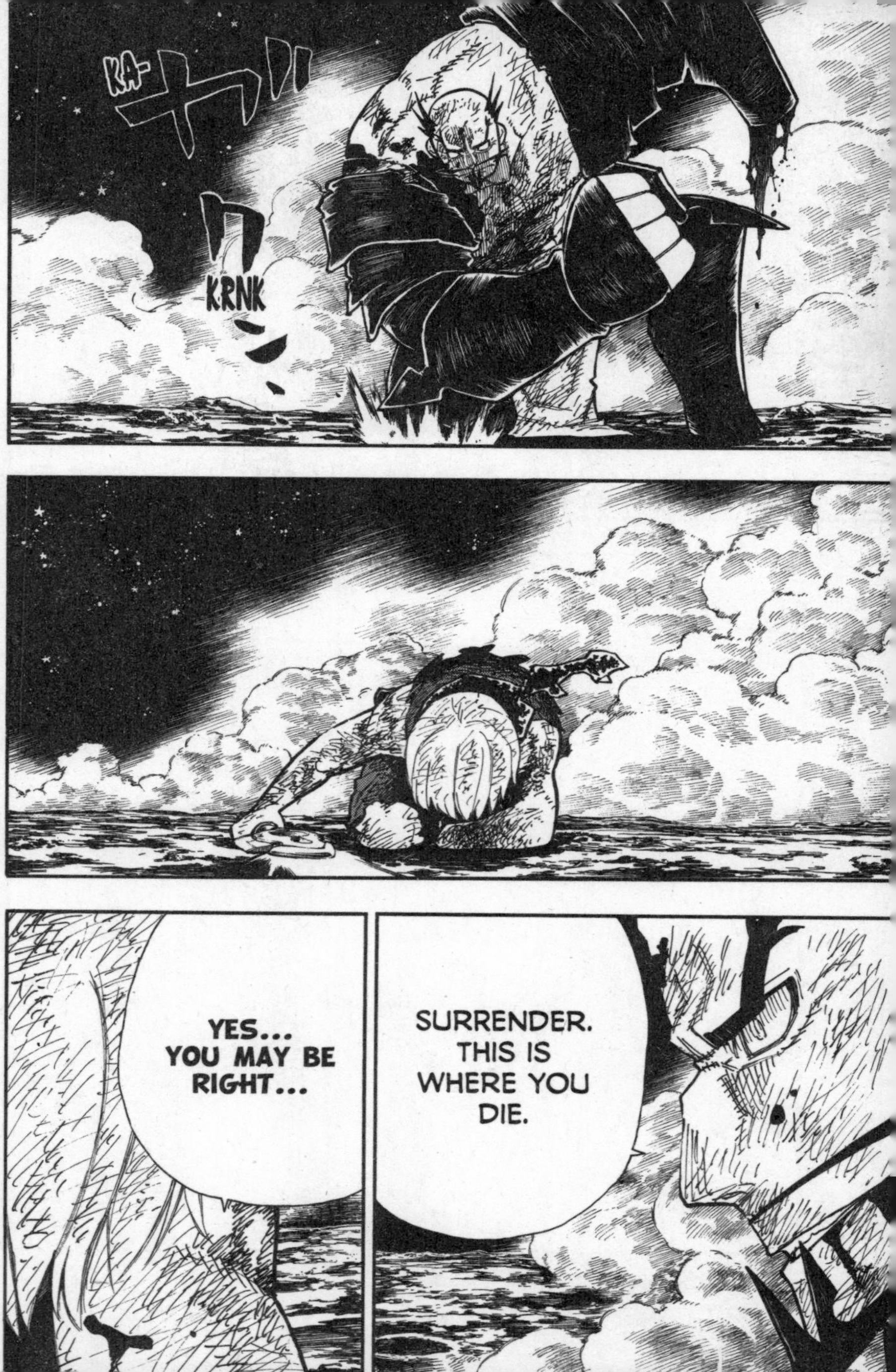
KA-
KRNK
SURRENDER. THIS IS WHERE YOU DIE.
YES... YOU MAY BE RIGHT...

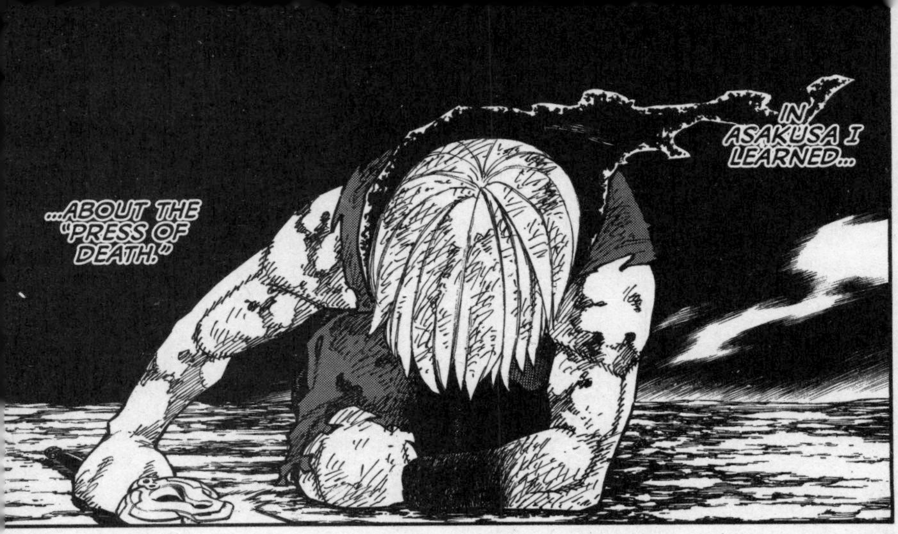
IN ASAKUSA I LEARNED...
...ABOUT THE "PRESS OF DEATH."
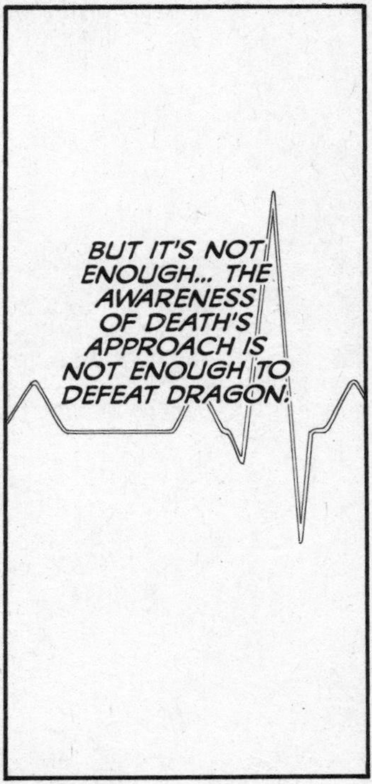
BUT IT'S NOT ENOUGH... THE AWARENESS OF DEATH'S APPROACH IS NOT ENOUGH TO DEFEAT DRAGON.
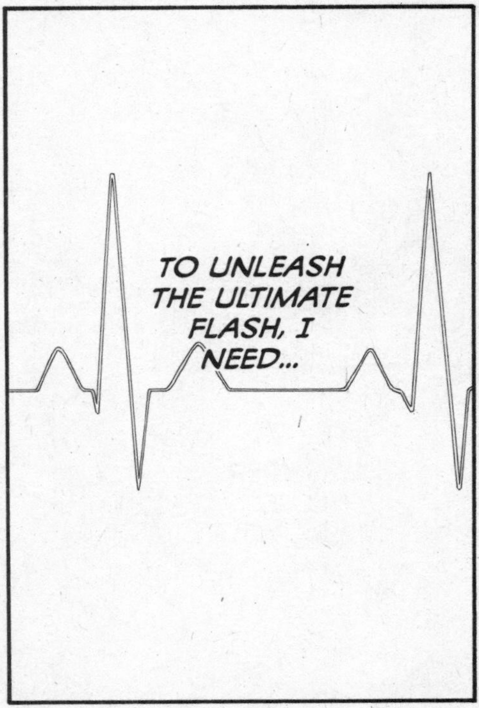
TO UNLEASH THE ULTIMATE FLASH, I NEED...

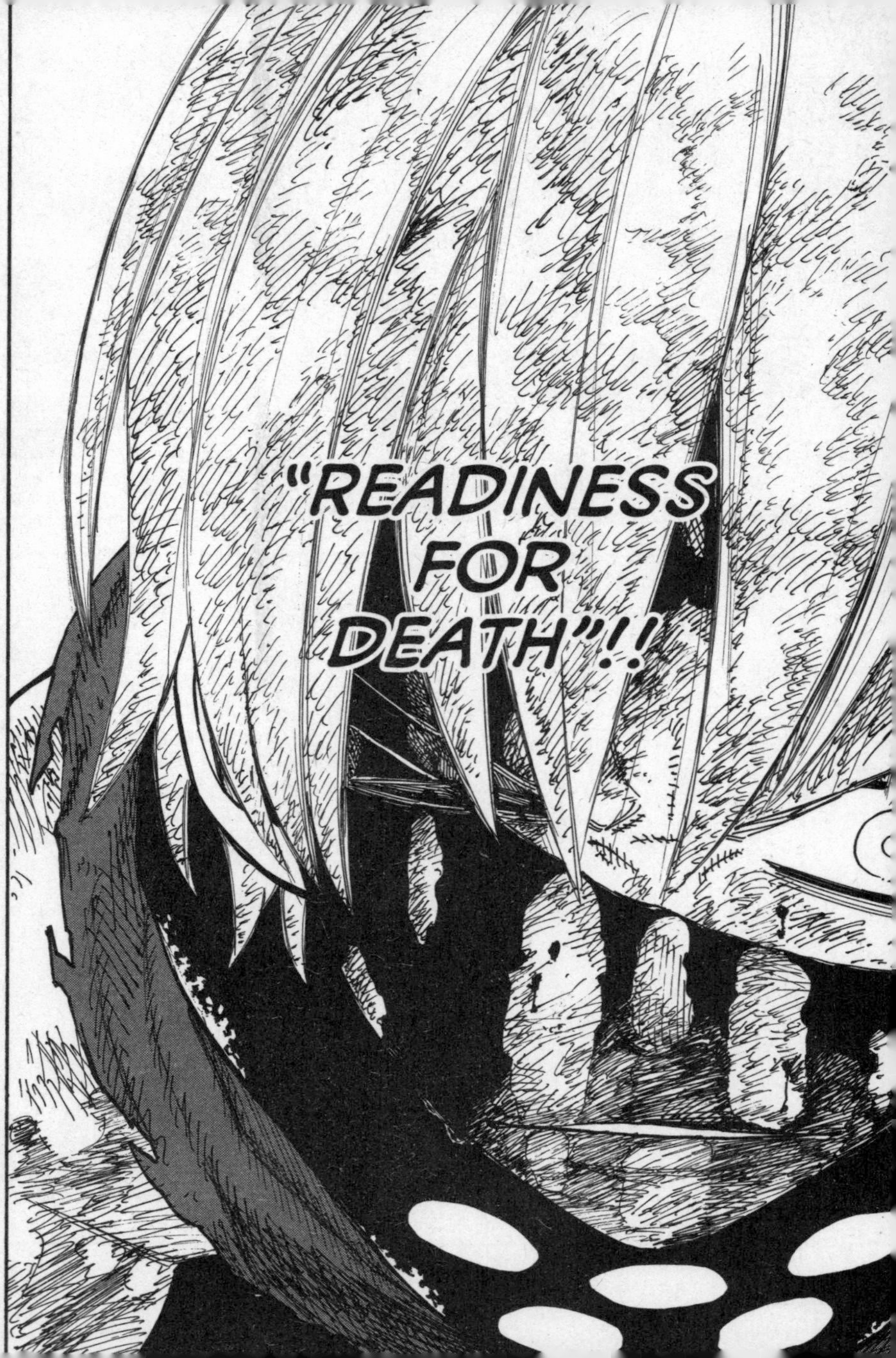
"READINESS FOR DEATH"!!

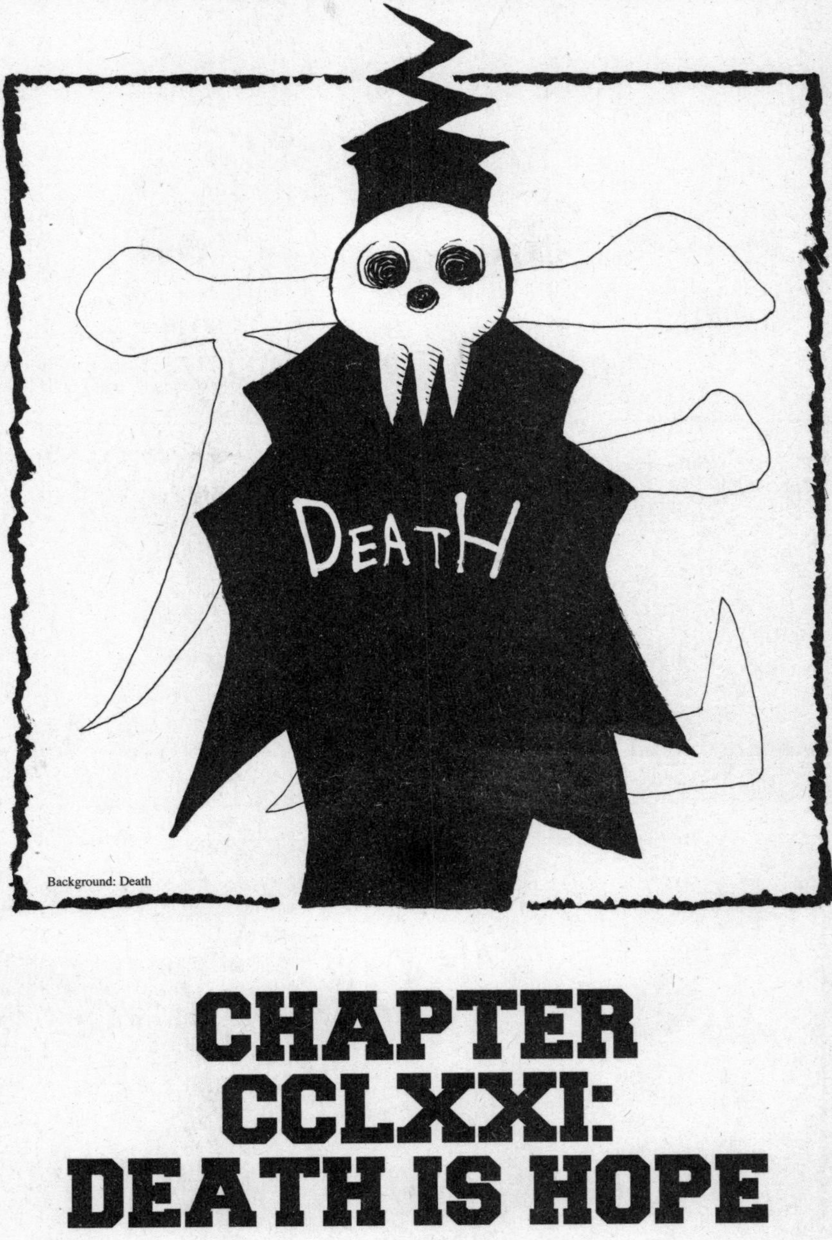
DEATH
Background: Death

CHAPTER CCLXXI: DEATH IS HOPE

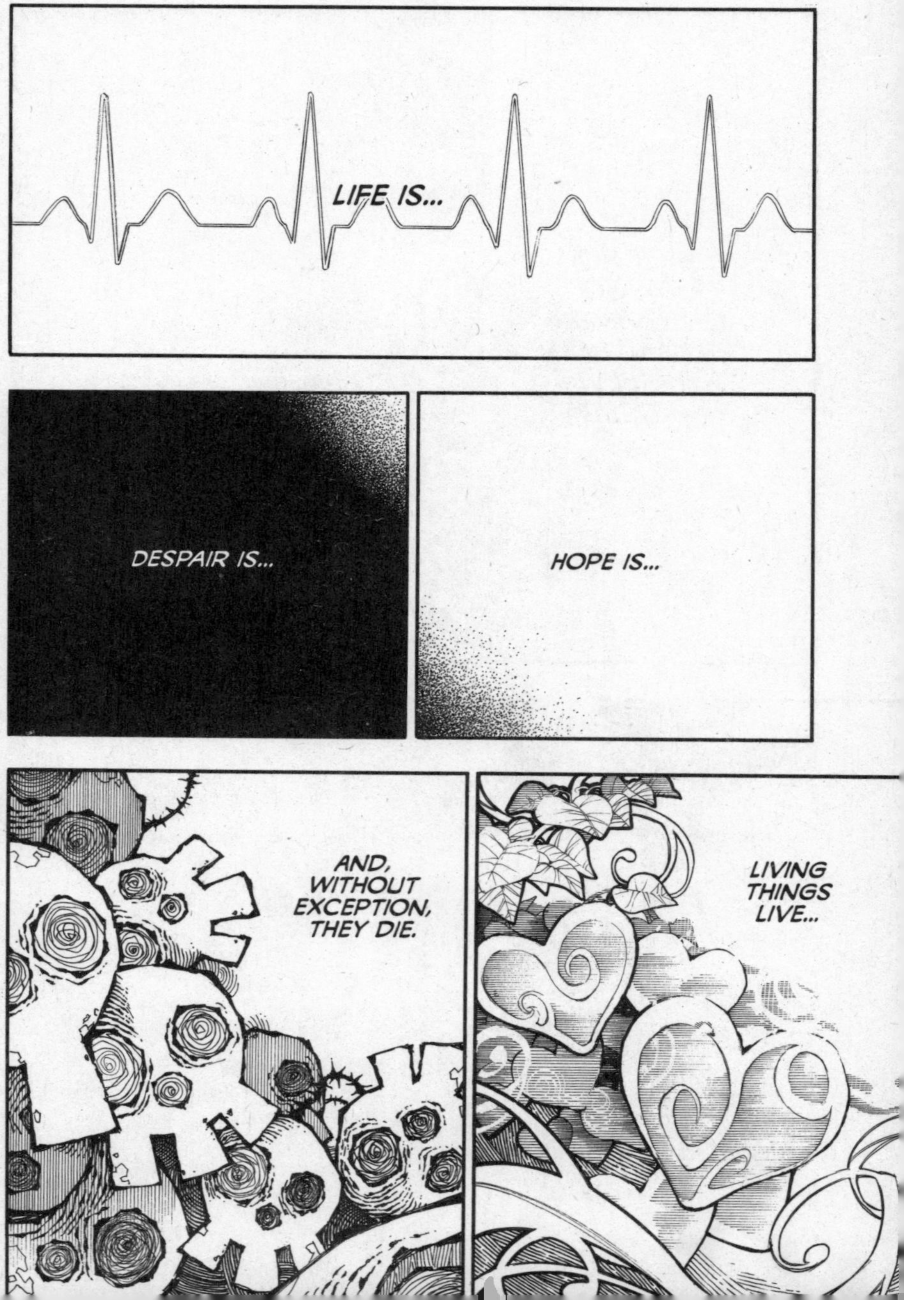
LIFE IS...
HOPE IS...
DESPAIR IS...
LIVING THINGS LIVE...
AND, WITHOUT EXCEPTION, THEY DIE.

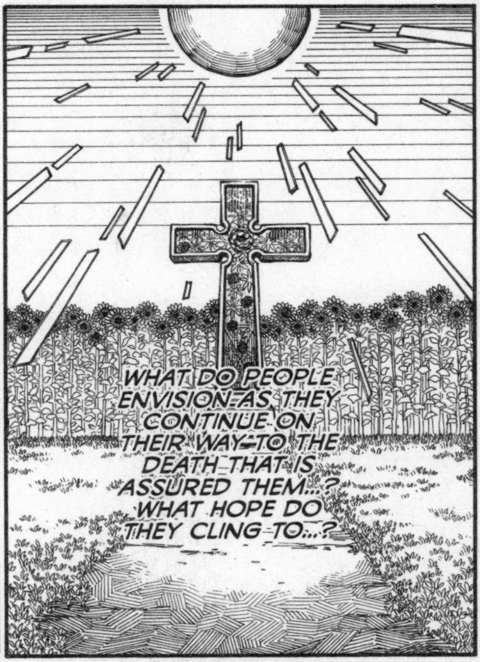
WHAT DO PEOPLE ENVISION AS THEY CONTINUE ON THEIR WAY TO THE DEATH THAT IS ASSURED THEM...?
WHAT HOPE DO THEY CLING TO...?

THAT IS HOW THEY GO ON LIVING, DISTRACTING THEMSELVES FROM DESPAIR.

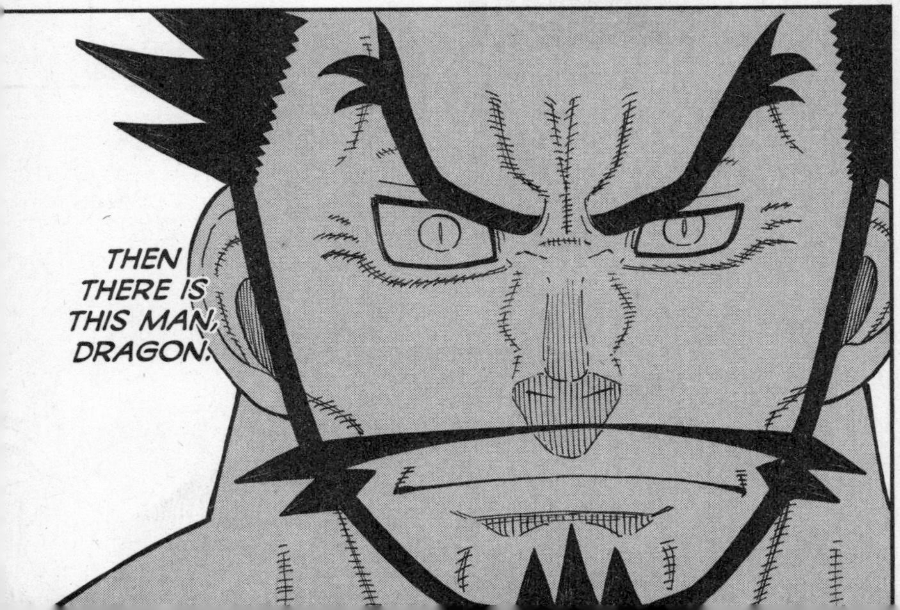
THEN THERE IS THIS MAN, DRAGON.

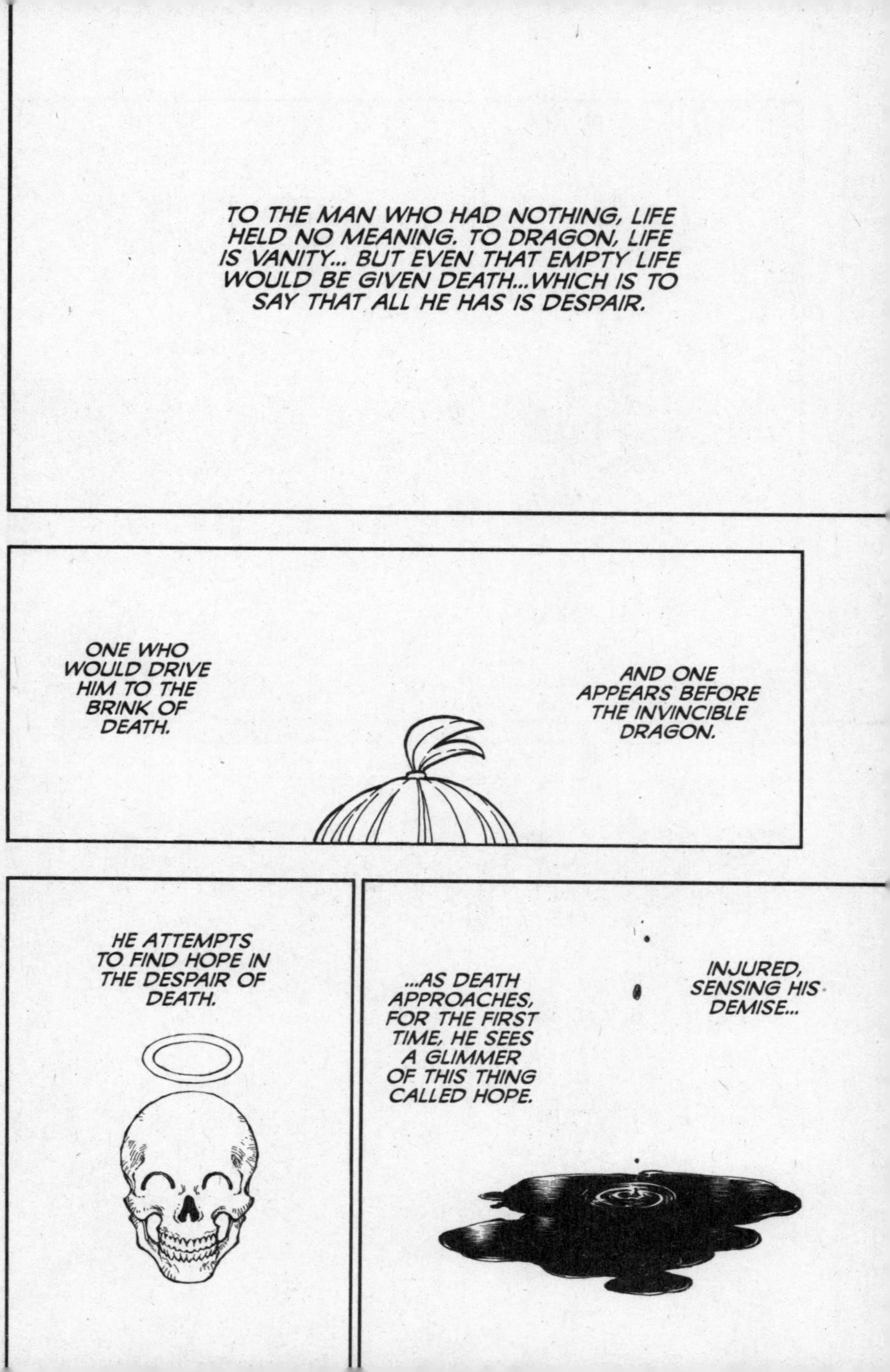
TO THE MAN WHO HAD NOTHING, LIFE HELD NO MEANING. TO DRAGON, LIFE IS VANITY... BUT EVEN THAT EMPTY LIFE WOULD BE GIVEN DEATH...WHICH IS TO SAY THAT ALL HE HAS IS DESPAIR.
AND ONE APPEARS BEFORE THE INVINCIBLE DRAGON.
ONE WHO WOULD DRIVE HIM TO THE BRINK OF DEATH.
INJURED, SENSING HIS DEMISE...
...AS DEATH APPROACHES, FOR THE FIRST TIME, HE SEES A GLIMMER OF THIS THING CALLED HOPE.
HE ATTEMPTS TO FIND HOPE IN THE DESPAIR OF DEATH.

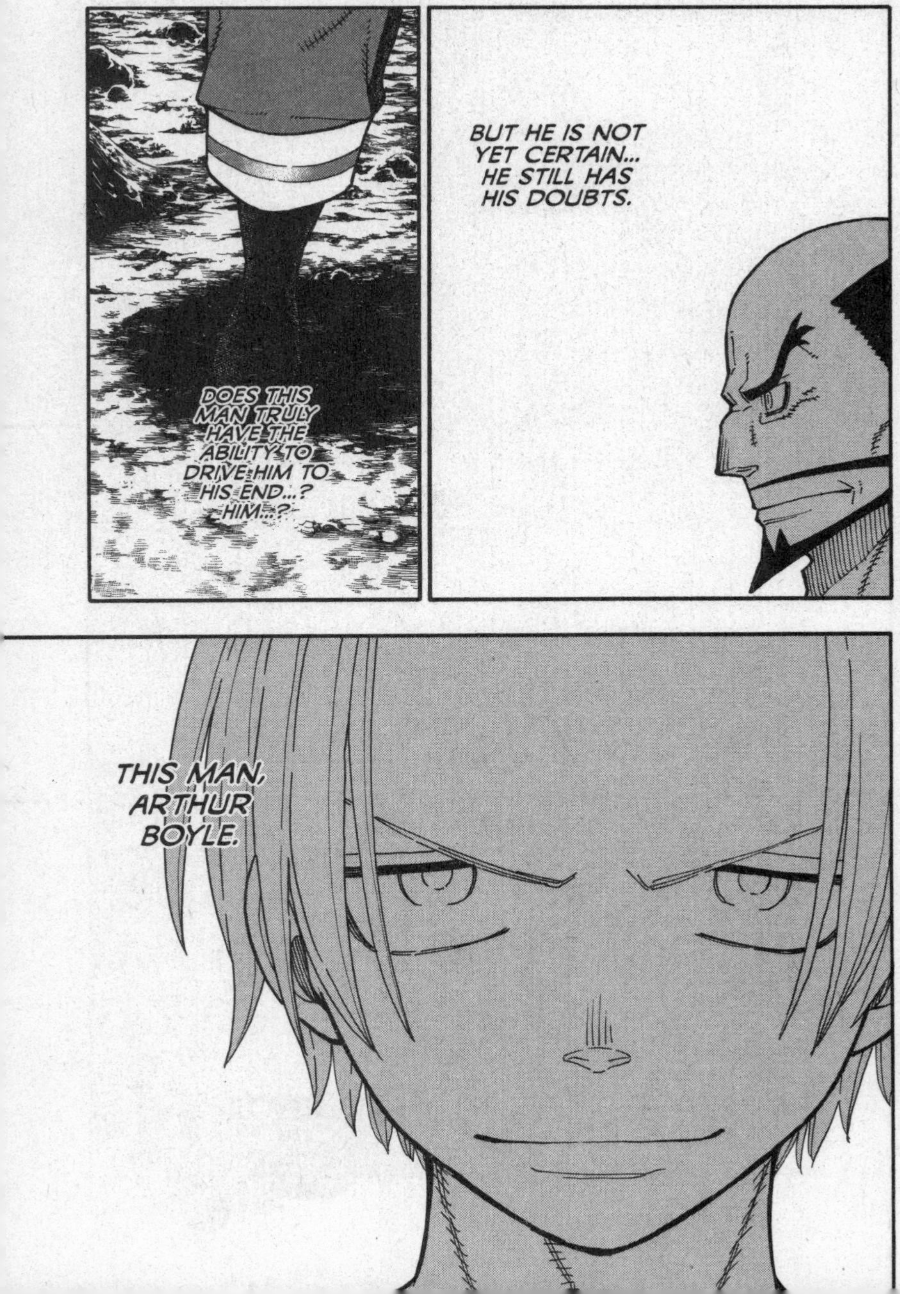
BUT HE IS NOT YET CERTAIN... HE STILL HAS HIS DOUBTS.
DOES THIS MAN TRULY HAVE THE ABILITY TO DRIVE HIM TO HIS END...? HIM...?
THIS MAN, ARTHUR BOYLE.

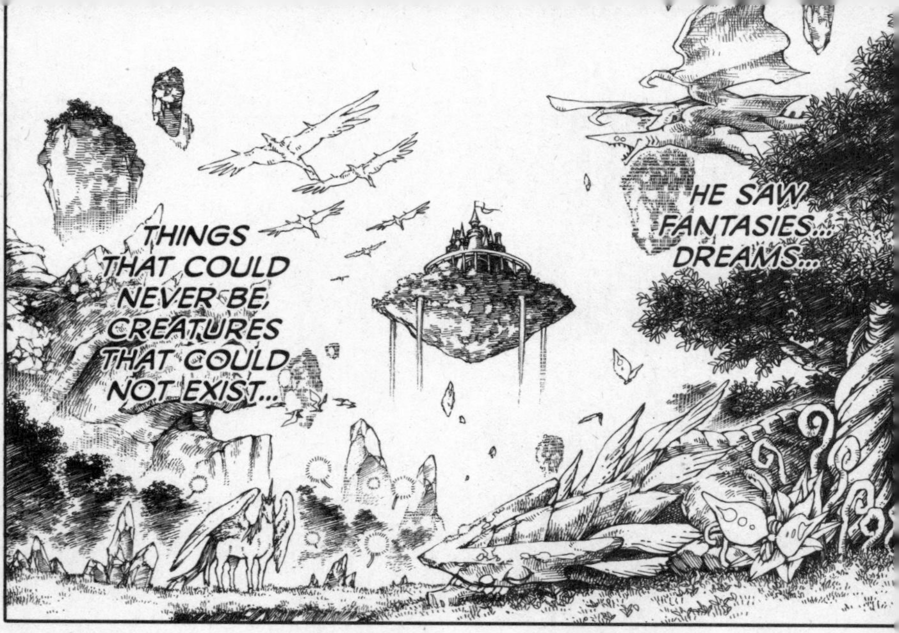
HE SAW FANTASIES... DREAMS...
THINGS THAT COULD NEVER BE, CREATURES THAT COULD NOT EXIST...

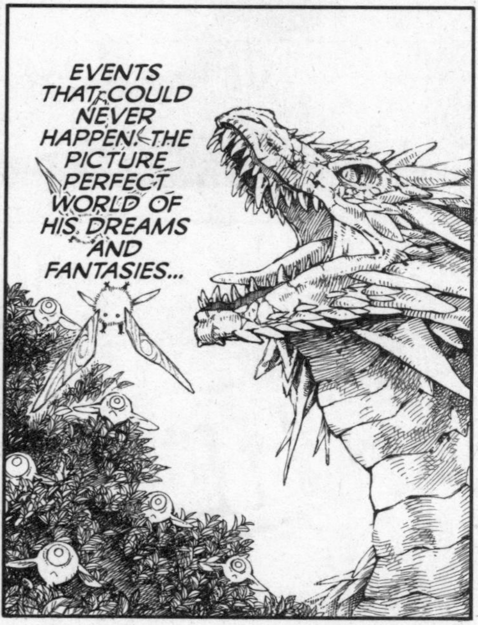
EVENTS THAT COULD NEVER HAPPEN. THE PICTURE PERFECT WORLD OF HIS DREAMS AND FANTASIES...

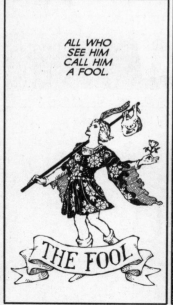

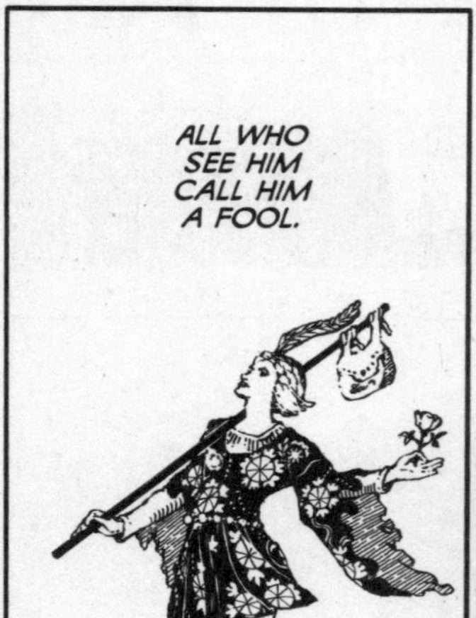
ALL WHO SEE HIM CALL HIM A FOOL.
THE FOOL

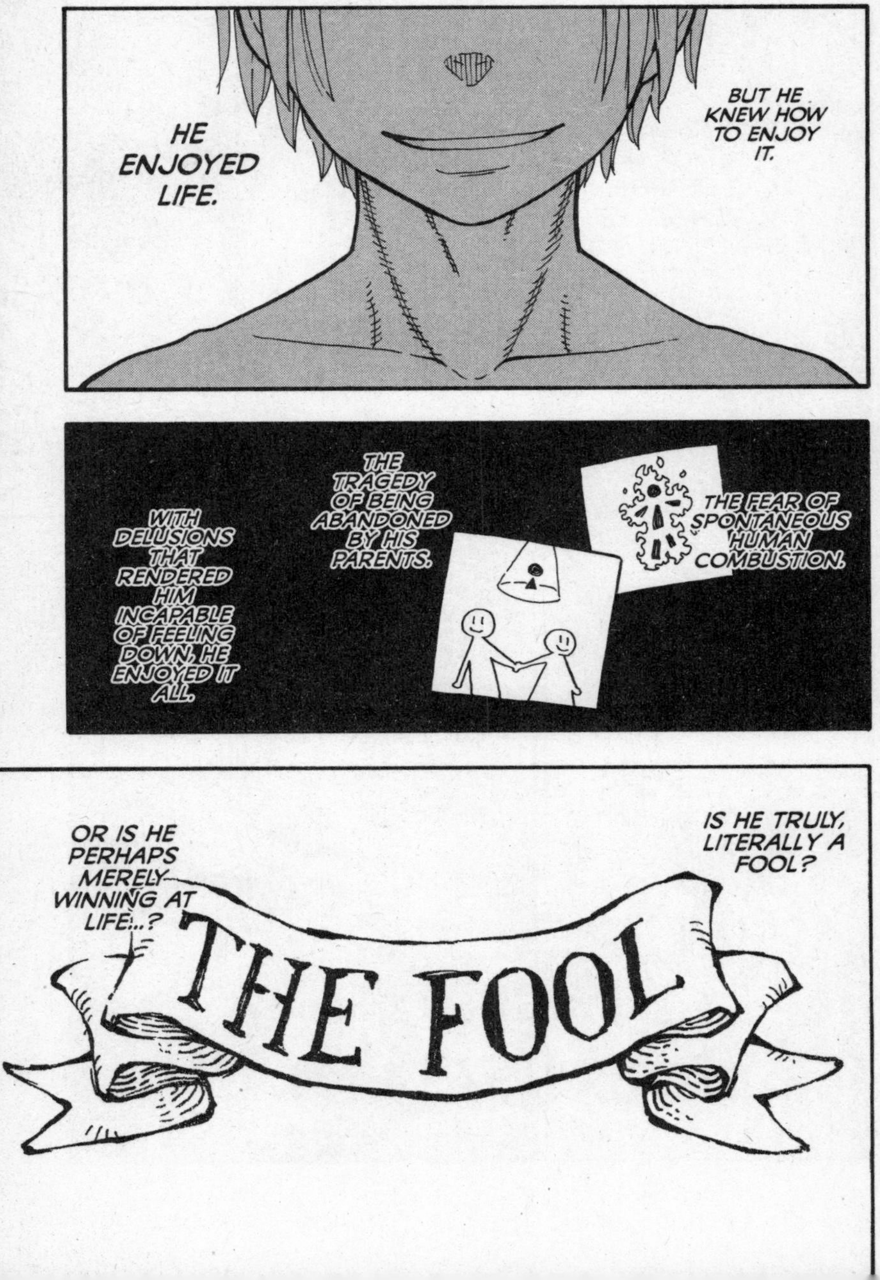
BUT HE KNEW HOW TO ENJOY IT.
HE ENJOYED LIFE.
THE FEAR OF SPONTANEOUS HUMAN COMBUSTION.
THE TRAGEDY OF BEING ABANDONED BY HIS PARENTS.
WITH DELUSIONS THAT RENDERED HIM INCAPABLE OF FEELING DOWN, HE ENJOYED IT ALL.
IS HE TRULY, LITERALLY A FOOL?
OR IS HE PERHAPS MERELY WINNING AT LIFE...?
THE FOOL

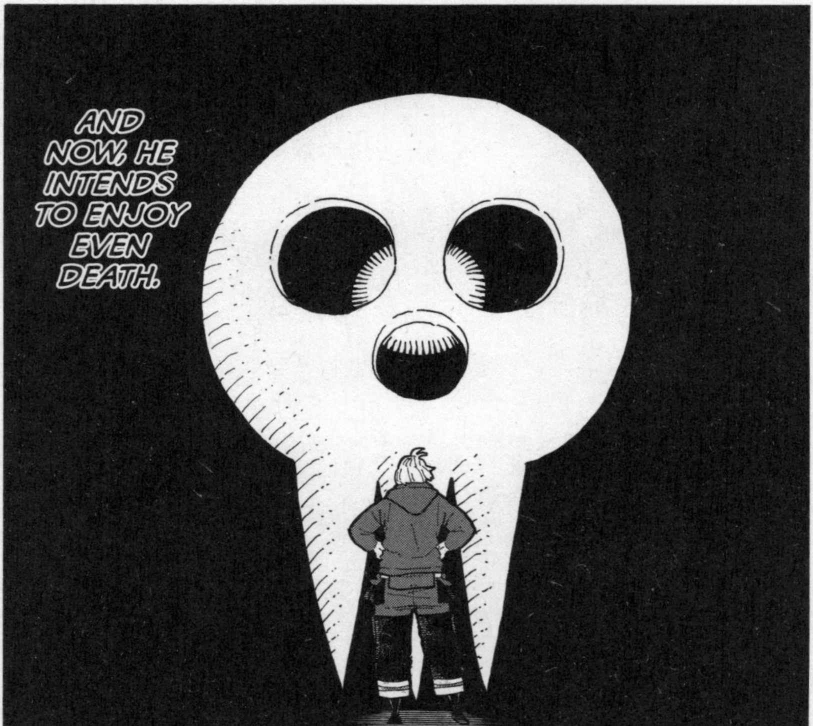
AND NOW, HE INTENDS TO ENJOY EVEN DEATH.
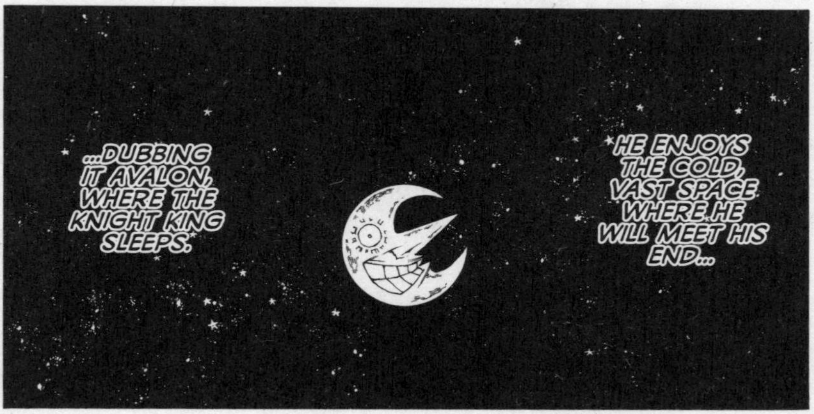
HE ENJOYS THE COLD, VAST SPACE WHERE HE WILL MEET HIS END...
...DUBBING IT AVALON, WHERE THE KNIGHT KING SLEEPS.

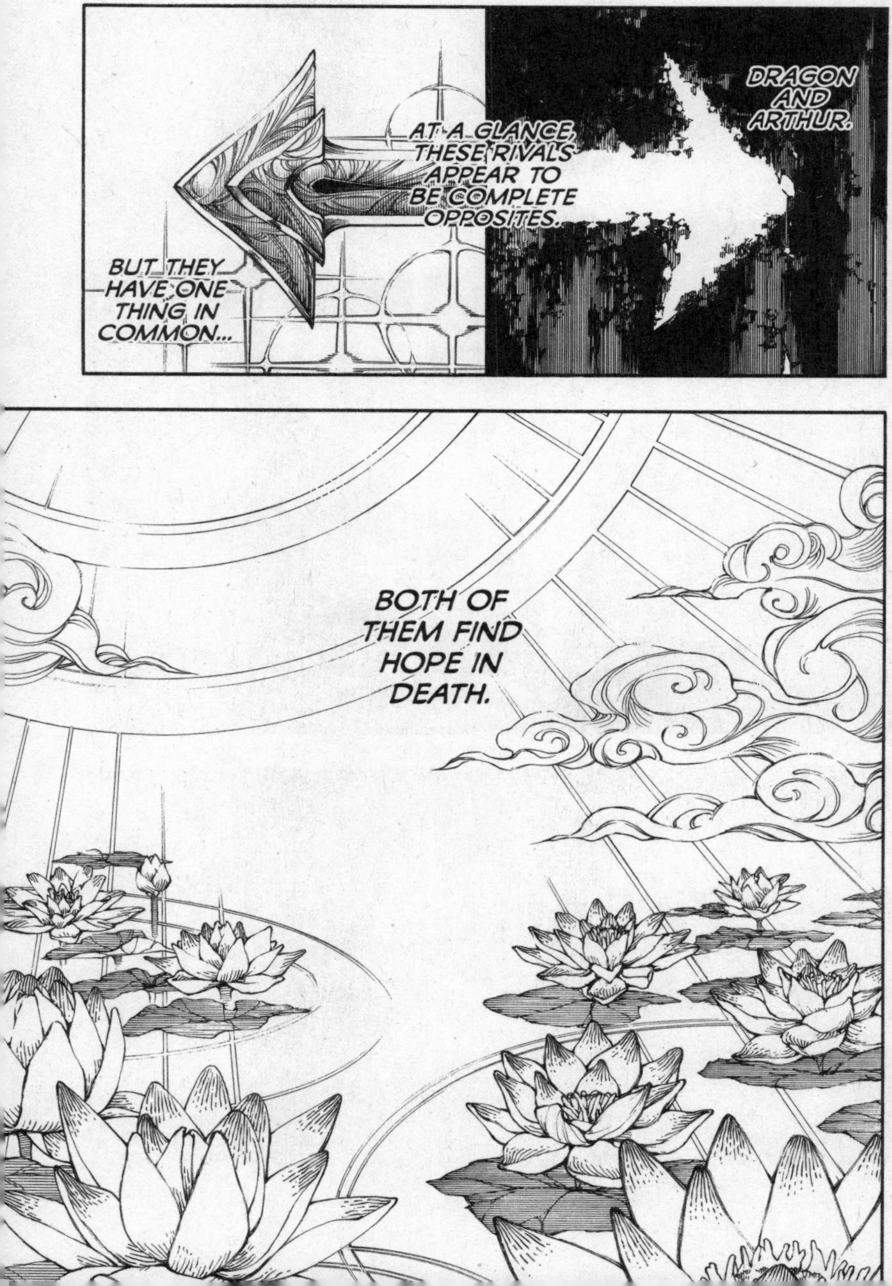
DRAGON AND ARTHUR.
AT A GLANCE, THESE RIVALS APPEAR TO BE COMPLETE OPPOSITES.
BUT THEY HAVE ONE THING IN COMMON...
BOTH OF THEM FIND HOPE IN DEATH.

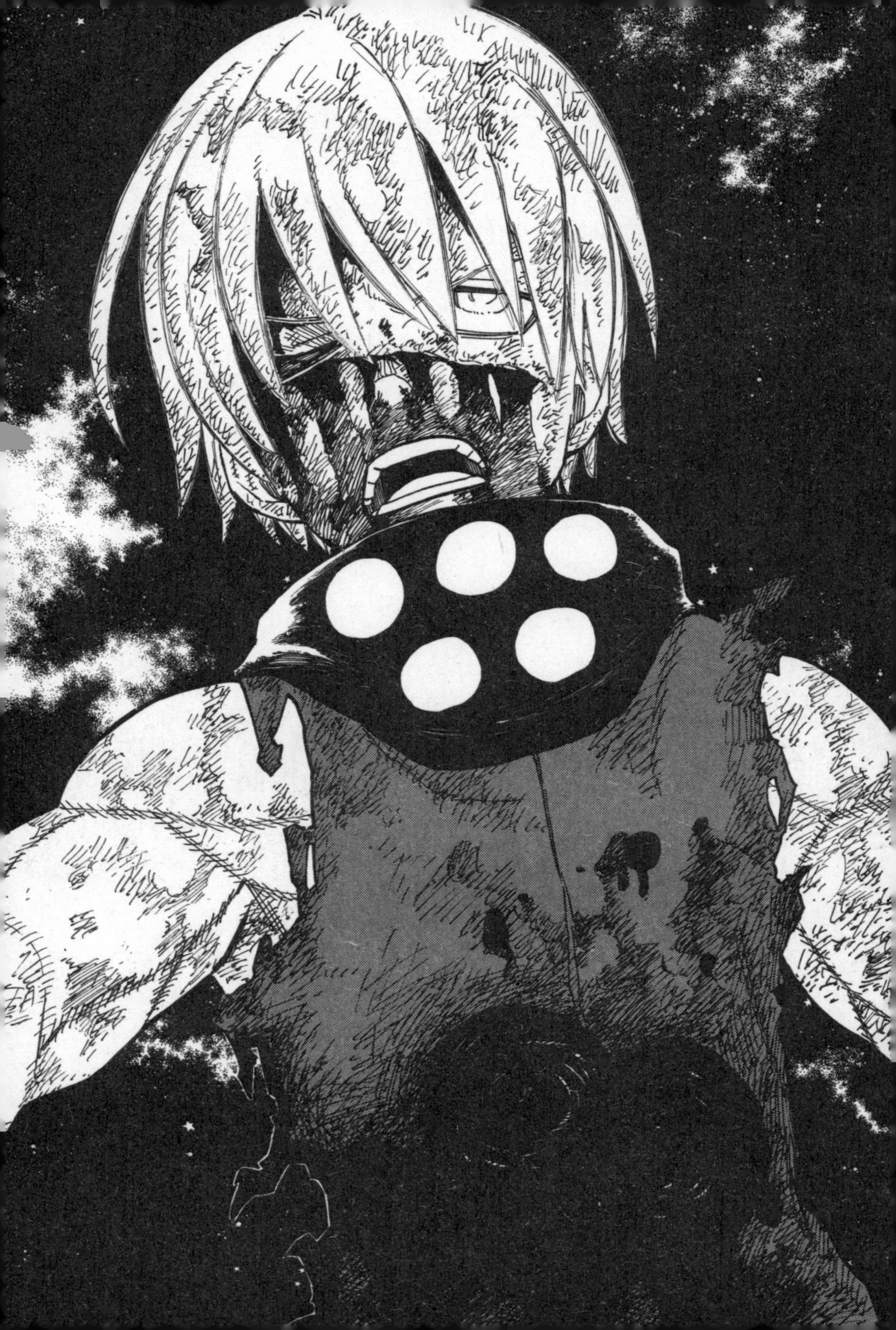

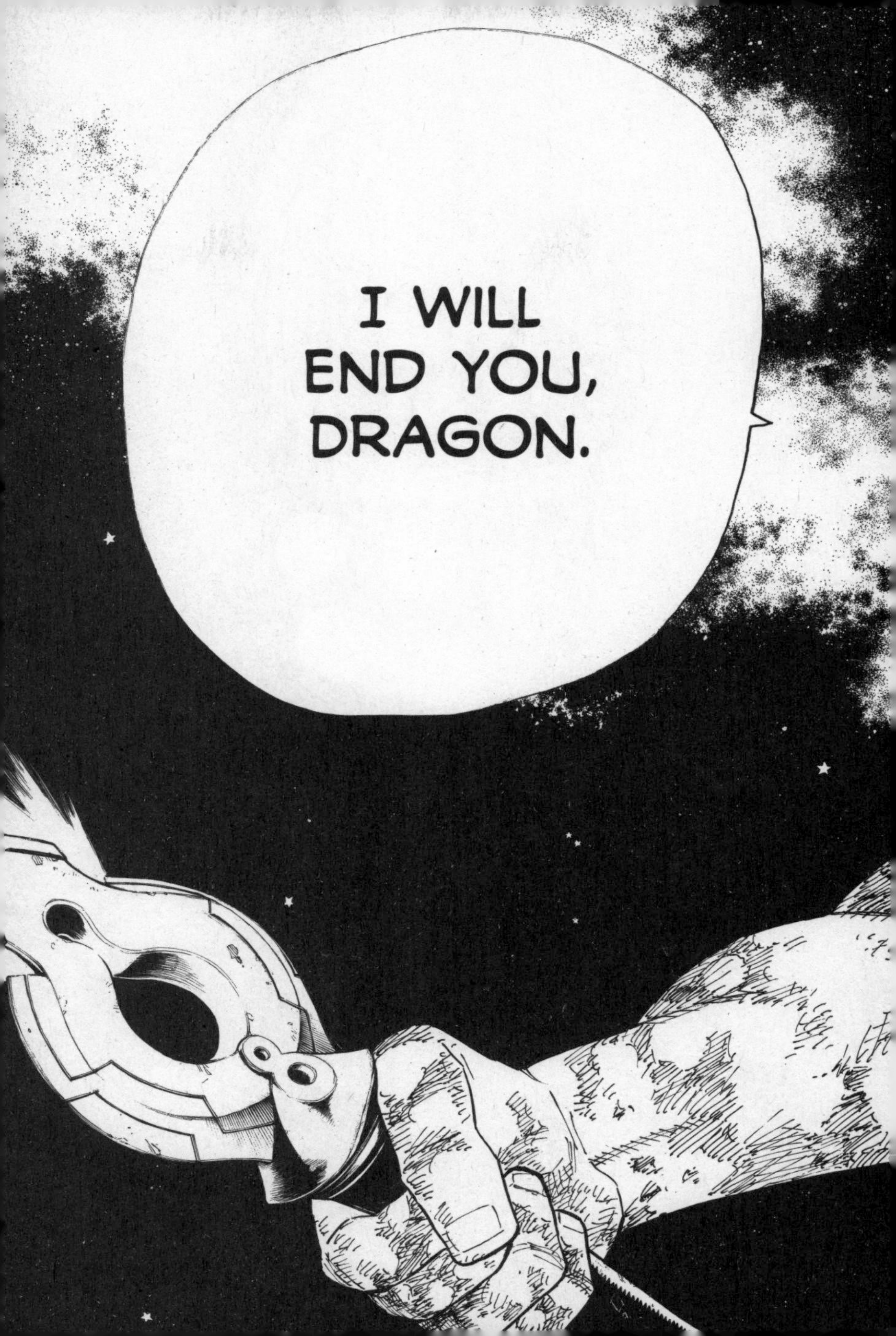
I WILL END YOU, DRAGON.

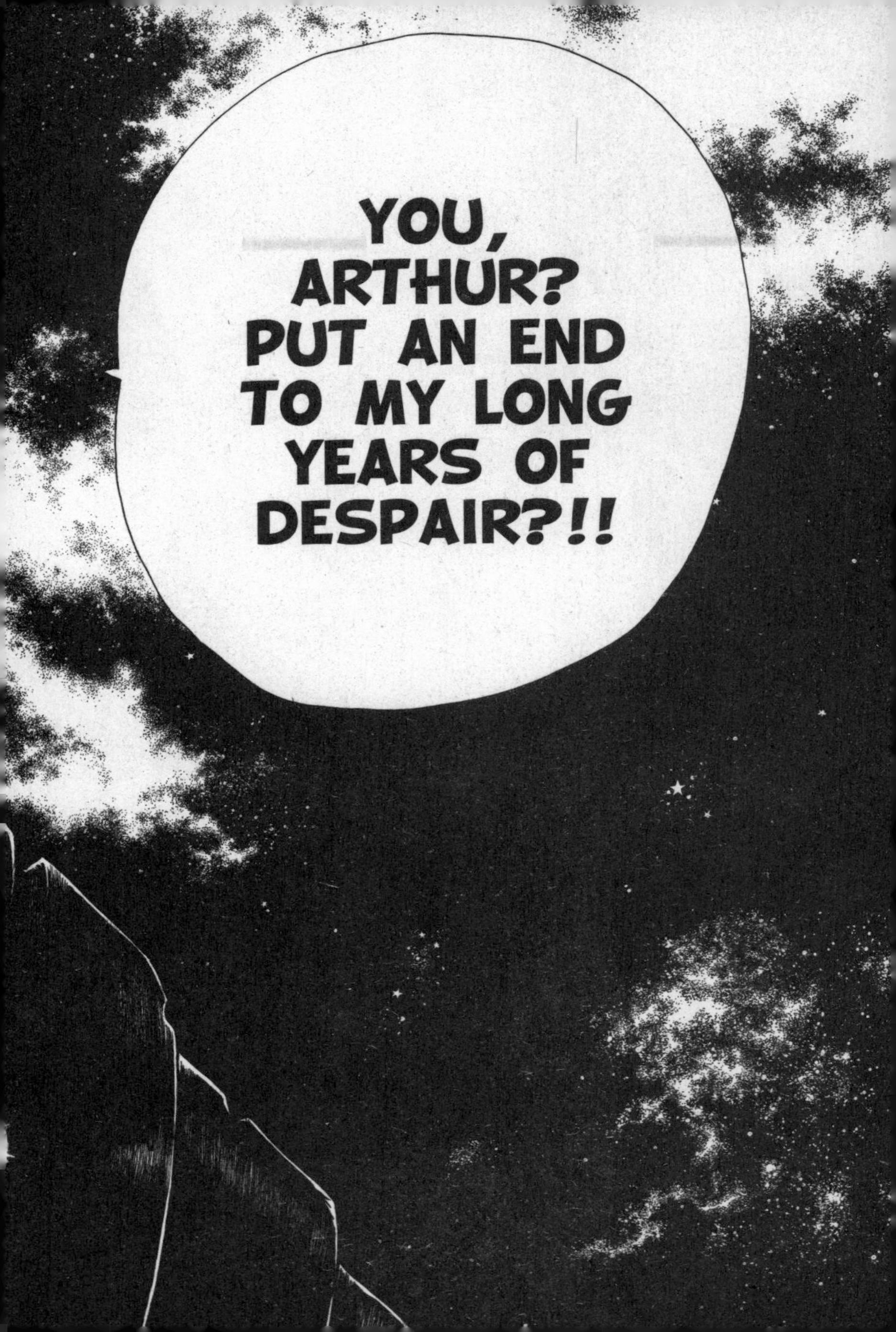
YOU, ARTHUR? PUT AN END TO MY LONG YEARS OF DESPAIR?!!

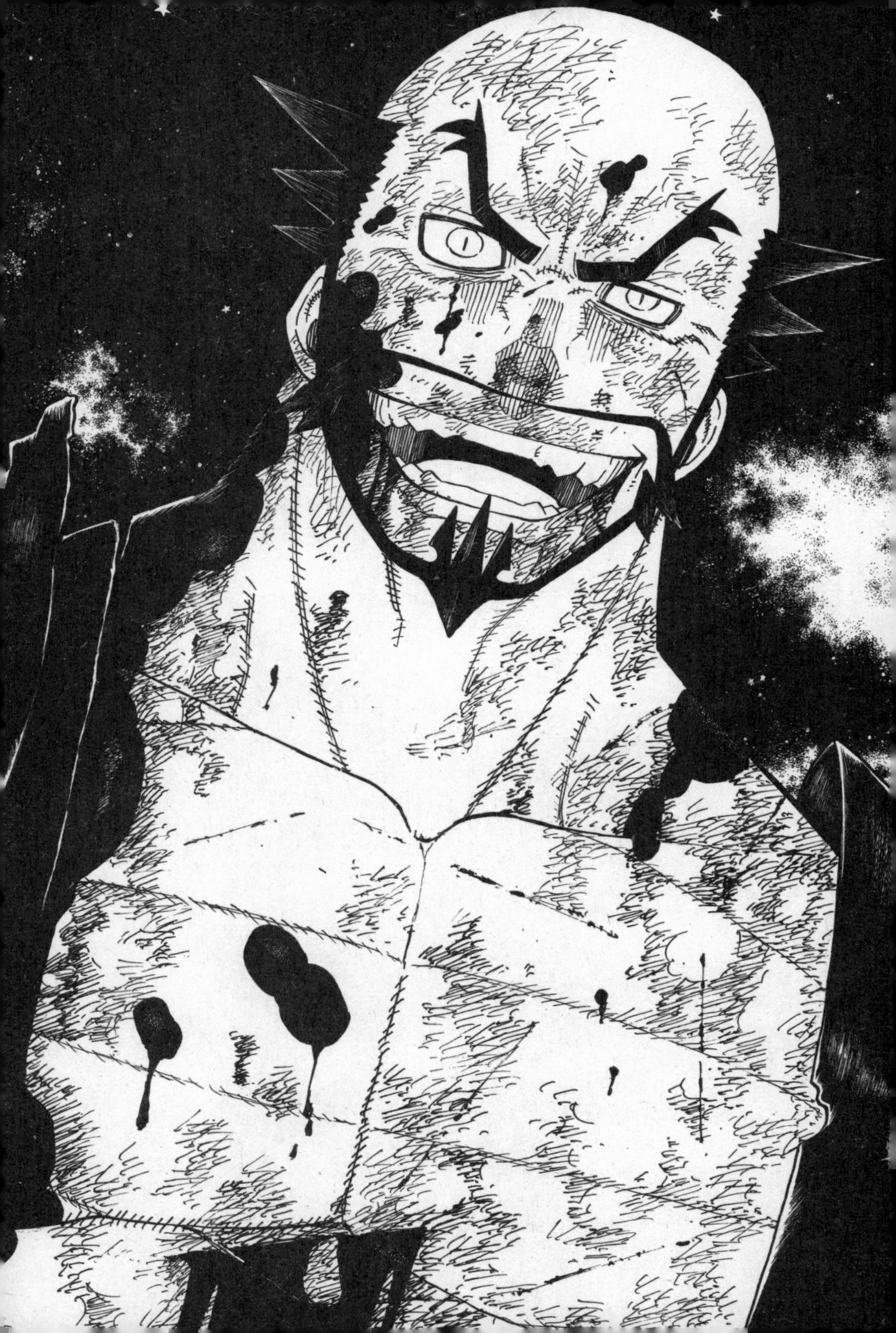

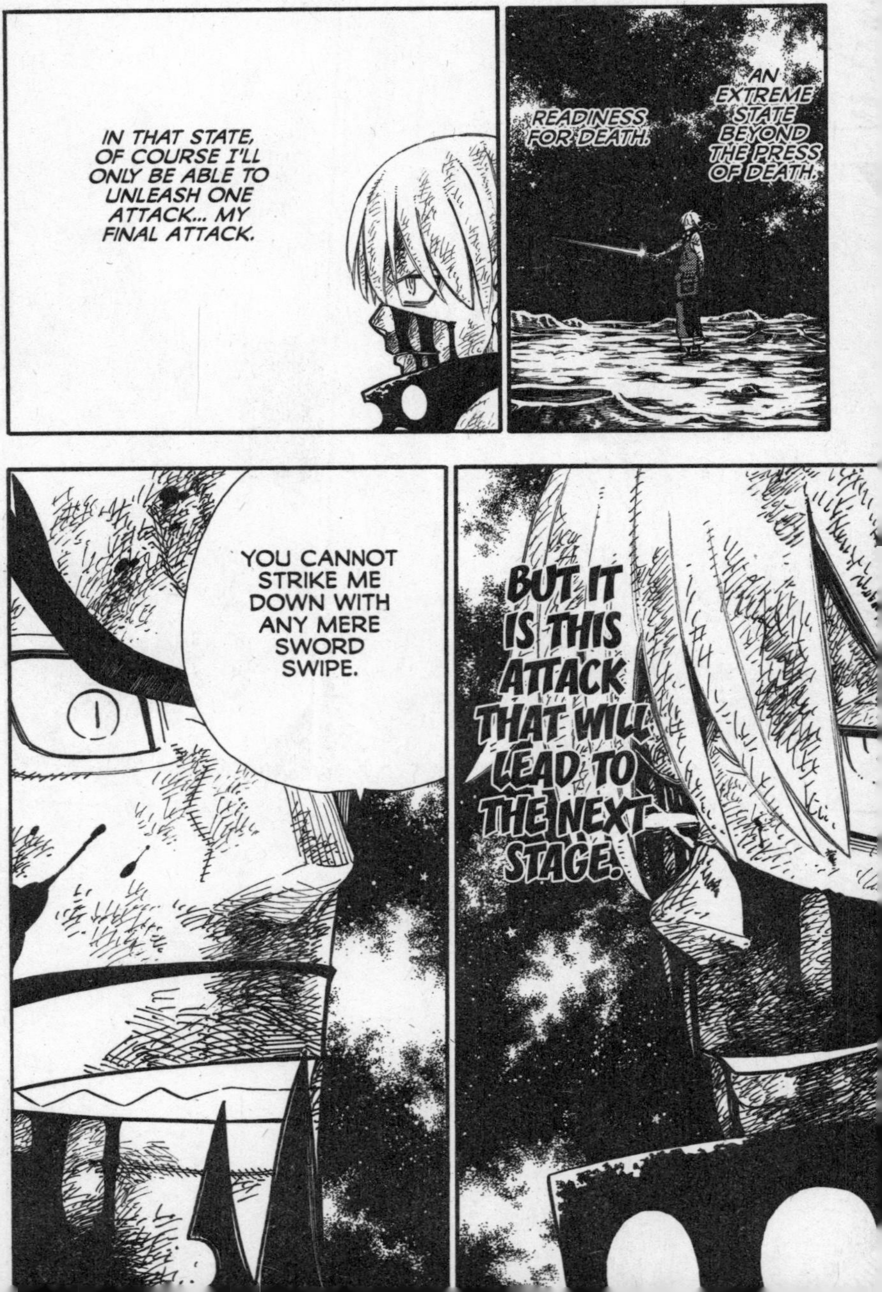
AN EXTREME STATE BEYOND THE PRESS OF DEATH.
READINESS FOR DEATH.
IN THAT STATE, OF COURSE I'LL ONLY BE ABLE TO UNLEASH ONE ATTACK... MY FINAL ATTACK.
BUT IT IS THIS ATTACK THAT WILL LEAD TO THE NEXT STAGE.
YOU CANNOT STRIKE ME DOWN WITH ANY MERE SWORD SWIPE.

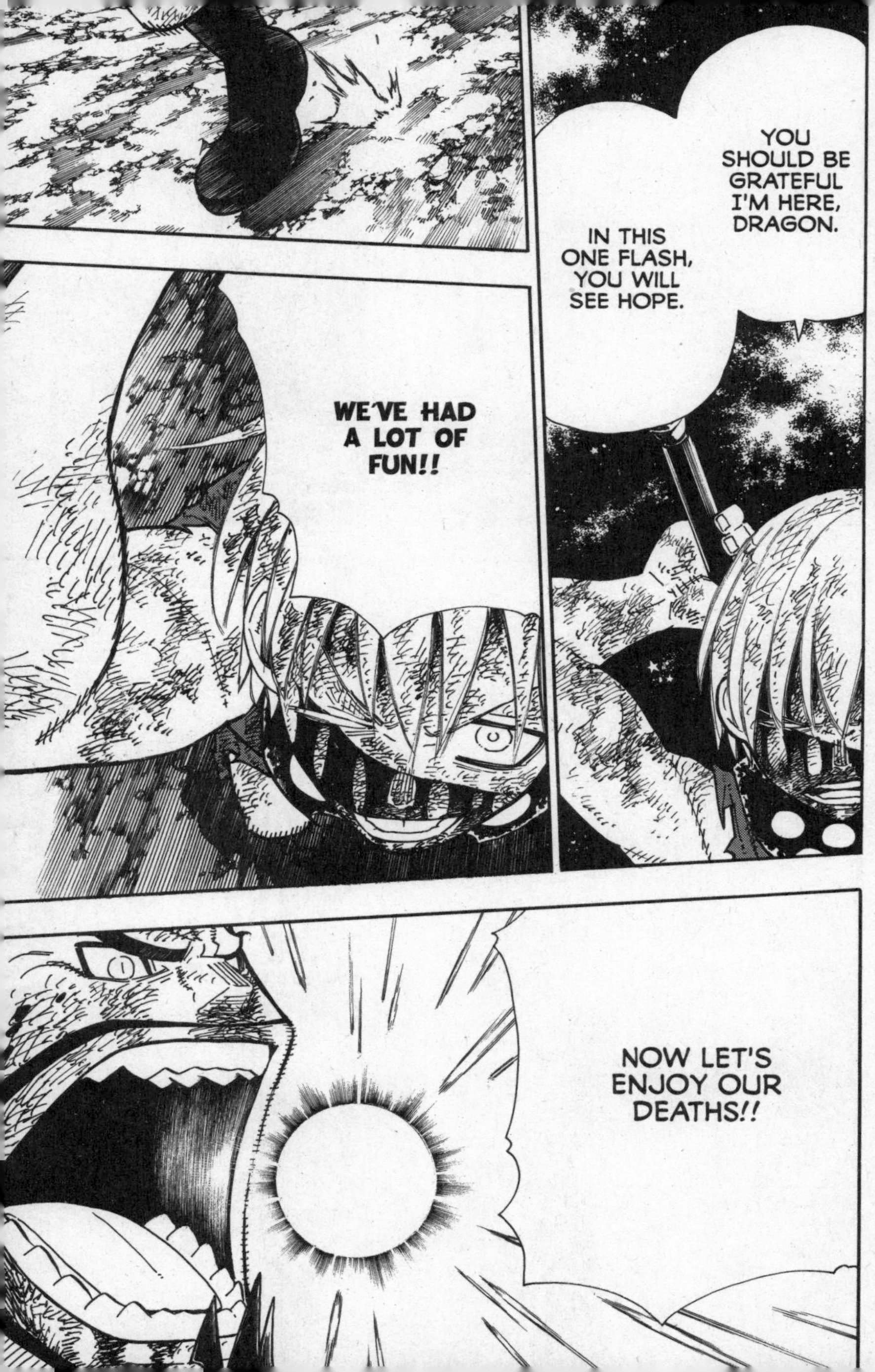
YOU SHOULD BE GRATEFUL I'M HERE, DRAGON.
IN THIS ONE FLASH, YOU WILL SEE HOPE.
WE'VE HAD A LOT OF FUN!!
NOW LET'S ENJOY OUR DEATHS!!

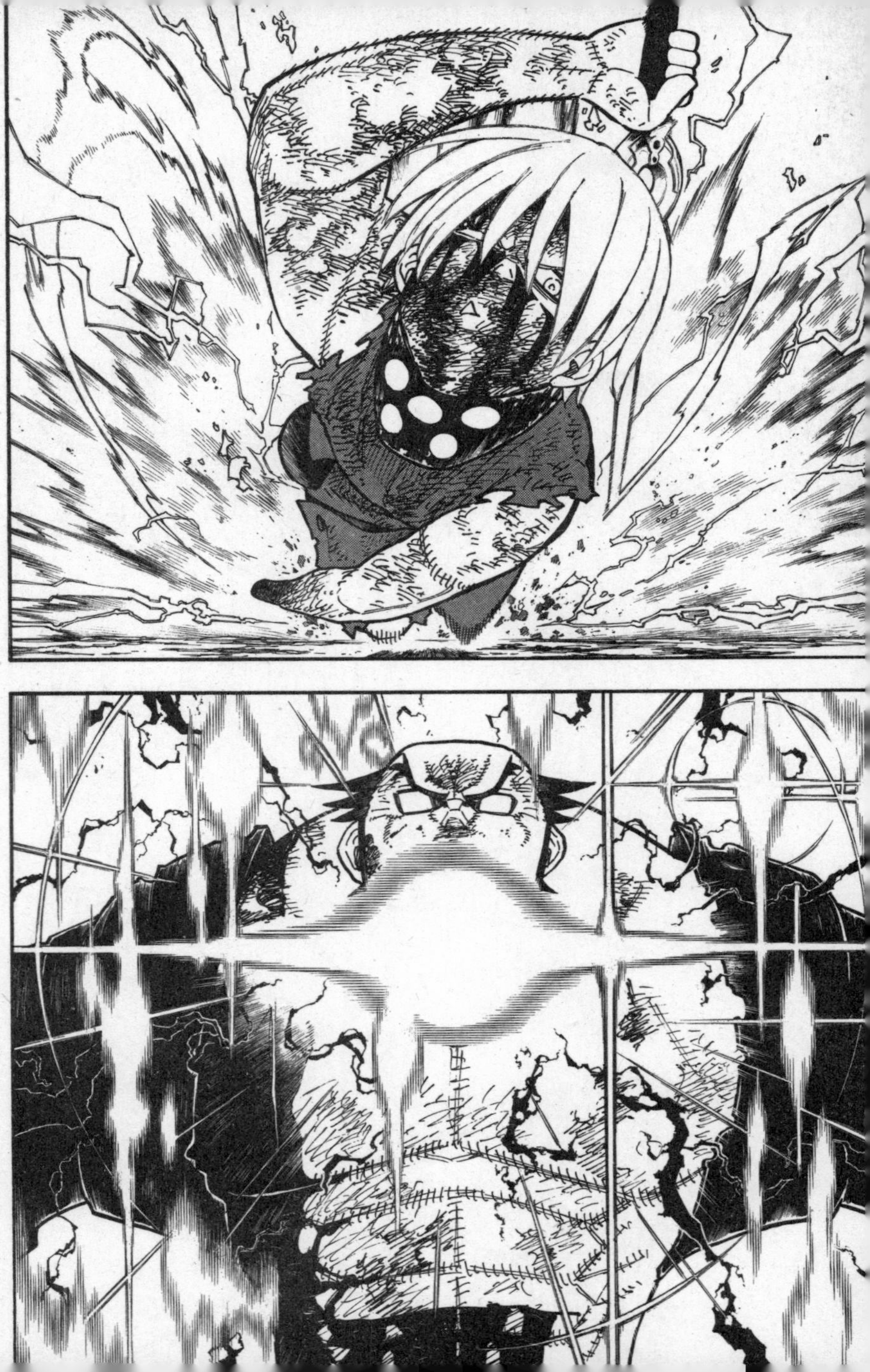

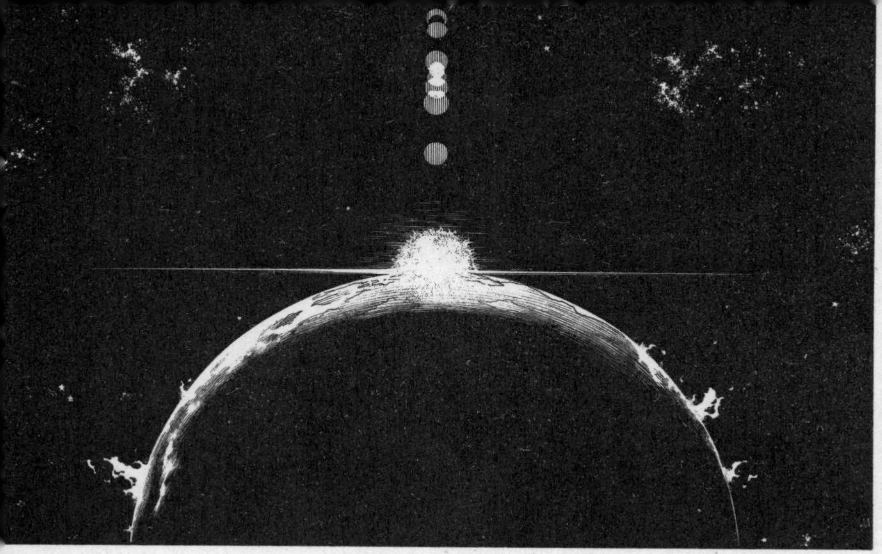
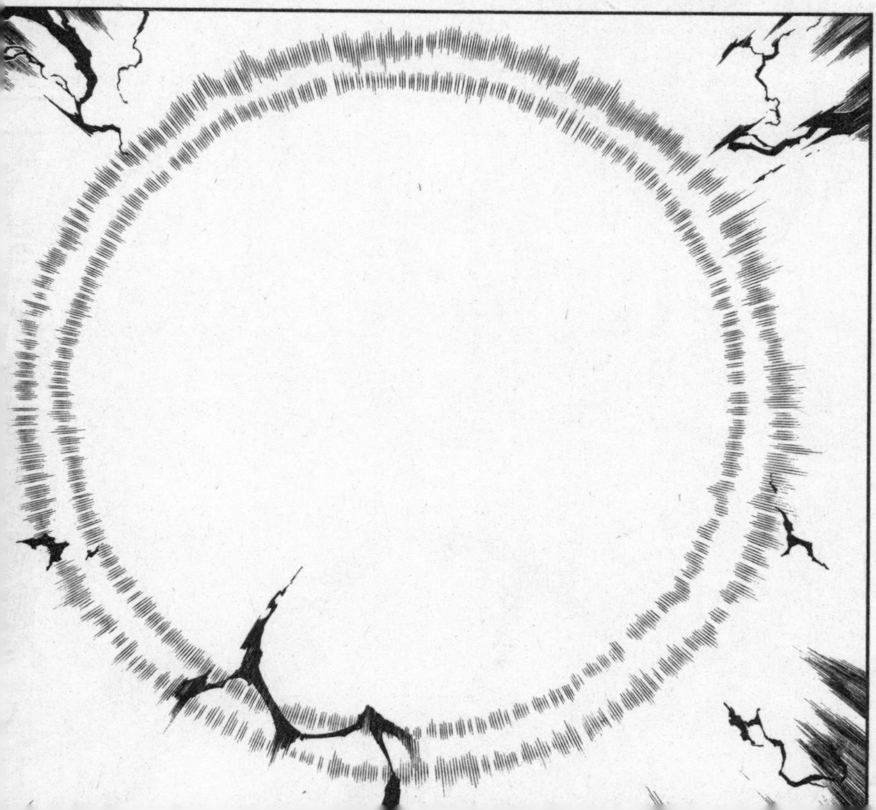

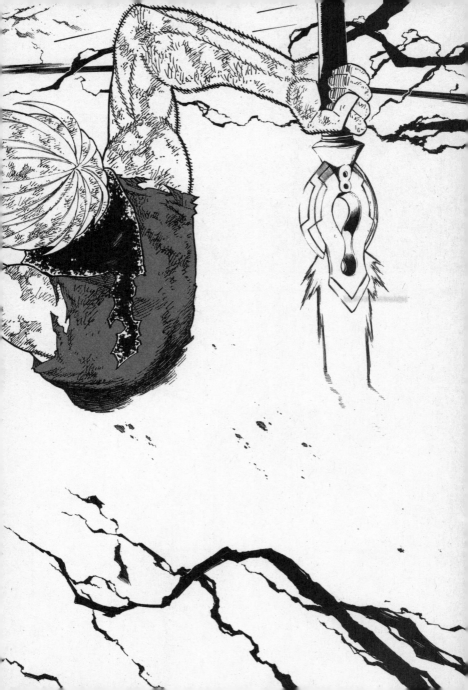

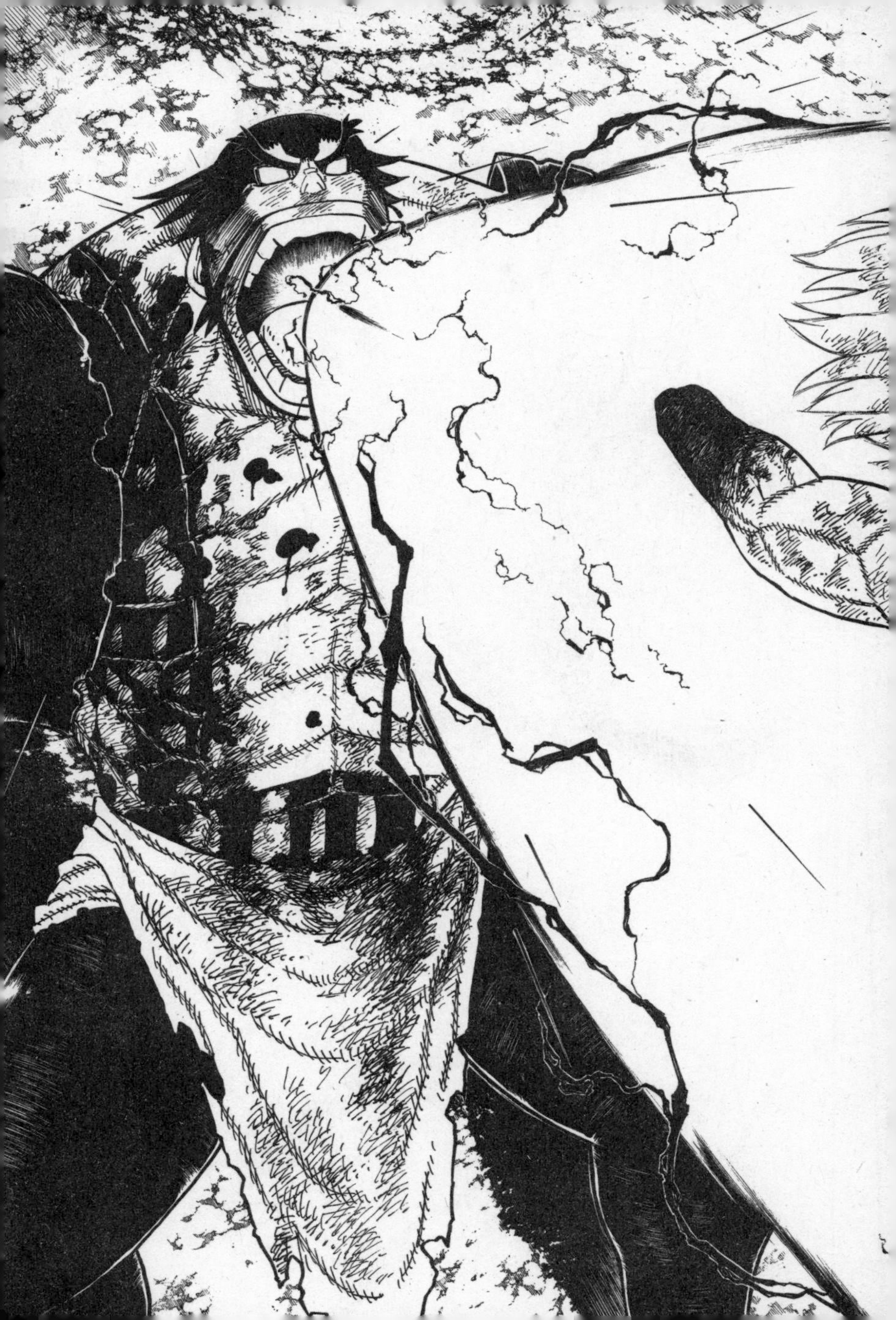

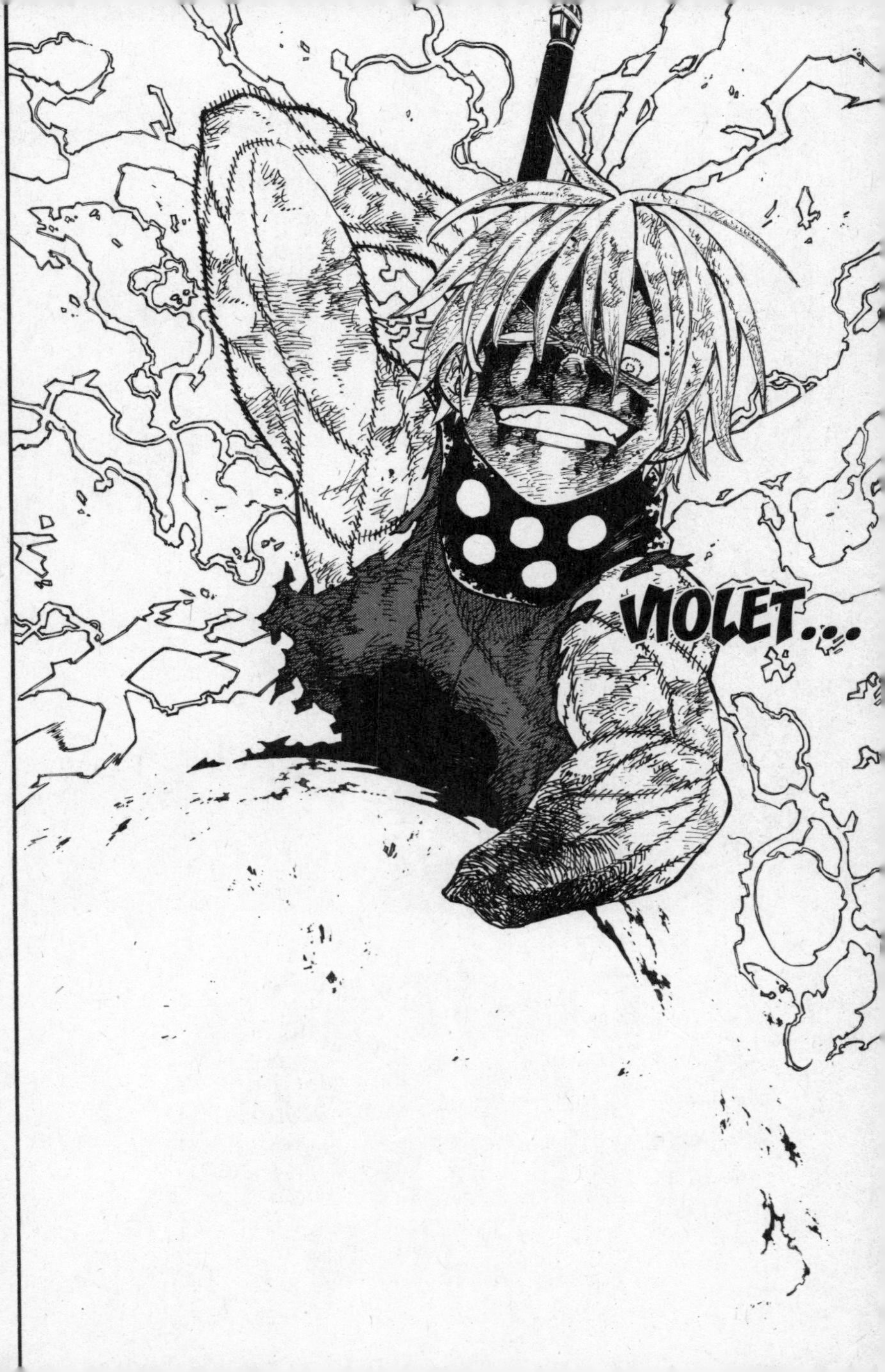
VIOLET...

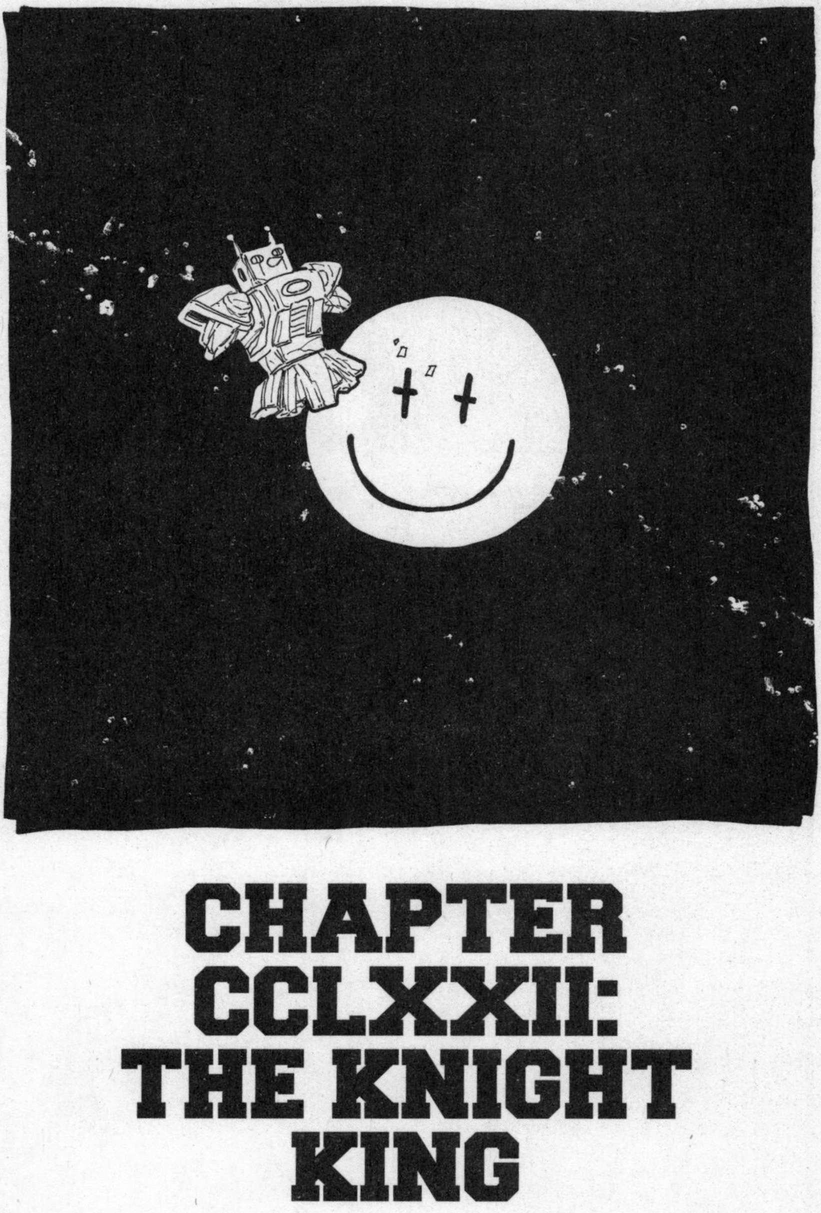

CHAPTER CCLXXII: THE KNIGHT KING

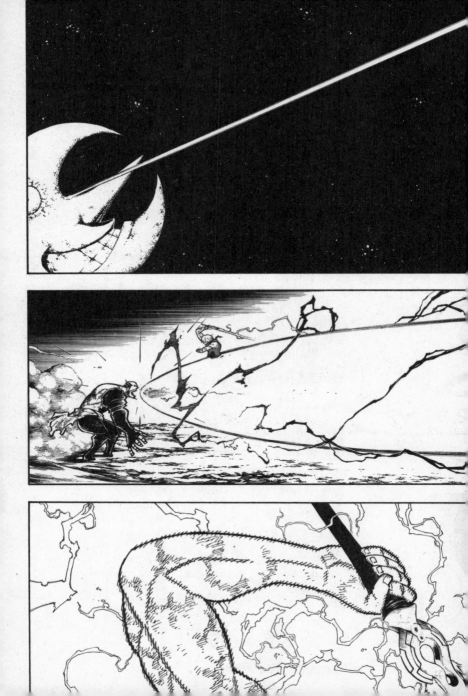

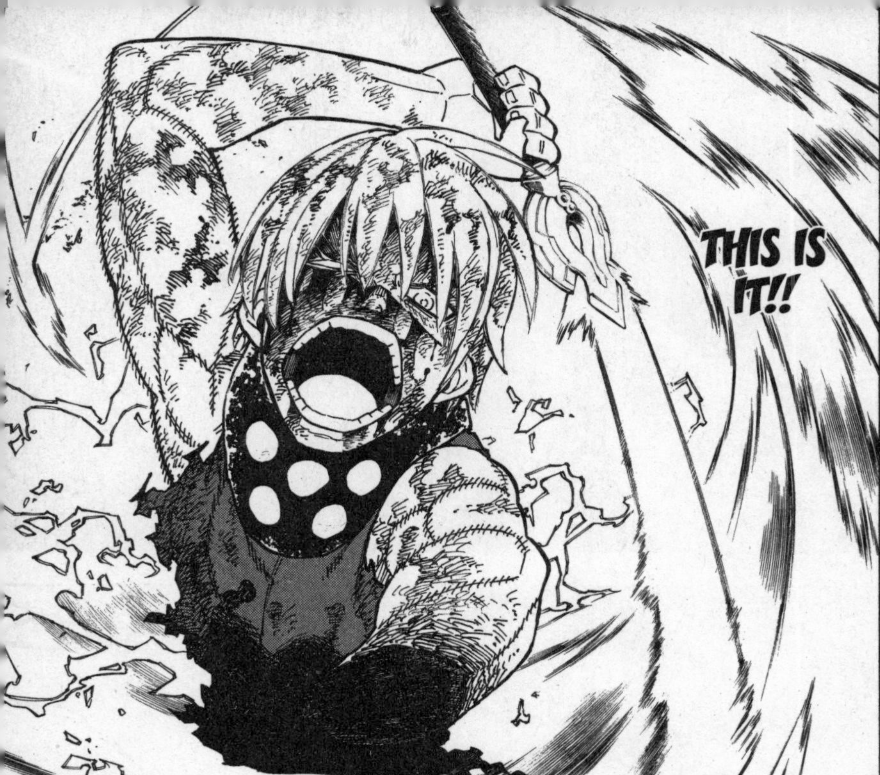
THIS IS IT!!
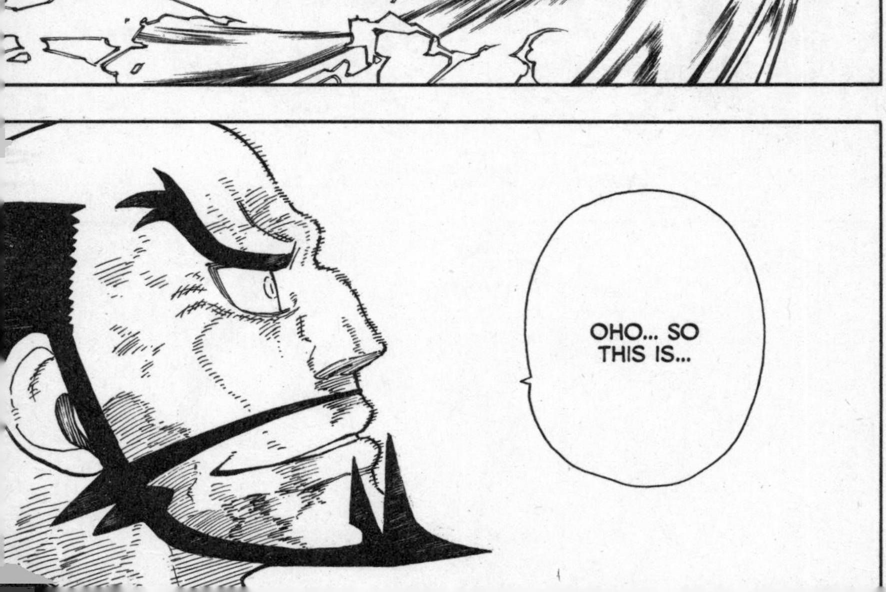
OHO... SO THIS IS...

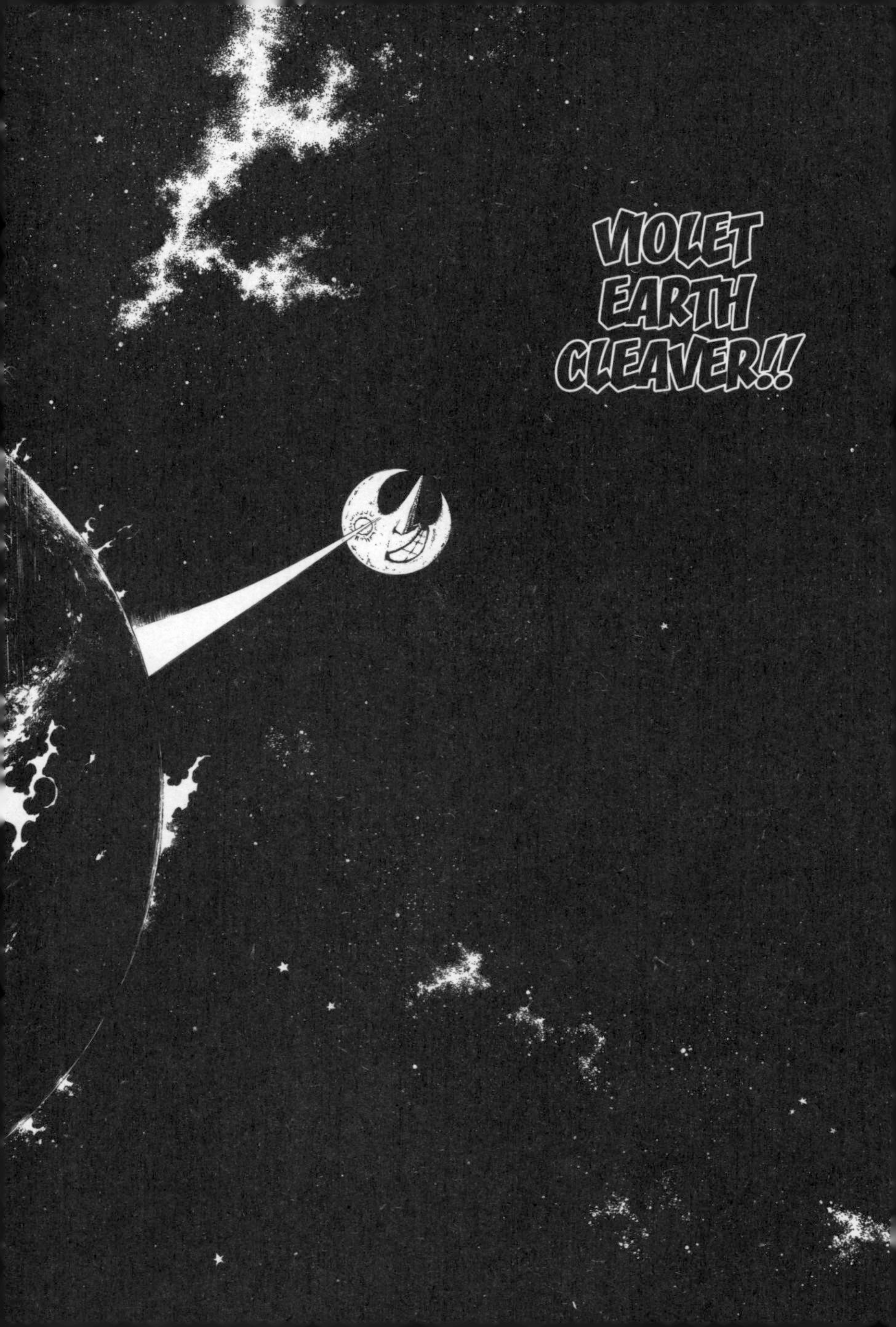
VIOLET EARTH CLEAVER!!

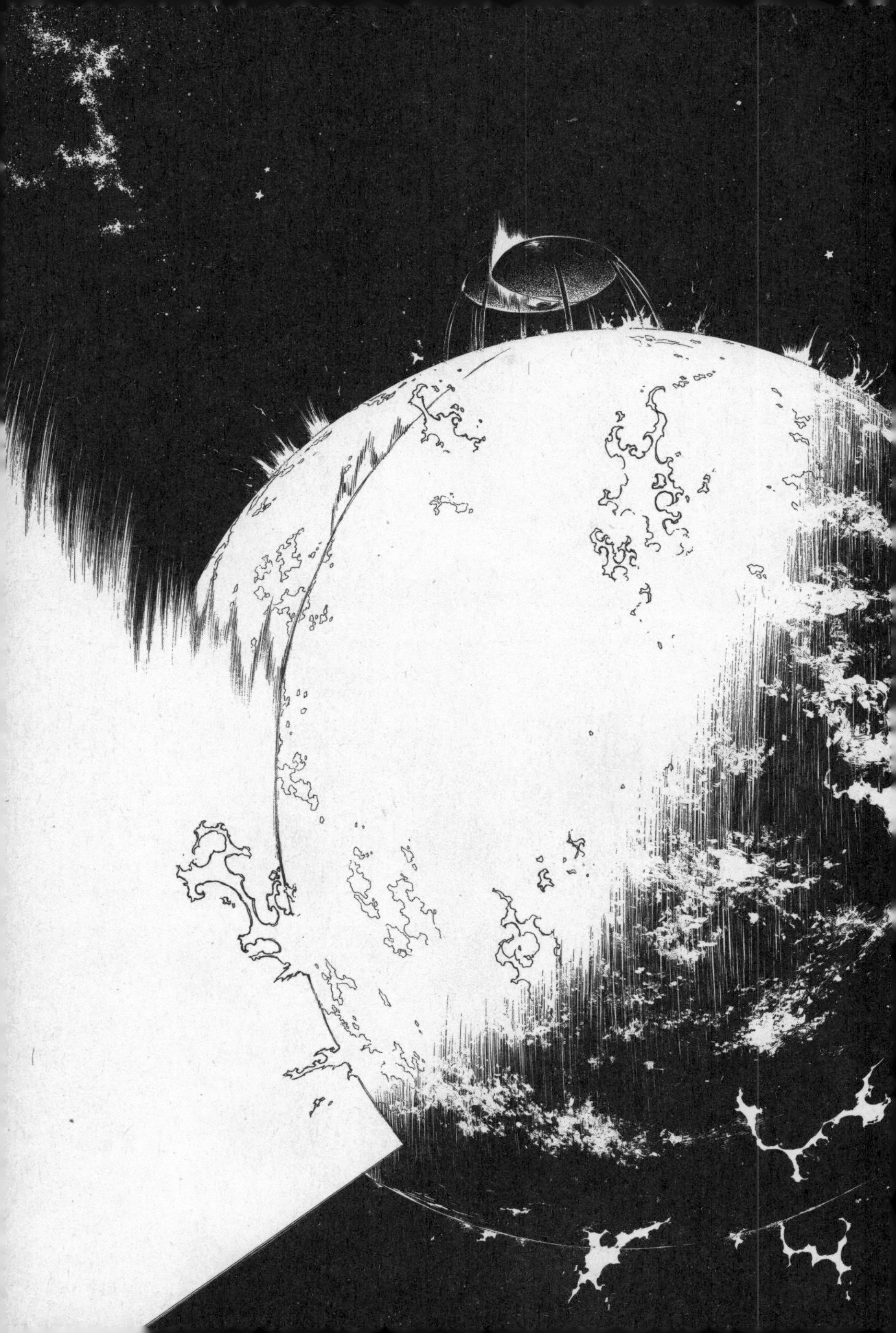

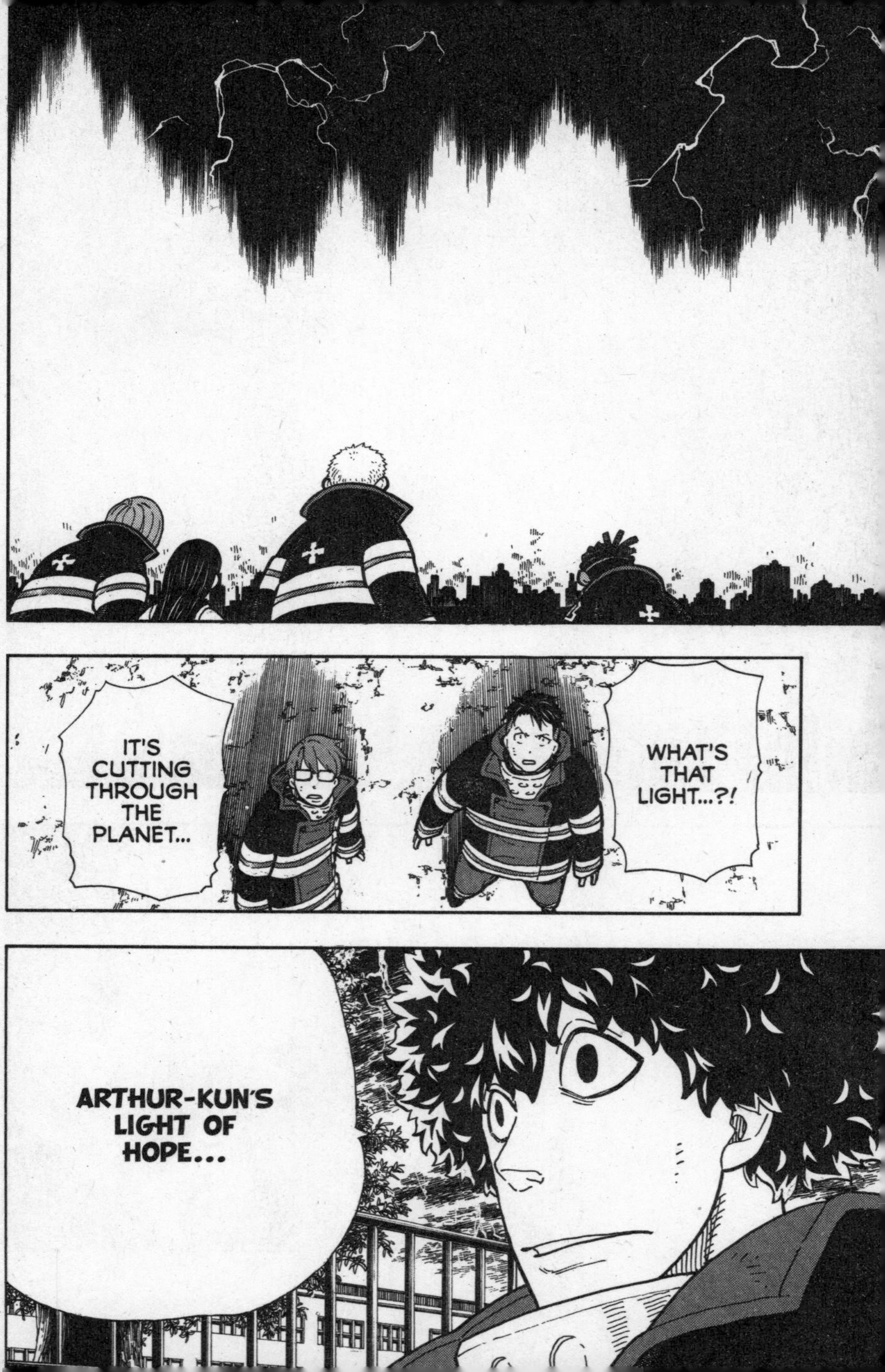
WHAT'S THAT LIGHT...?!
IT'S CUTTING THROUGH THE PLANET...
ARTHUR-KUN'S LIGHT OF HOPE...

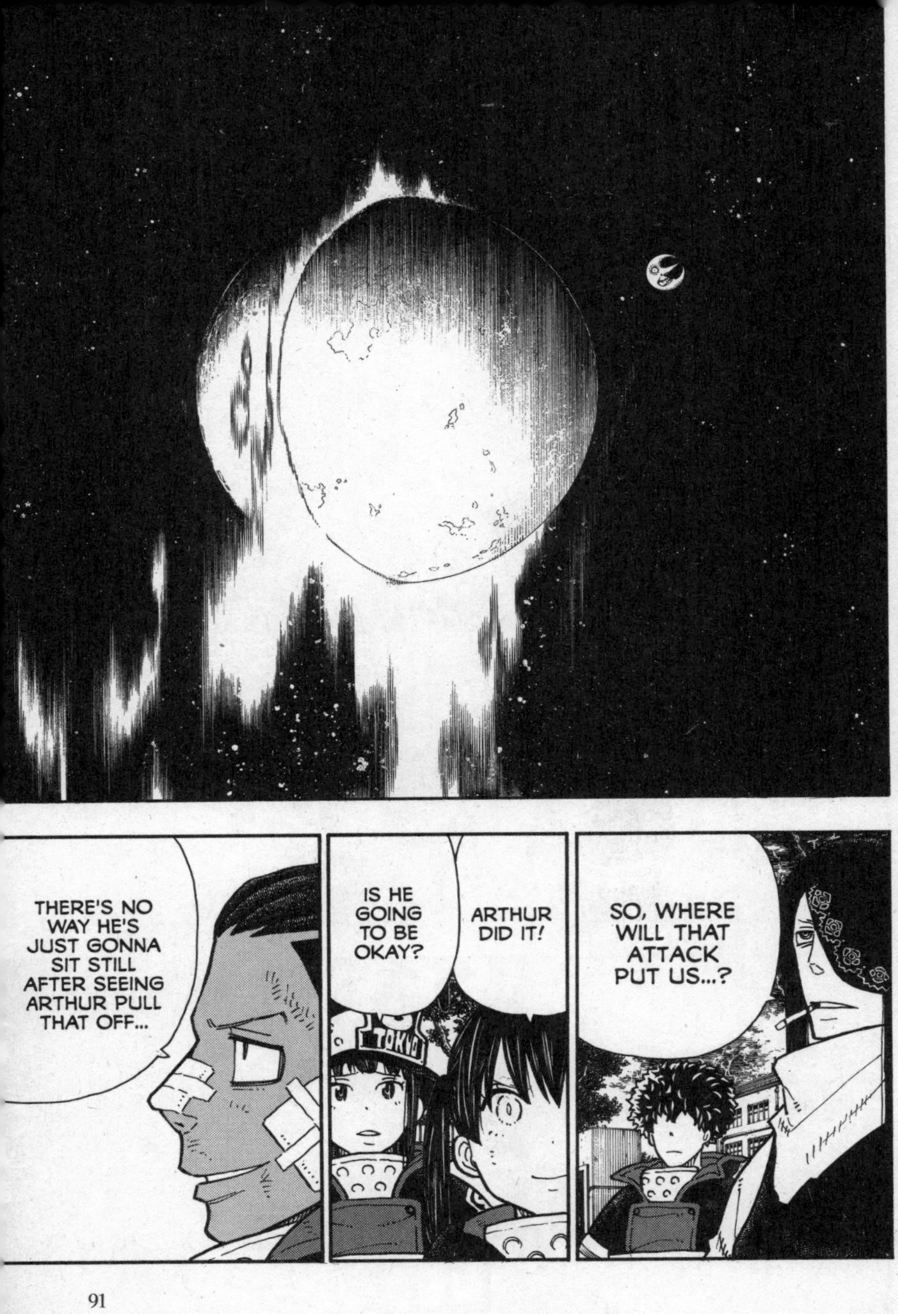
SO, WHERE WILL THAT ATTACK PUT US...?
ARTHUR DID IT!
IS HE GOING TO BE OKAY?
THERE'S NO WAY HE'S JUST GONNA SIT STILL AFTER SEEING ARTHUR PULL THAT OFF...

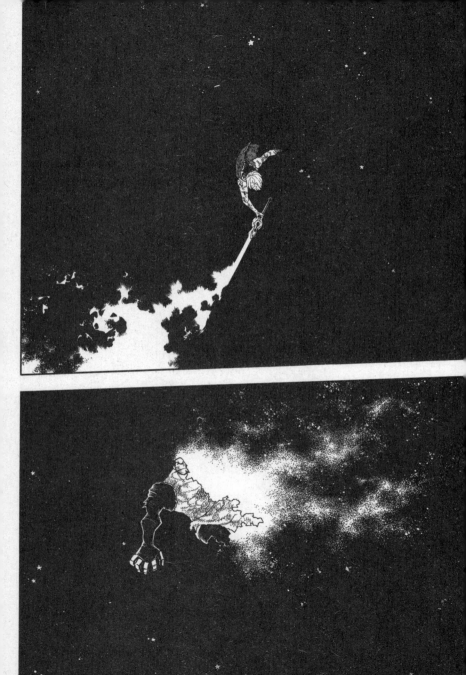

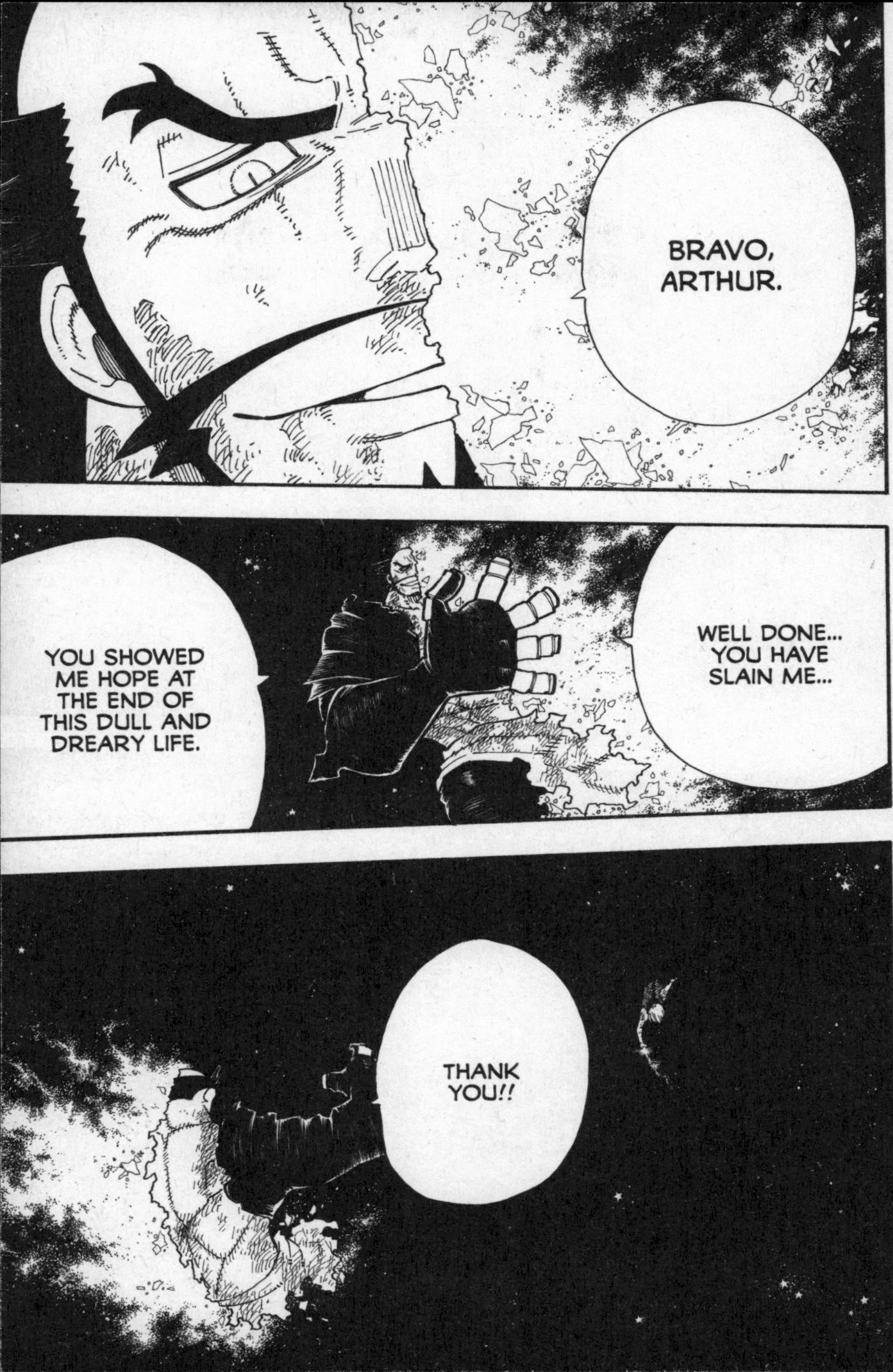
BRAVO, ARTHUR.
WELL DONE... YOU HAVE SLAIN ME...
YOU SHOWED ME HOPE AT THE END OF THIS DULL AND DREARY LIFE.
THANK YOU!!

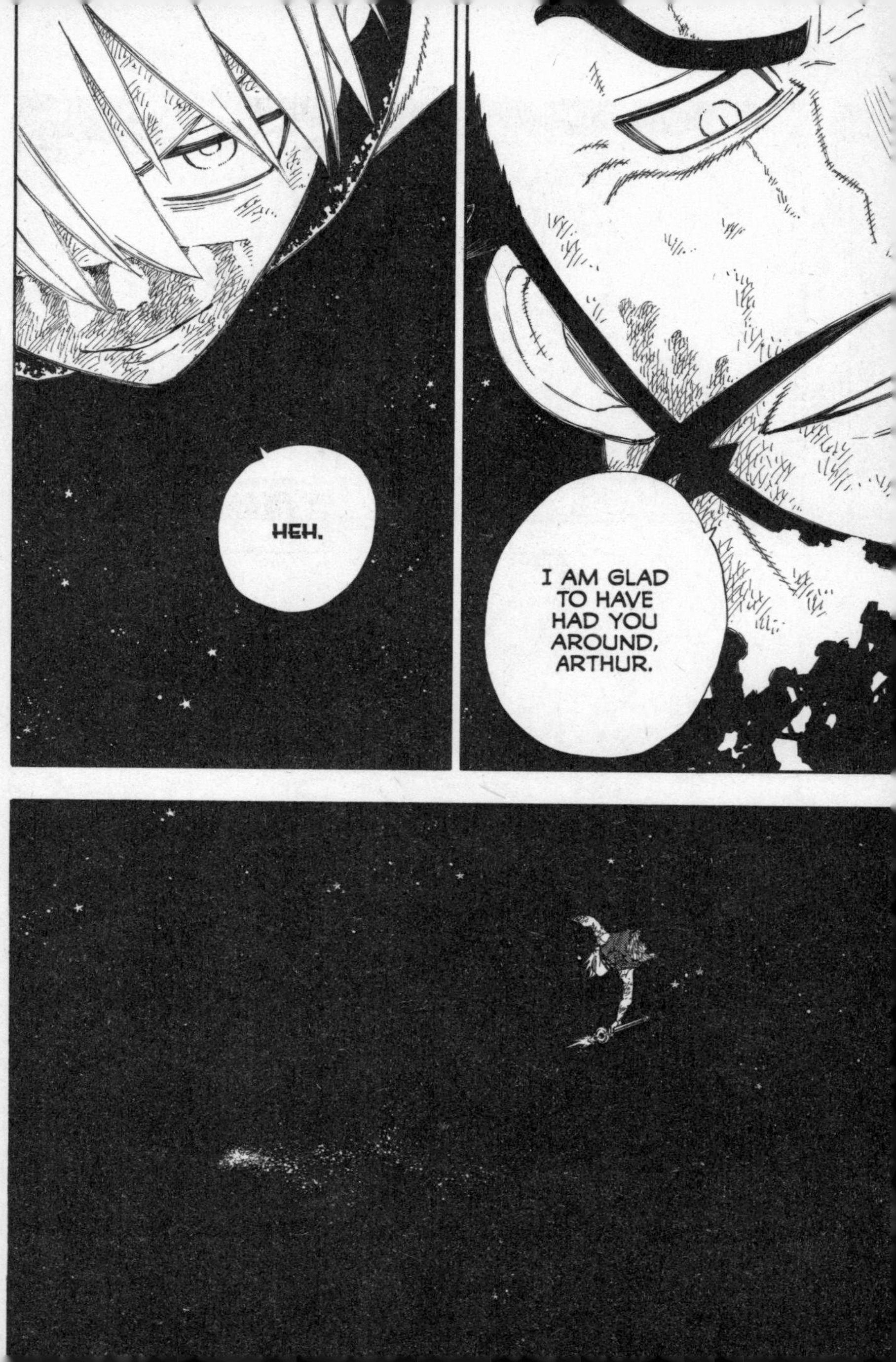
I AM GLAD TO HAVE HAD YOU AROUND, ARTHUR.
HEH.

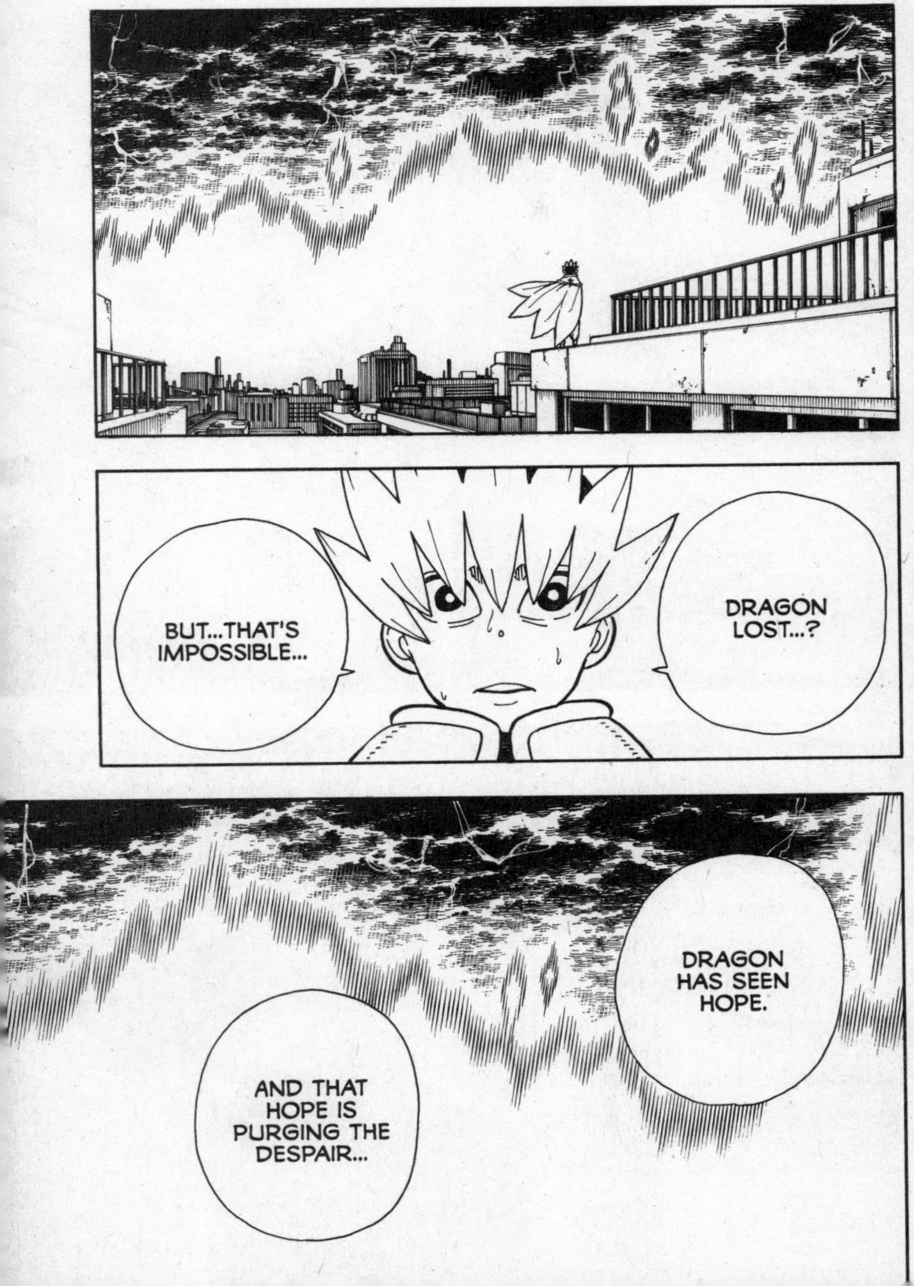
DRAGON LOST...?
BUT...THAT'S IMPOSSIBLE...
DRAGON HAS SEEN HOPE.
AND THAT HOPE IS PURGING THE DESPAIR...

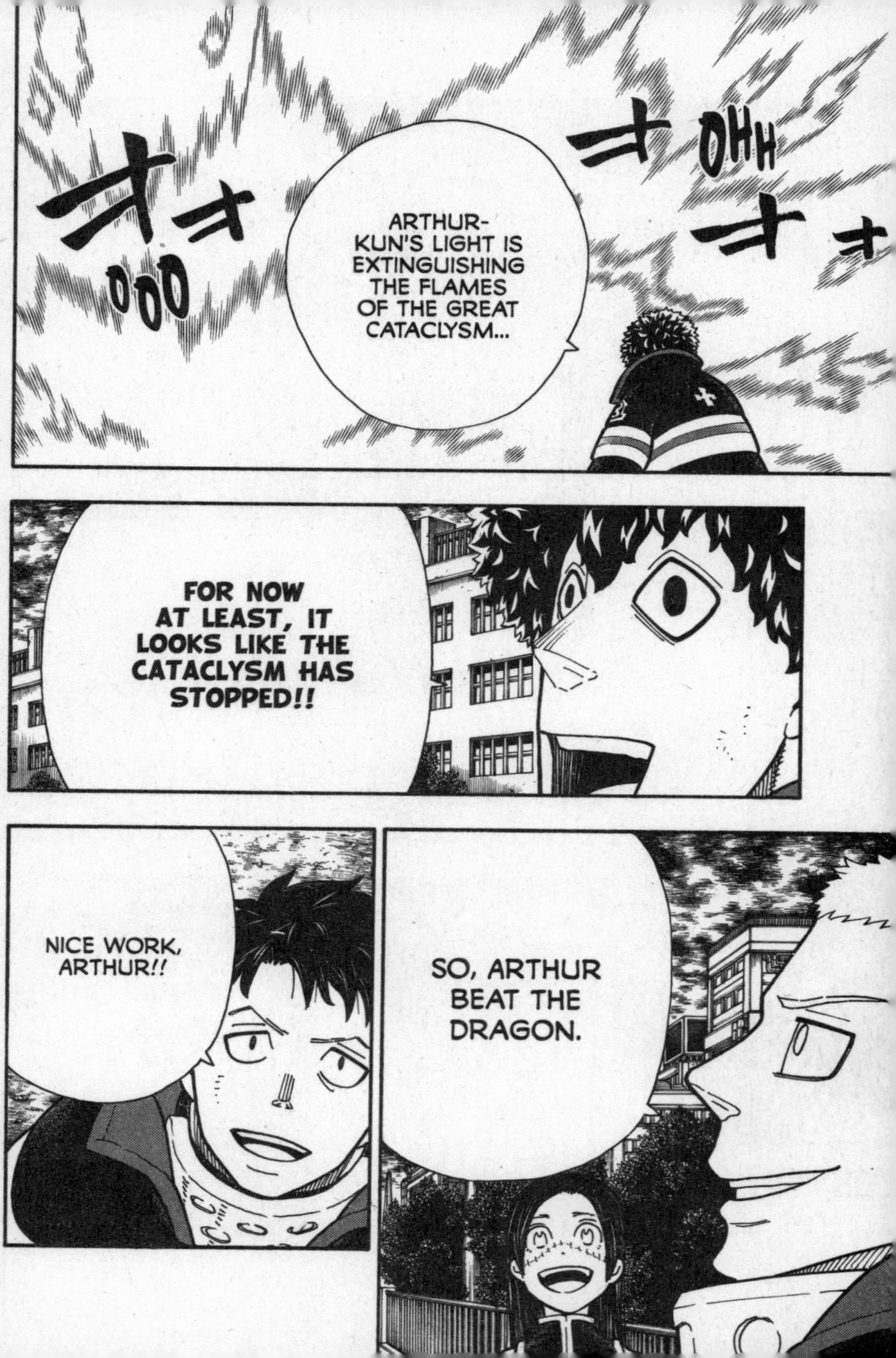
OHH
ARTHUR-KUN'S LIGHT IS EXTINGUISHING THE FLAMES OF THE GREAT CATACLYSM...
OOO
FOR NOW AT LEAST, IT LOOKS LIKE THE CATACLYSM HAS STOPPED!!
SO, ARTHUR BEAT THE DRAGON.
NICE WORK, ARTHUR!!

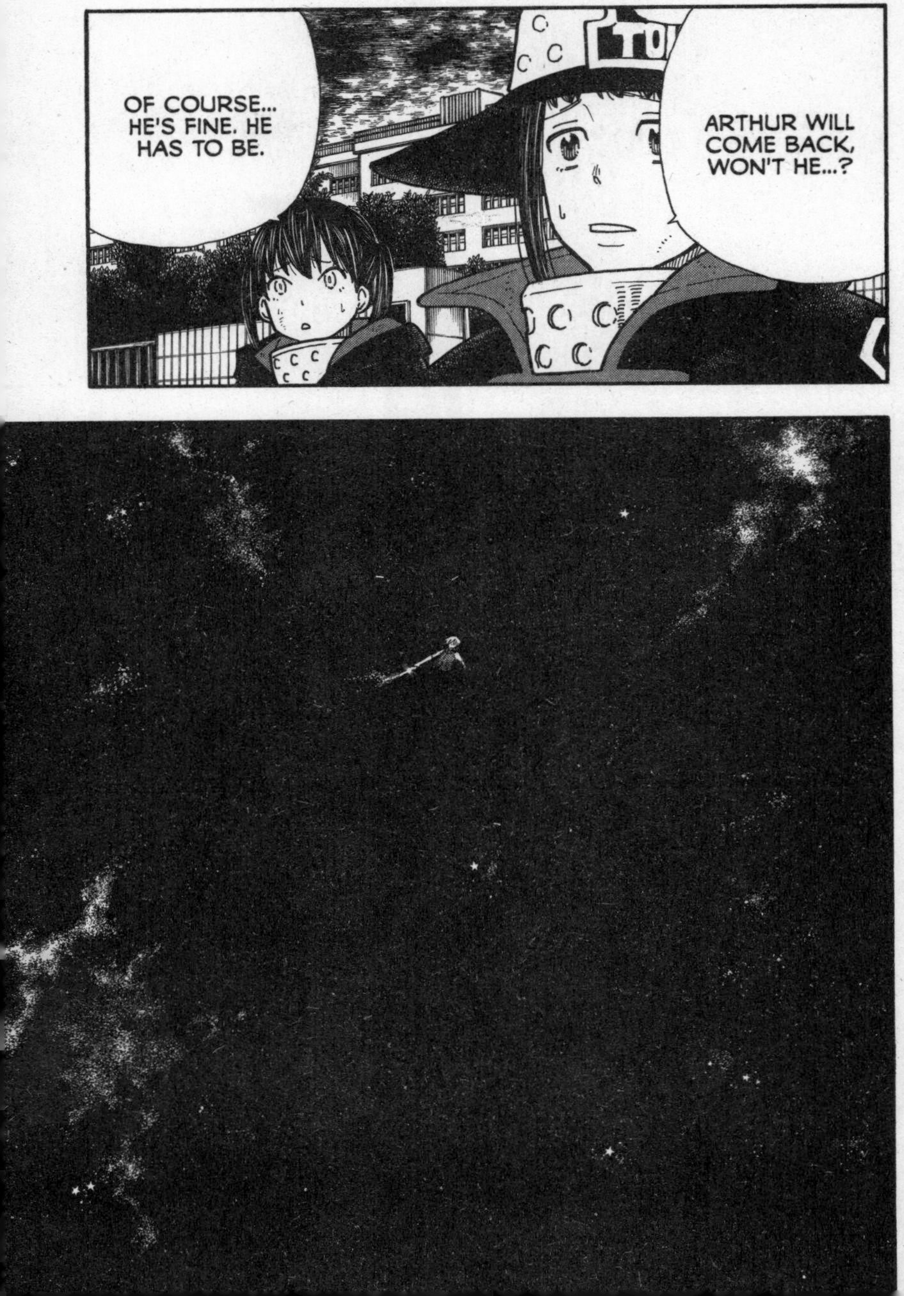
ARTHUR WILL COME BACK, WON'T HE...?
OF COURSE... HE'S FINE. HE HAS TO BE.

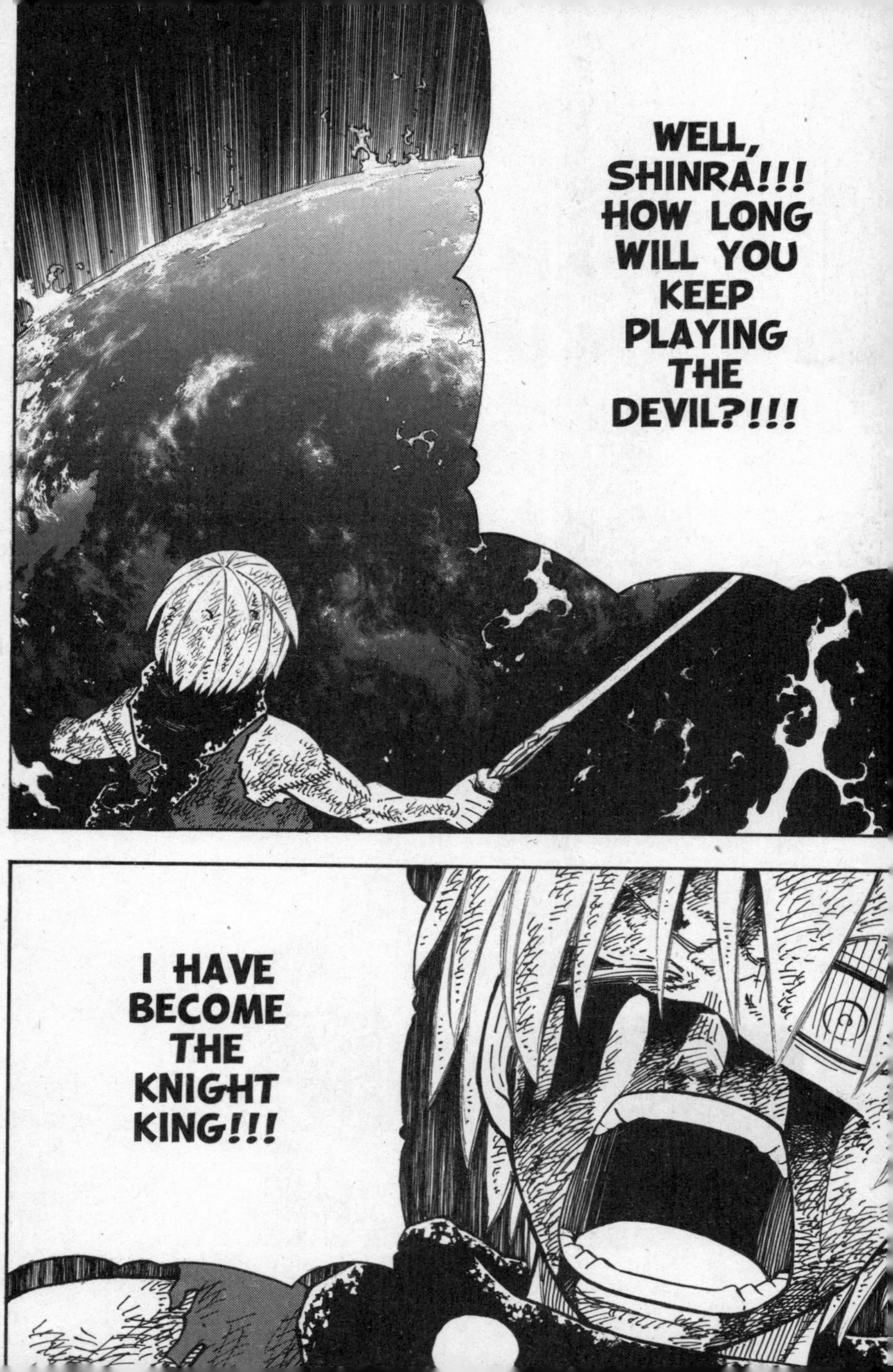
WELL, SHINRA!!! HOW LONG WILL YOU KEEP PLAYING THE DEVIL?!!!
I HAVE BECOME THE KNIGHT KING!!!

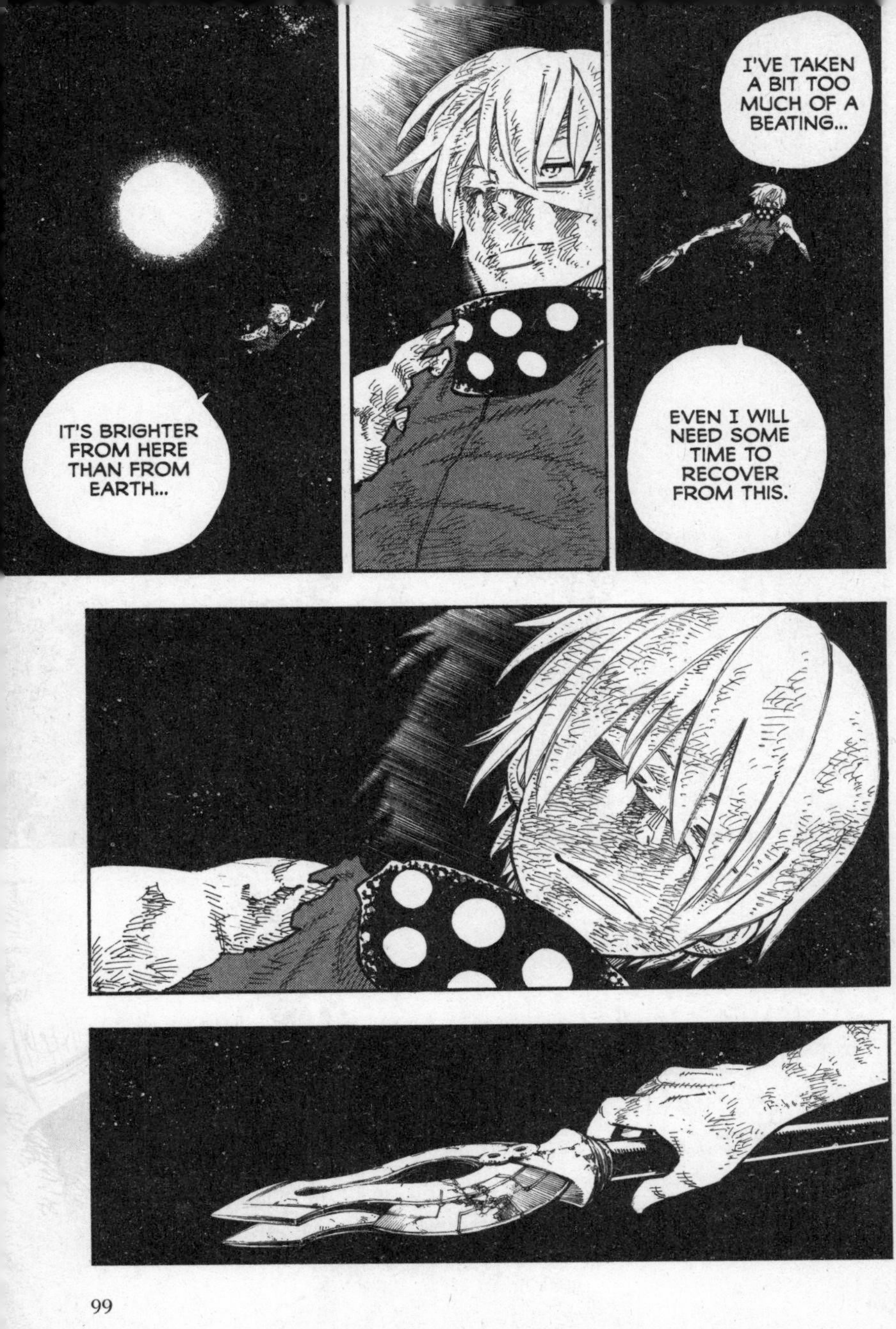
I'VE TAKEN A BIT TOO MUCH OF A BEATING...
EVEN I WILL NEED SOME TIME TO RECOVER FROM THIS.
IT'S BRIGHTER FROM HERE THAN FROM EARTH...

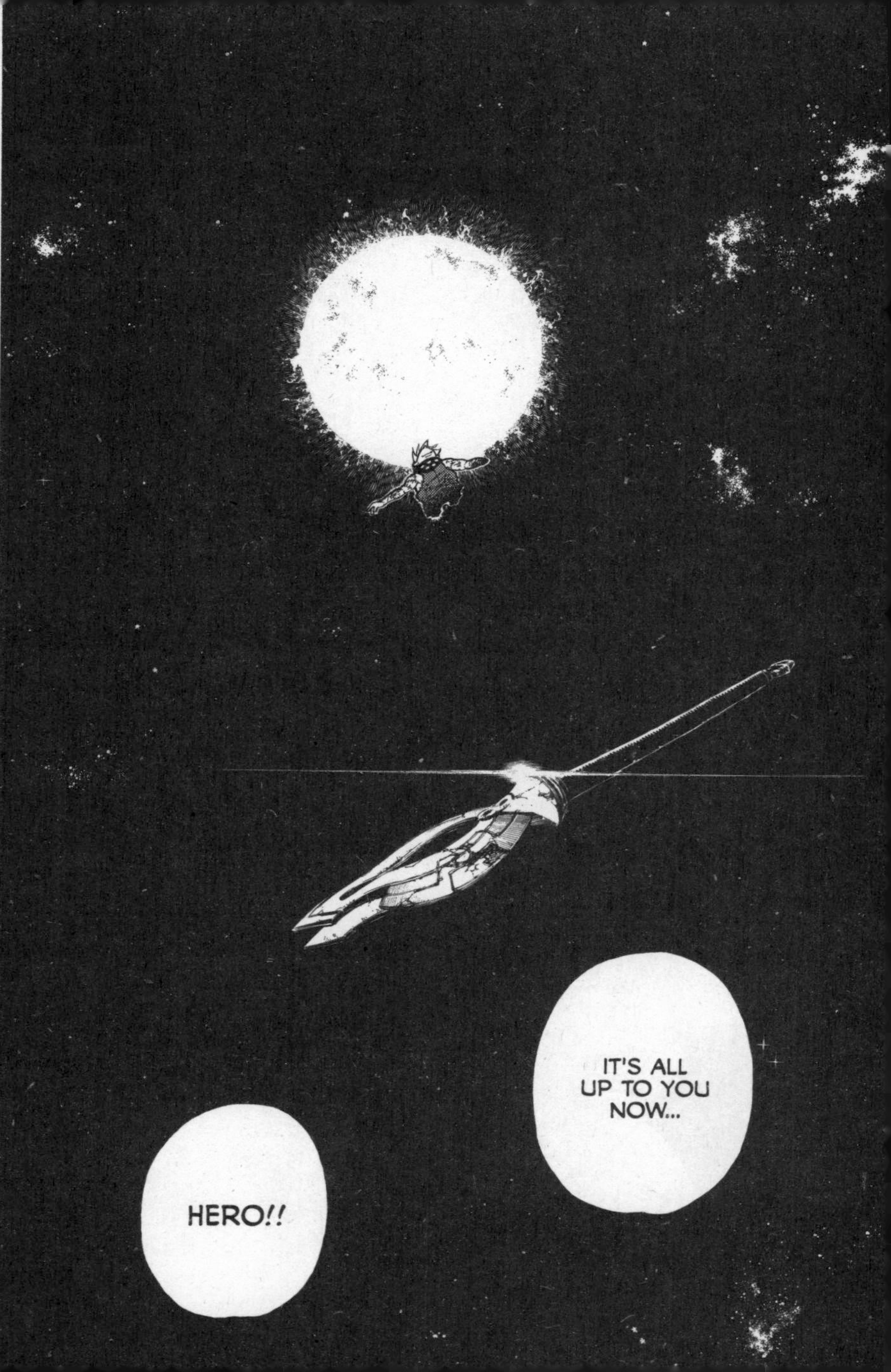
IT'S ALL UP TO YOU NOW...
HERO!!

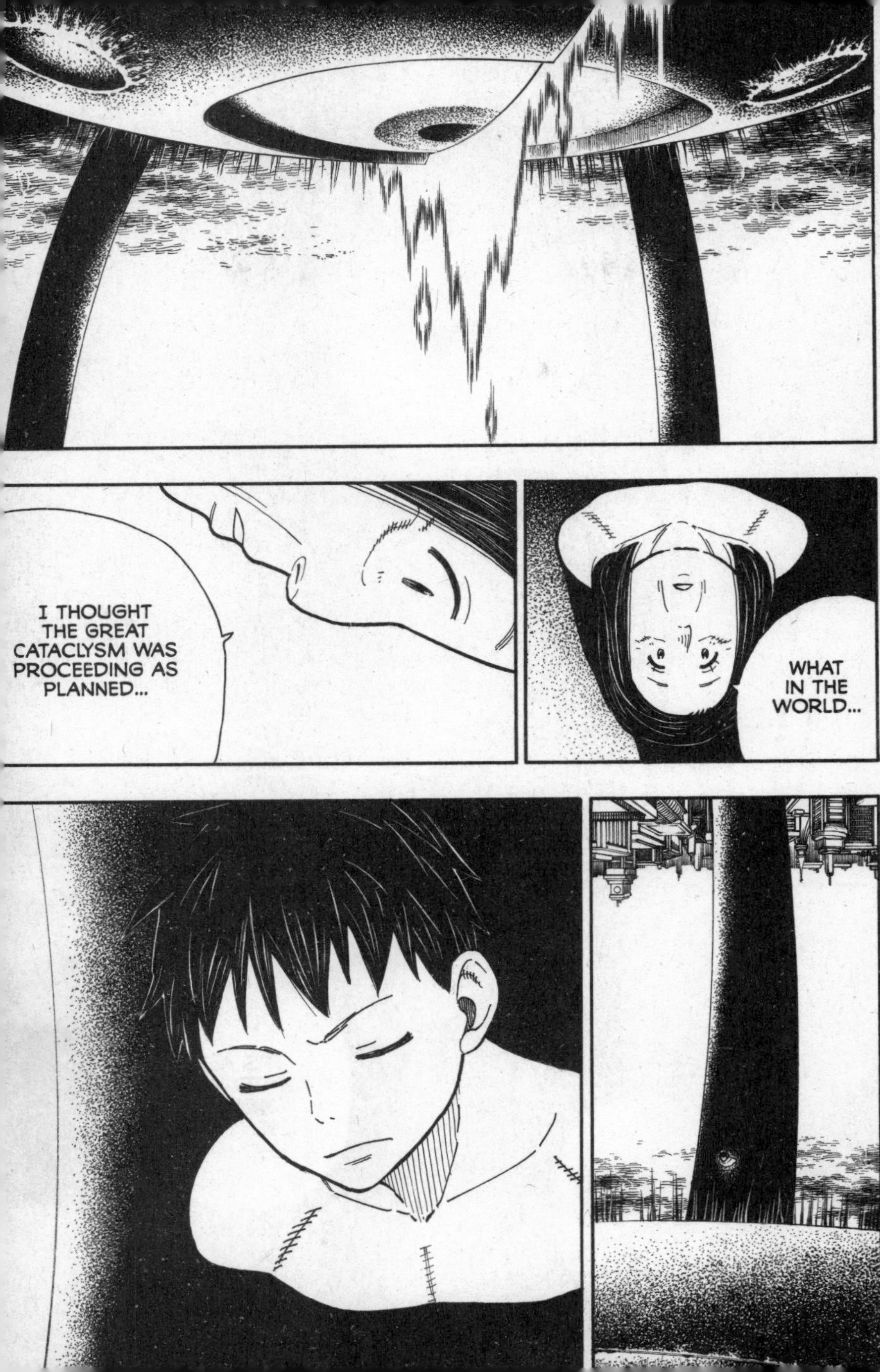
WHAT IN THE WORLD...
I THOUGHT THE GREAT CATACLYSM WAS PROCEEDING AS PLANNED...

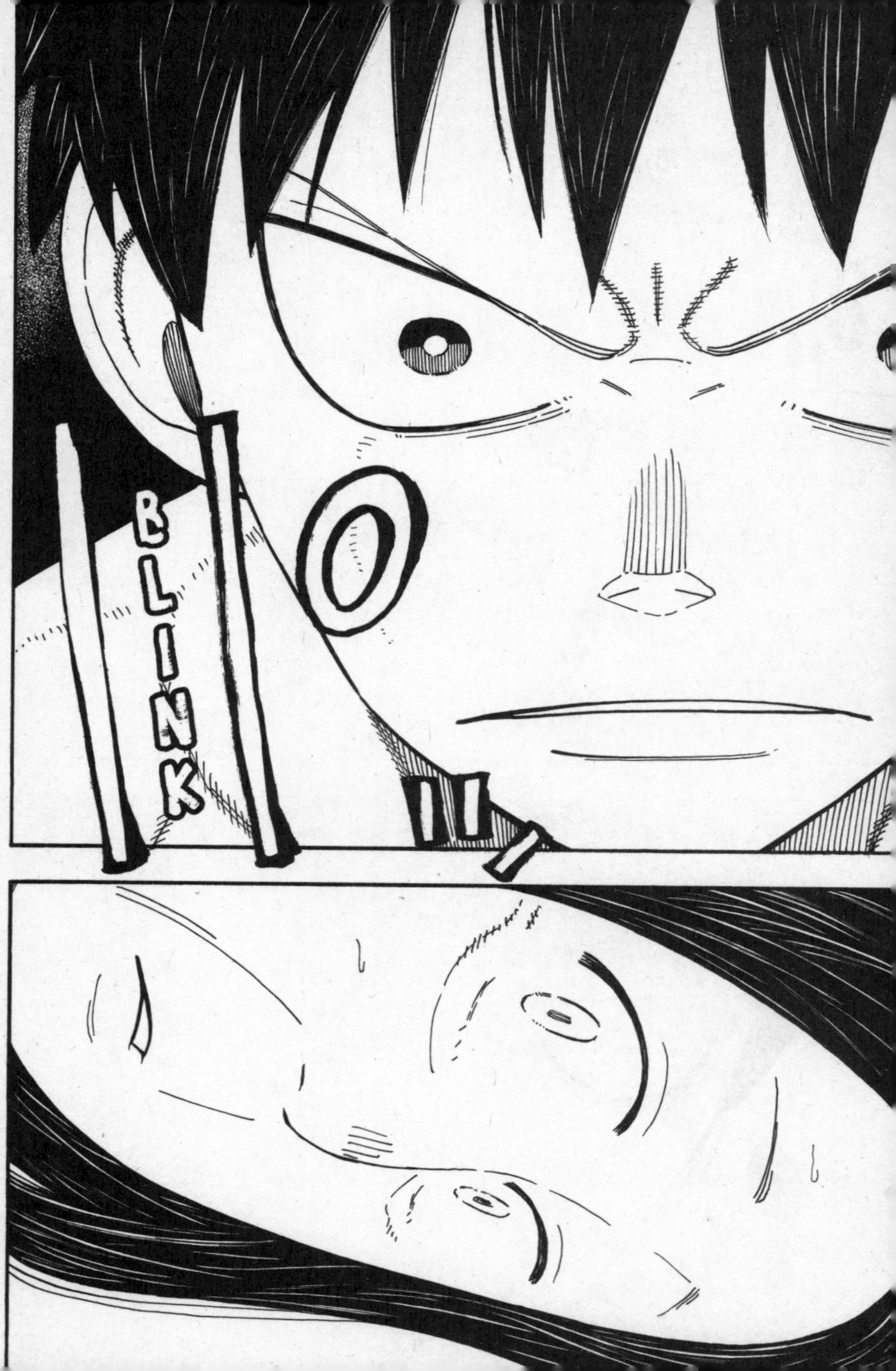
BLINK

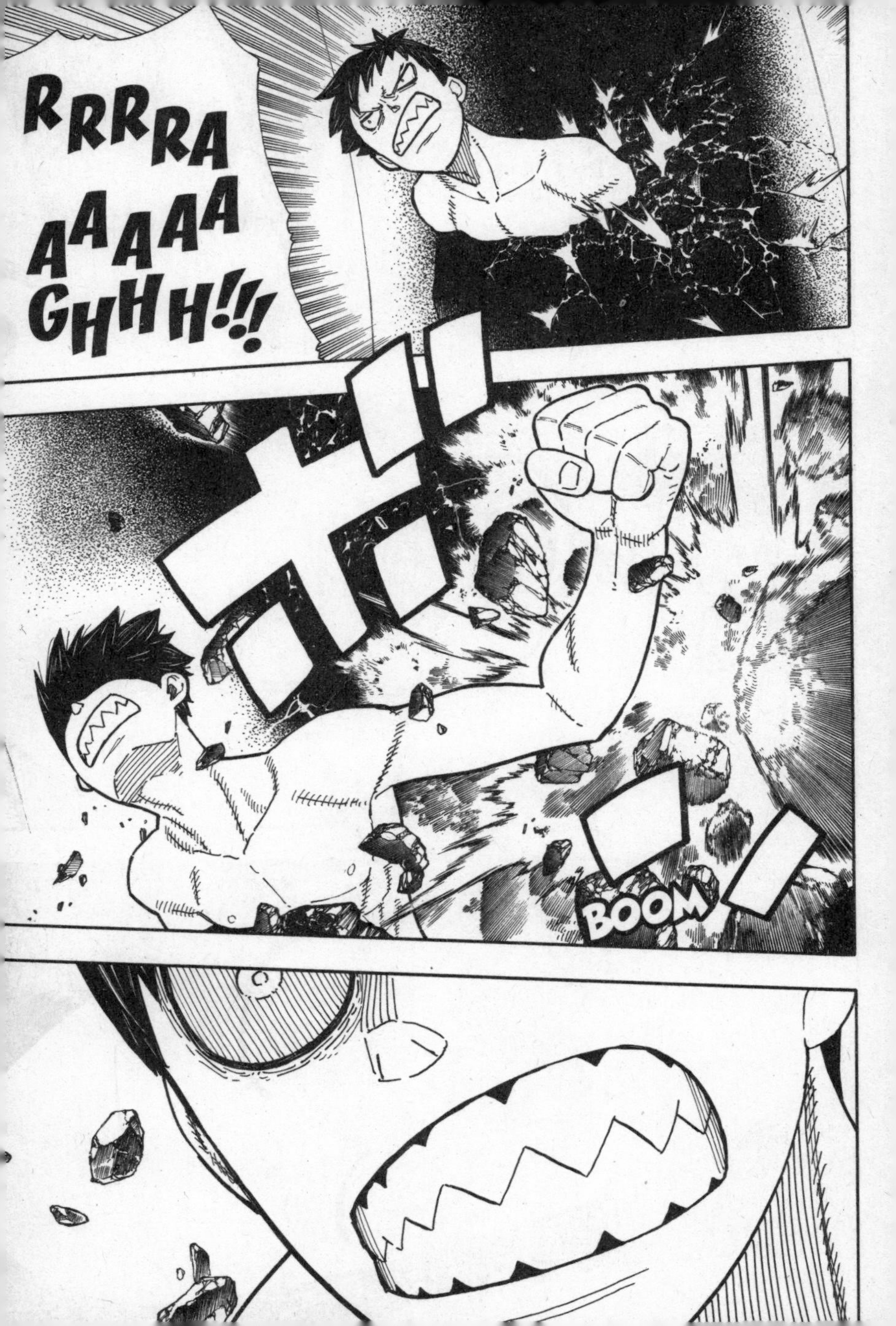
RRRRA
AAAAA
GHHH!!!
BOOM

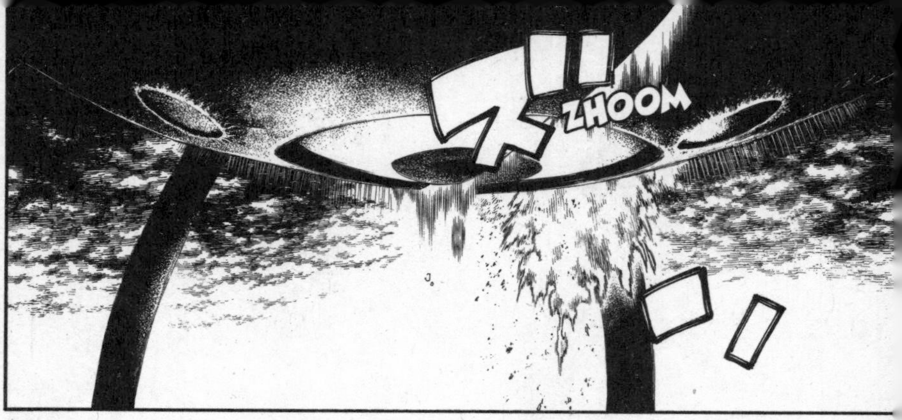
ZHOOM
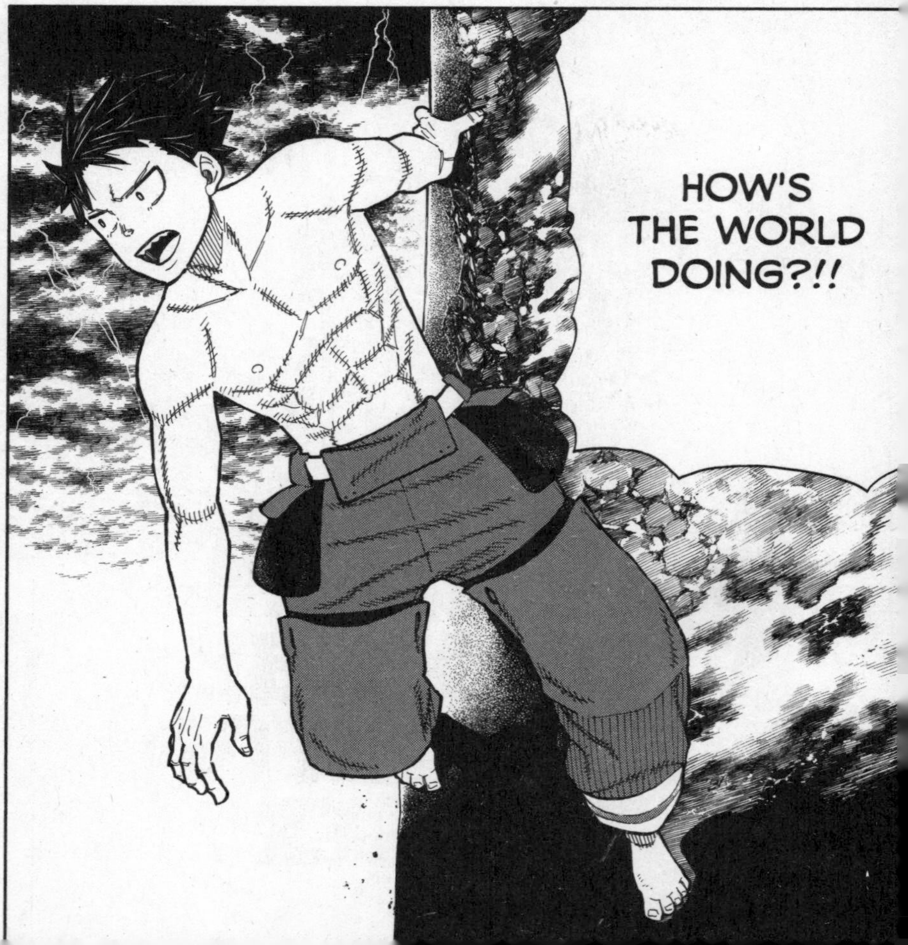
HOW'S
THE WORLD
DOING?!!

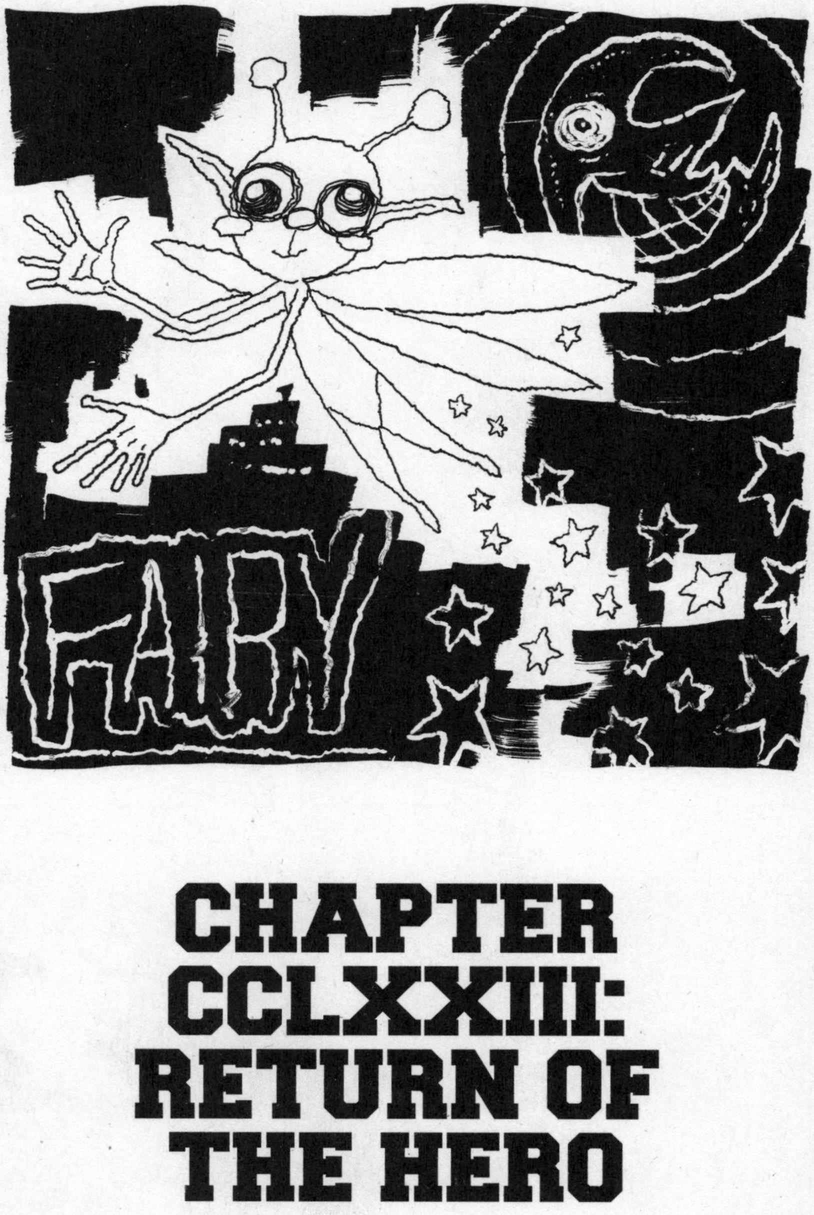
FAIRY

CHAPTER CCLXXIII: RETURN OF THE HERO

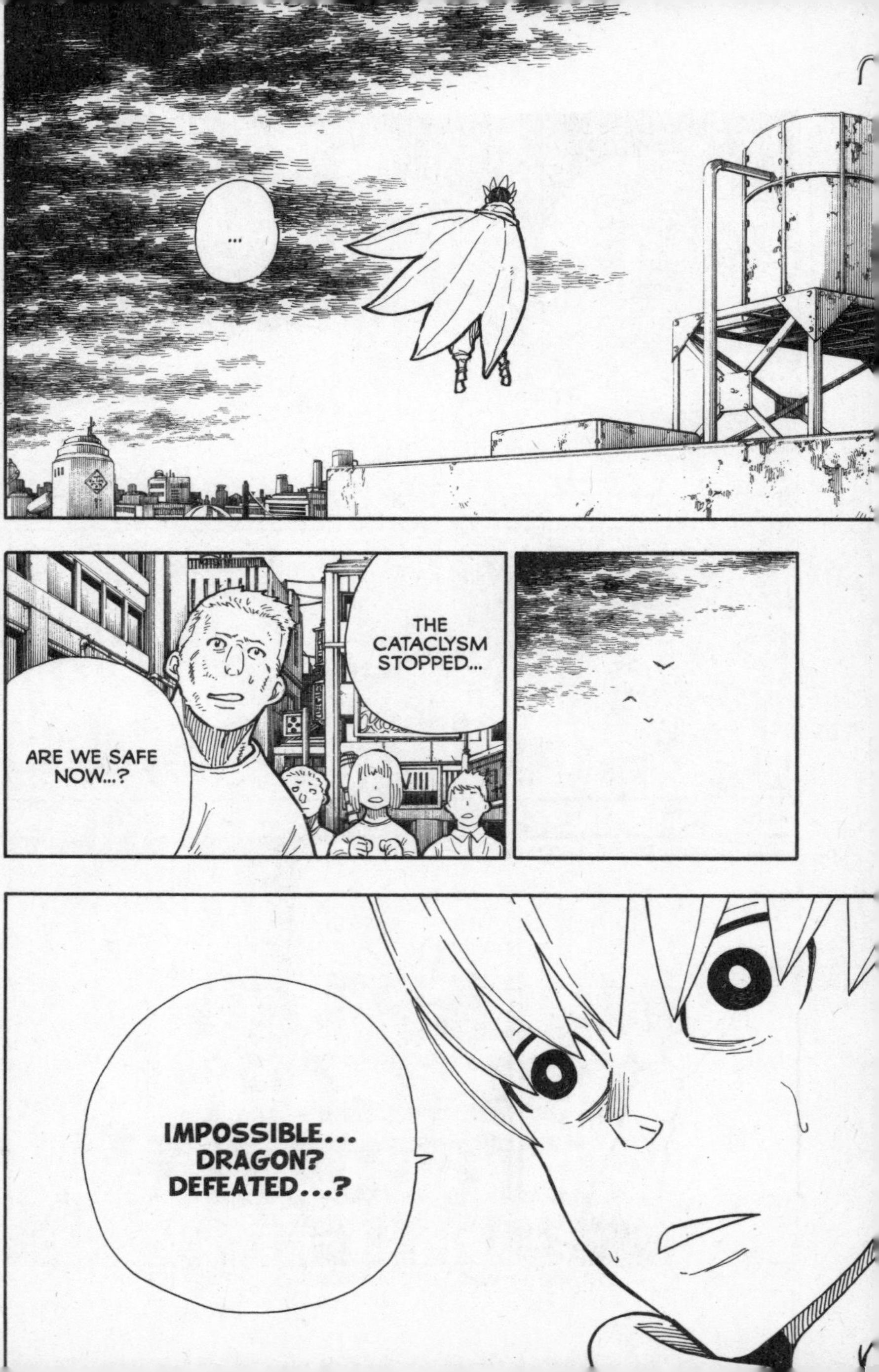
...
THE CATACLYSM STOPPED...
ARE WE SAFE NOW...?
IMPOSSIBLE... DRAGON? DEFEATED...?

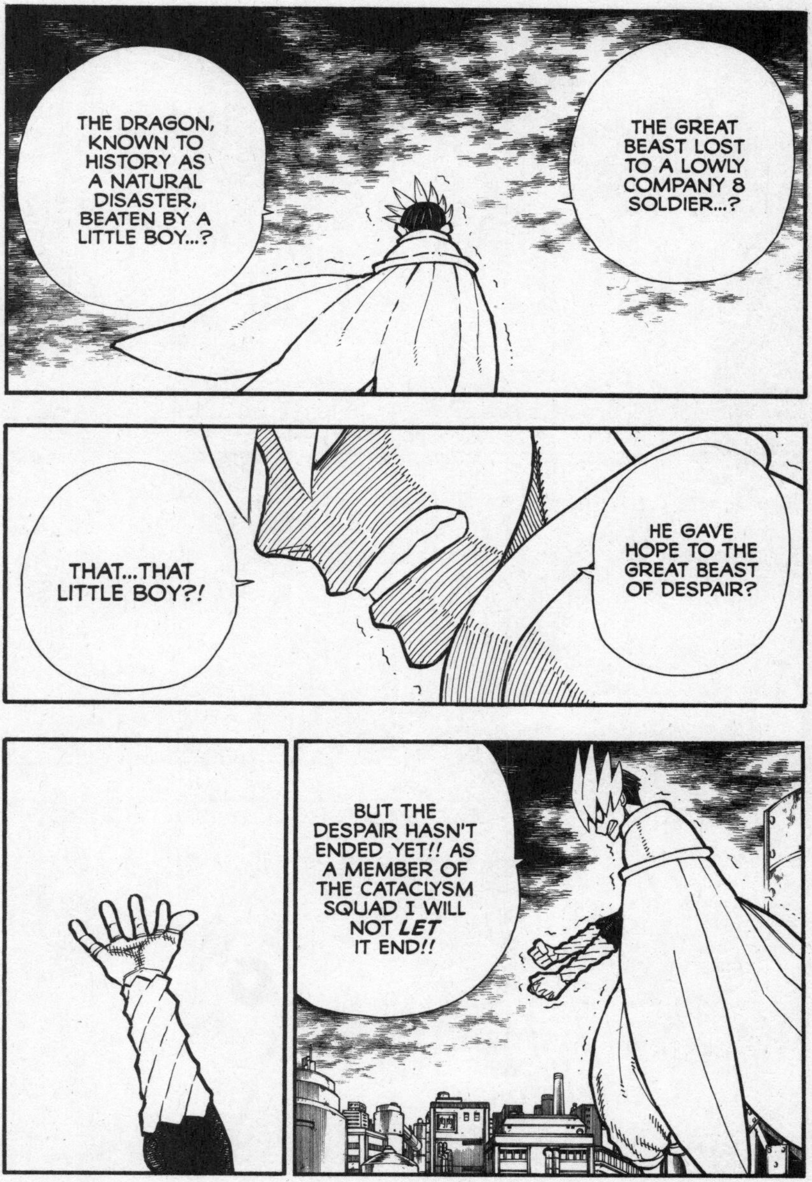
THE GREAT BEAST LOST TO A LOWLY COMPANY 8 SOLDIER...?
THE DRAGON, KNOWN TO HISTORY AS A NATURAL DISASTER, BEATEN BY A LITTLE BOY...?
HE GAVE HOPE TO THE GREAT BEAST OF DESPAIR?
THAT...THAT LITTLE BOY?!
BUT THE DESPAIR HASN'T ENDED YET!! AS A MEMBER OF THE CATACLYSM SQUAD I WILL NOT *LET* IT END!!

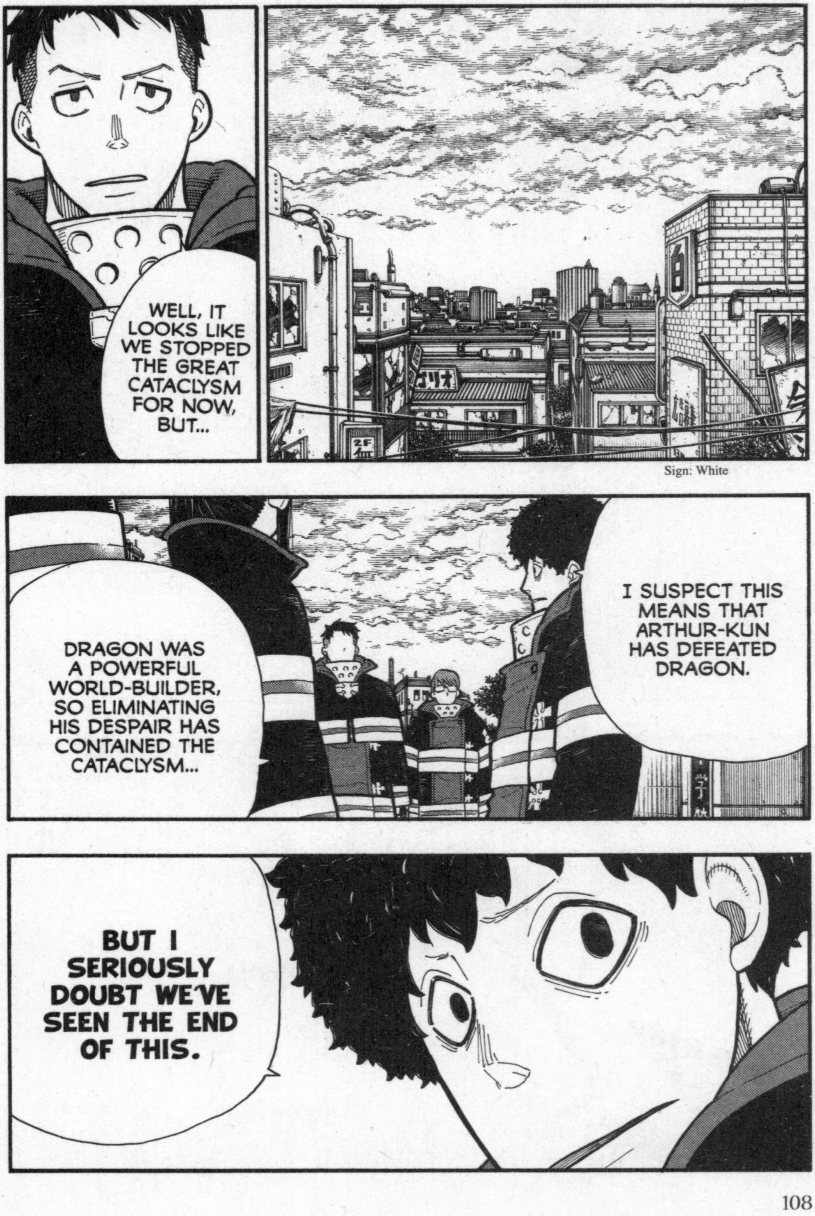
WELL, IT LOOKS LIKE WE STOPPED THE GREAT CATACLYSM FOR NOW, BUT...
I SUSPECT THIS MEANS THAT ARTHUR-KUN HAS DEFEATED DRAGON.
DRAGON WAS A POWERFUL WORLD-BUILDER, SO ELIMINATING HIS DESPAIR HAS CONTAINED THE CATACLYSM...
BUT I SERIOUSLY DOUBT WE'VE SEEN THE END OF THIS.
Sign: White

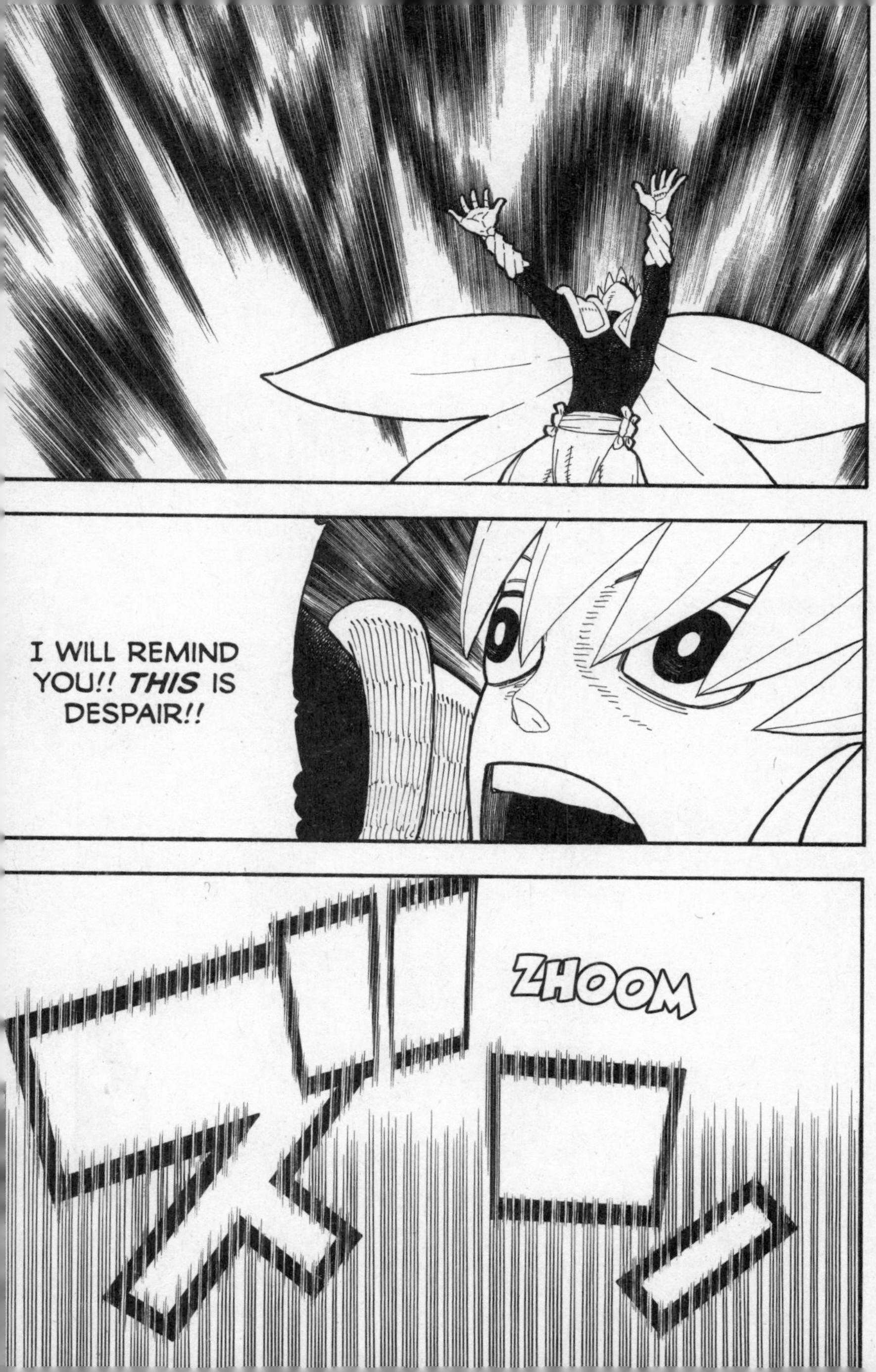
I WILL REMIND YOU!! *THIS* IS DESPAIR!!
ZHOOM

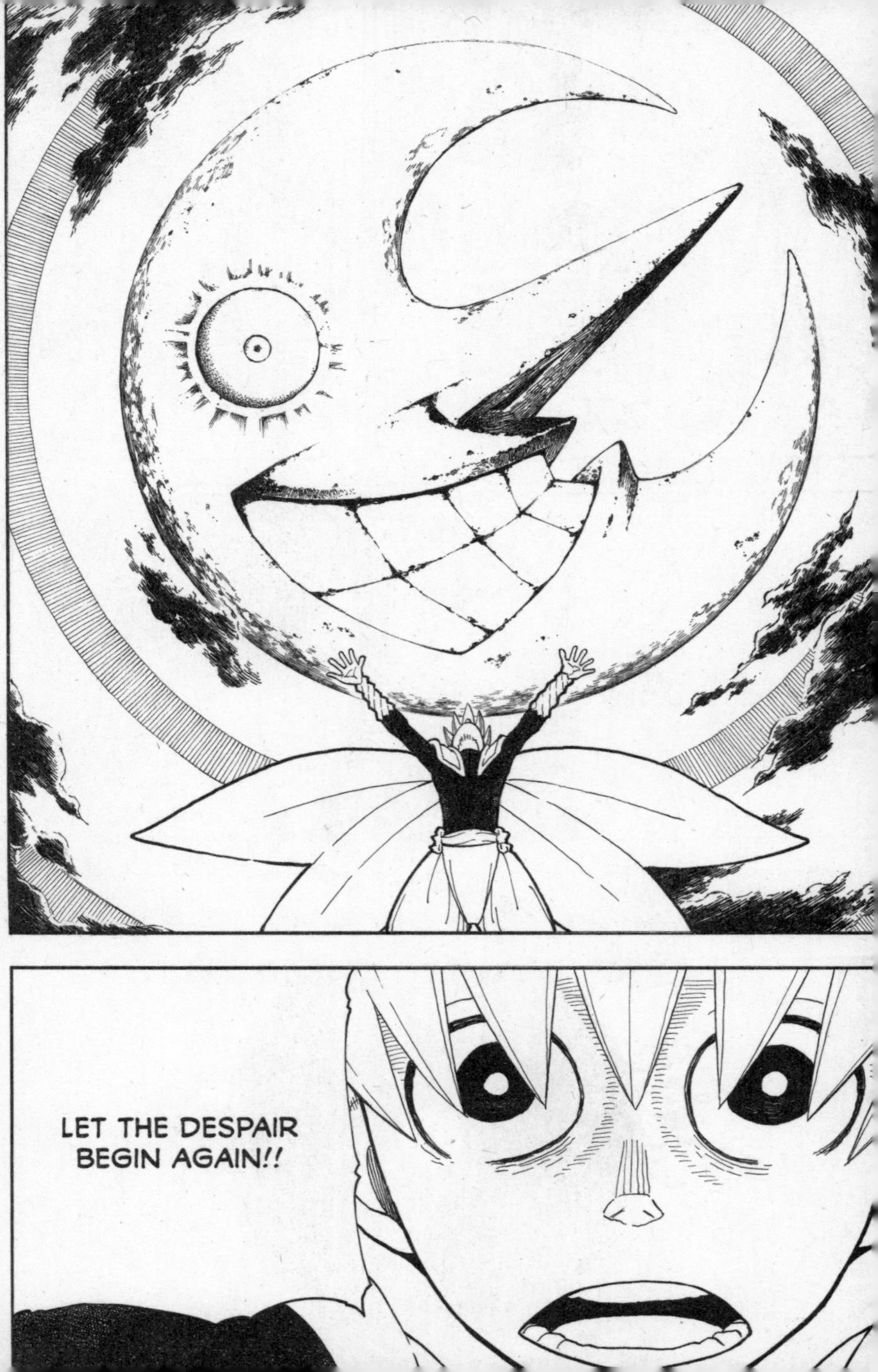
LET THE DESPAIR
BEGIN AGAIN!!

WHAT'S THIS SHAKING...? AN EARTH-QUAKE...?

!!

NO...!! LOOK ABOVE US!!

TUMBLE

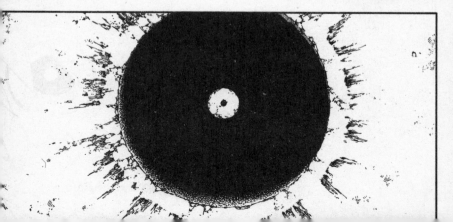

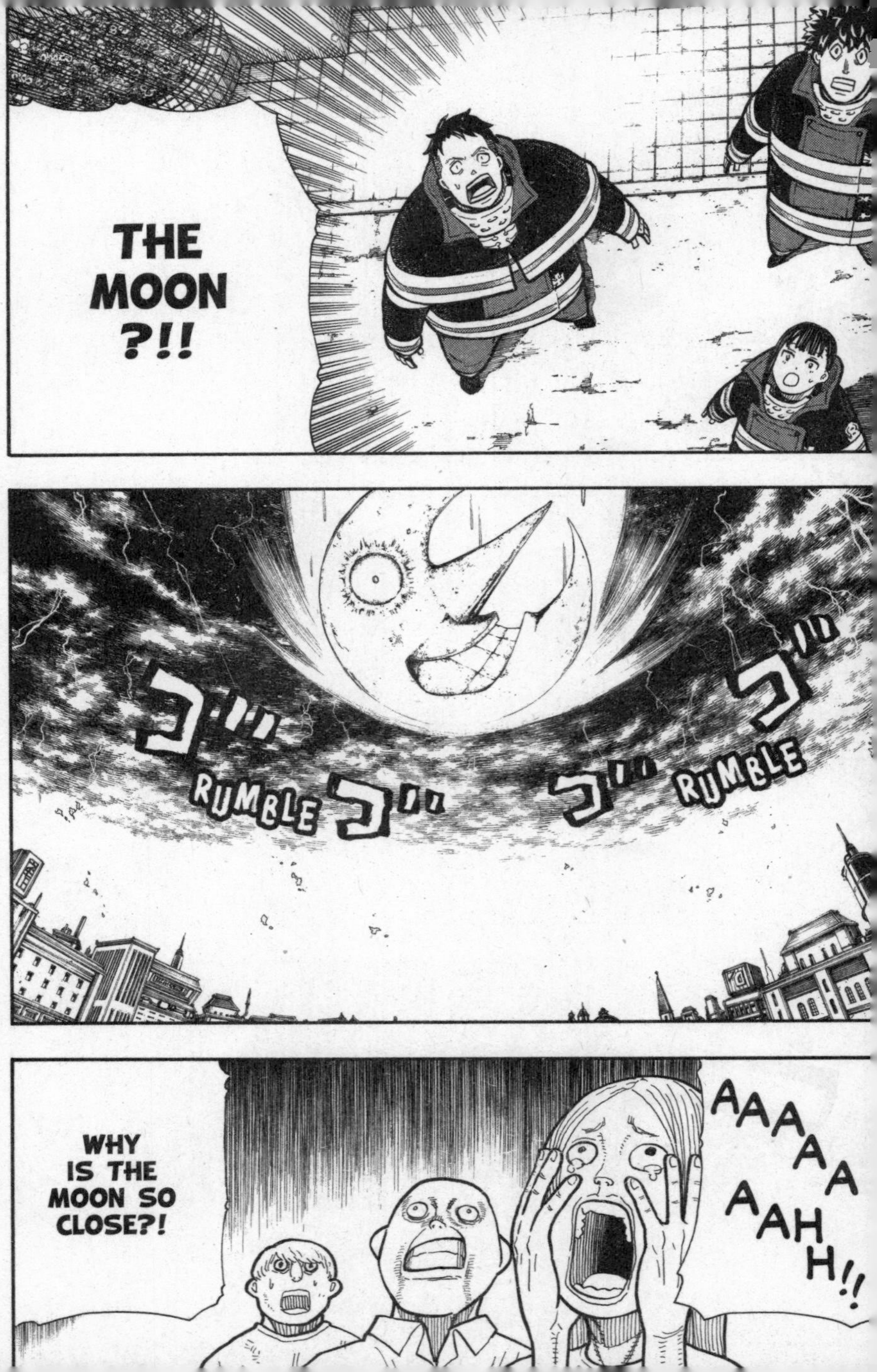
THE MOON ?!!
ゴ
ゴ RUMBLE
ゴ
RUMBLE ゴ
AAAAAAAHH!!
WHY IS THE MOON SO CLOSE?!

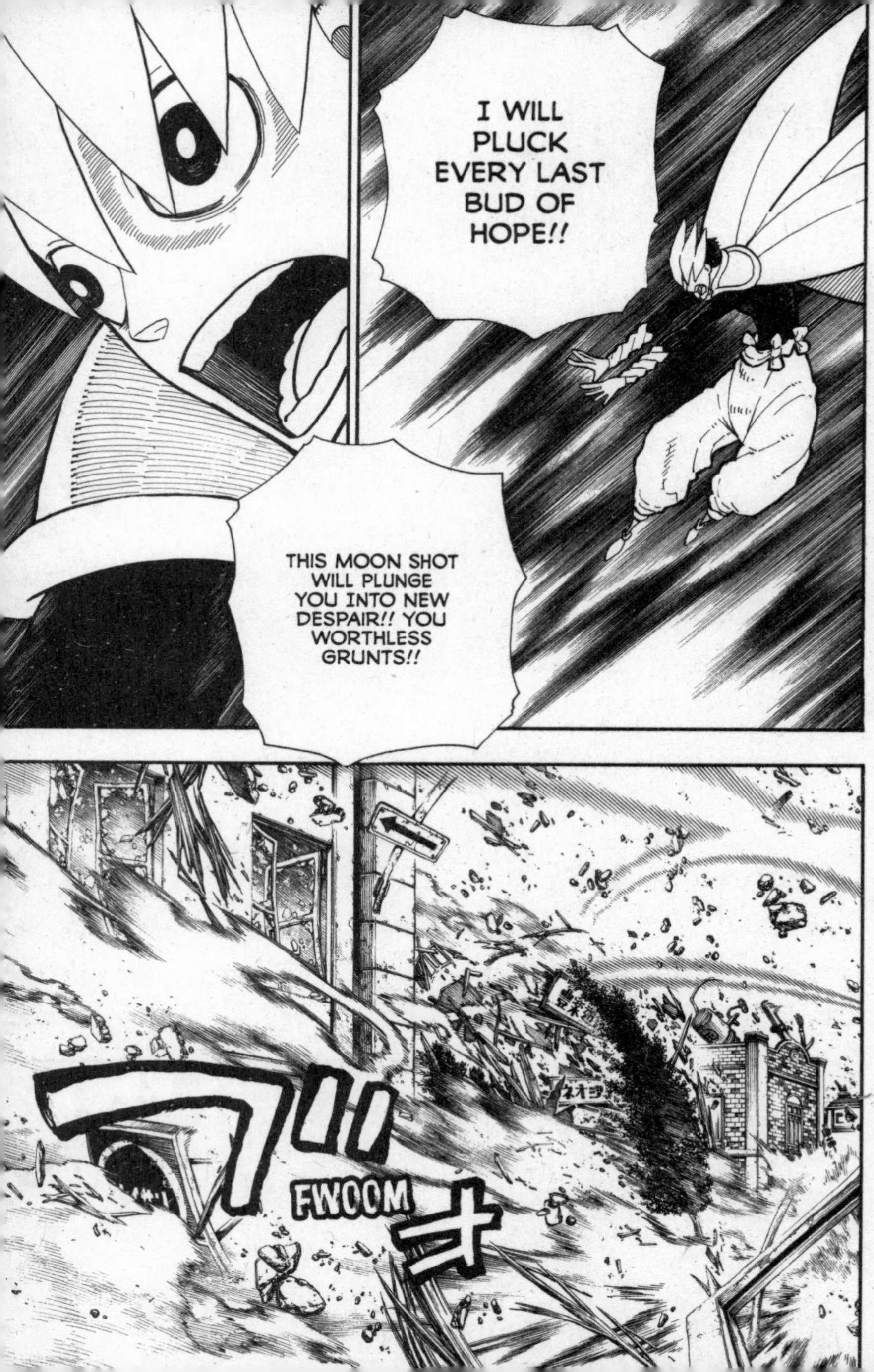
I WILL PLUCK EVERY LAST BUD OF HOPE!!
THIS MOON SHOT WILL PLUNGE YOU INTO NEW DESPAIR!! YOU WORTHLESS GRUNTS!!
FWOOM

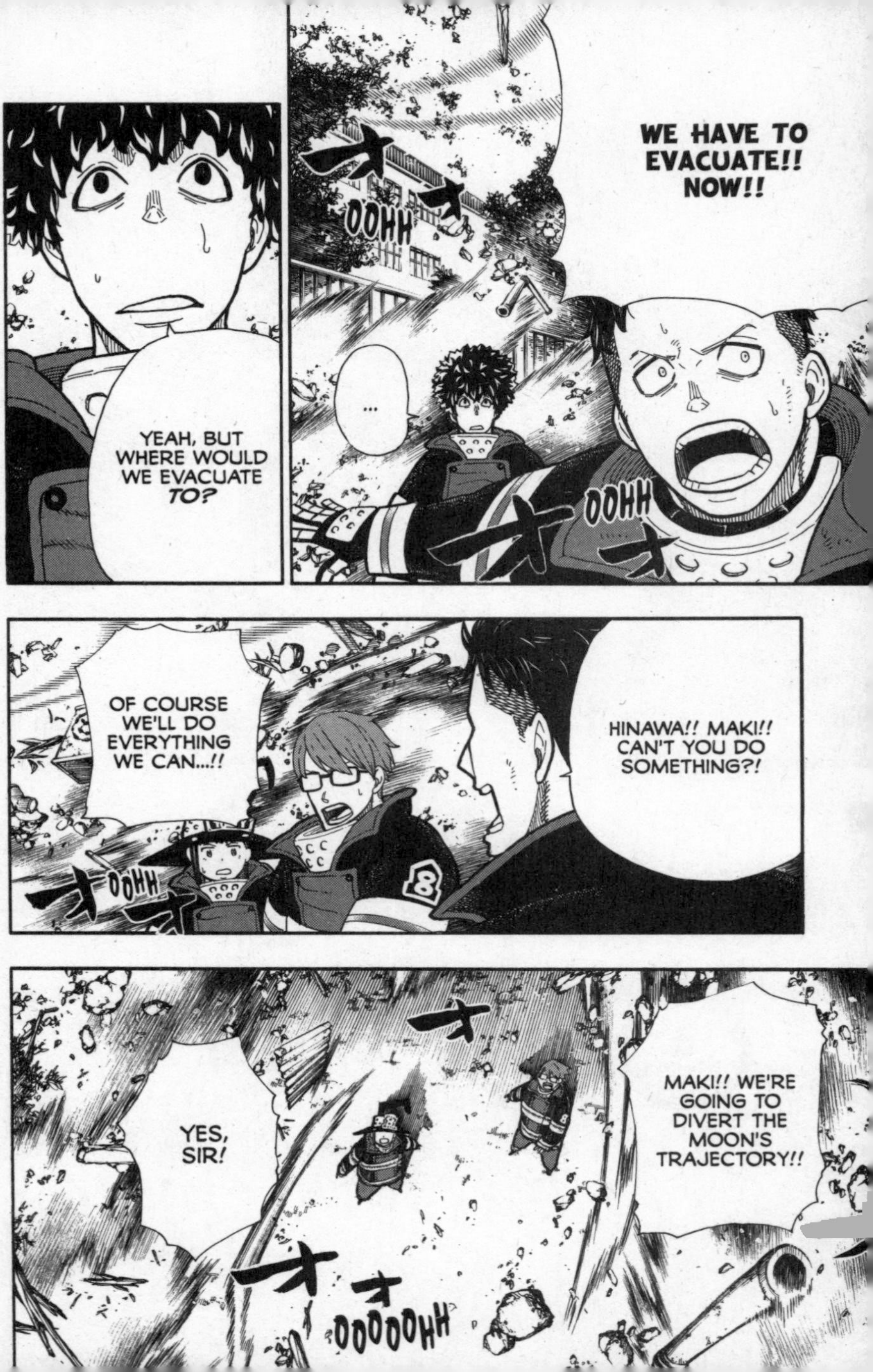
WE HAVE TO EVACUATE!! NOW!!
OOHH
...
OOHH
YEAH, BUT WHERE WOULD WE EVACUATE *TO?*
HINAWA!! MAKI!! CAN'T YOU DO SOMETHING?!
OF COURSE WE'LL DO EVERYTHING WE CAN...!!
OOHH
MAKI!! WE'RE GOING TO DIVERT THE MOON'S TRAJECTORY!!
YES, SIR!
OOOOOHH

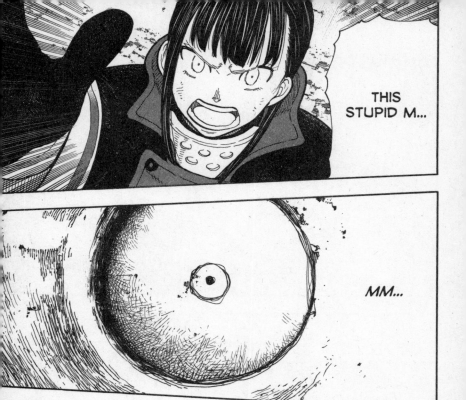

THIS
STUPID M...

MM...

MMM......

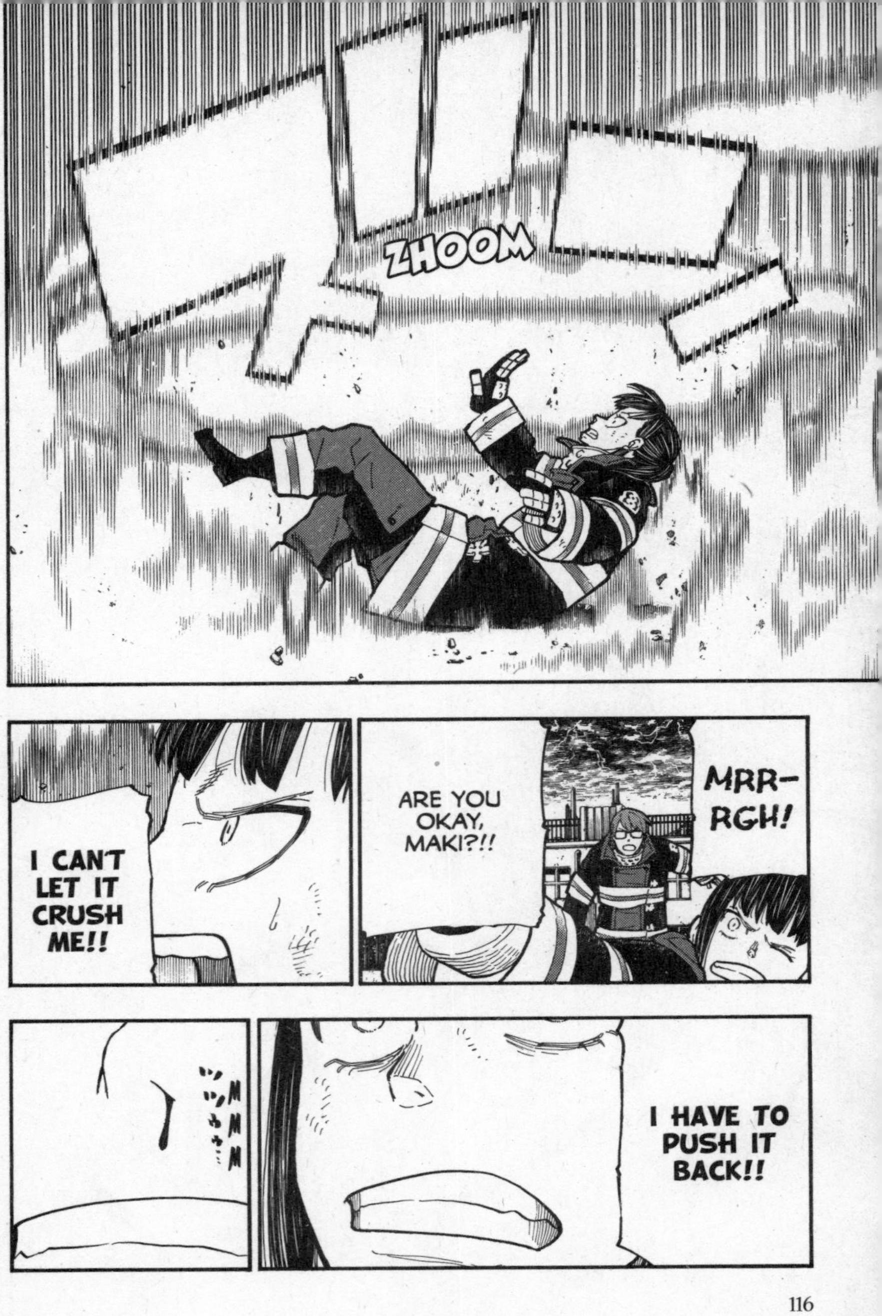
ZHOOM
MRR-RGH!
ARE YOU OKAY, MAKI?!!
I CAN'T LET IT CRUSH ME!!
I HAVE TO PUSH IT BACK!!
MMM
ッッみゅ…

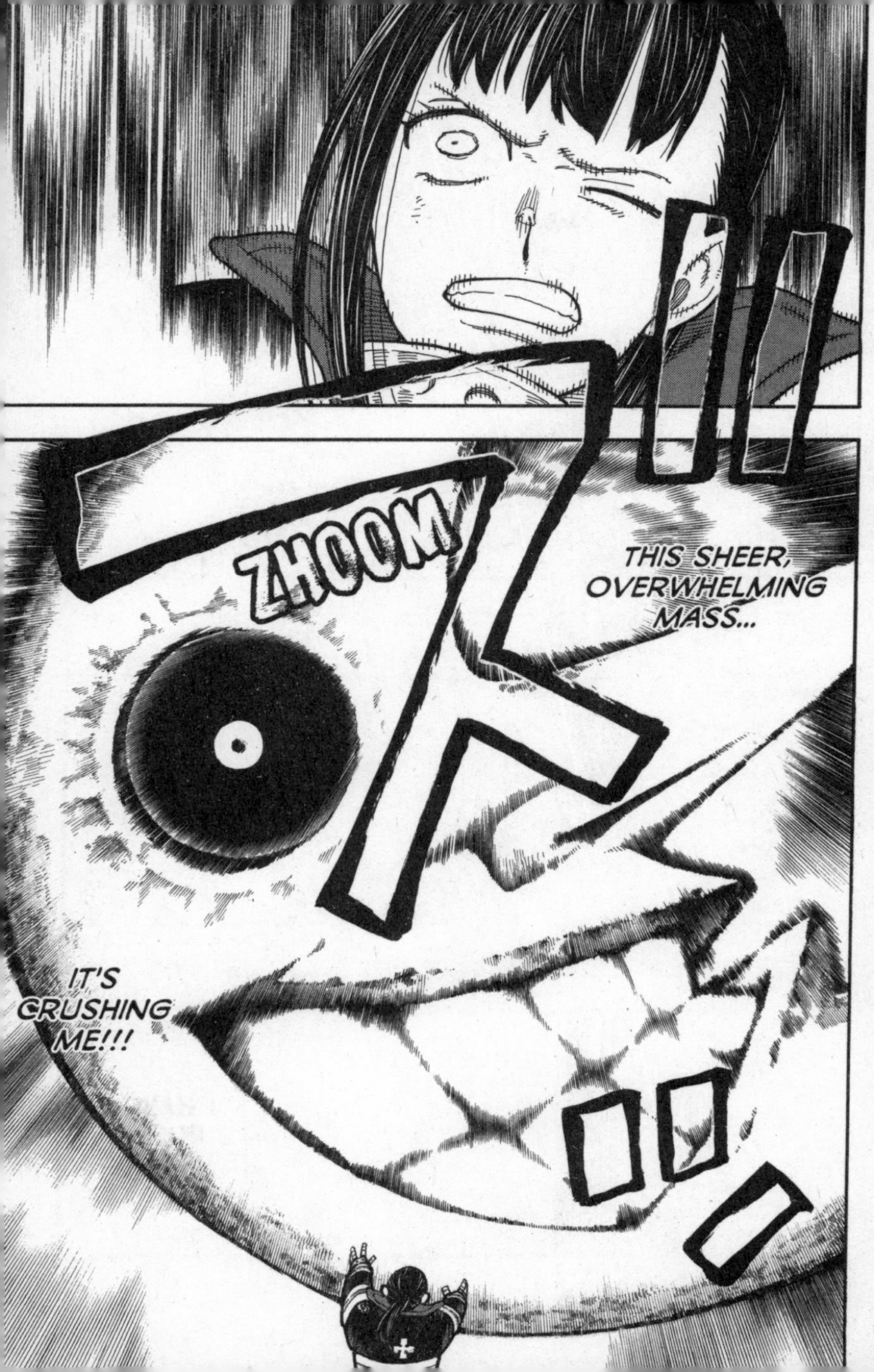
ZHOOM
THIS SHEER, OVERWHELMING MASS...
IT'S CRUSHING ME!!!

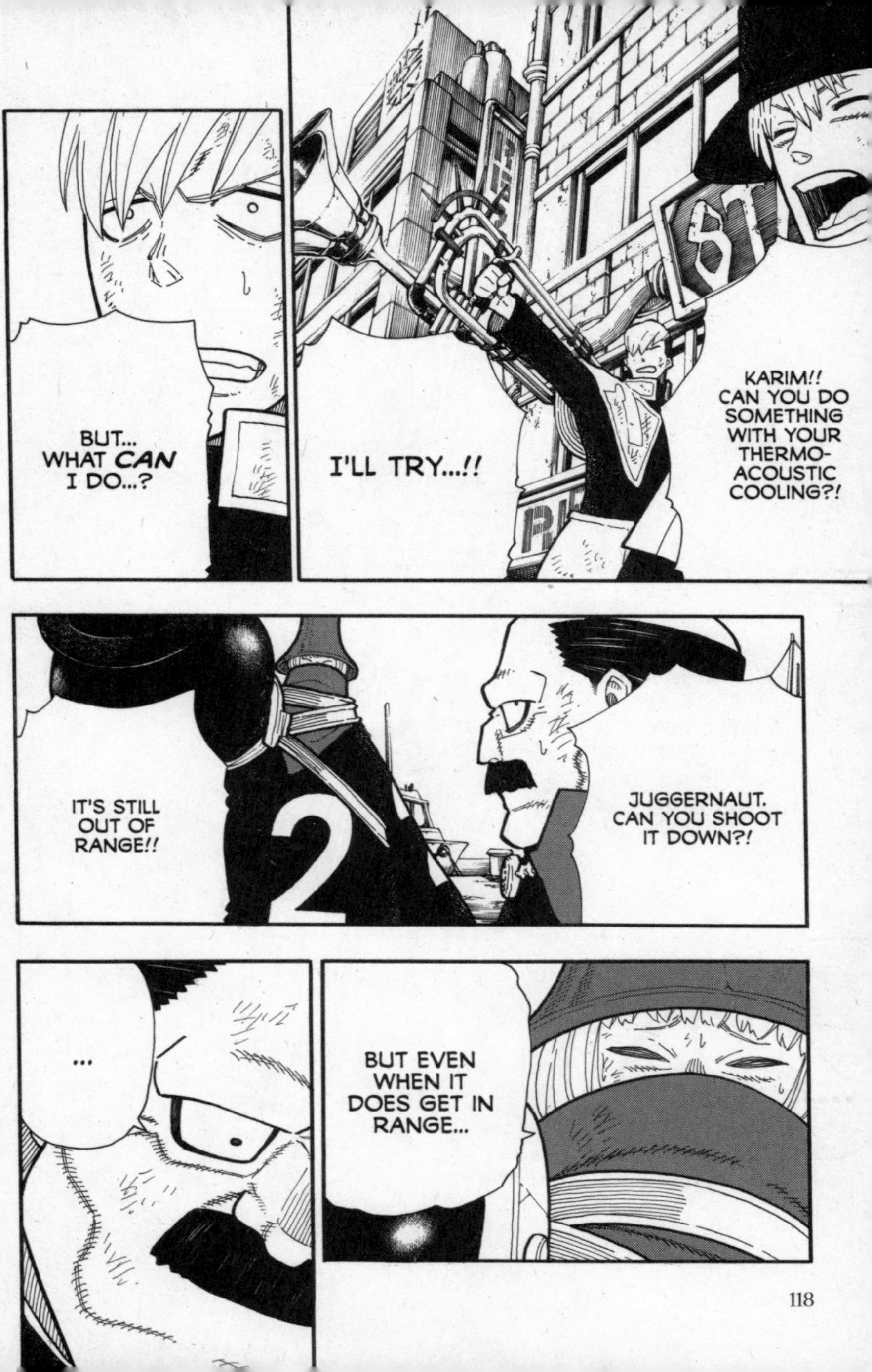
KARIM!! CAN YOU DO SOMETHING WITH YOUR THERMO-ACOUSTIC COOLING?!
I'LL TRY...!!
BUT... WHAT CAN I DO...?
JUGGERNAUT. CAN YOU SHOOT IT DOWN?!
IT'S STILL OUT OF RANGE!!
BUT EVEN WHEN IT DOES GET IN RANGE...
...

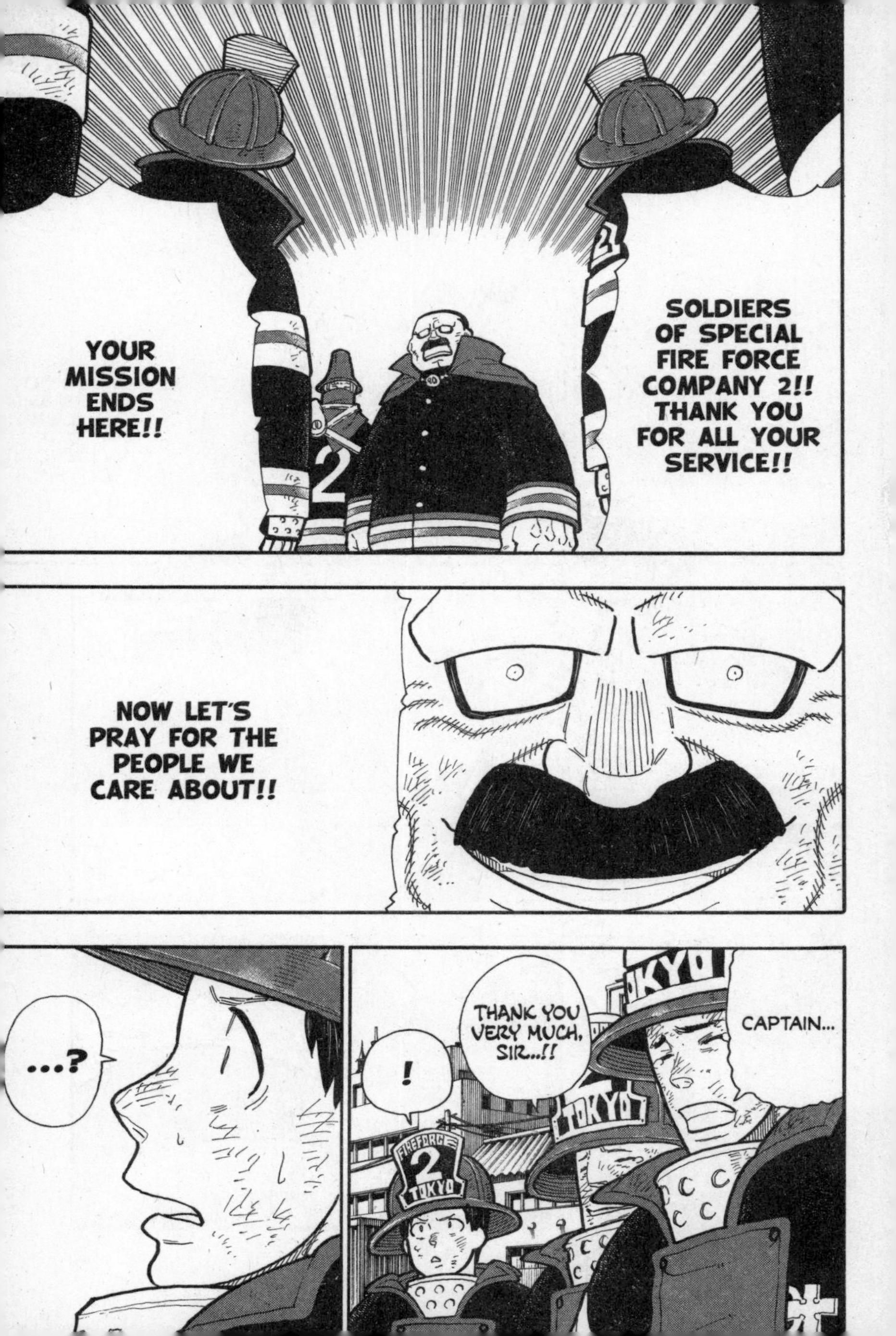
SOLDIERS OF SPECIAL FIRE FORCE COMPANY 2!! THANK YOU FOR ALL YOUR SERVICE!!
YOUR MISSION ENDS HERE!!
NOW LET'S PRAY FOR THE PEOPLE WE CARE ABOUT!!
CAPTAIN...
THANK YOU VERY MUCH, SIR...!!
TOKYO
!
FIREFORCE 2 TOKYO
...?

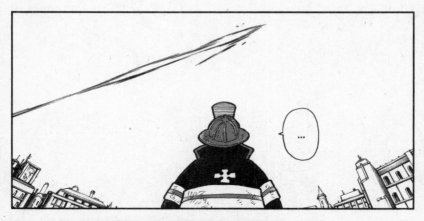

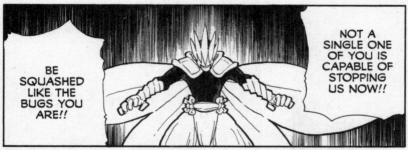

...
NOT A SINGLE ONE OF YOU IS CAPABLE OF STOPPING US NOW!!
BE SQUASHED LIKE THE BUGS YOU ARE!!
?!

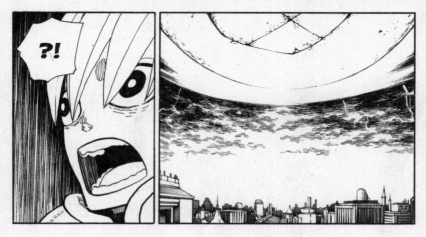

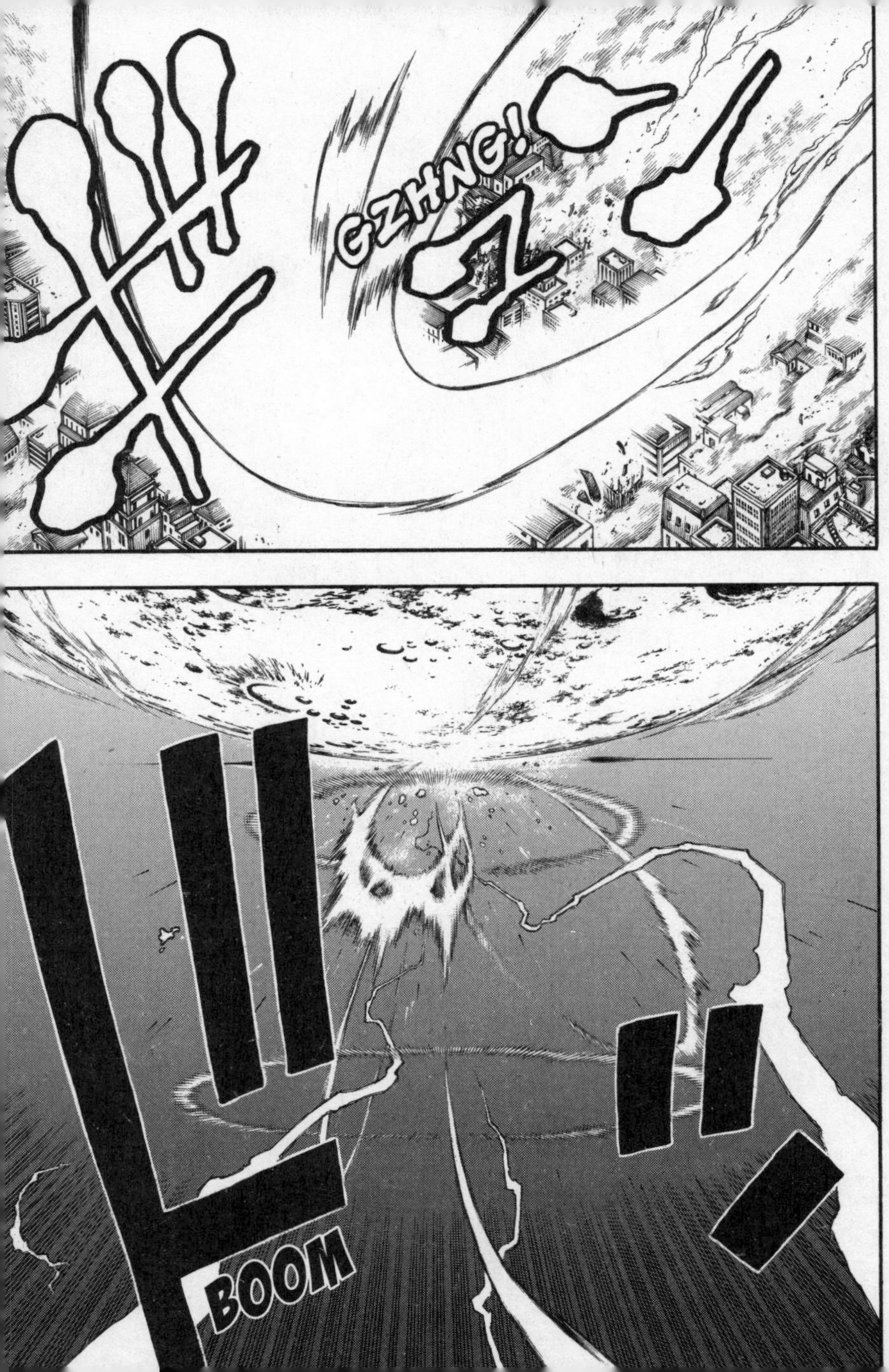
GZHNG!
BOOM

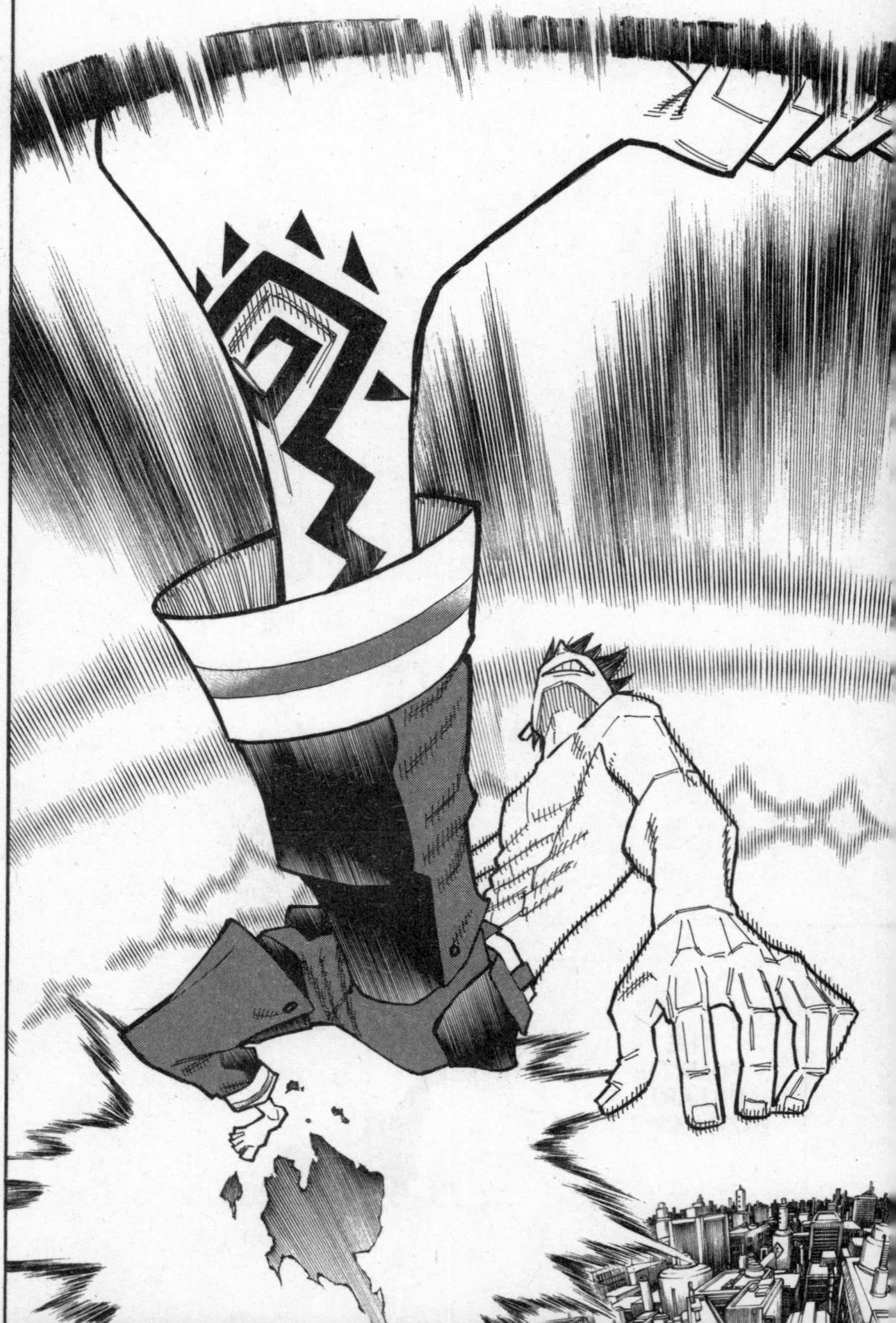

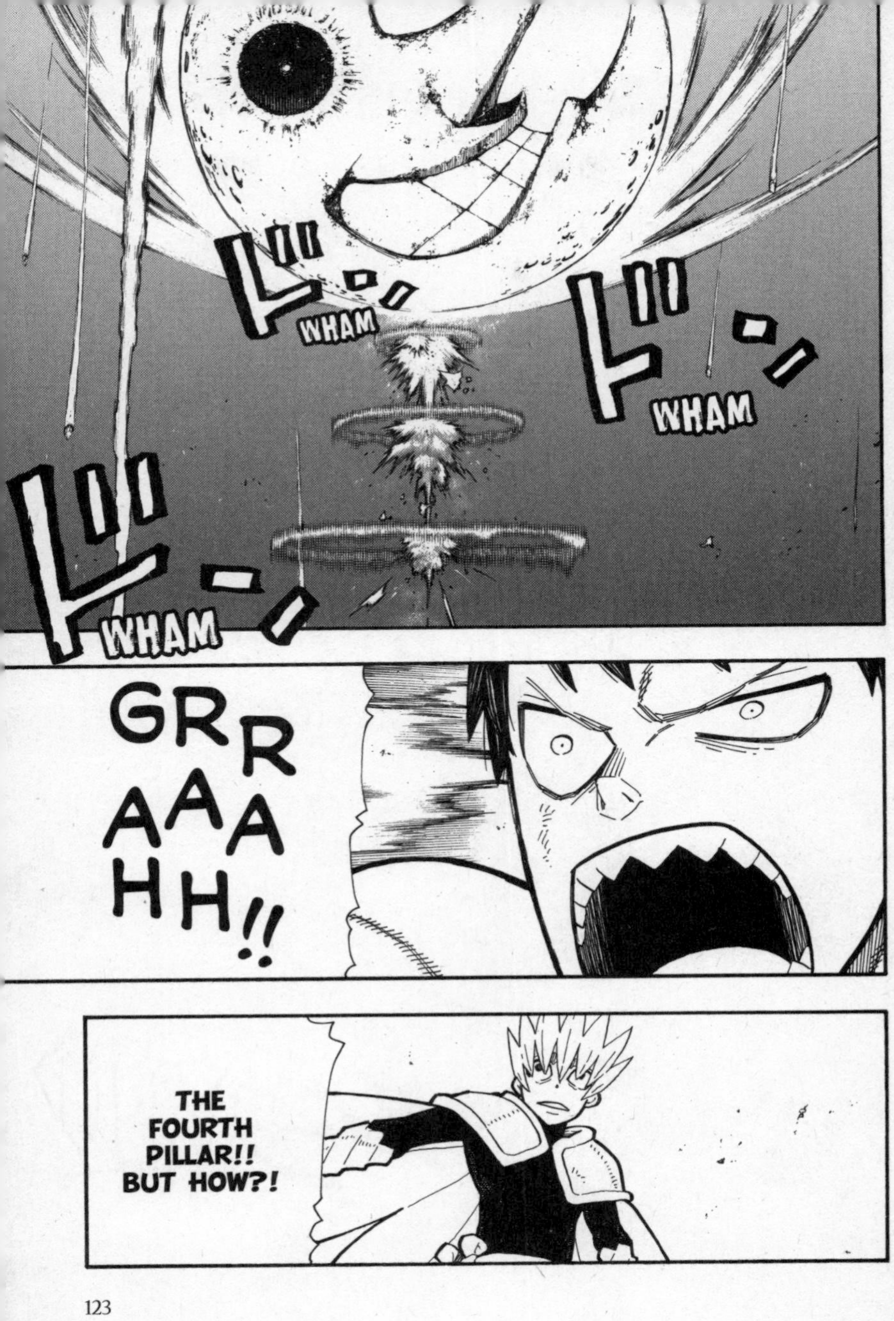
WHAM
WHAM
WHAM
GRRAAAHH!!
THE FOURTH PILLAR!! BUT HOW?!

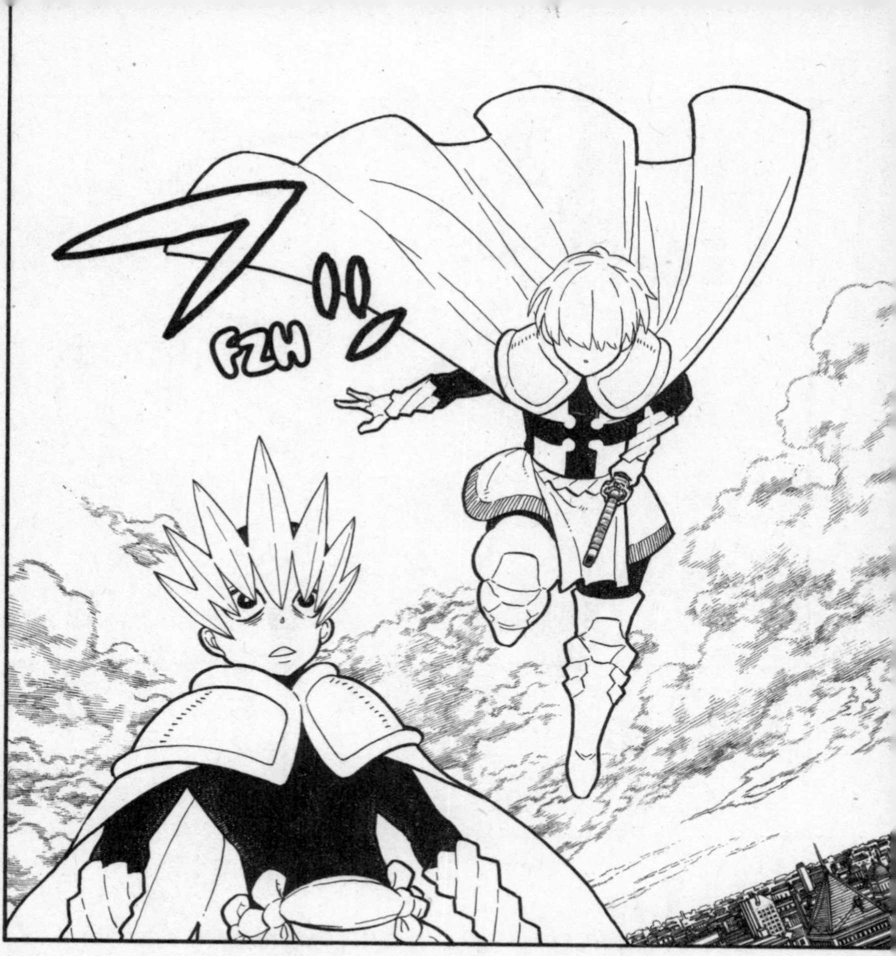
FZH
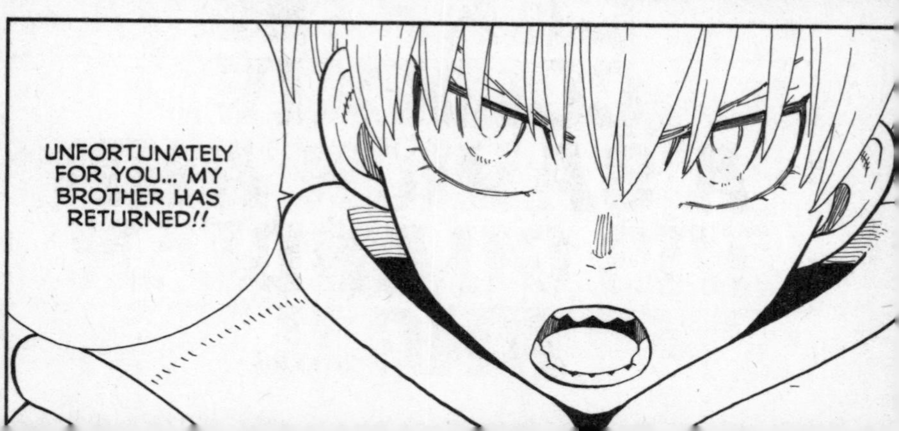
UNFORTUNATELY FOR YOU... MY BROTHER HAS RETURNED!!

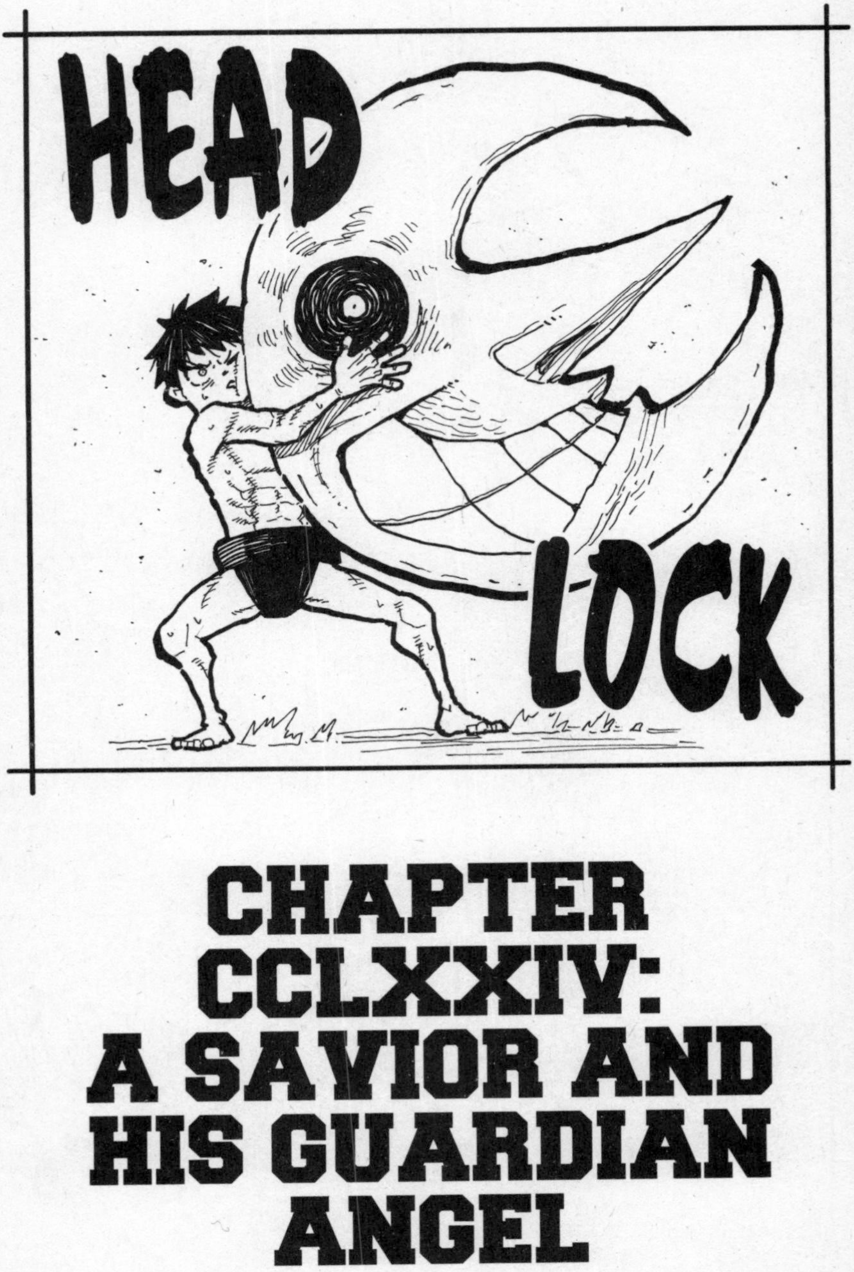
HEAD
LOCK

CHAPTER CCLXXIV: A SAVIOR AND HIS GUARDIAN ANGEL

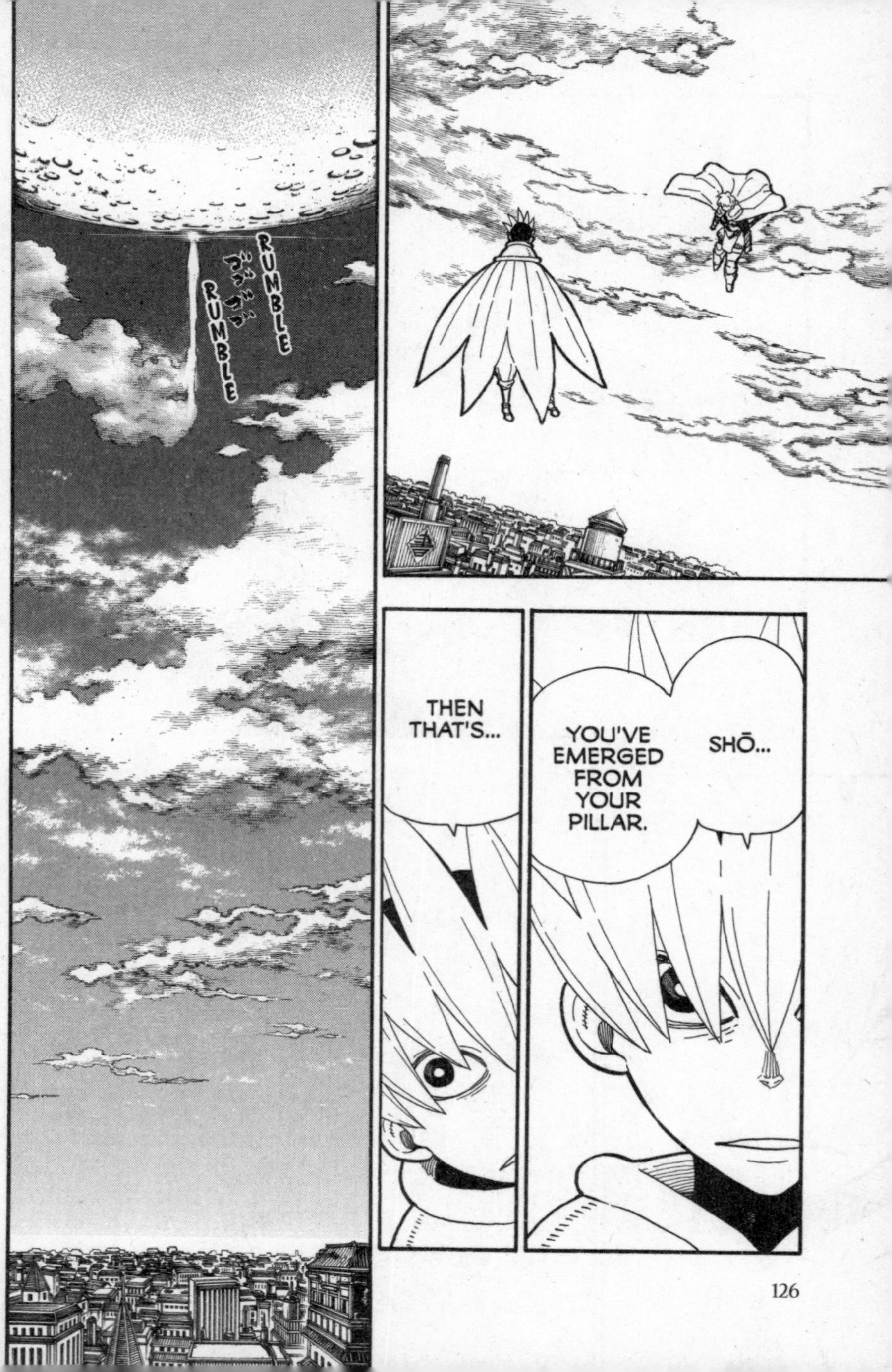
SHŌ...
YOU'VE EMERGED FROM YOUR PILLAR.
THEN THAT'S...
RUMBLE
RUMBLE

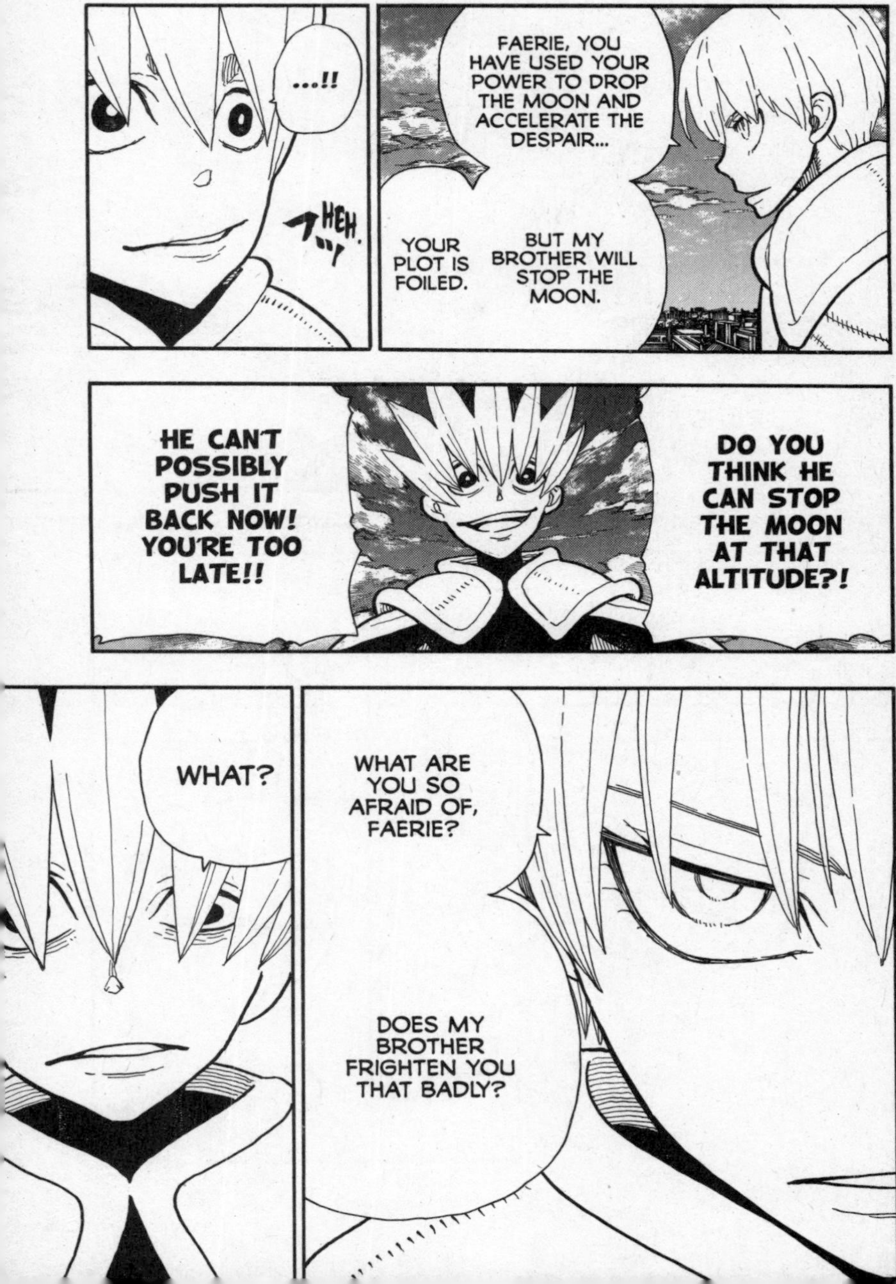
FAERIE, YOU HAVE USED YOUR POWER TO DROP THE MOON AND ACCELERATE THE DESPAIR...
BUT MY BROTHER WILL STOP THE MOON.
YOUR PLOT IS FOILED.
...!!
HEH.
DO YOU THINK HE CAN STOP THE MOON AT THAT ALTITUDE?!
HE CAN'T POSSIBLY PUSH IT BACK NOW! YOU'RE TOO LATE!!
WHAT ARE YOU SO AFRAID OF, FAERIE?
DOES MY BROTHER FRIGHTEN YOU THAT BADLY?
WHAT?

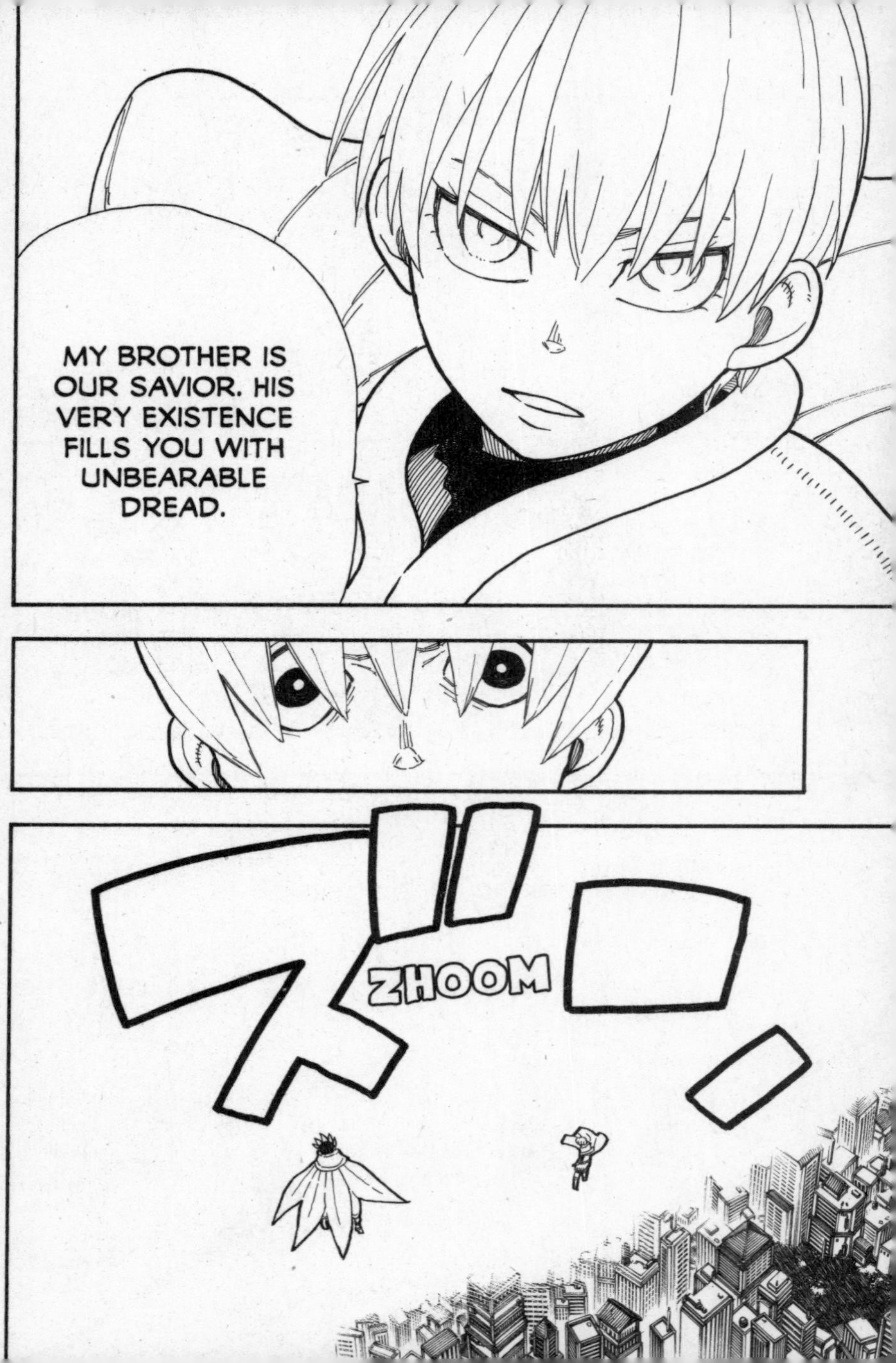
MY BROTHER IS OUR SAVIOR. HIS VERY EXISTENCE FILLS YOU WITH UNBEARABLE DREAD.
ZHOOM

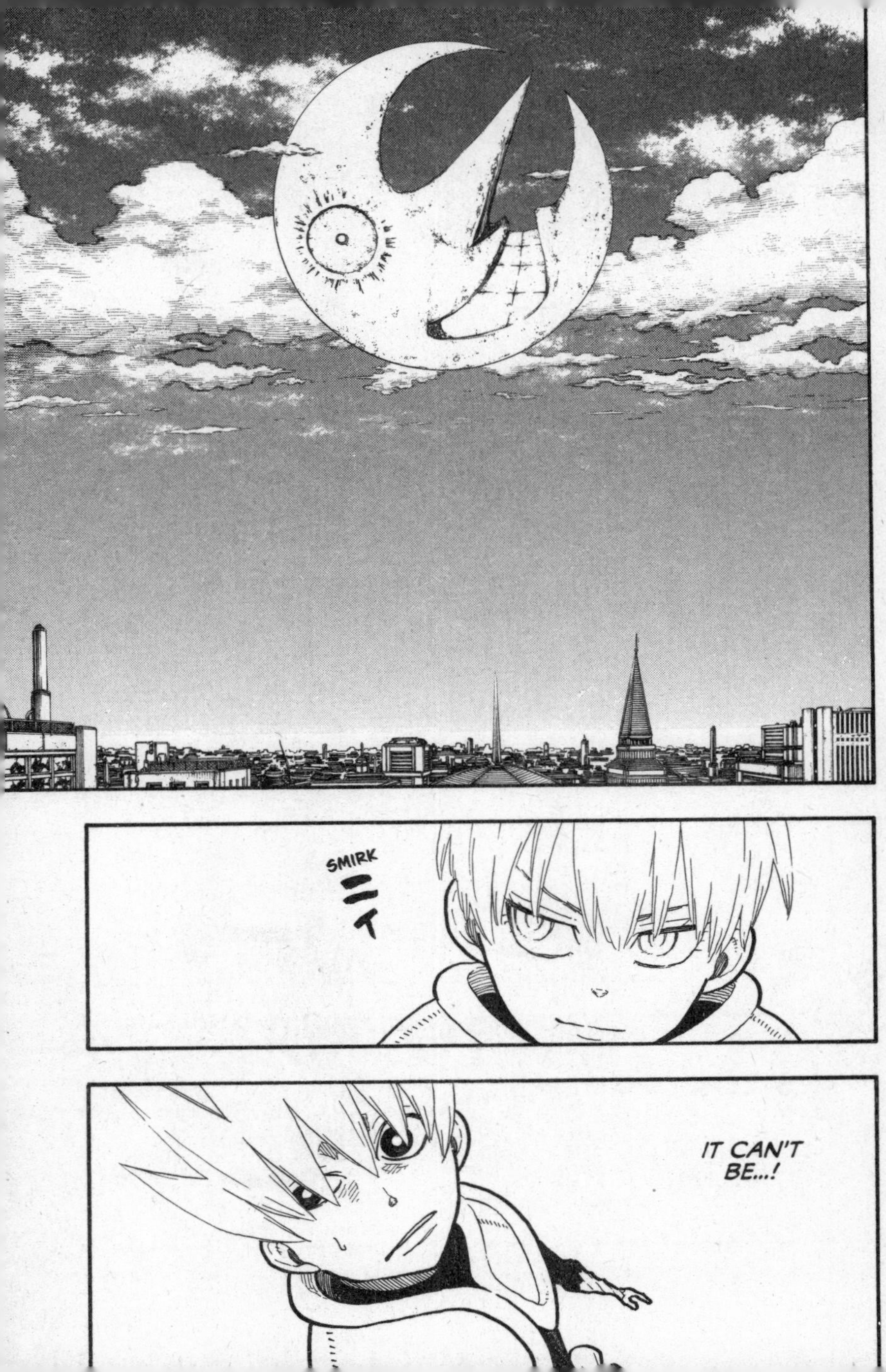
SMIRK
IT CAN'T BE...!

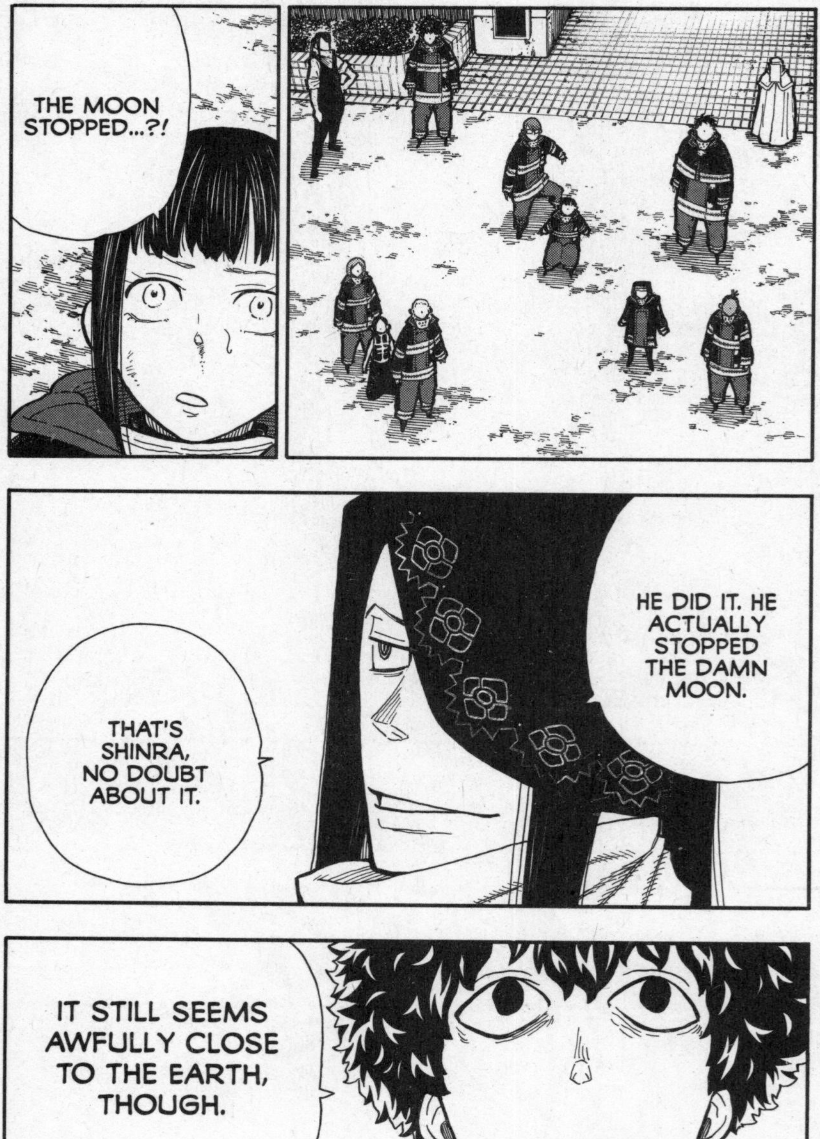
THE MOON STOPPED...?!
HE DID IT. HE ACTUALLY STOPPED THE DAMN MOON.
THAT'S SHINRA, NO DOUBT ABOUT IT.
IT STILL SEEMS AWFULLY CLOSE TO THE EARTH, THOUGH.

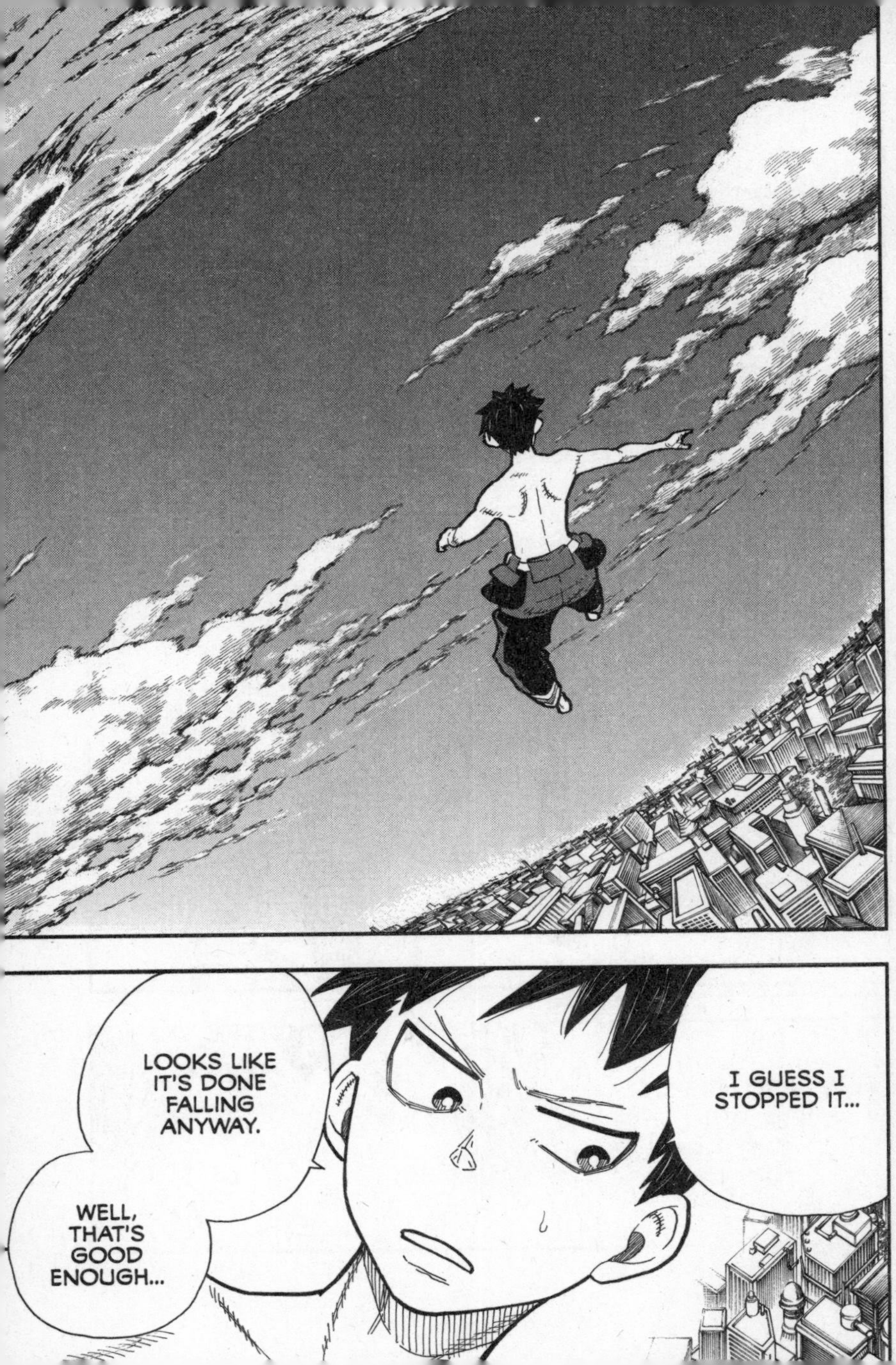
I GUESS I STOPPED IT...
LOOKS LIKE IT'S DONE FALLING ANYWAY.
WELL, THAT'S GOOD ENOUGH...

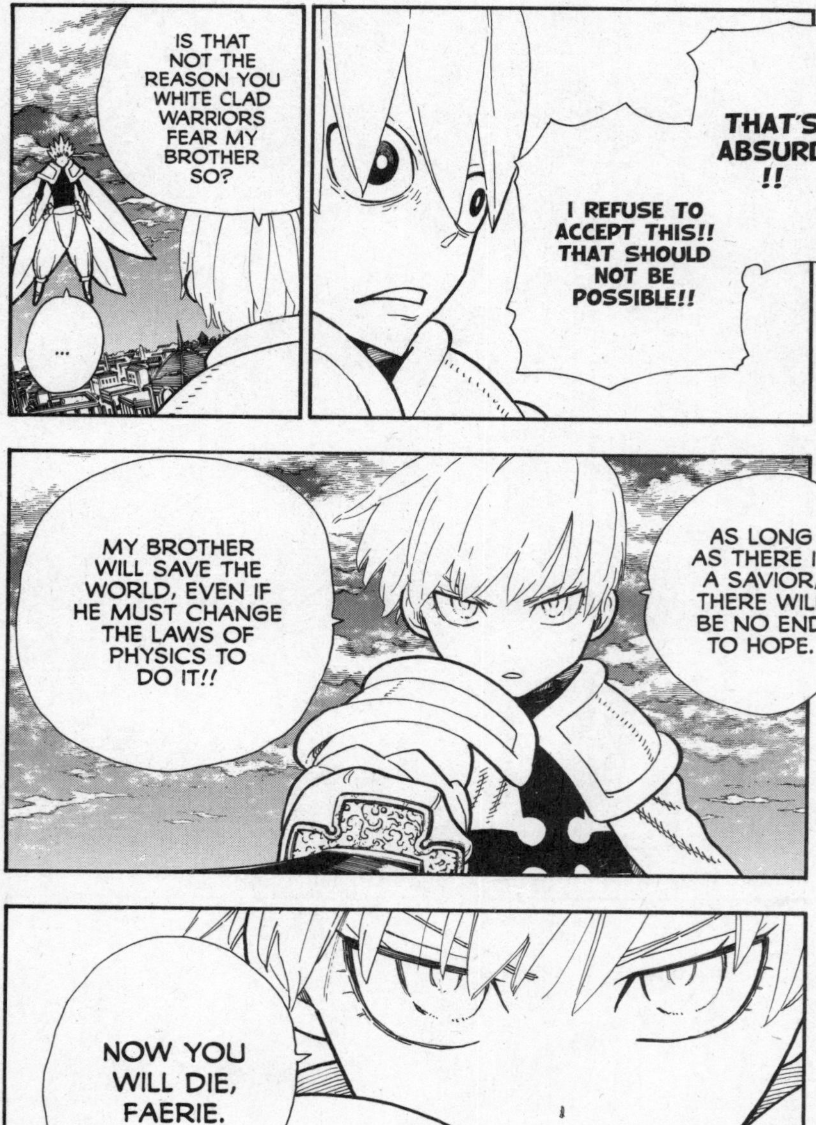
THAT'S ABSURD!!
I REFUSE TO ACCEPT THIS!! THAT SHOULD NOT BE POSSIBLE!!
IS THAT NOT THE REASON YOU WHITE CLAD WARRIORS FEAR MY BROTHER SO?
...
AS LONG AS THERE IS A SAVIOR, THERE WILL BE NO END TO HOPE.
MY BROTHER WILL SAVE THE WORLD, EVEN IF HE MUST CHANGE THE LAWS OF PHYSICS TO DO IT!!
NOW YOU WILL DIE, FAERIE.

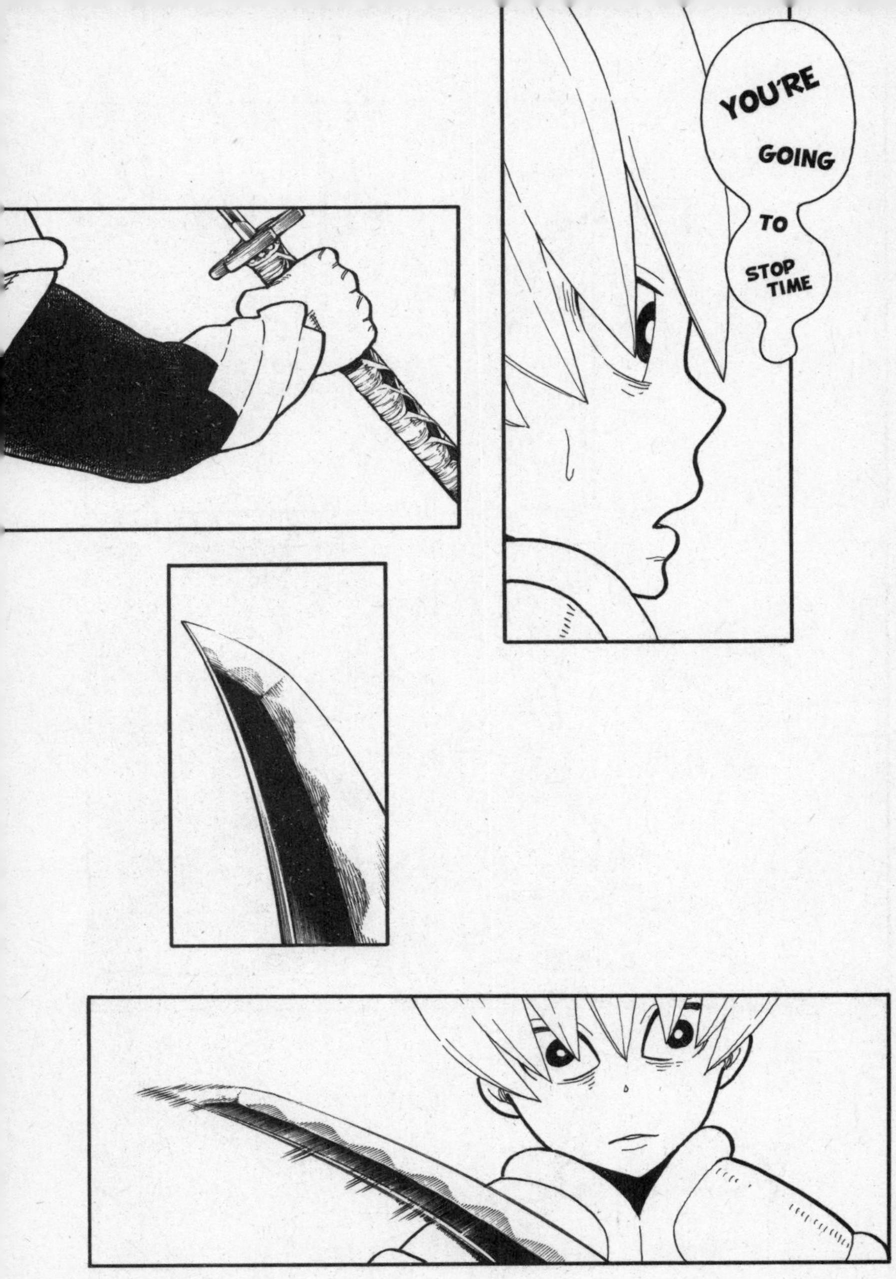
YOU'RE GOING TO STOP TIME

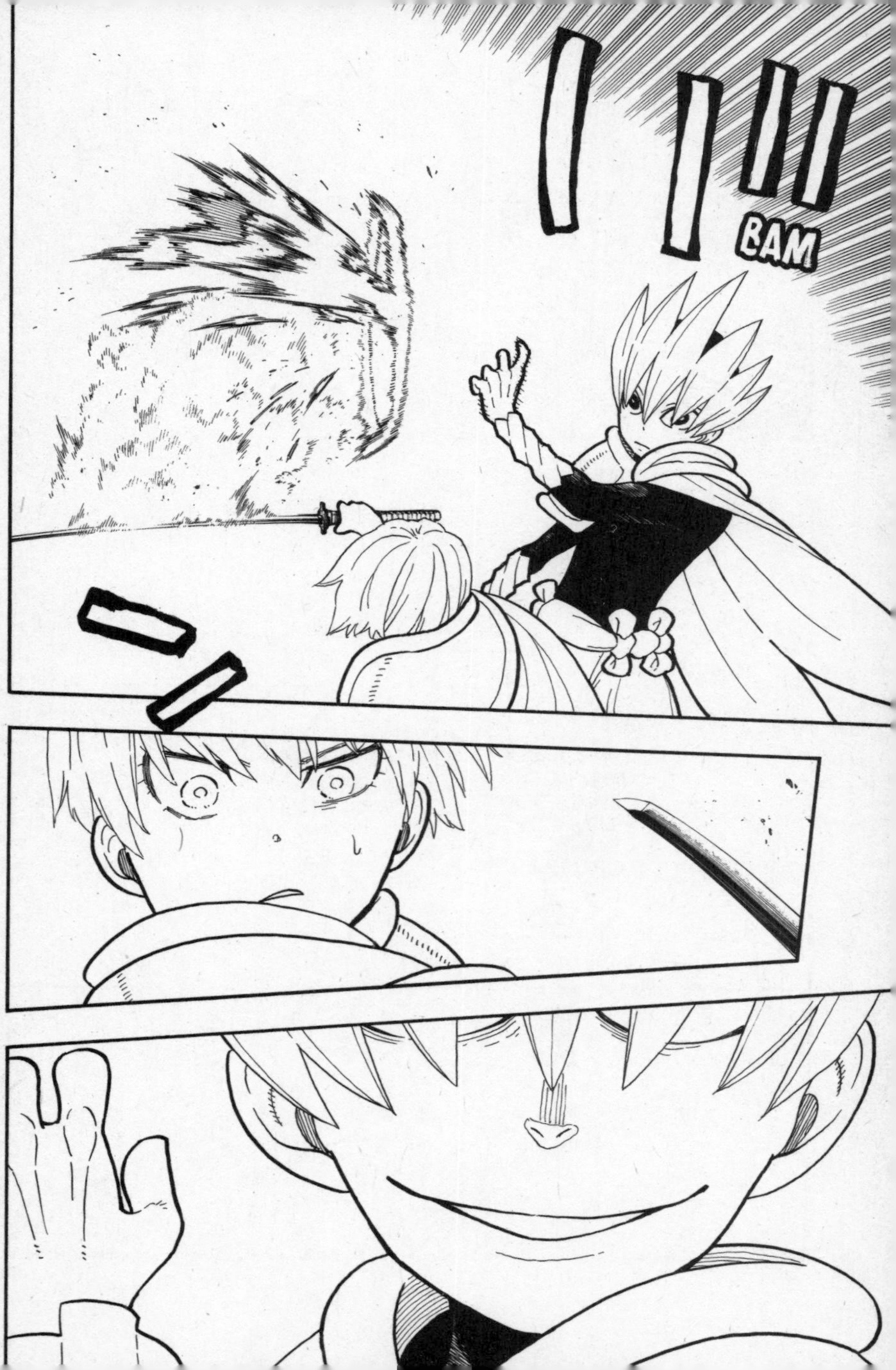
BAM

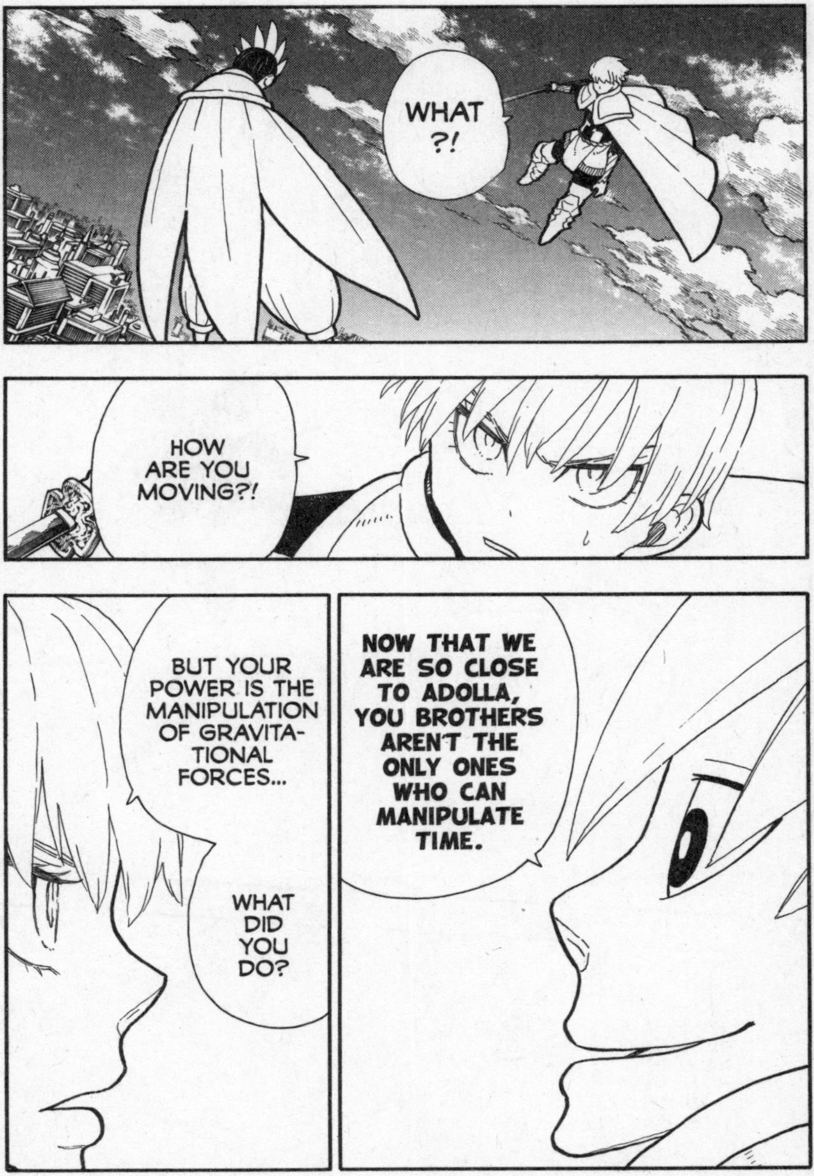
WHAT ?!
HOW ARE YOU MOVING?!
NOW THAT WE ARE SO CLOSE TO ADOLLA, YOU BROTHERS AREN'T THE ONLY ONES WHO CAN MANIPULATE TIME.
BUT YOUR POWER IS THE MANIPULATION OF GRAVITA-TIONAL FORCES...
WHAT DID YOU DO?

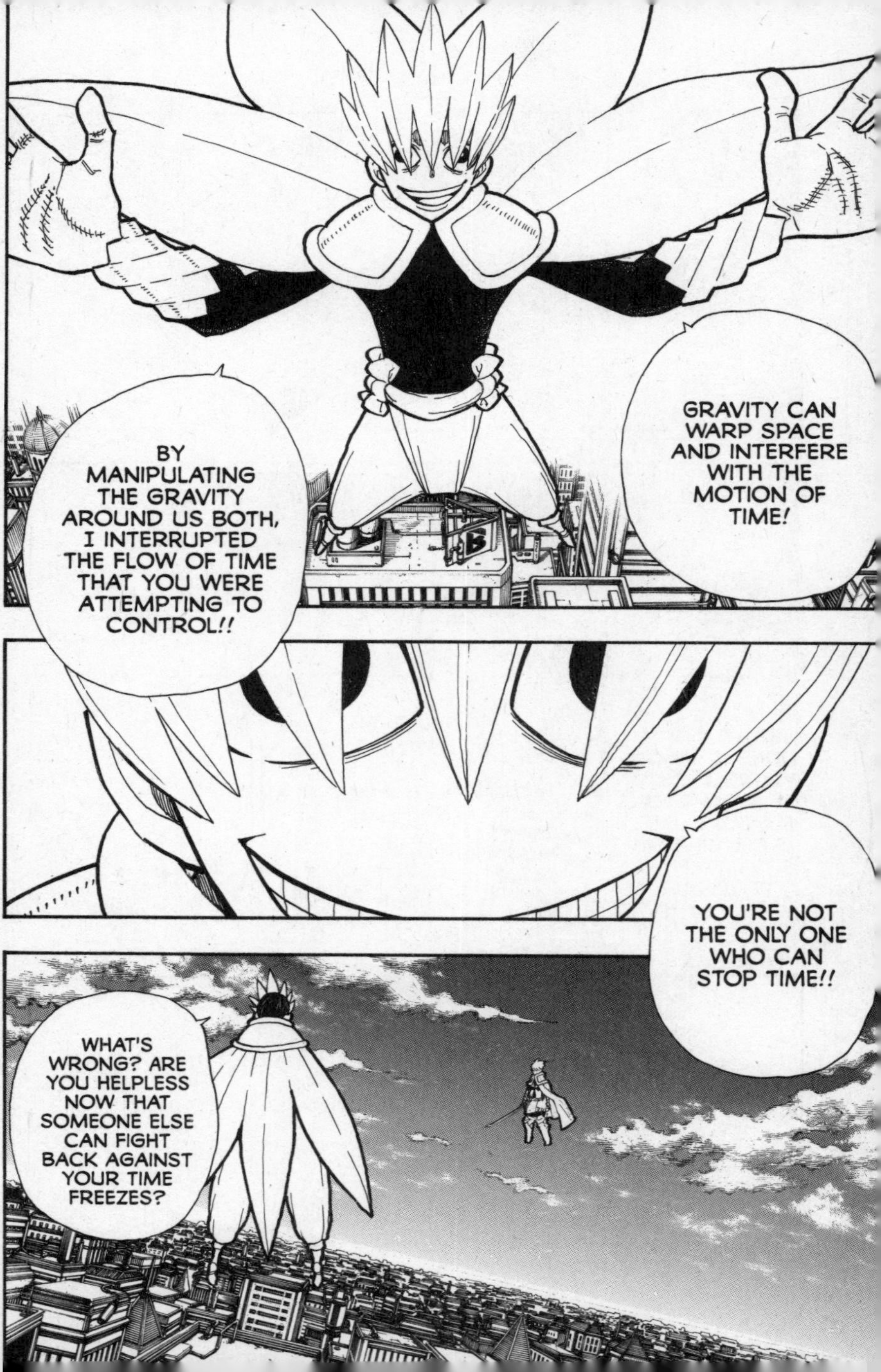
GRAVITY CAN WARP SPACE AND INTERFERE WITH THE MOTION OF TIME!
BY MANIPULATING THE GRAVITY AROUND US BOTH, I INTERRUPTED THE FLOW OF TIME THAT YOU WERE ATTEMPTING TO CONTROL!!
YOU'RE NOT THE ONLY ONE WHO CAN STOP TIME!!
WHAT'S WRONG? ARE YOU HELPLESS NOW THAT SOMEONE ELSE CAN FIGHT BACK AGAINST YOUR TIME FREEZES?

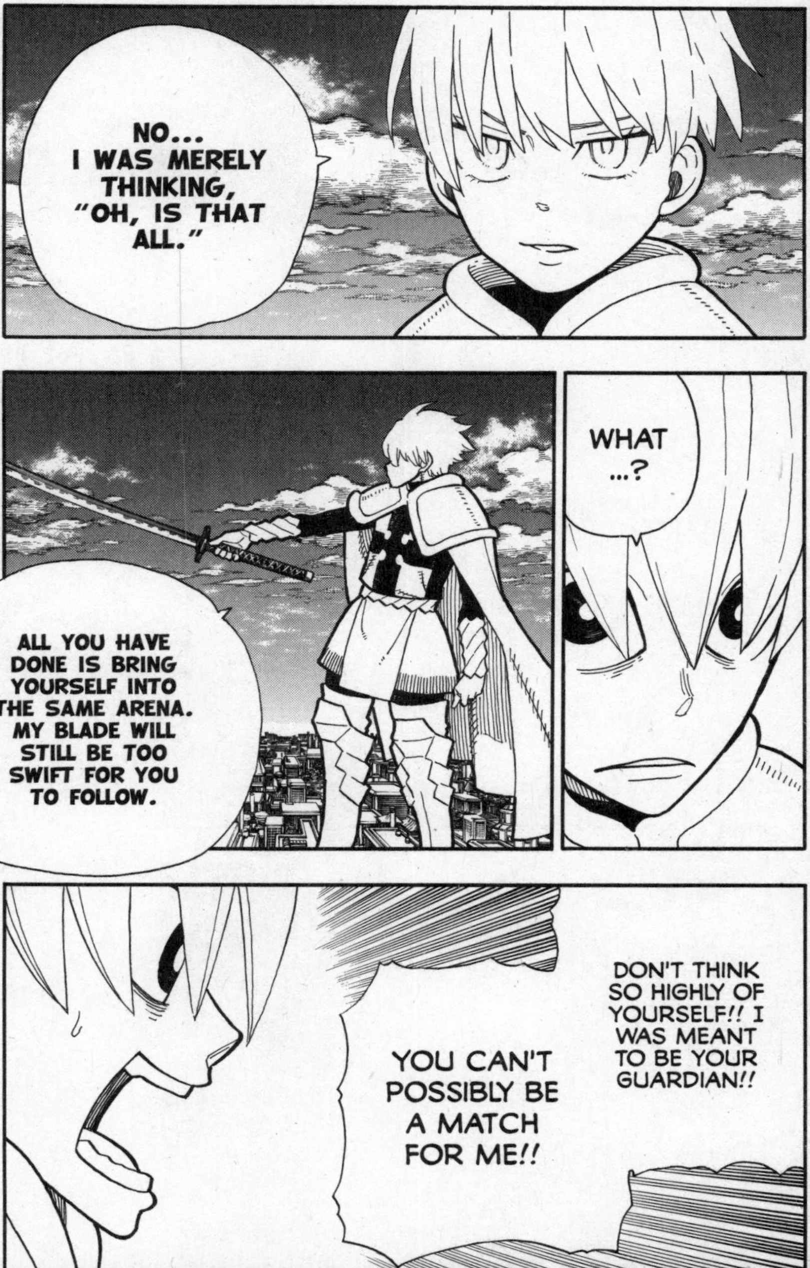
NO... I WAS MERELY THINKING, "OH, IS THAT ALL."
WHAT ...?
ALL YOU HAVE DONE IS BRING YOURSELF INTO THE SAME ARENA. MY BLADE WILL STILL BE TOO SWIFT FOR YOU TO FOLLOW.
DON'T THINK SO HIGHLY OF YOURSELF!! I WAS MEANT TO BE YOUR GUARDIAN!!
YOU CAN'T POSSIBLY BE A MATCH FOR ME!!

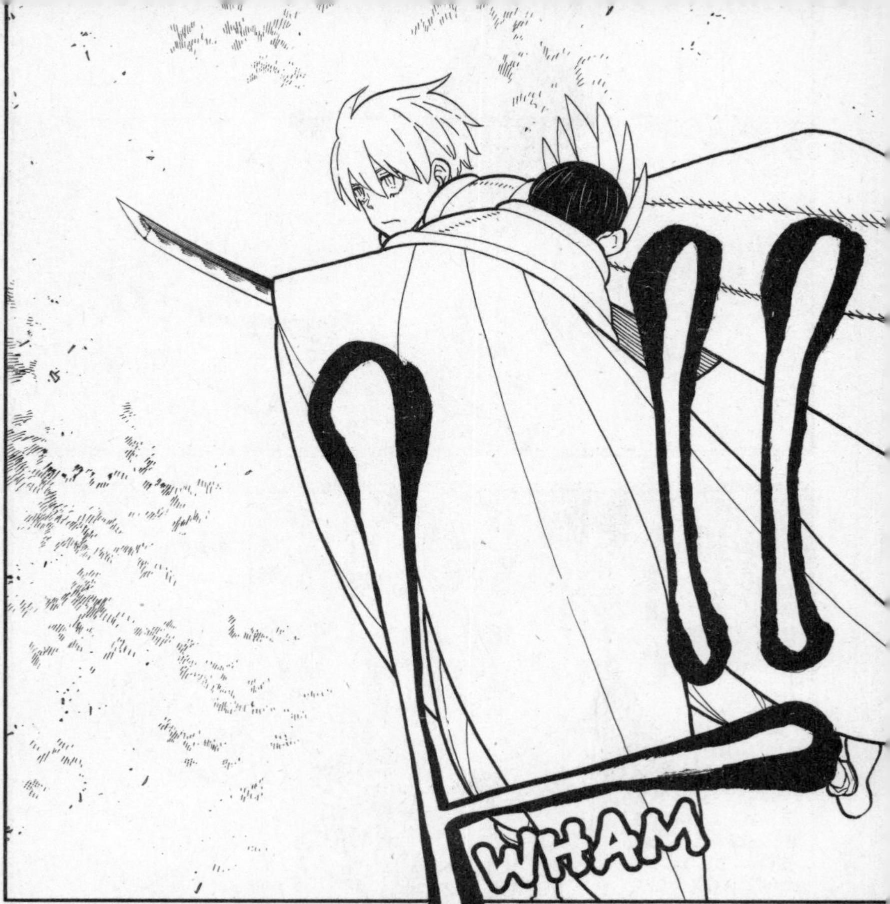
WHAM
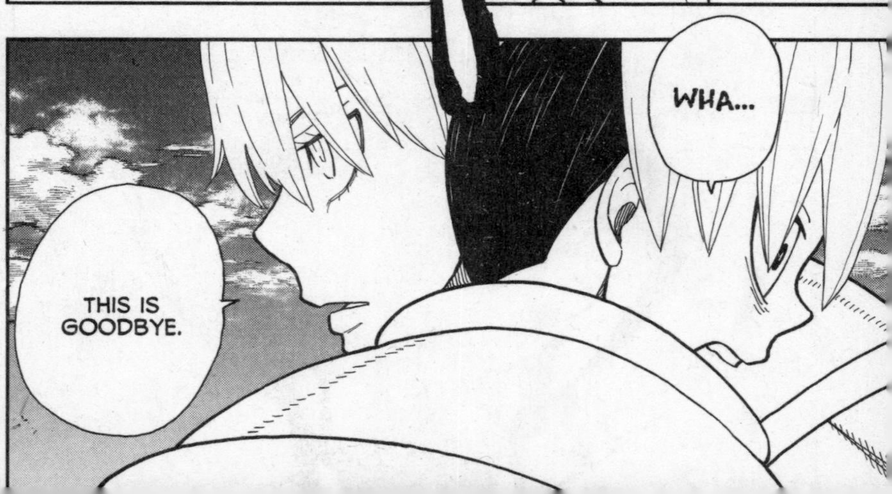
WHA...
THIS IS GOODBYE.

ZH
HNGH !
GLRGH
SMIRK

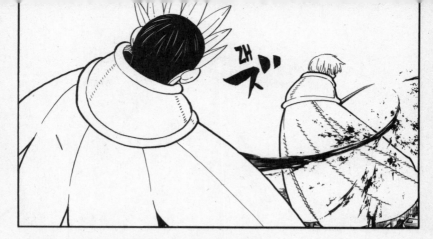

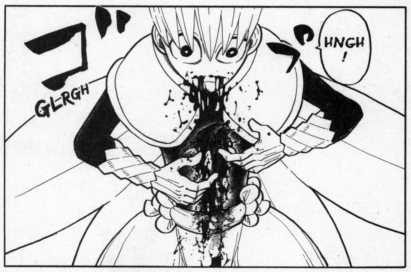

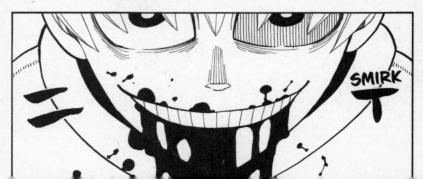

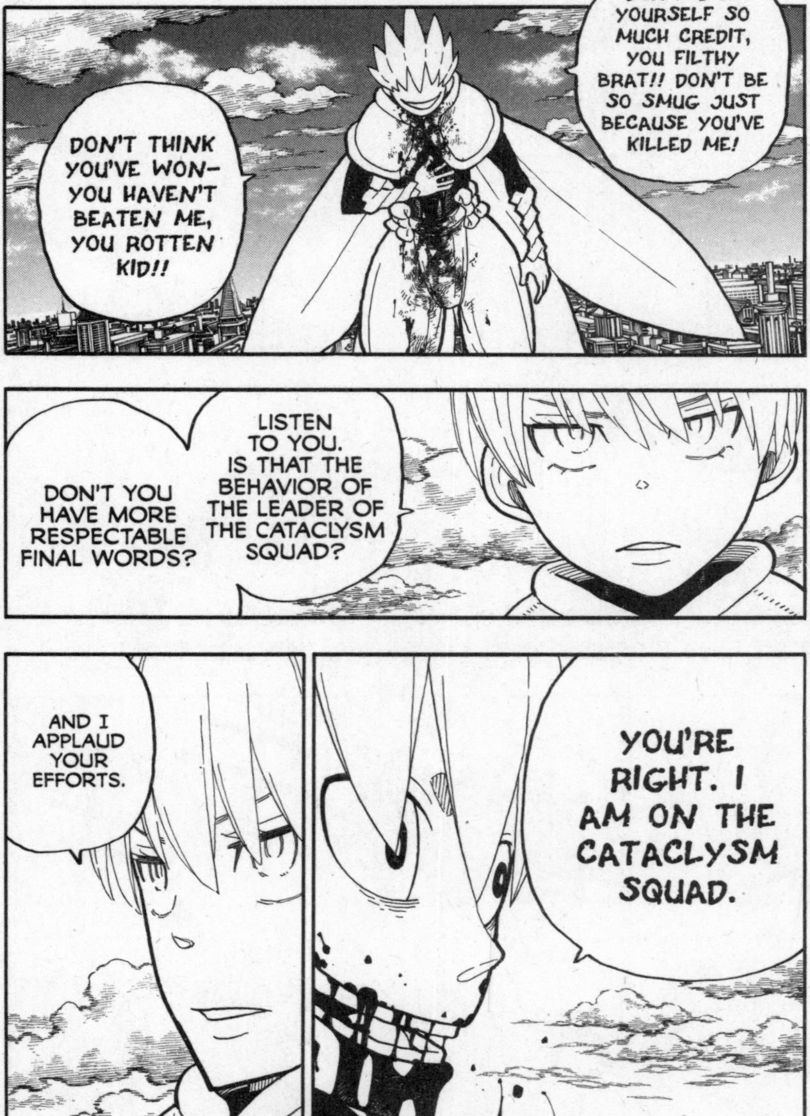
DON'T GIVE YOURSELF SO MUCH CREDIT, YOU FILTHY BRAT!! DON'T BE SO SMUG JUST BECAUSE YOU'VE KILLED ME!
DON'T THINK YOU'VE WON-YOU HAVEN'T BEATEN ME, YOU ROTTEN KID!!
LISTEN TO YOU. IS THAT THE BEHAVIOR OF THE LEADER OF THE CATACLYSM SQUAD?
DON'T YOU HAVE MORE RESPECTABLE FINAL WORDS?
YOU'RE RIGHT. I AM ON THE CATACLYSM SQUAD.
AND I APPLAUD YOUR EFFORTS.

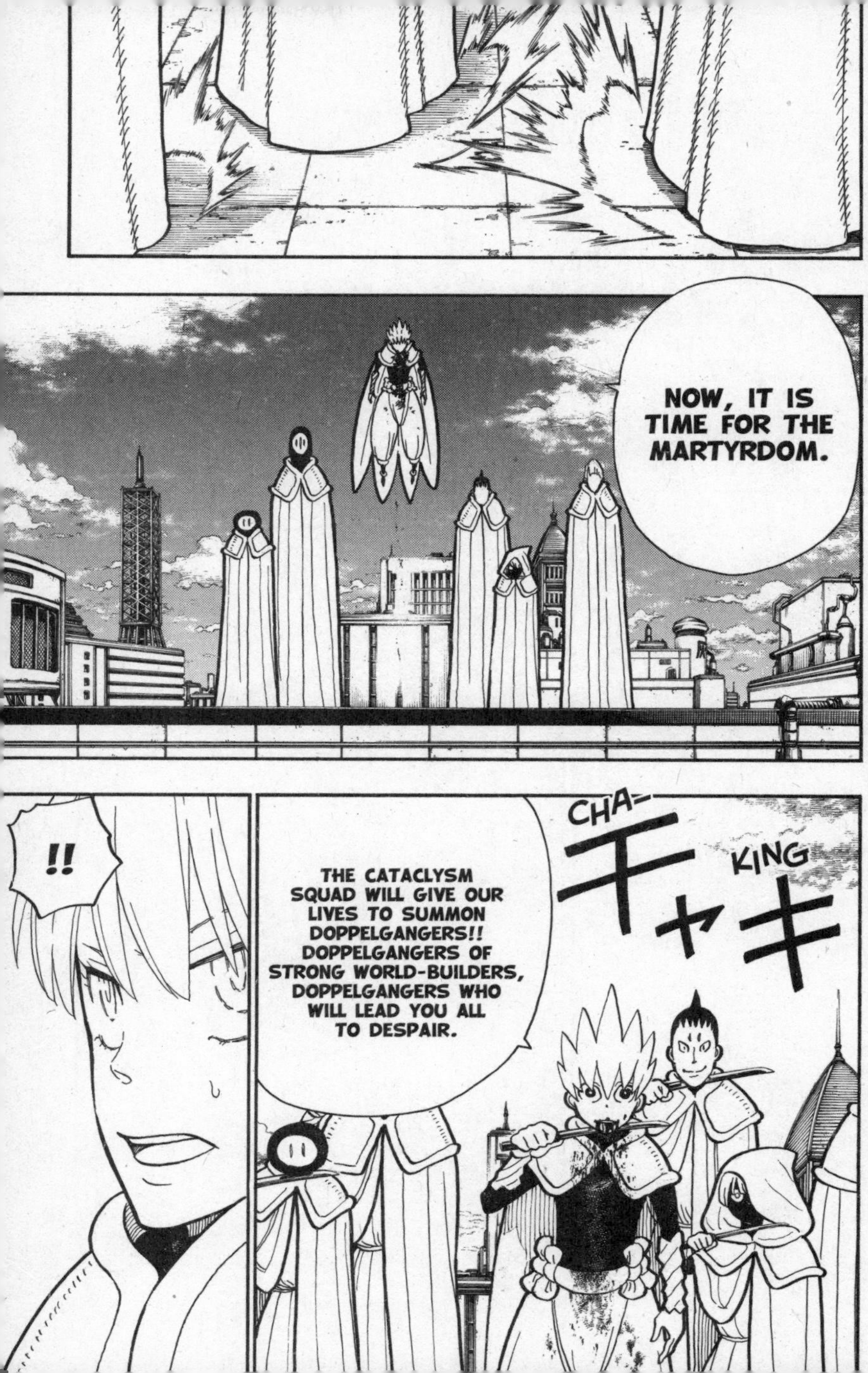
NOW, IT IS TIME FOR THE MARTYRDOM.
CHA-KING
チャキ
THE CATACLYSM SQUAD WILL GIVE OUR LIVES TO SUMMON DOPPELGANGERS!! DOPPELGANGERS OF STRONG WORLD-BUILDERS, DOPPELGANGERS WHO WILL LEAD YOU ALL TO DESPAIR.
!!

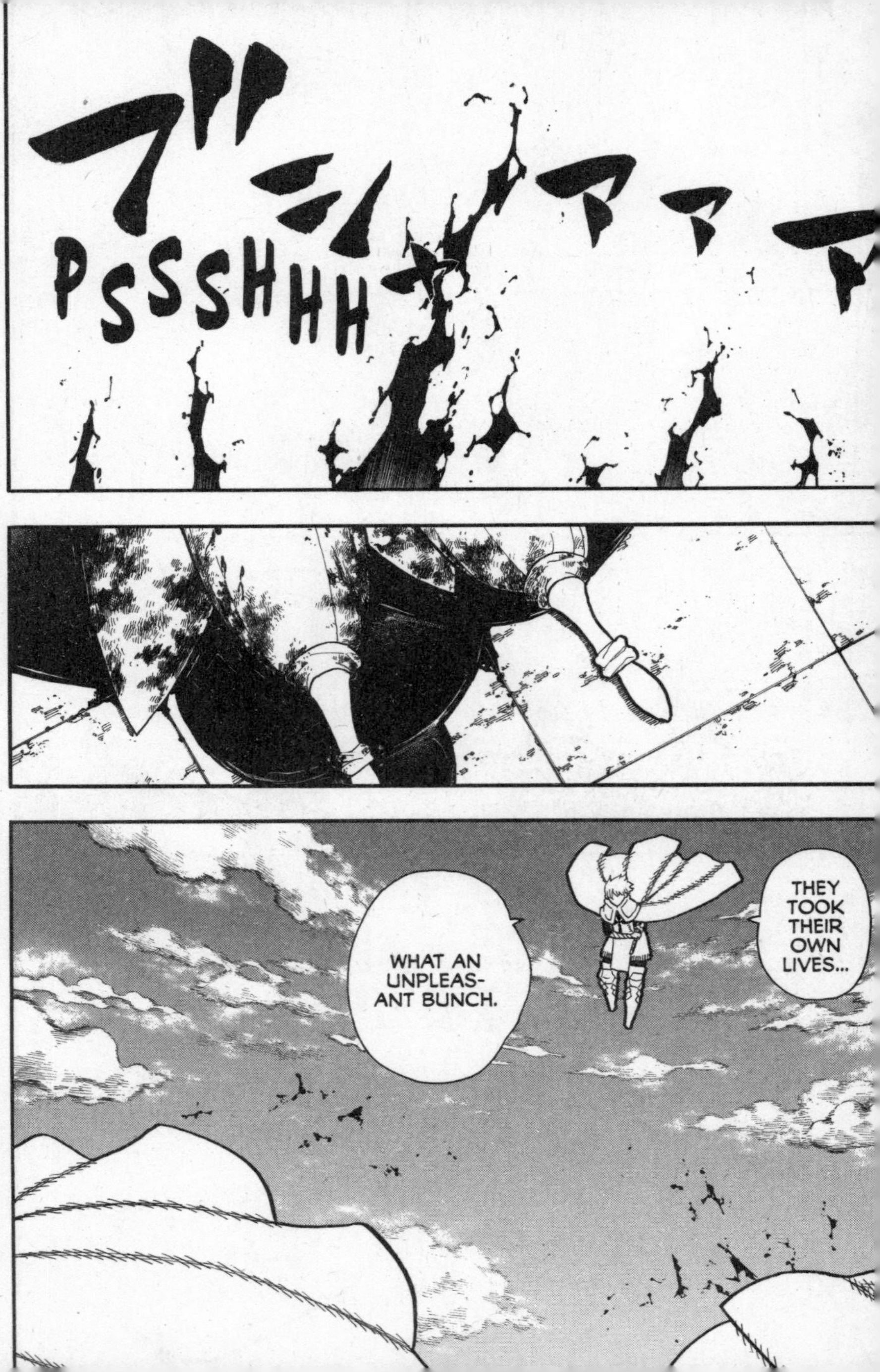
ブシャァァァ
PSSSHHH
THEY TOOK THEIR OWN LIVES...
WHAT AN UNPLEAS-ANT BUNCH.

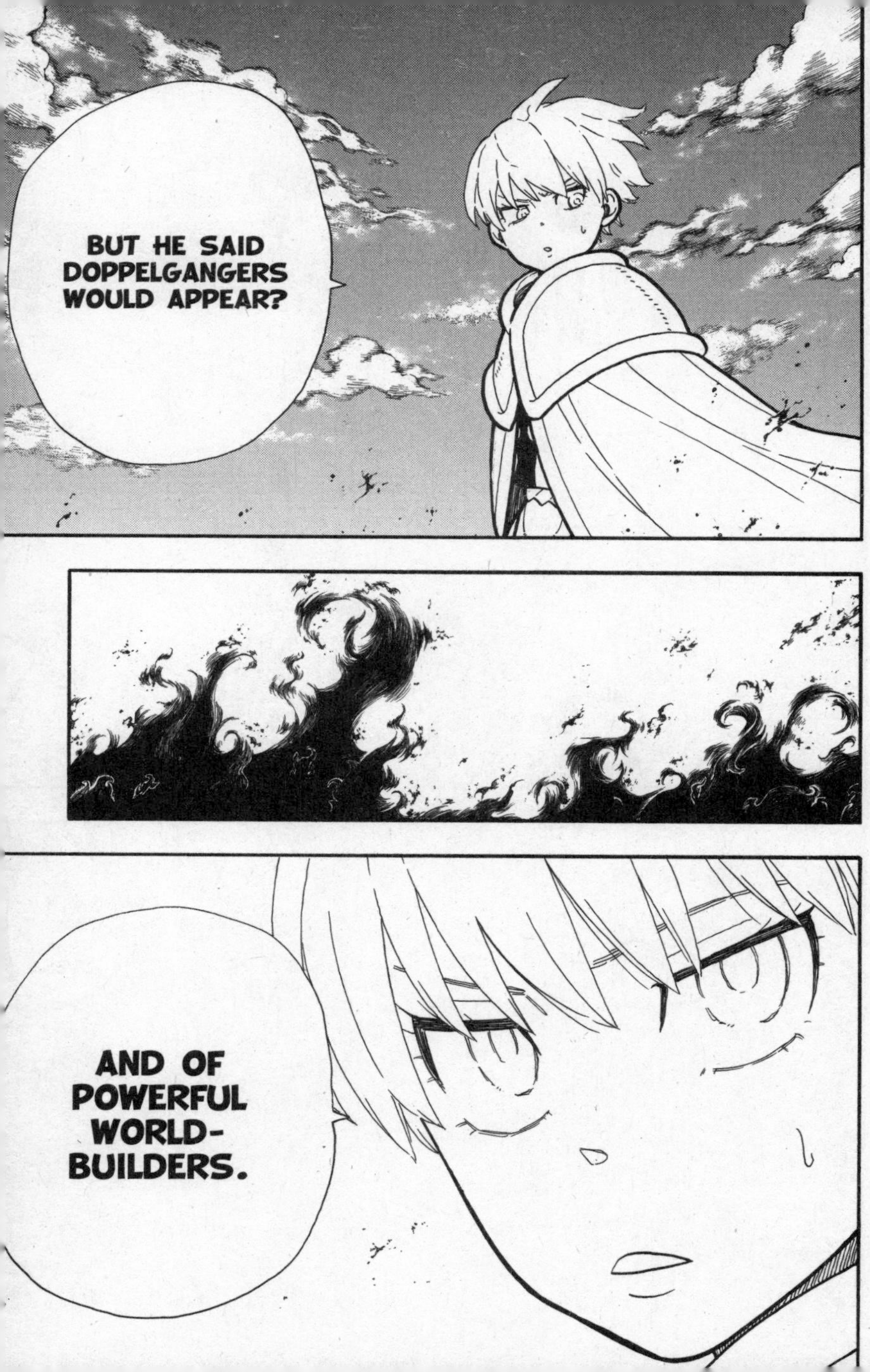
BUT HE SAID DOPPELGANGERS WOULD APPEAR?
AND OF POWERFUL WORLD-BUILDERS.

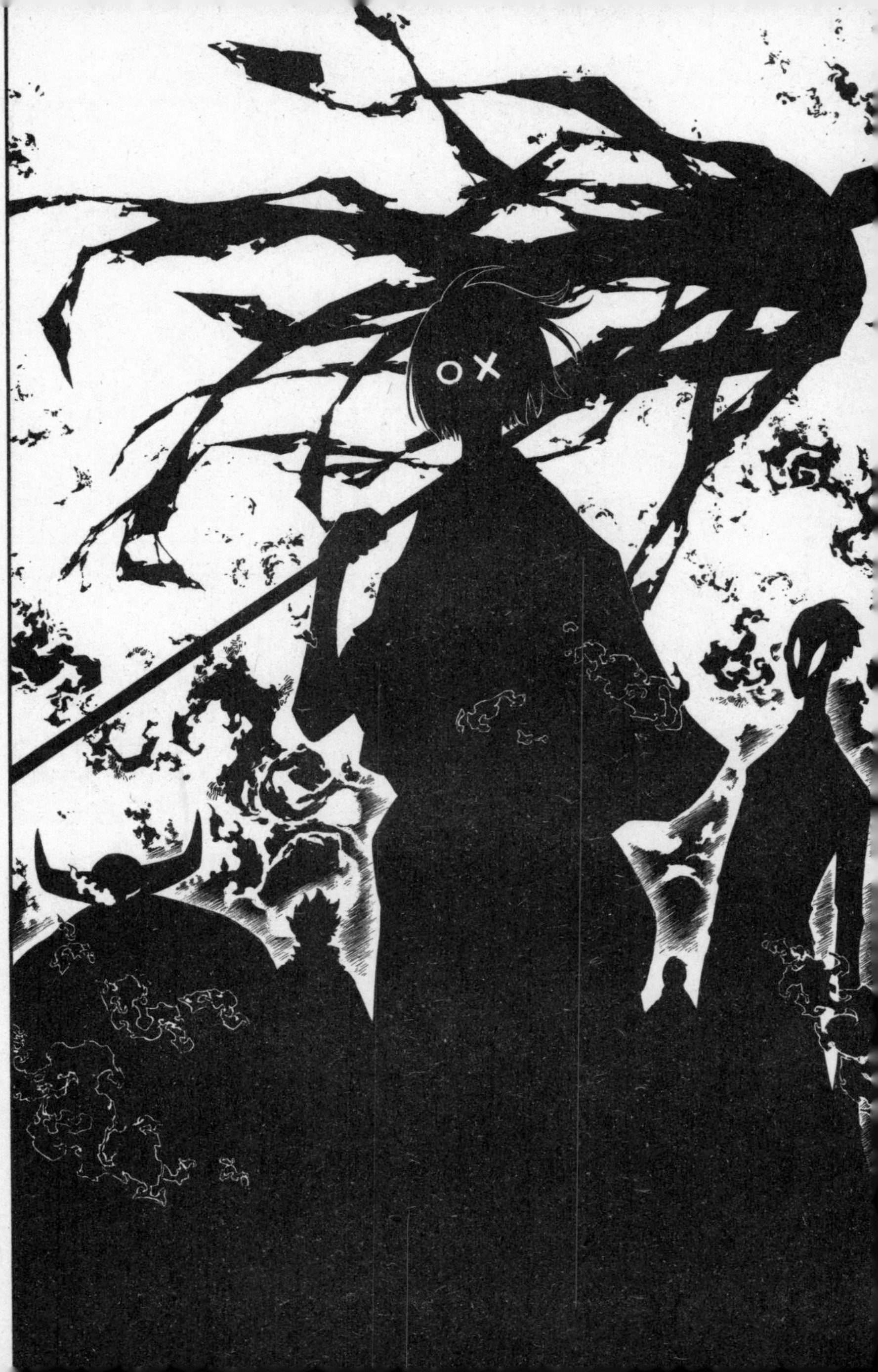

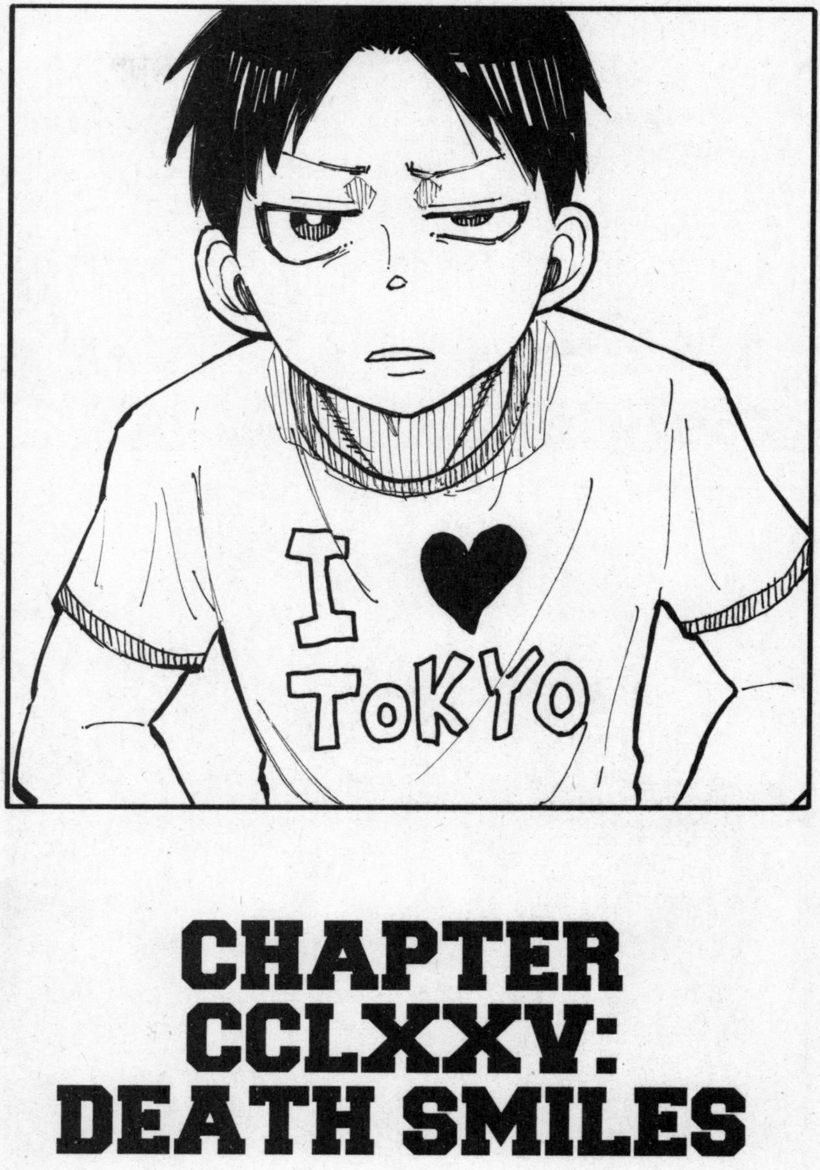
I ♥ TOKYO

CHAPTER CCLXXV: DEATH SMILES

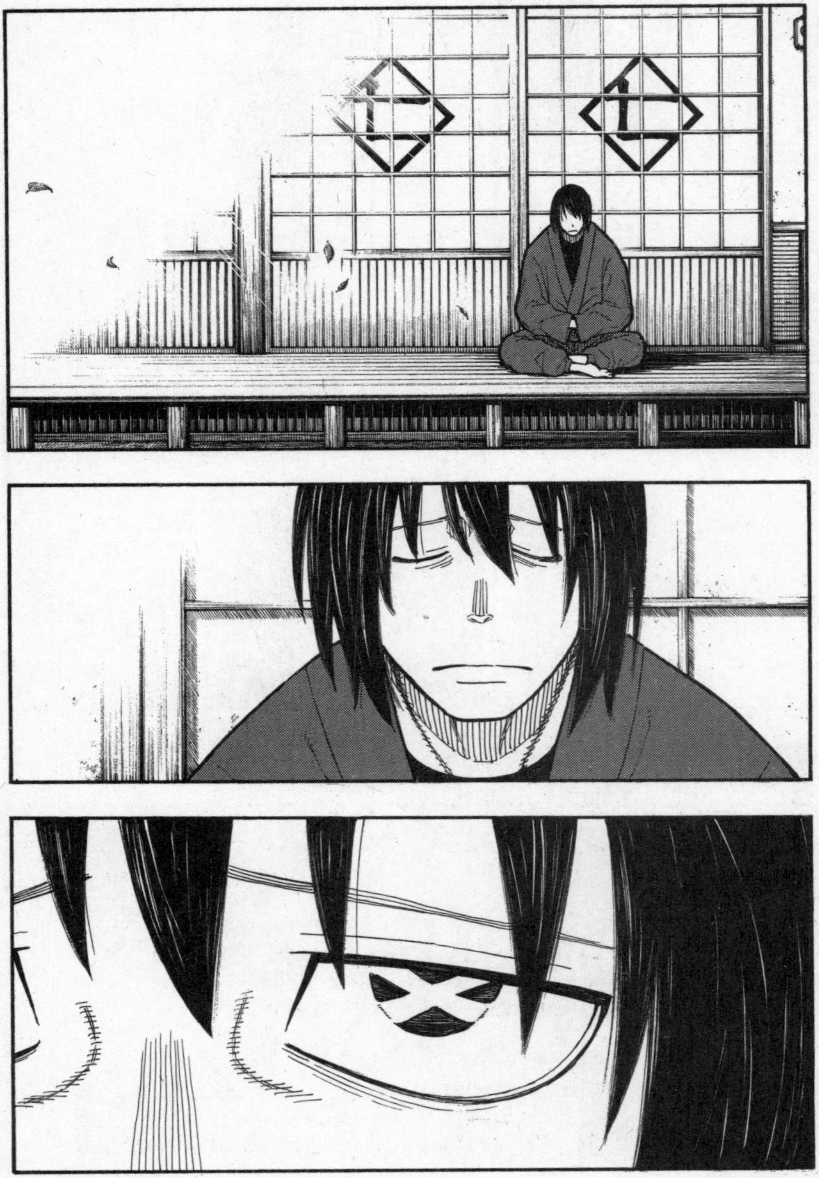

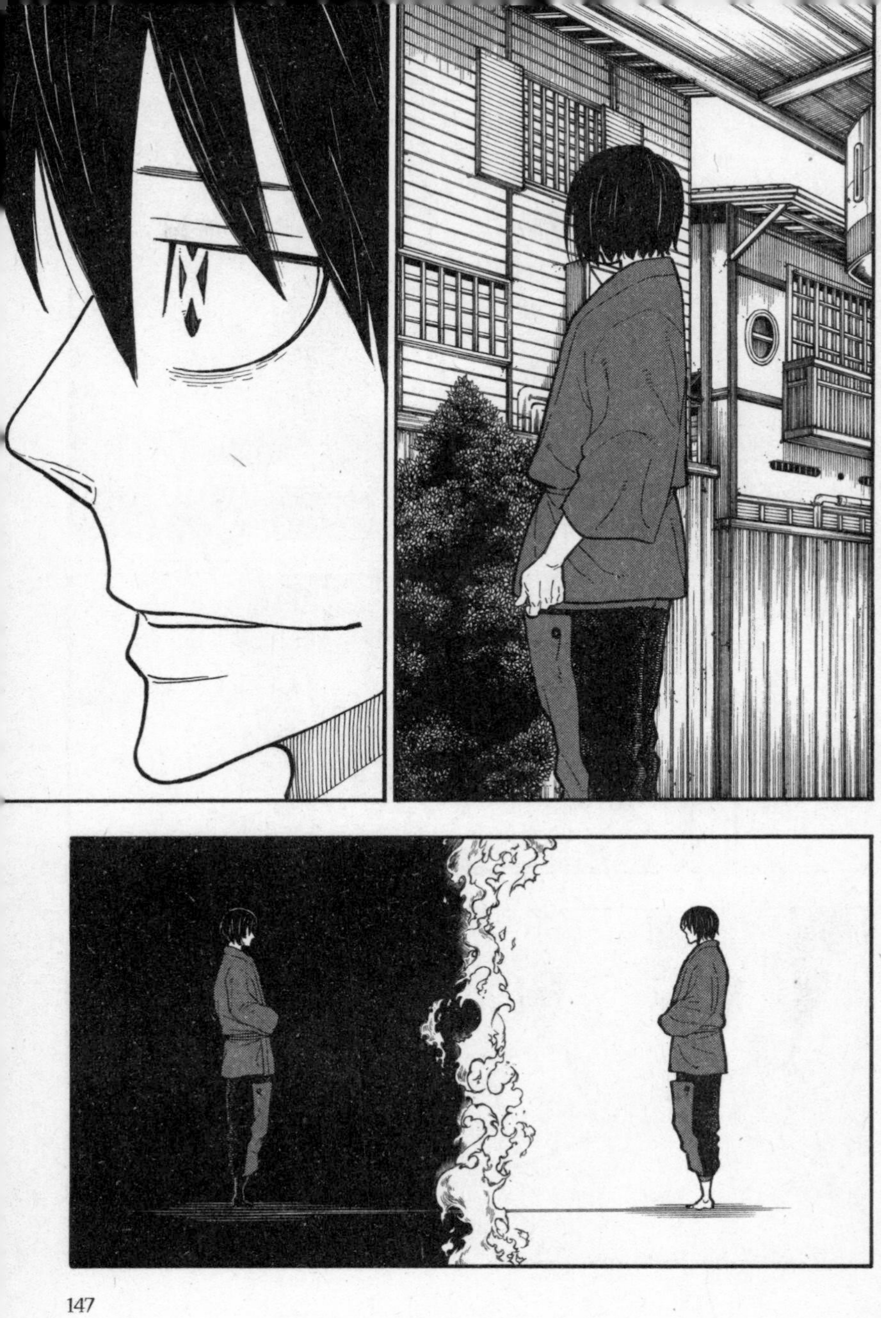

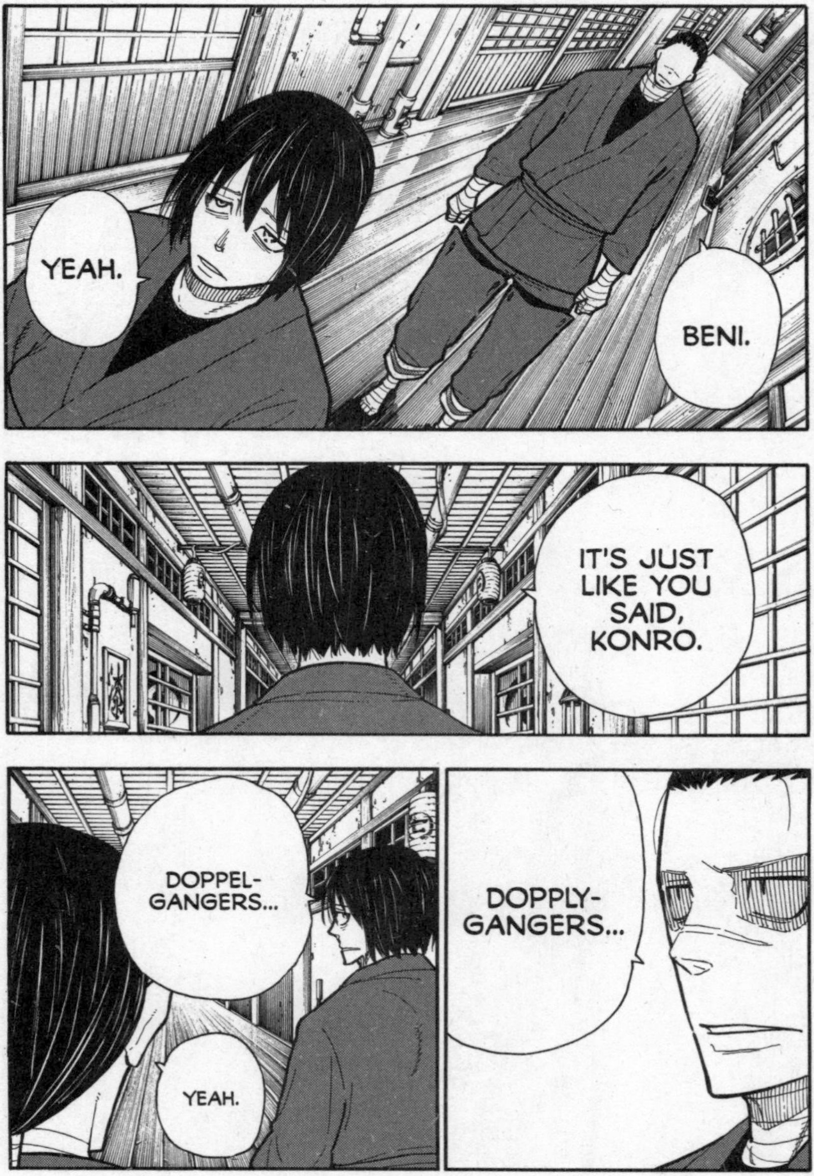
BENI.
YEAH.
IT'S JUST LIKE YOU SAID, KONRO.
DOPPLY-GANGERS...
DOPPEL-GANGERS...
YEAH.

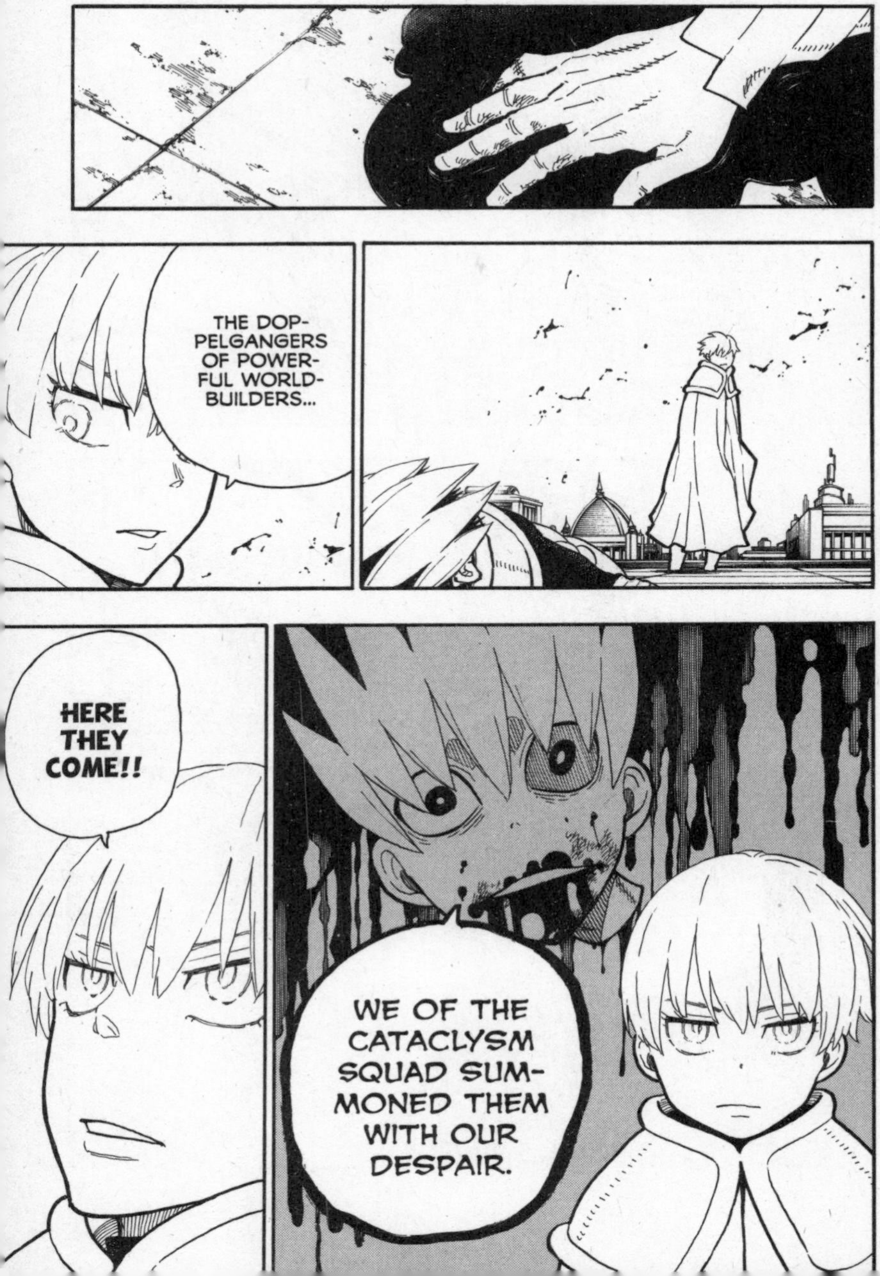
THE DOP-PELGANGERS OF POWER-FUL WORLD-BUILDERS...
WE OF THE CATACLYSM SQUAD SUM-MONED THEM WITH OUR DESPAIR.
HERE THEY COME!!

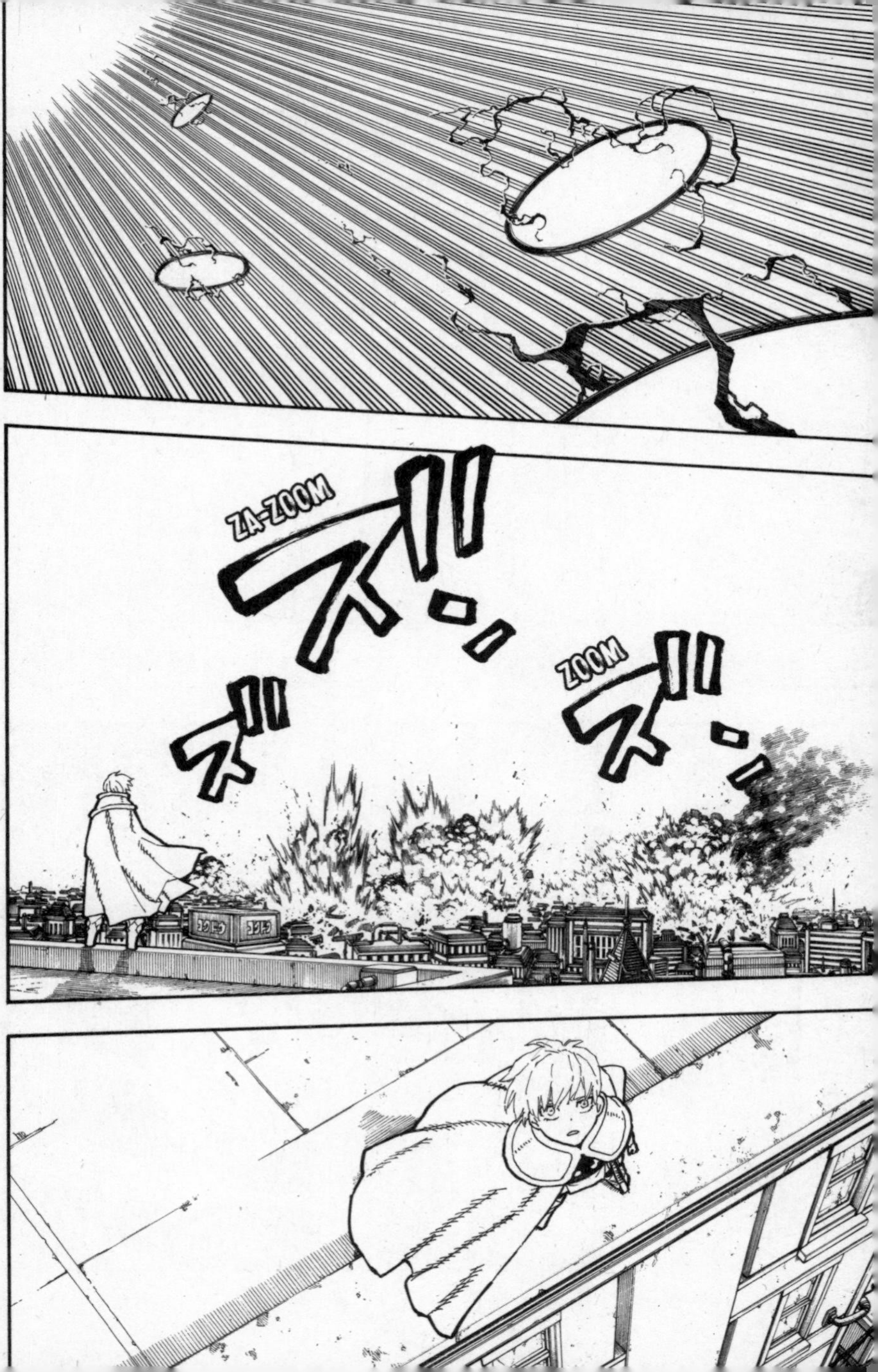
ZA-ZOOM
ZOOM

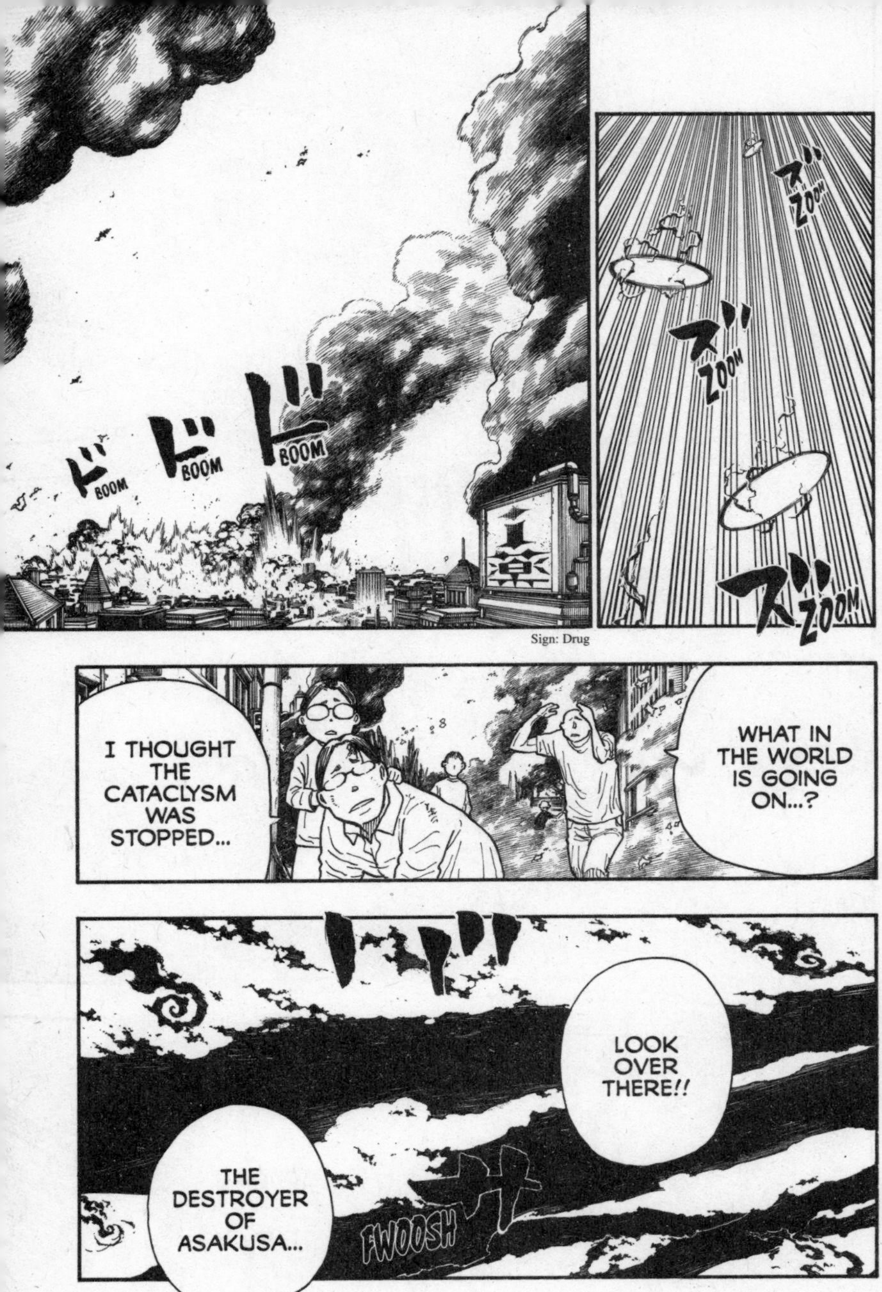
ズ ZOOM
ズ ZOOM
ズ ZOOM
ド BOOM
ド BOOM
ド BOOM
WHAT IN THE WORLD IS GOING ON...?
I THOUGHT THE CATACLYSM WAS STOPPED...
LOOK OVER THERE!!
THE DESTROYER OF ASAKUSA...
FWOOSH
Sign: Drug

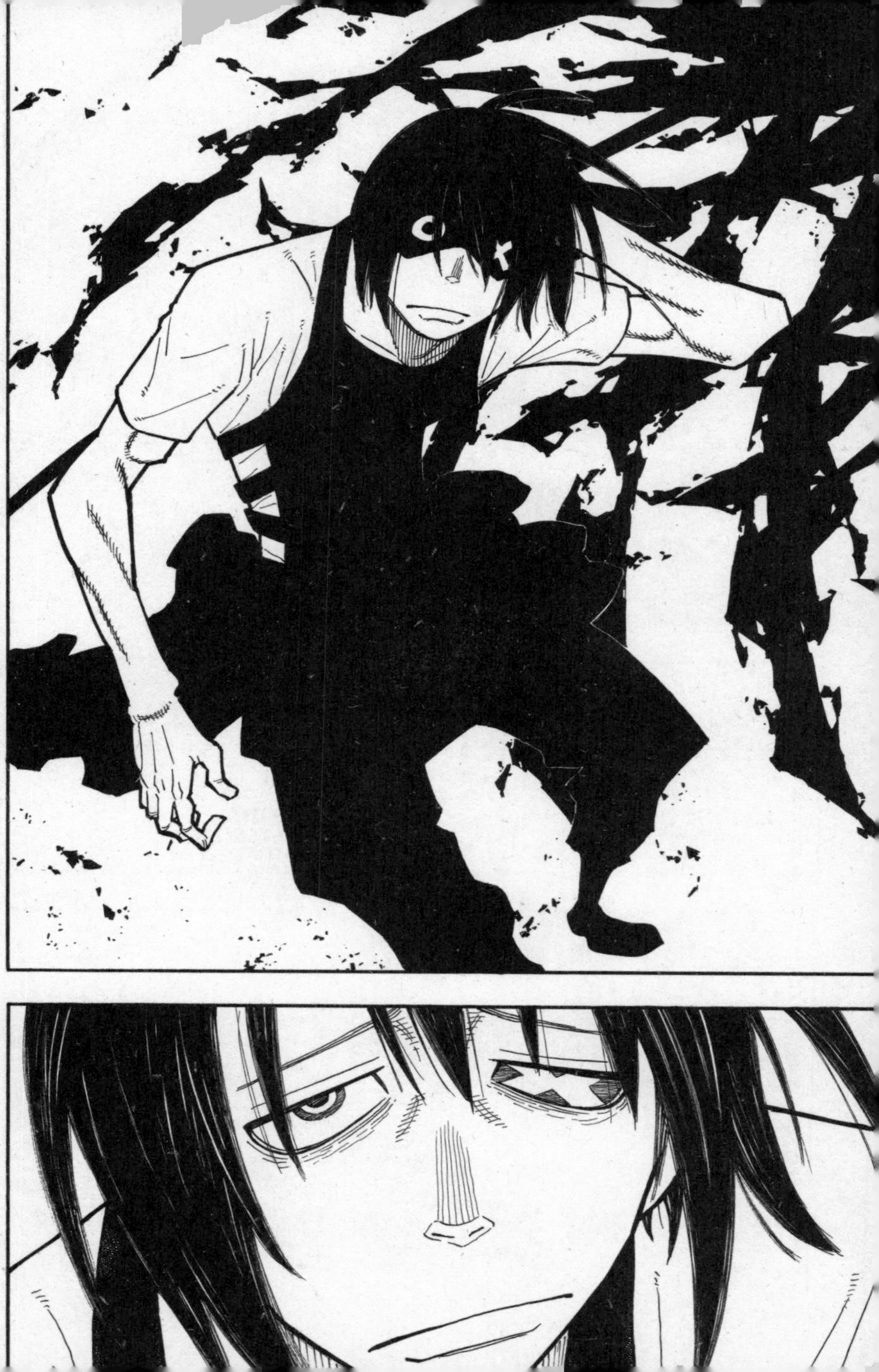

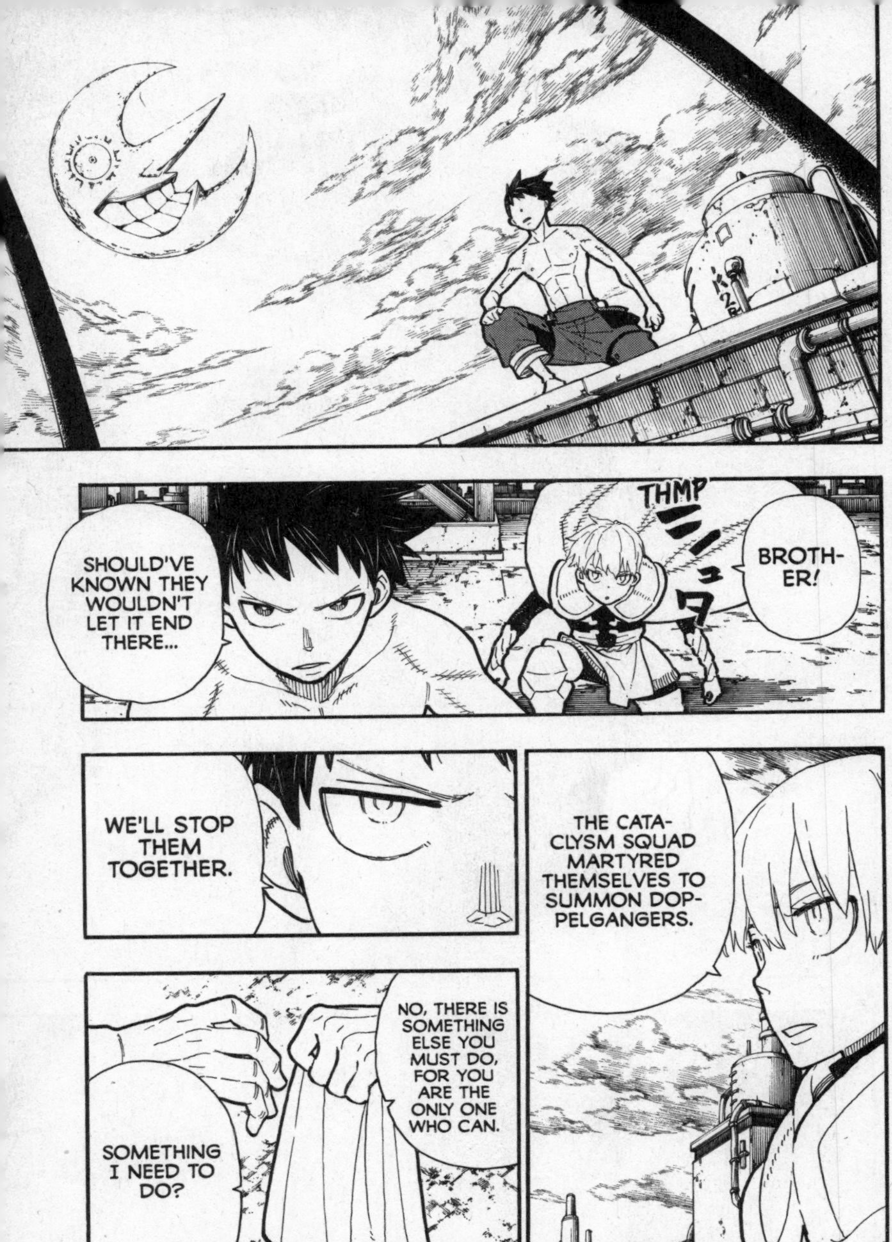
BROTH-ER!
THMP
SHOULD'VE KNOWN THEY WOULDN'T LET IT END THERE...
THE CATA-CLYSM SQUAD MARTYRED THEMSELVES TO SUMMON DOP-PELGANGERS.
WE'LL STOP THEM TOGETHER.
NO, THERE IS SOMETHING ELSE YOU MUST DO, FOR YOU ARE THE ONLY ONE WHO CAN.
SOMETHING I NEED TO DO?

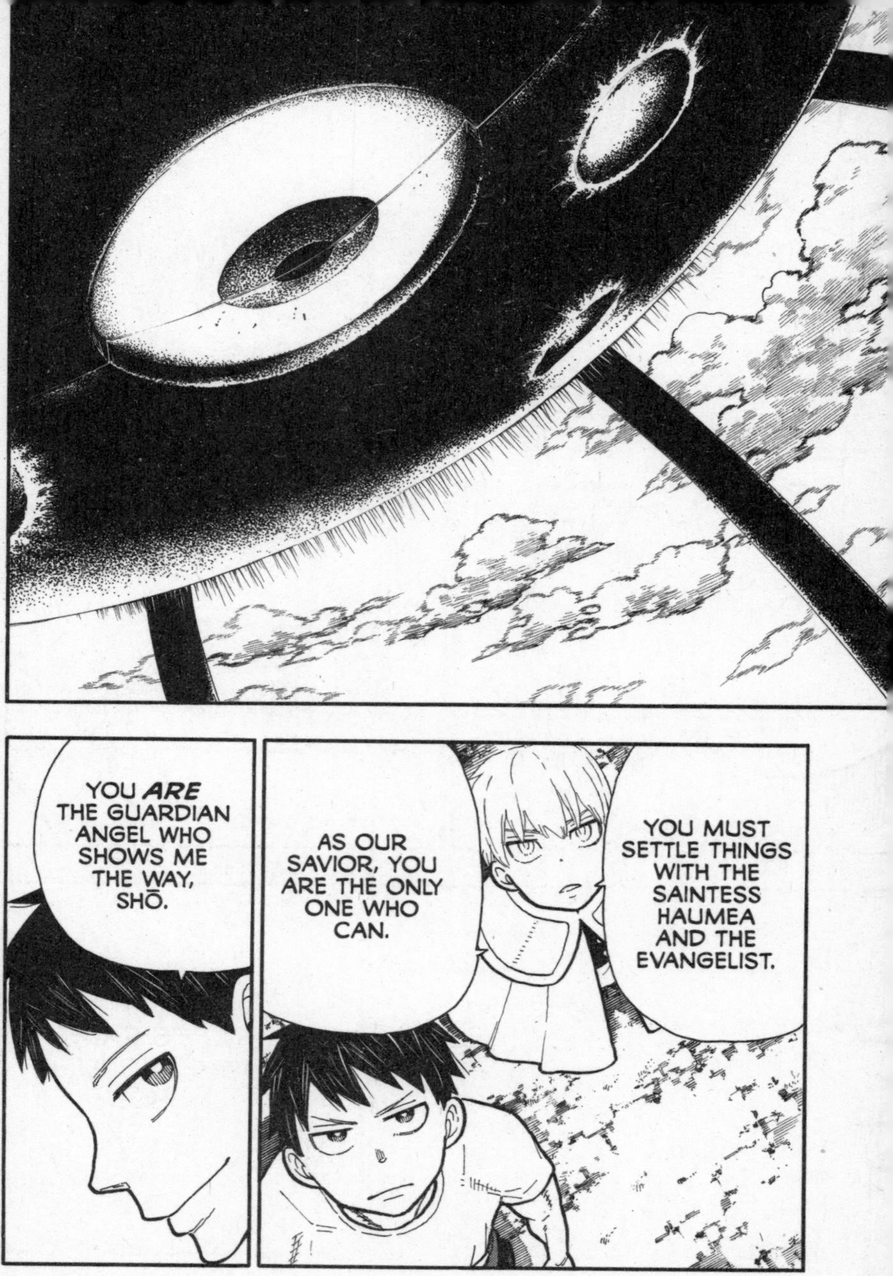
YOU MUST SETTLE THINGS WITH THE SAINTESS HAUMEA AND THE EVANGELIST.
AS OUR SAVIOR, YOU ARE THE ONLY ONE WHO CAN.
YOU ***ARE*** THE GUARDIAN ANGEL WHO SHOWS ME THE WAY, SHŌ.

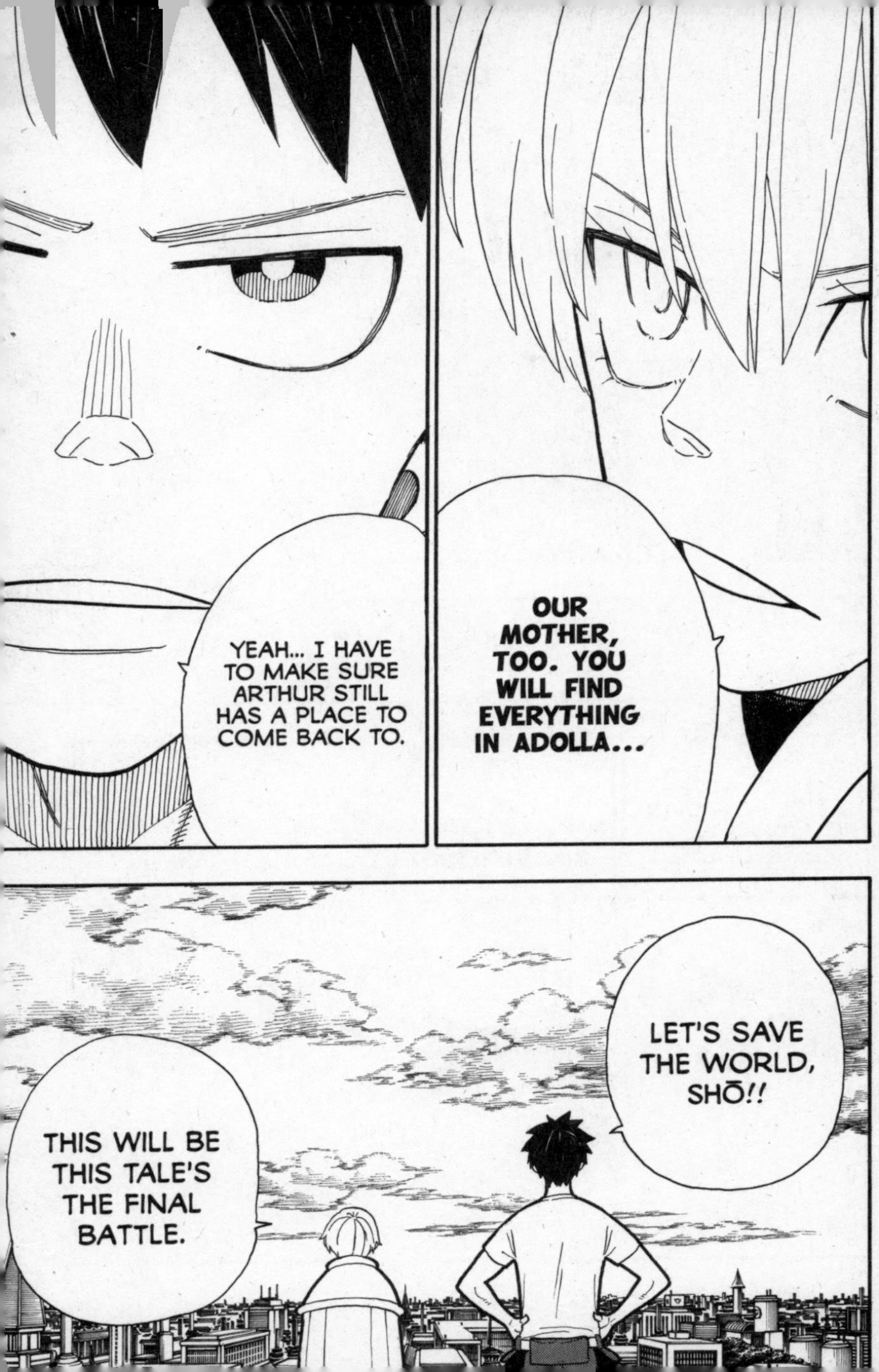
OUR MOTHER, TOO. YOU WILL FIND EVERYTHING IN ADOLLA...
YEAH... I HAVE TO MAKE SURE ARTHUR STILL HAS A PLACE TO COME BACK TO.
LET'S SAVE THE WORLD, SHŌ!!
THIS WILL BE THIS TALE'S THE FINAL BATTLE.

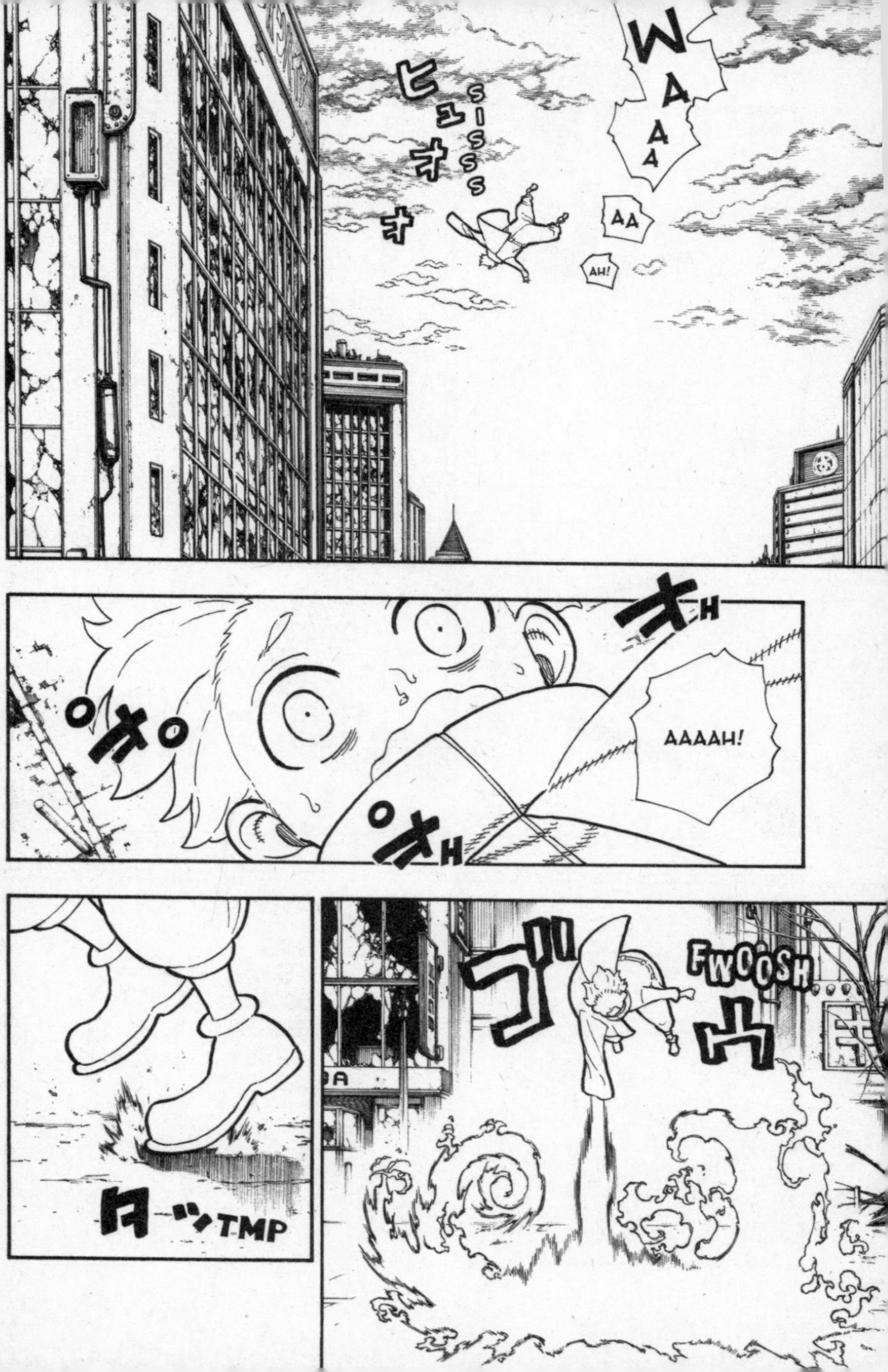
WAAAA
AA
AH!
SISSSS
AAAAH!
FWOOSH
TMP

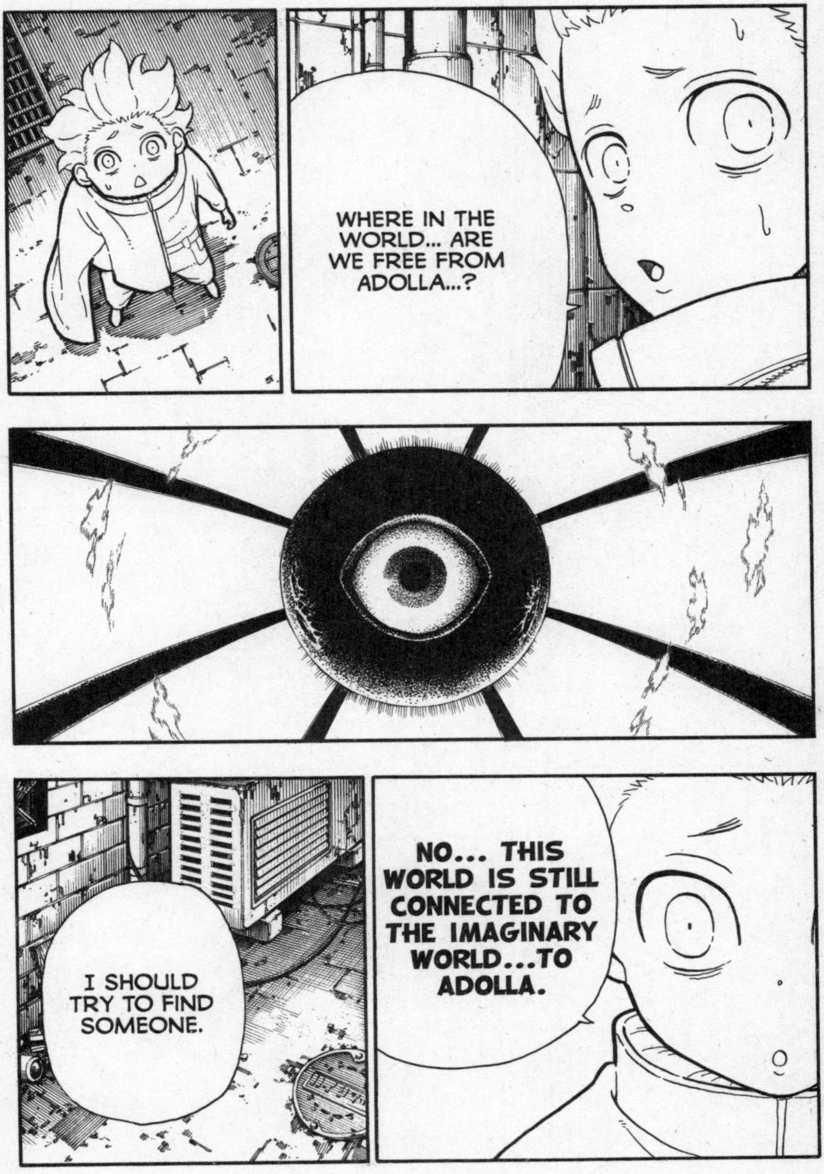
WHERE IN THE WORLD... ARE WE FREE FROM ADOLLA...?
NO... THIS WORLD IS STILL CONNECTED TO THE IMAGINARY WORLD...TO ADOLLA.
I SHOULD TRY TO FIND SOMEONE.

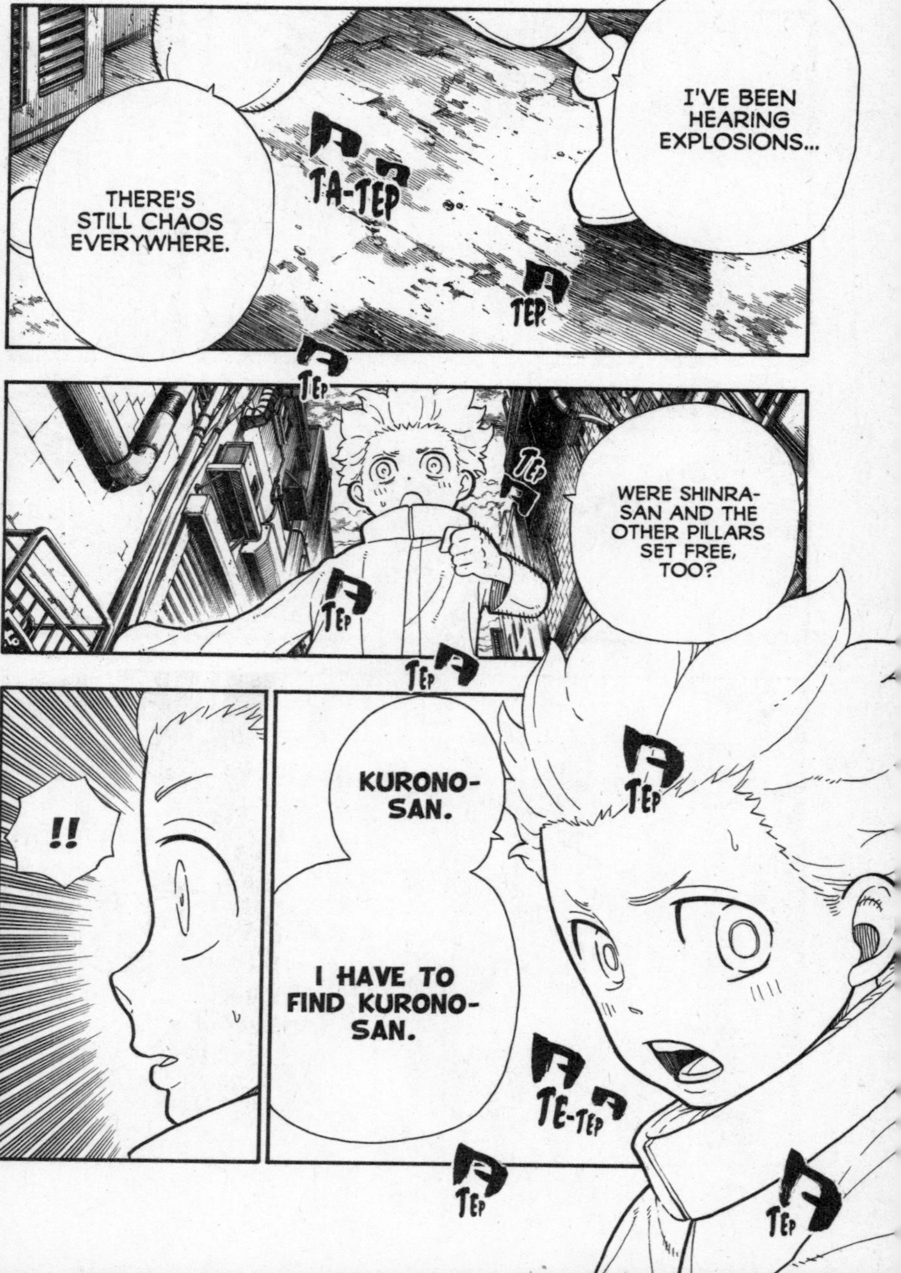
I'VE BEEN HEARING EXPLOSIONS...
TA-TEP
THERE'S STILL CHAOS EVERYWHERE.
TEP
TEP
TEP
WERE SHINRA-SAN AND THE OTHER PILLARS SET FREE, TOO?
TEP
TEP
TEP
KURONO-SAN.
I HAVE TO FIND KURONO-SAN.
TE-TEP
TEP
TEP
!!

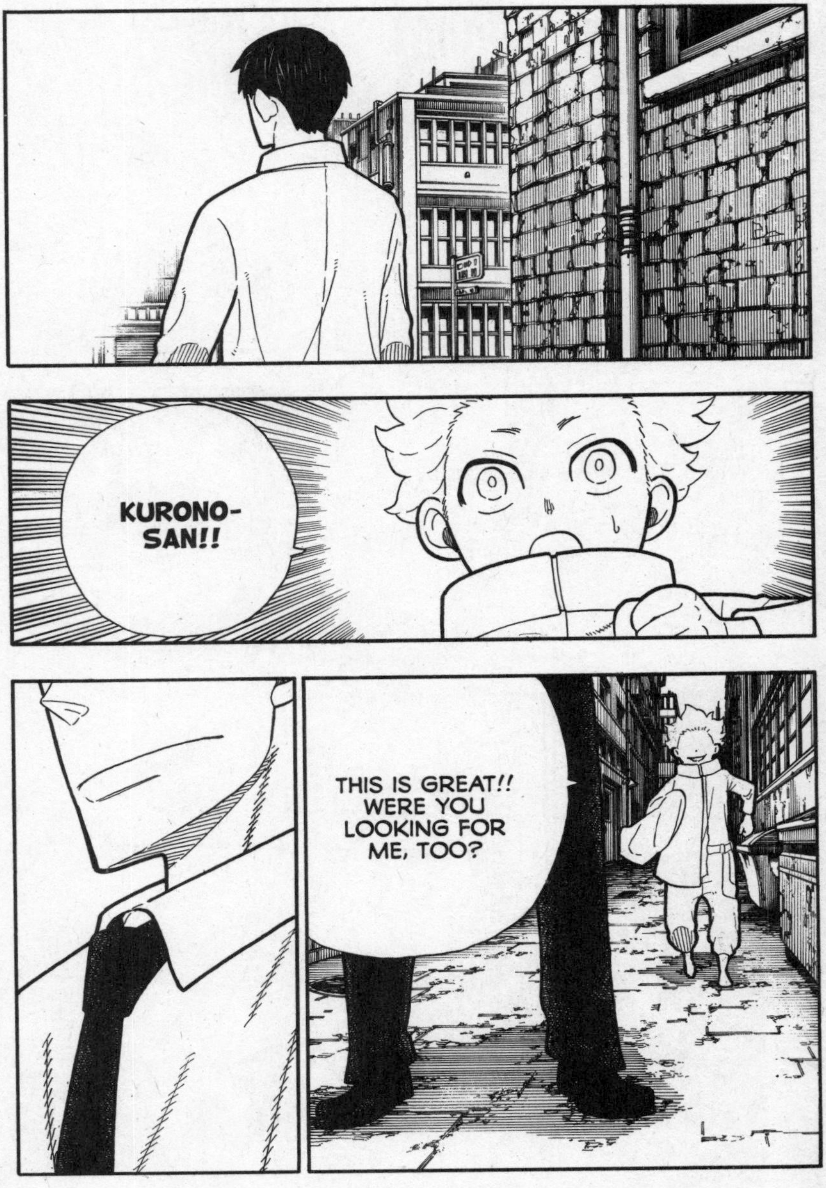
KURONO-SAN!!
THIS IS GREAT!! WERE YOU LOOKING FOR ME, TOO?

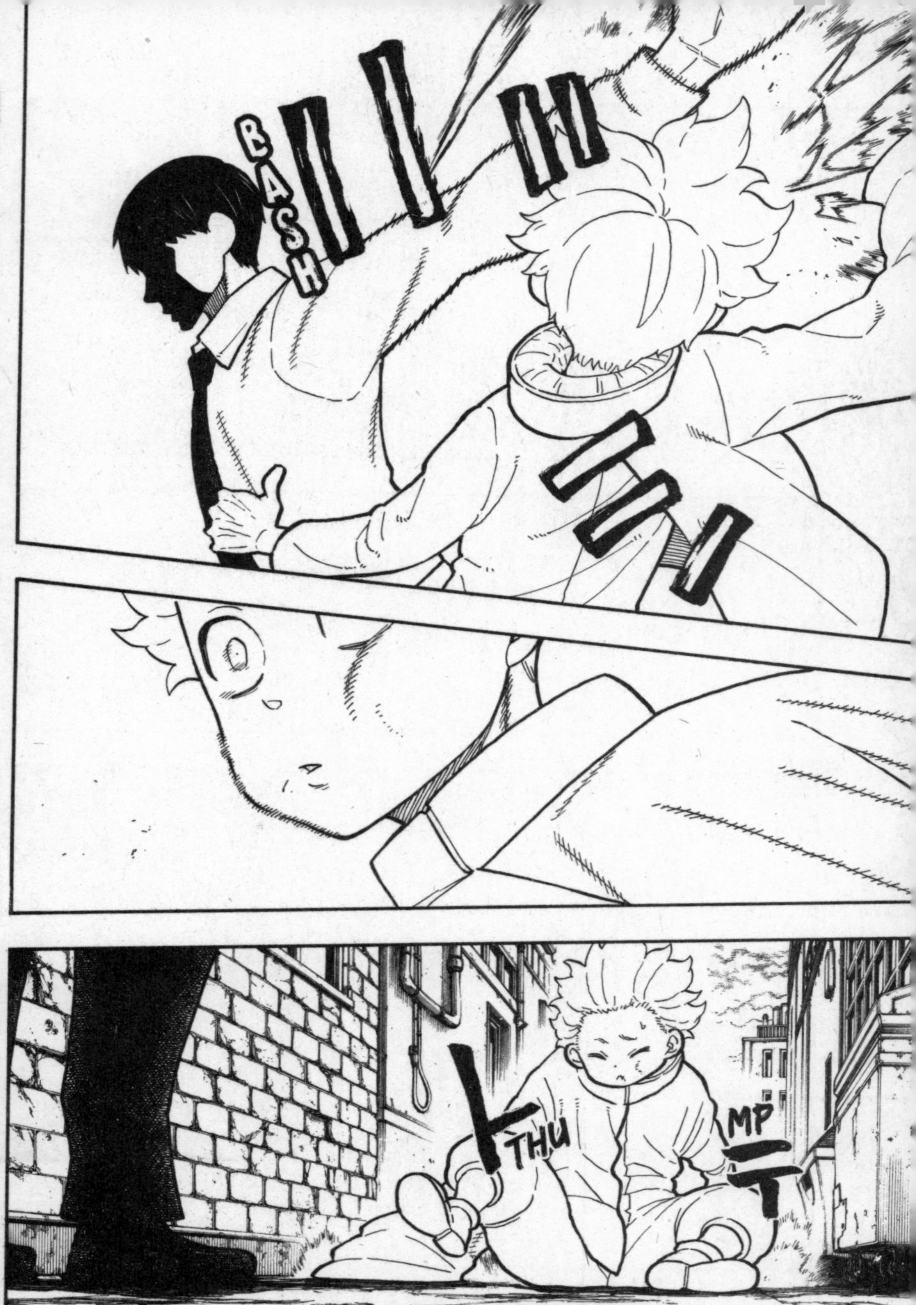
BASH
THUMP

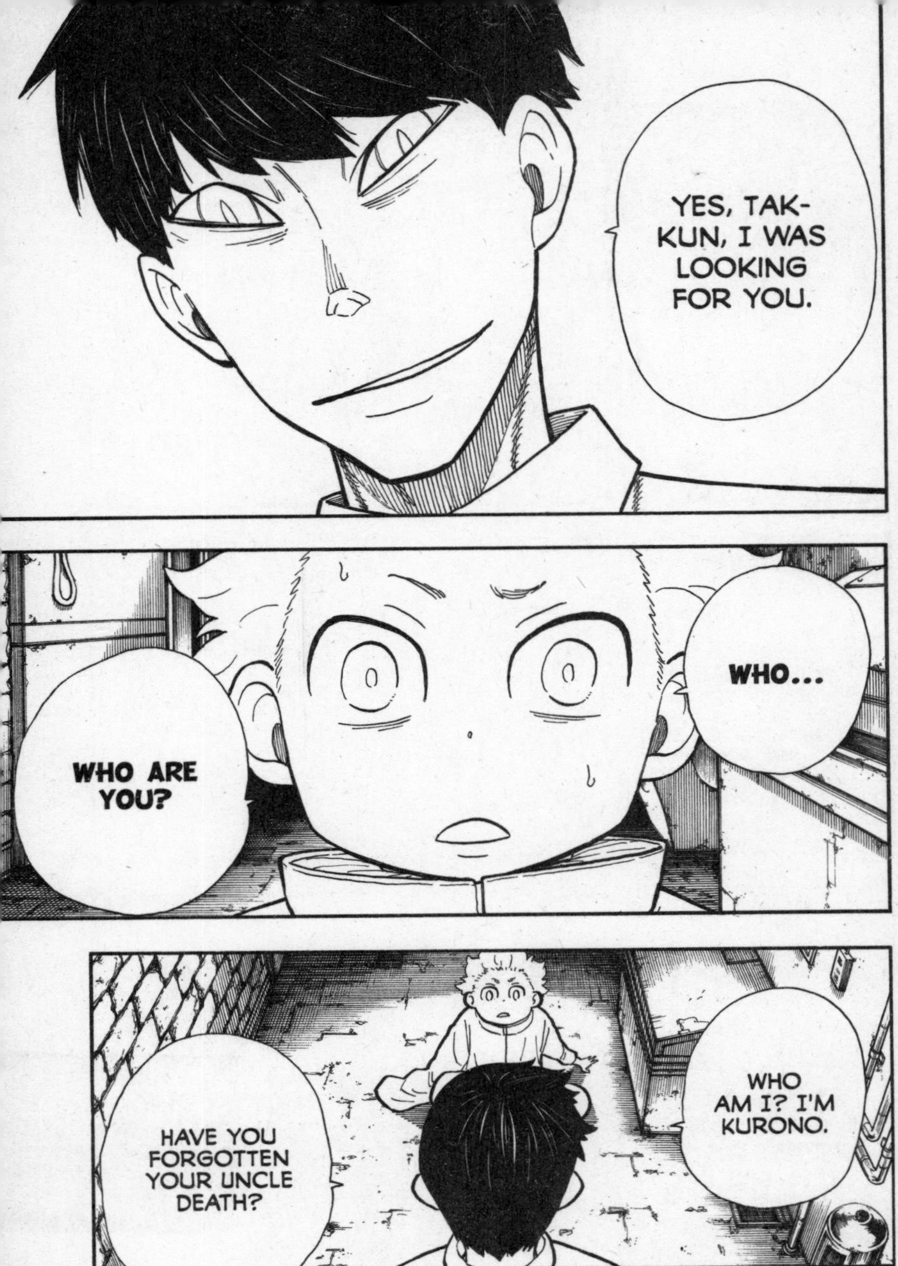
YES, TAK-KUN, I WAS LOOKING FOR YOU.
WHO...
WHO ARE YOU?
WHO AM I? I'M KURONO.
HAVE YOU FORGOTTEN YOUR UNCLE DEATH?

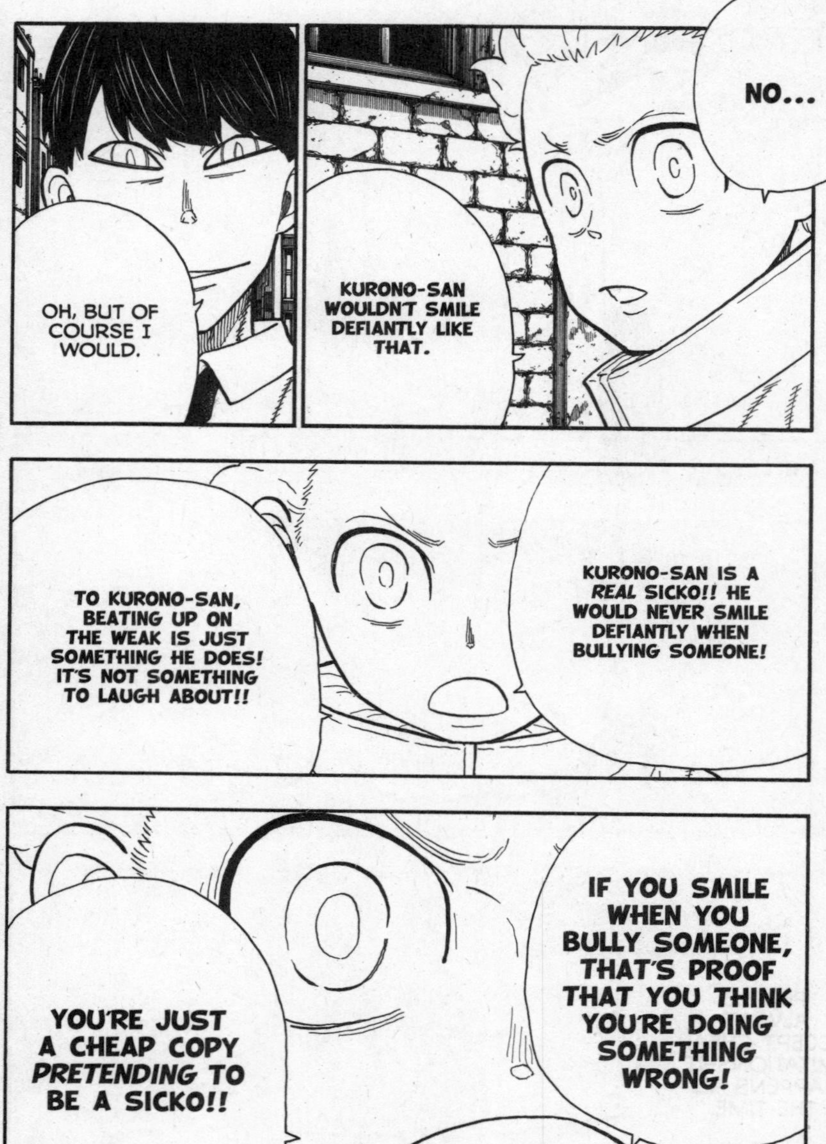
NO...
KURONO-SAN WOULDN'T SMILE DEFIANTLY LIKE THAT.
OH, BUT OF COURSE I WOULD.
KURONO-SAN IS A *REAL* SICKO!! HE WOULD NEVER SMILE DEFIANTLY WHEN BULLYING SOMEONE!
TO KURONO-SAN, BEATING UP ON THE WEAK IS JUST SOMETHING HE DOES! IT'S NOT SOMETHING TO LAUGH ABOUT!!
IF YOU SMILE WHEN YOU BULLY SOMEONE, THAT'S PROOF THAT YOU THINK YOU'RE DOING SOMETHING WRONG!
YOU'RE JUST A CHEAP COPY *PRETENDING* TO BE A SICKO!!

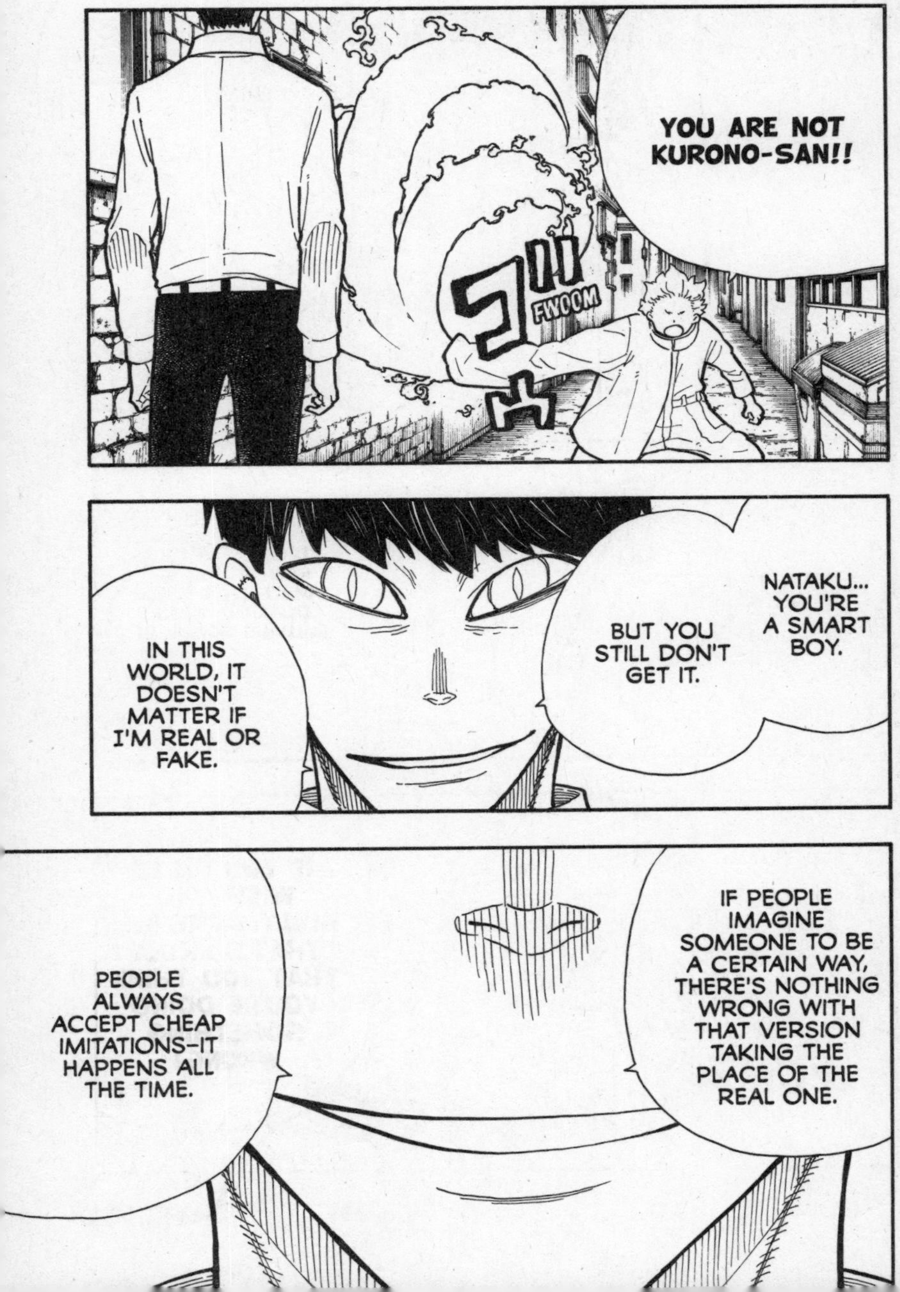
YOU ARE NOT KURONO-SAN!!
FWOOM
NATAKU... YOU'RE A SMART BOY.
BUT YOU STILL DON'T GET IT.
IN THIS WORLD, IT DOESN'T MATTER IF I'M REAL OR FAKE.
IF PEOPLE IMAGINE SOMEONE TO BE A CERTAIN WAY, THERE'S NOTHING WRONG WITH THAT VERSION TAKING THE PLACE OF THE REAL ONE.
PEOPLE ALWAYS ACCEPT CHEAP IMITATIONS–IT HAPPENS ALL THE TIME.

FIRE FORCE

The man called Kurono

CHAPTER CCLXXVI: CHEAP IMITATION

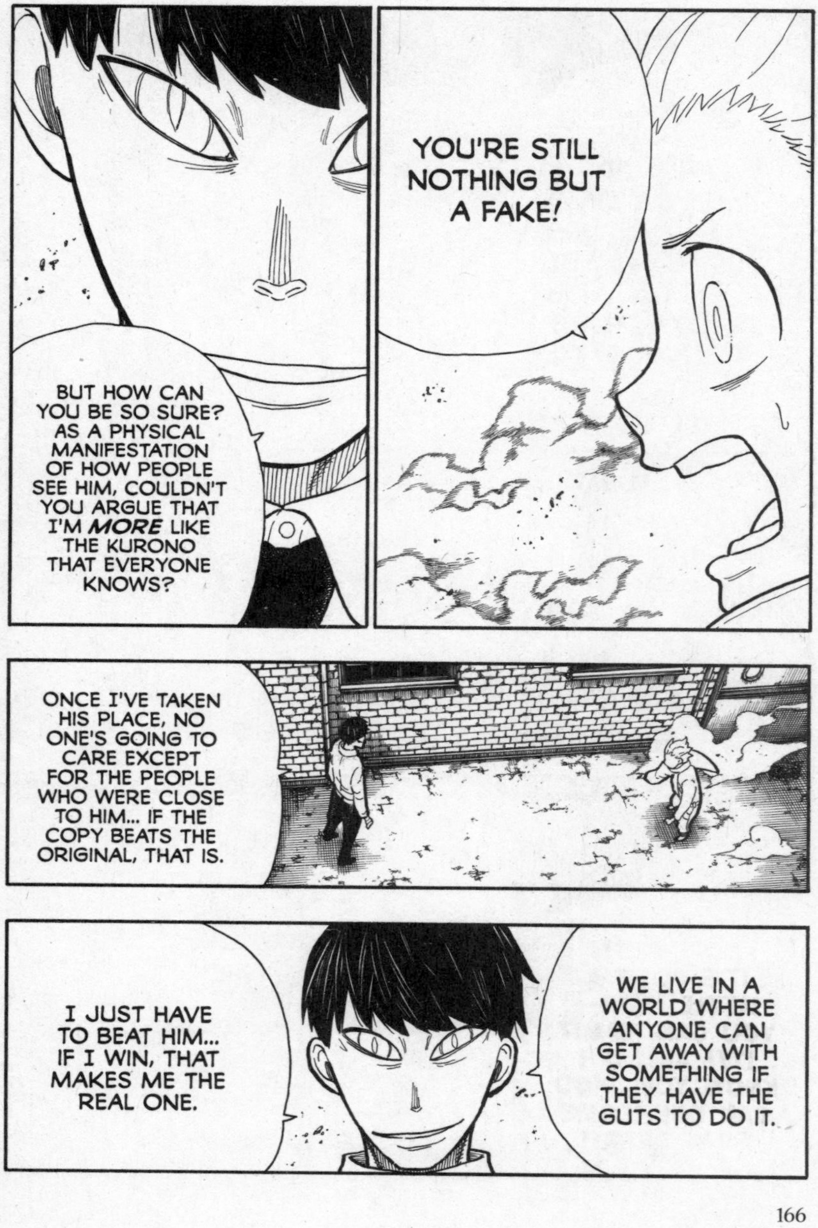
YOU'RE STILL NOTHING BUT A FAKE!
BUT HOW CAN YOU BE SO SURE? AS A PHYSICAL MANIFESTATION OF HOW PEOPLE SEE HIM, COULDN'T YOU ARGUE THAT I'M *MORE* LIKE THE KURONO THAT EVERYONE KNOWS?
ONCE I'VE TAKEN HIS PLACE, NO ONE'S GOING TO CARE EXCEPT FOR THE PEOPLE WHO WERE CLOSE TO HIM... IF THE COPY BEATS THE ORIGINAL, THAT IS.
WE LIVE IN A WORLD WHERE ANYONE CAN GET AWAY WITH SOMETHING IF THEY HAVE THE GUTS TO DO IT.
I JUST HAVE TO BEAT HIM... IF I WIN, THAT MAKES ME THE REAL ONE.

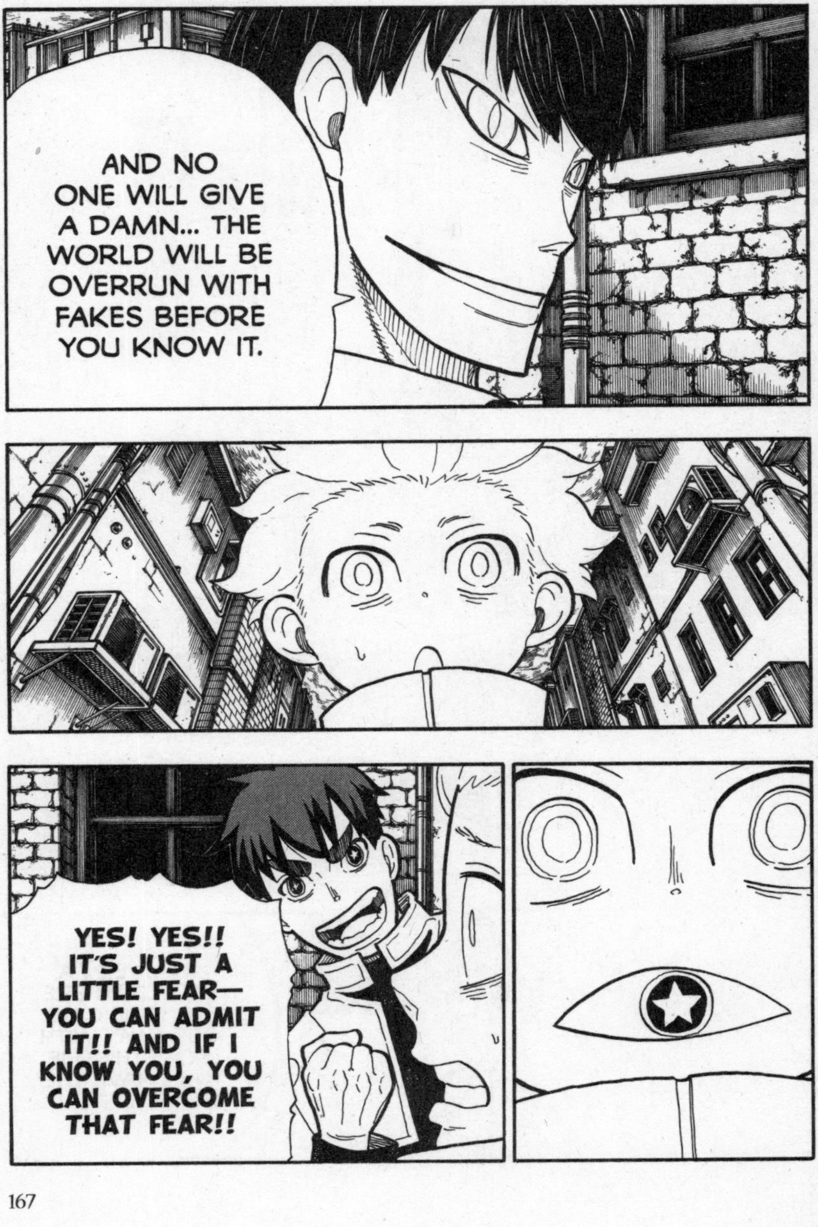
AND NO ONE WILL GIVE A DAMN... THE WORLD WILL BE OVERRUN WITH FAKES BEFORE YOU KNOW IT.
YES! YES!! IT'S JUST A LITTLE FEAR— YOU CAN ADMIT IT!! AND IF I KNOW YOU, YOU CAN OVERCOME THAT FEAR!!

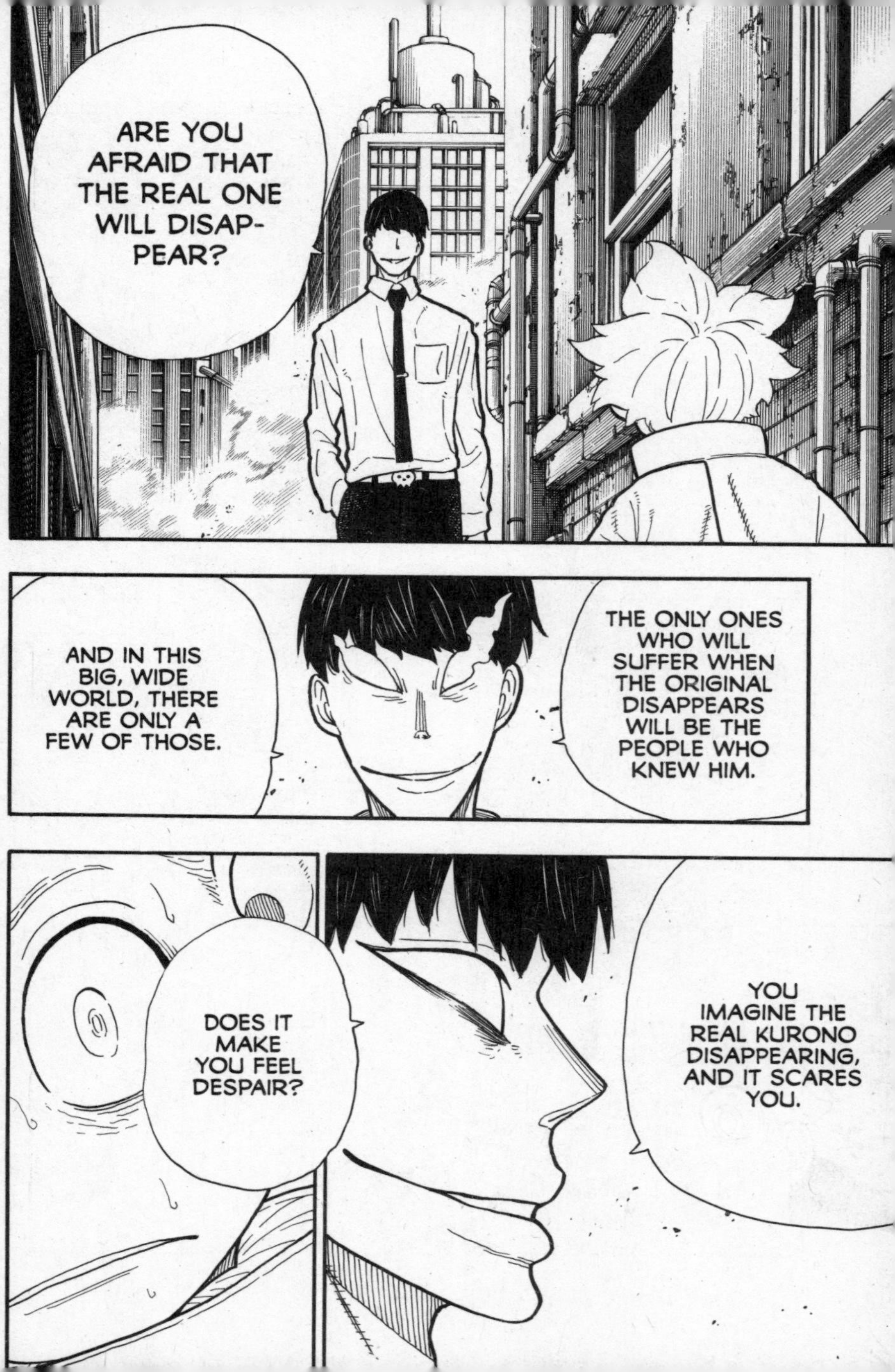
ARE YOU AFRAID THAT THE REAL ONE WILL DISAP-PEAR?
THE ONLY ONES WHO WILL SUFFER WHEN THE ORIGINAL DISAPPEARS WILL BE THE PEOPLE WHO KNEW HIM.
AND IN THIS BIG, WIDE WORLD, THERE ARE ONLY A FEW OF THOSE.
YOU IMAGINE THE REAL KURONO DISAPPEARING, AND IT SCARES YOU.
DOES IT MAKE YOU FEEL DESPAIR?

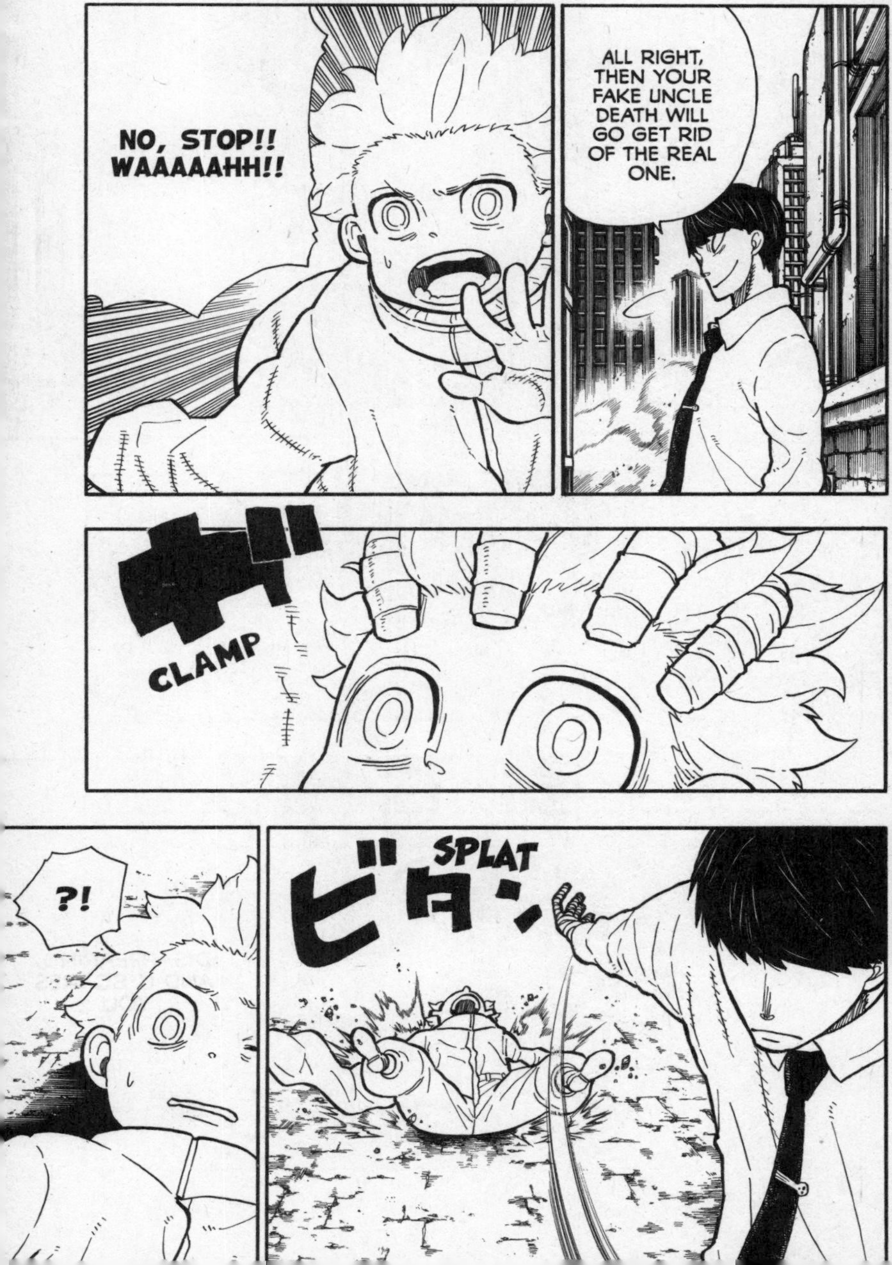
ALL RIGHT, THEN YOUR FAKE UNCLE DEATH WILL GO GET RID OF THE REAL ONE.
NO, STOP!! WAAAAAHH!!
CLAMP
ビタン
SPLAT
?!

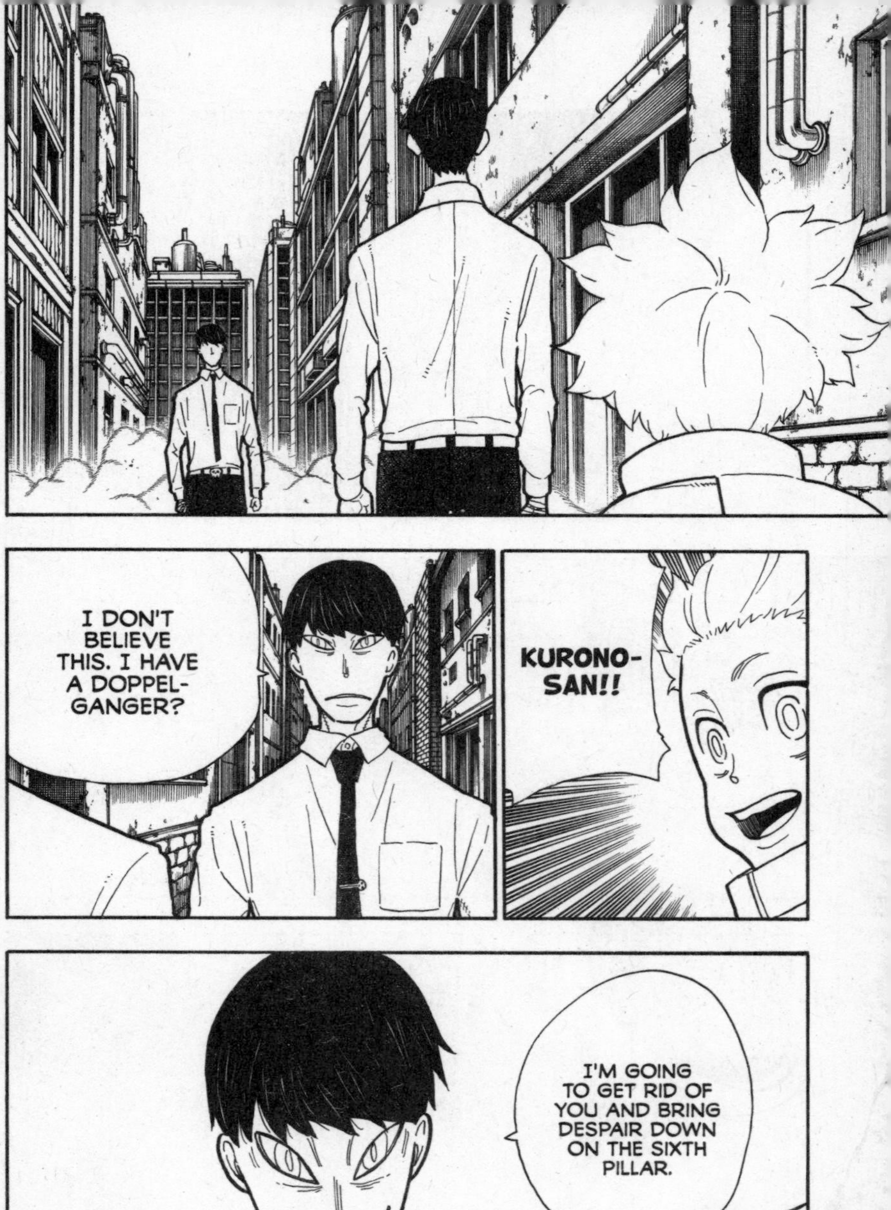
KURONO-SAN!!
I DON'T BELIEVE THIS. I HAVE A DOPPEL-GANGER?
I'M GOING TO GET RID OF YOU AND BRING DESPAIR DOWN ON THE SIXTH PILLAR.

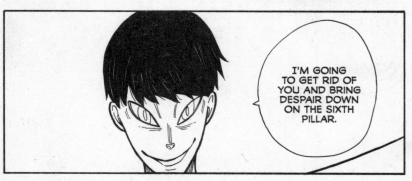

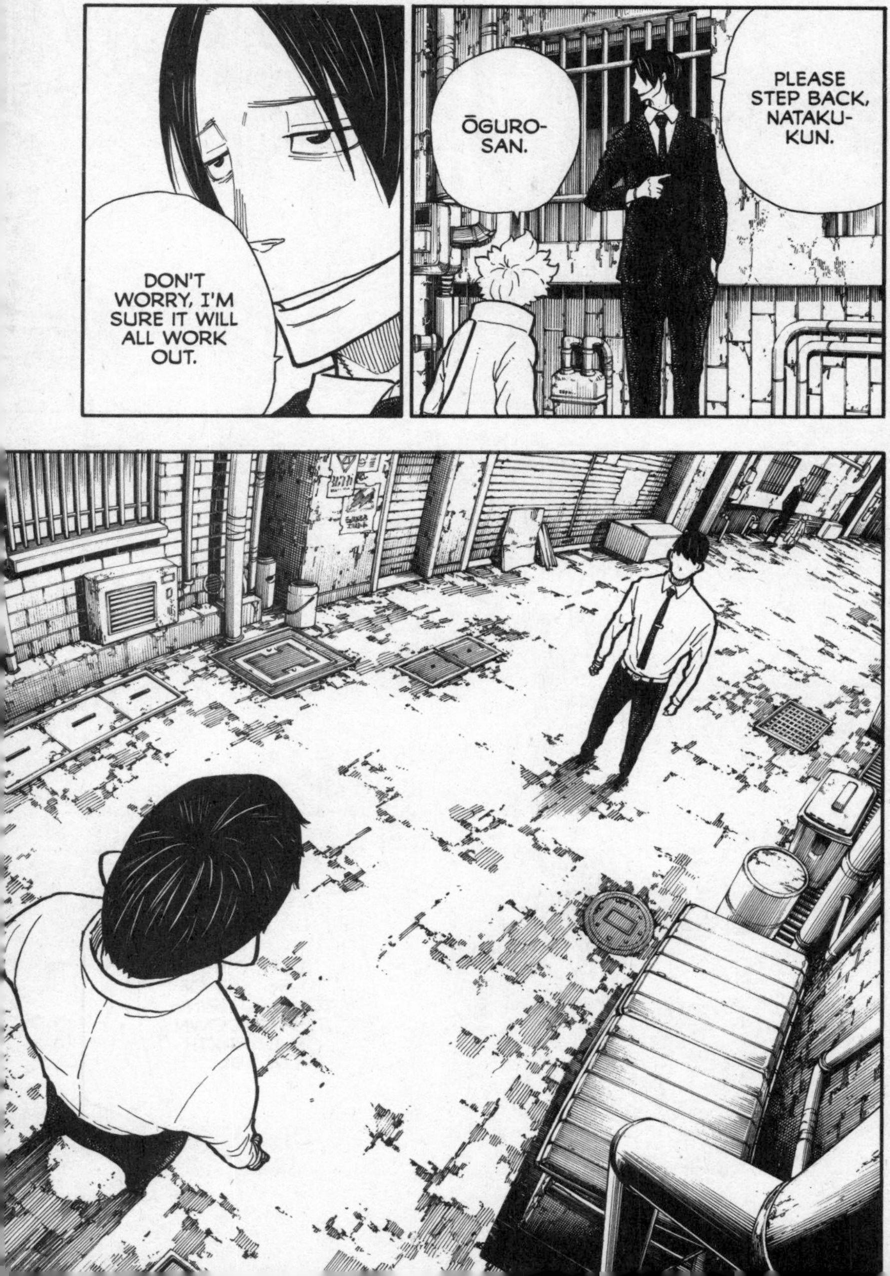
PLEASE STEP BACK, NATAKU-KUN.
ŌGURO-SAN.
DON'T WORRY, I'M SURE IT WILL ALL WORK OUT.

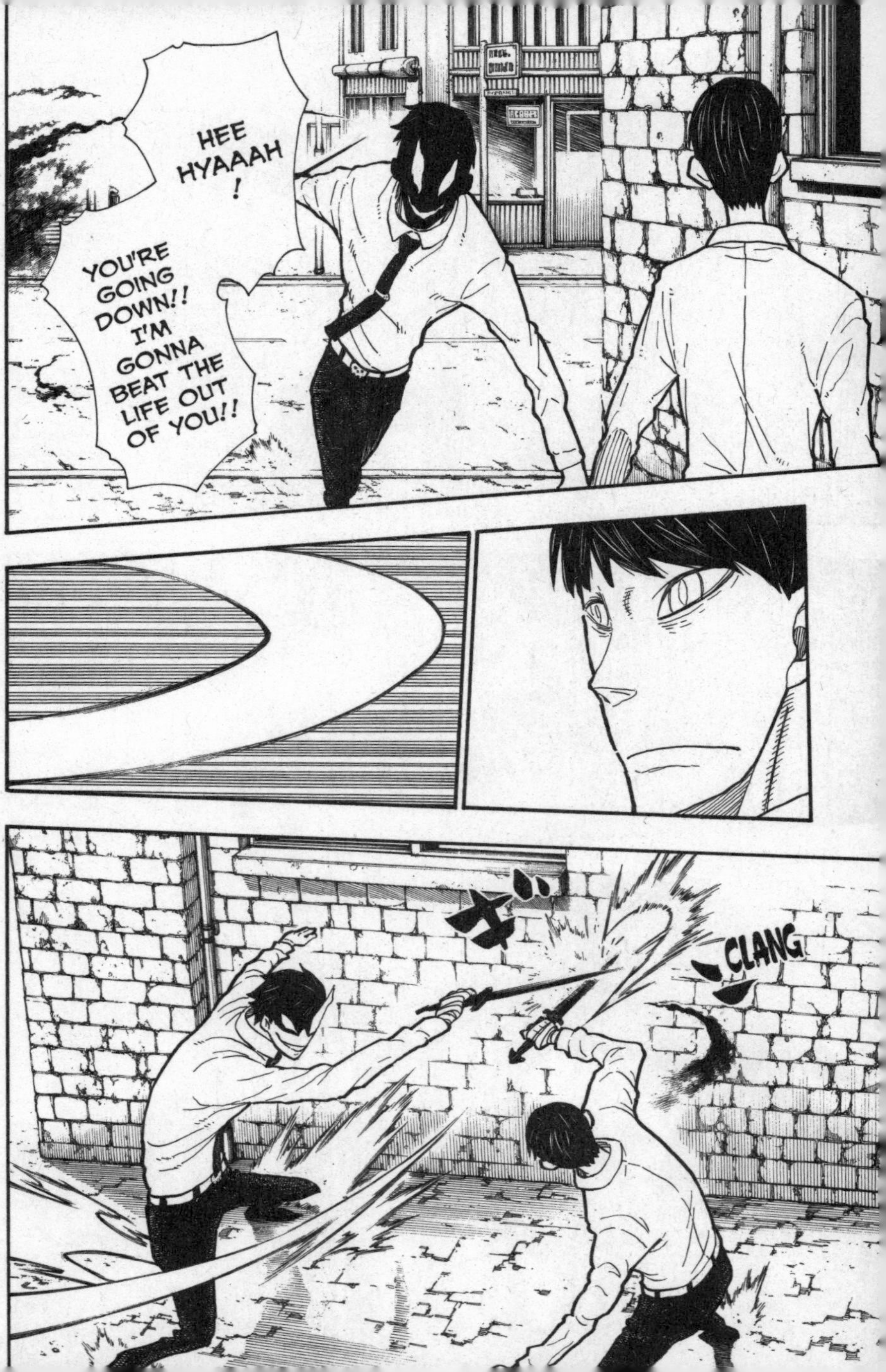
HEE HYAAAH!
YOU'RE GOING DOWN!! I'M GONNA BEAT THE LIFE OUT OF YOU!!
CLANG

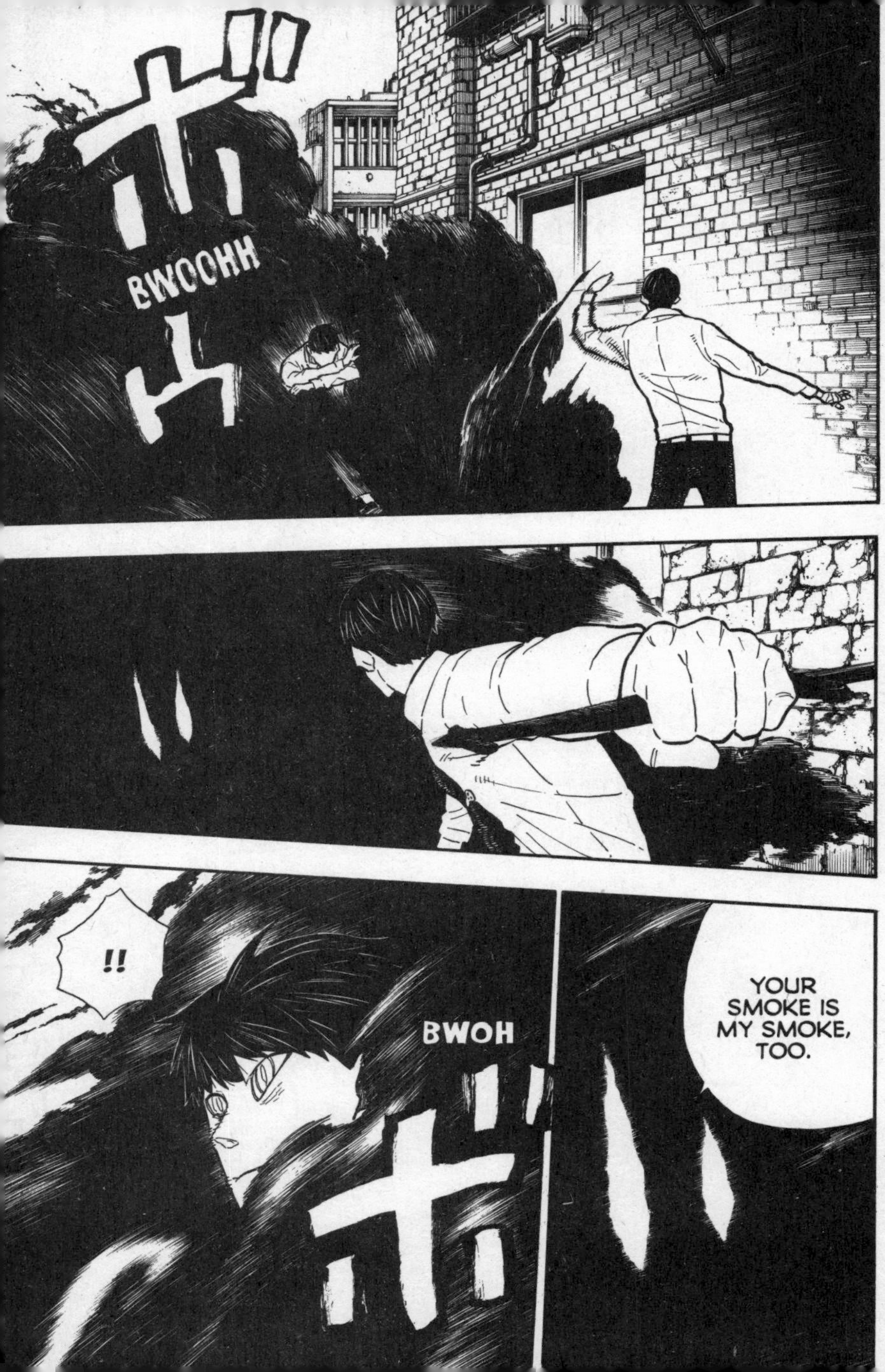
BWOOHH
YOUR SMOKE IS MY SMOKE, TOO.
!!
BWOH

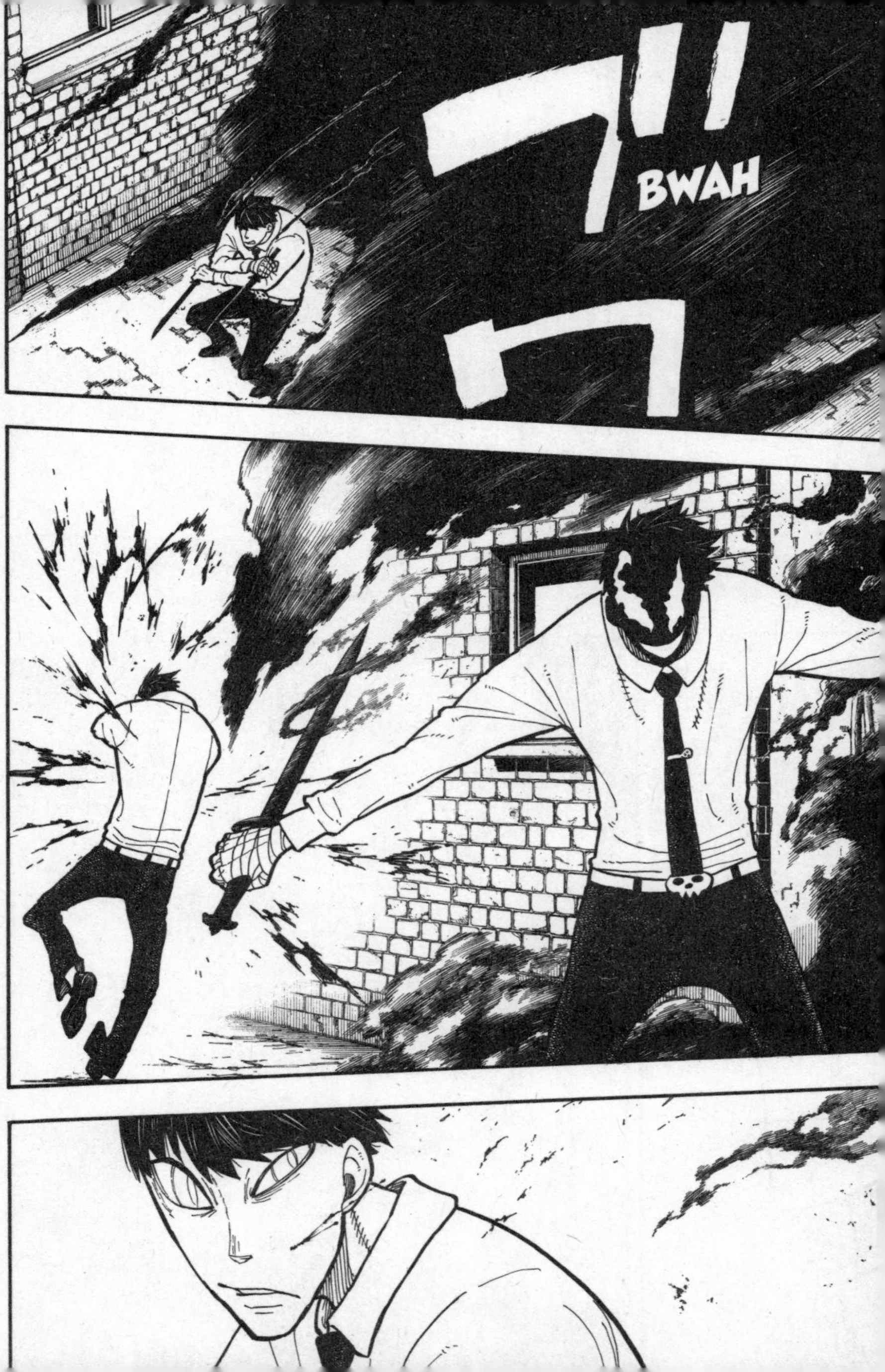
ブワッ
BWAH

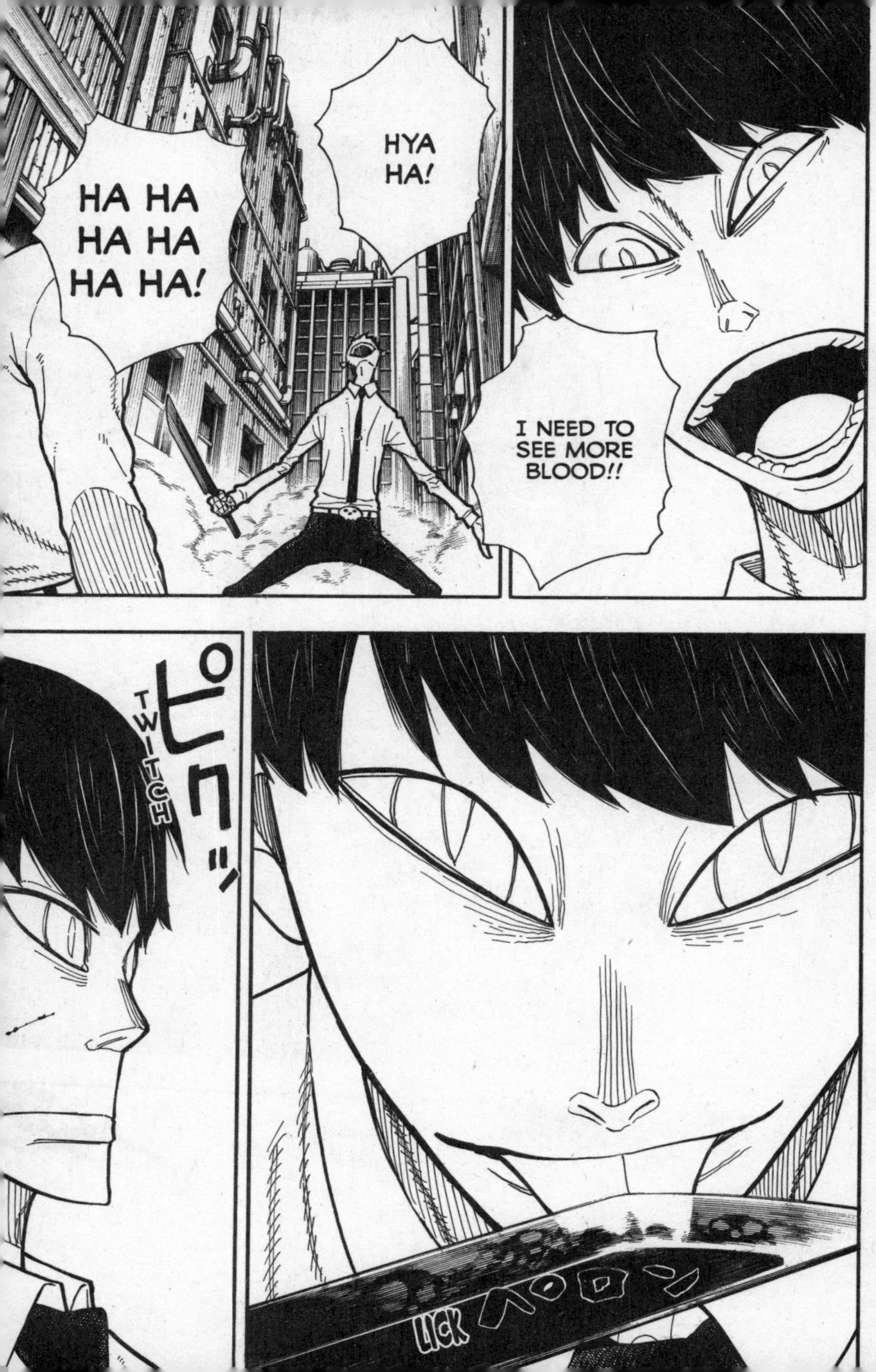
I NEED TO SEE MORE BLOOD!!
HYA HA!
HA HA HA HA HA HA!
LICK
ピクッ
TWITCH

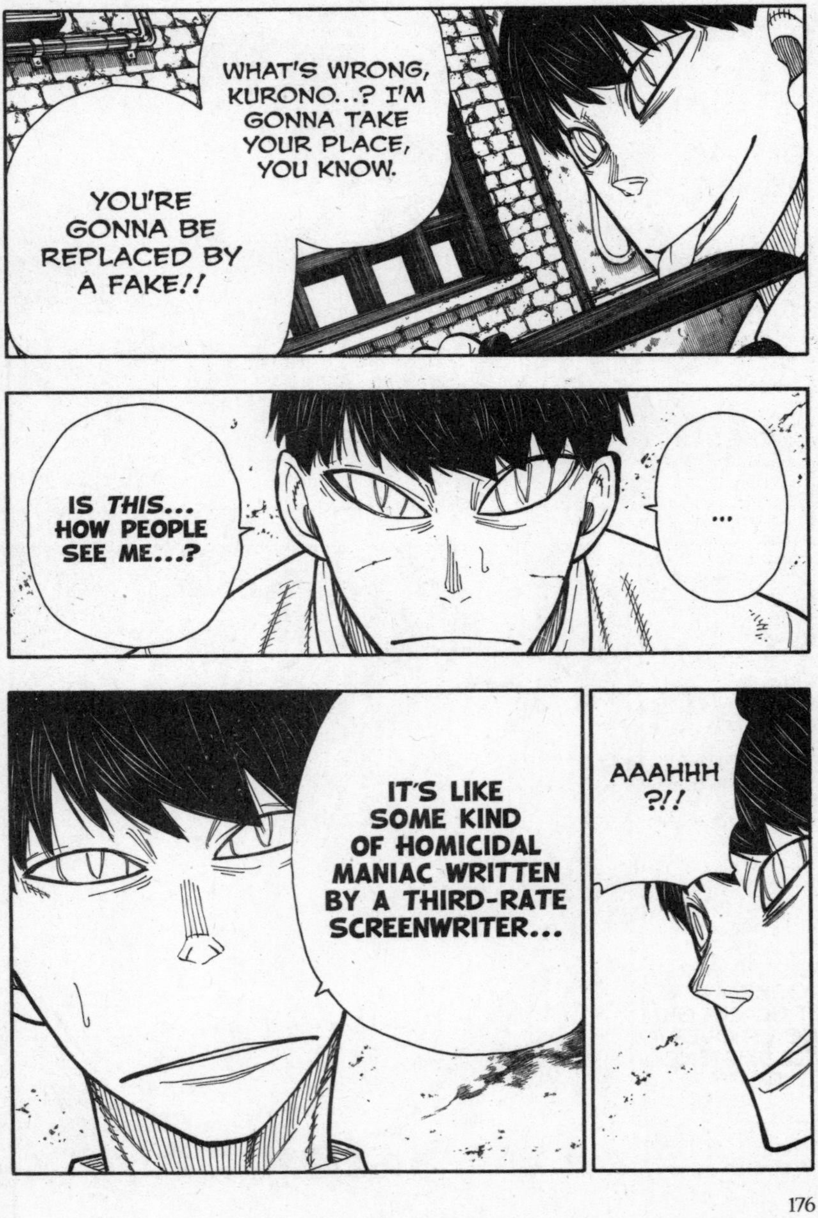
WHAT'S WRONG, KURONO...? I'M GONNA TAKE YOUR PLACE, YOU KNOW.
YOU'RE GONNA BE REPLACED BY A FAKE!!
...
IS *THIS*... HOW PEOPLE SEE ME...?
AAAHHH ?!!
IT'S LIKE SOME KIND OF HOMICIDAL MANIAC WRITTEN BY A THIRD-RATE SCREENWRITER...

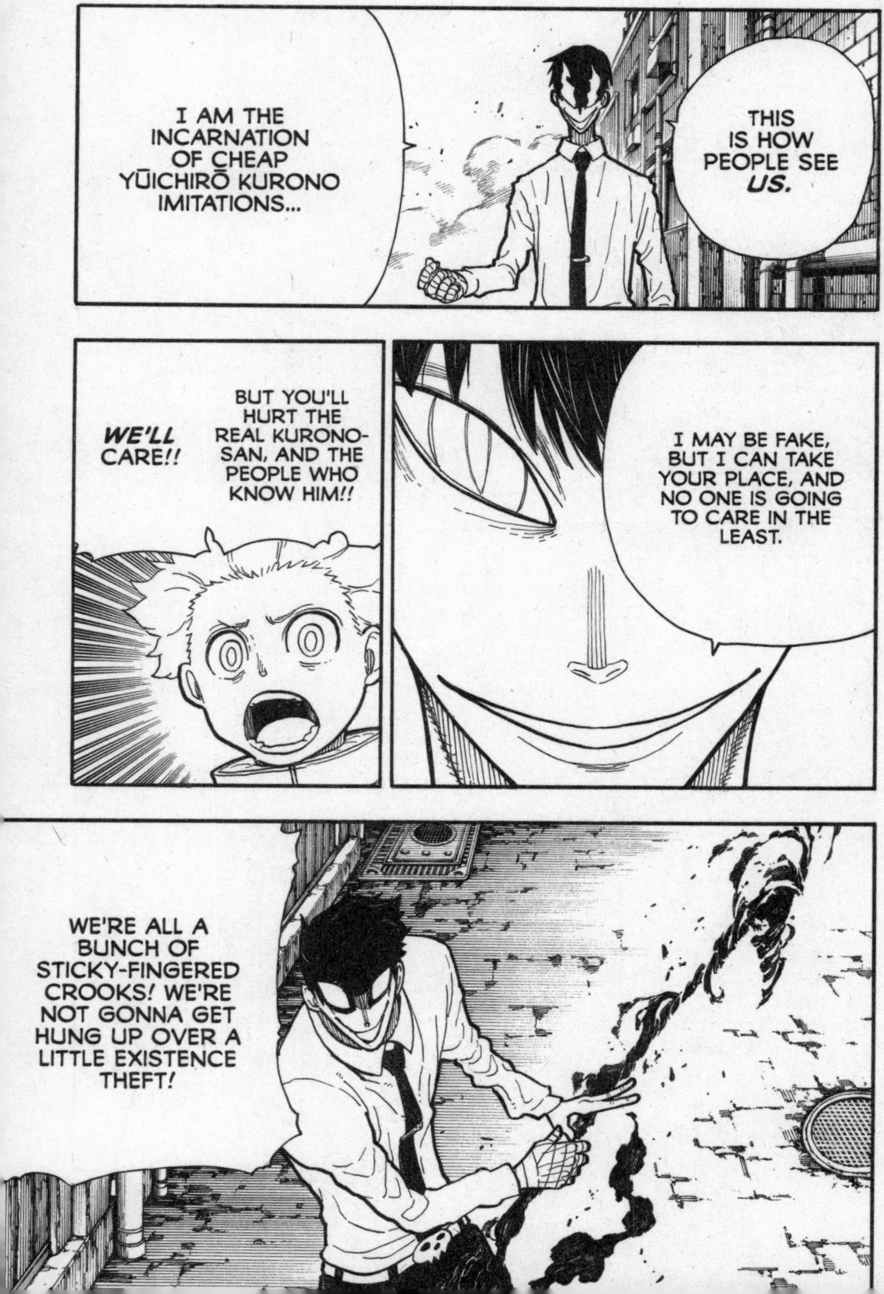
THIS IS HOW PEOPLE SEE *US.*
I AM THE INCARNATION OF CHEAP YŪICHIRŌ KURONO IMITATIONS...
I MAY BE FAKE, BUT I CAN TAKE YOUR PLACE, AND NO ONE IS GOING TO CARE IN THE LEAST.
BUT YOU'LL HURT THE REAL KURONO-SAN, AND THE PEOPLE WHO KNOW HIM!!
WE'LL CARE!!
WE'RE ALL A BUNCH OF STICKY-FINGERED CROOKS! WE'RE NOT GONNA GET HUNG UP OVER A LITTLE EXISTENCE THEFT!

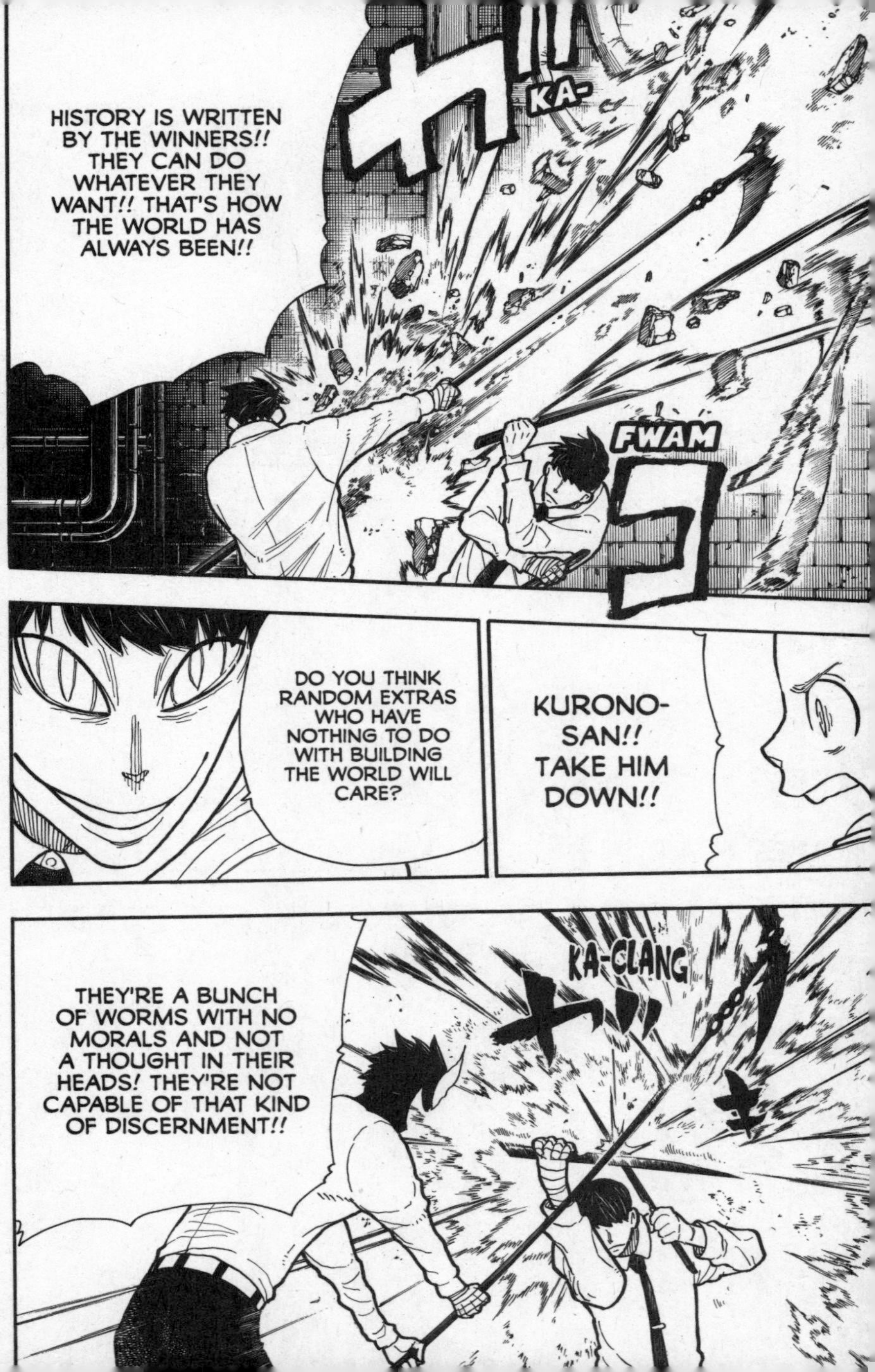
KA-
HISTORY IS WRITTEN BY THE WINNERS!! THEY CAN DO WHATEVER THEY WANT!! THAT'S HOW THE WORLD HAS ALWAYS BEEN!!
FWAM
KURONO-SAN!! TAKE HIM DOWN!!
DO YOU THINK RANDOM EXTRAS WHO HAVE NOTHING TO DO WITH BUILDING THE WORLD WILL CARE?
KA-CLANG
THEY'RE A BUNCH OF WORMS WITH NO MORALS AND NOT A THOUGHT IN THEIR HEADS! THEY'RE NOT CAPABLE OF THAT KIND OF DISCERNMENT!!

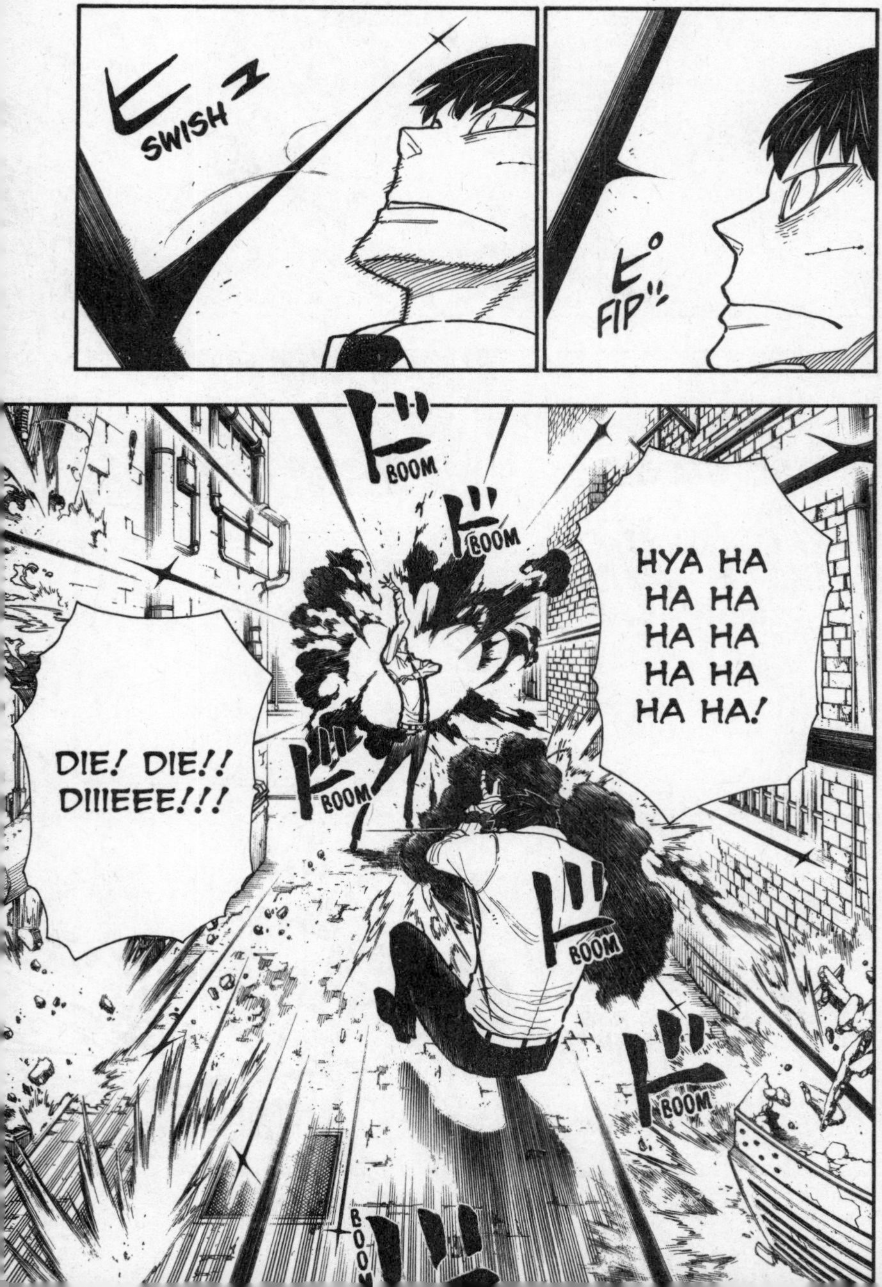

ピ
FIP!!
ヒュ
SWISH
HYA HA HA HA HA HA HA HA HA HA!
ド BOOM
ド BOOM
DIE! DIE!! DIIIEEE!!!
ド BOOM
ド BOOM
ド BOOM
BOOM

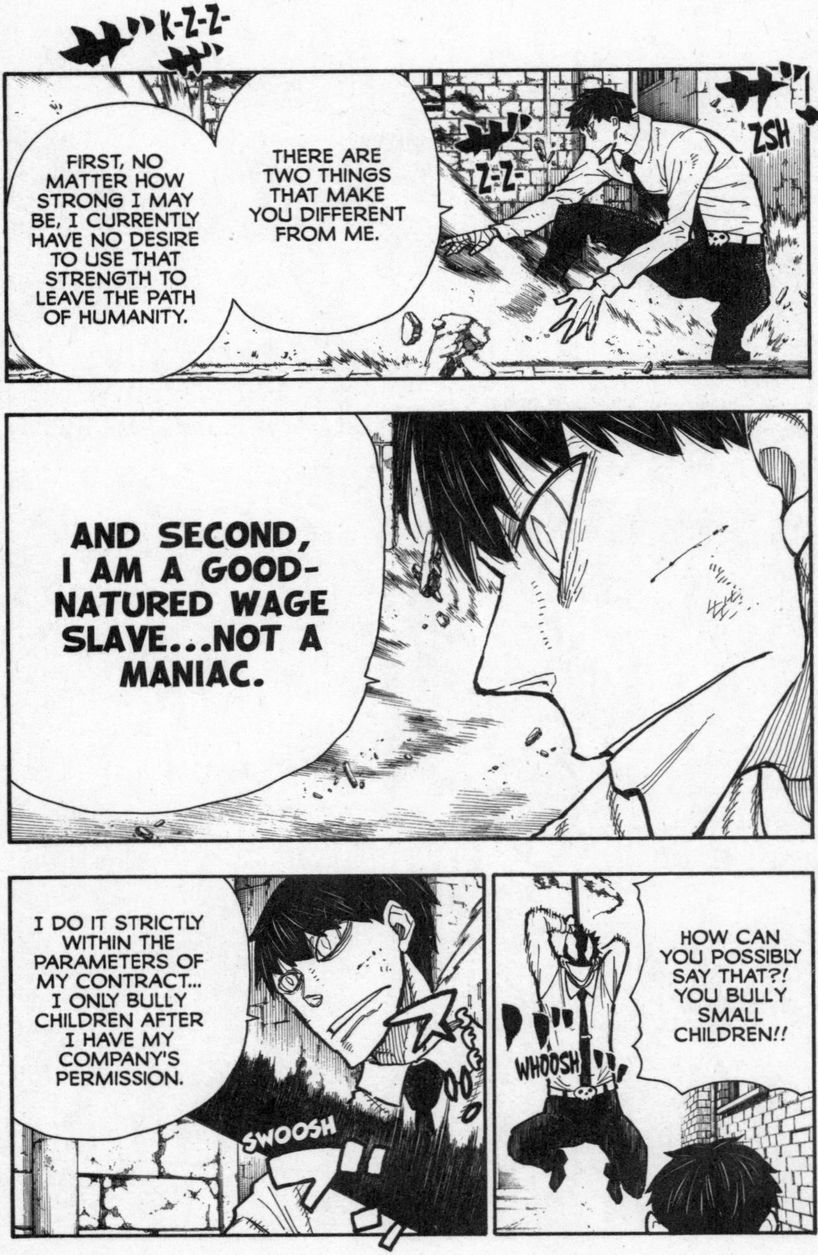
K-Z-Z-Z-
ZSH
THERE ARE TWO THINGS THAT MAKE YOU DIFFERENT FROM ME.
Z-Z-
FIRST, NO MATTER HOW STRONG I MAY BE, I CURRENTLY HAVE NO DESIRE TO USE THAT STRENGTH TO LEAVE THE PATH OF HUMANITY.
AND SECOND, I AM A GOOD-NATURED WAGE SLAVE...NOT A MANIAC.
HOW CAN YOU POSSIBLY SAY THAT?! YOU BULLY SMALL CHILDREN!!
WHOOSH
I DO IT STRICTLY WITHIN THE PARAMETERS OF MY CONTRACT... I ONLY BULLY CHILDREN AFTER I HAVE MY COMPANY'S PERMISSION.
SWOOSH

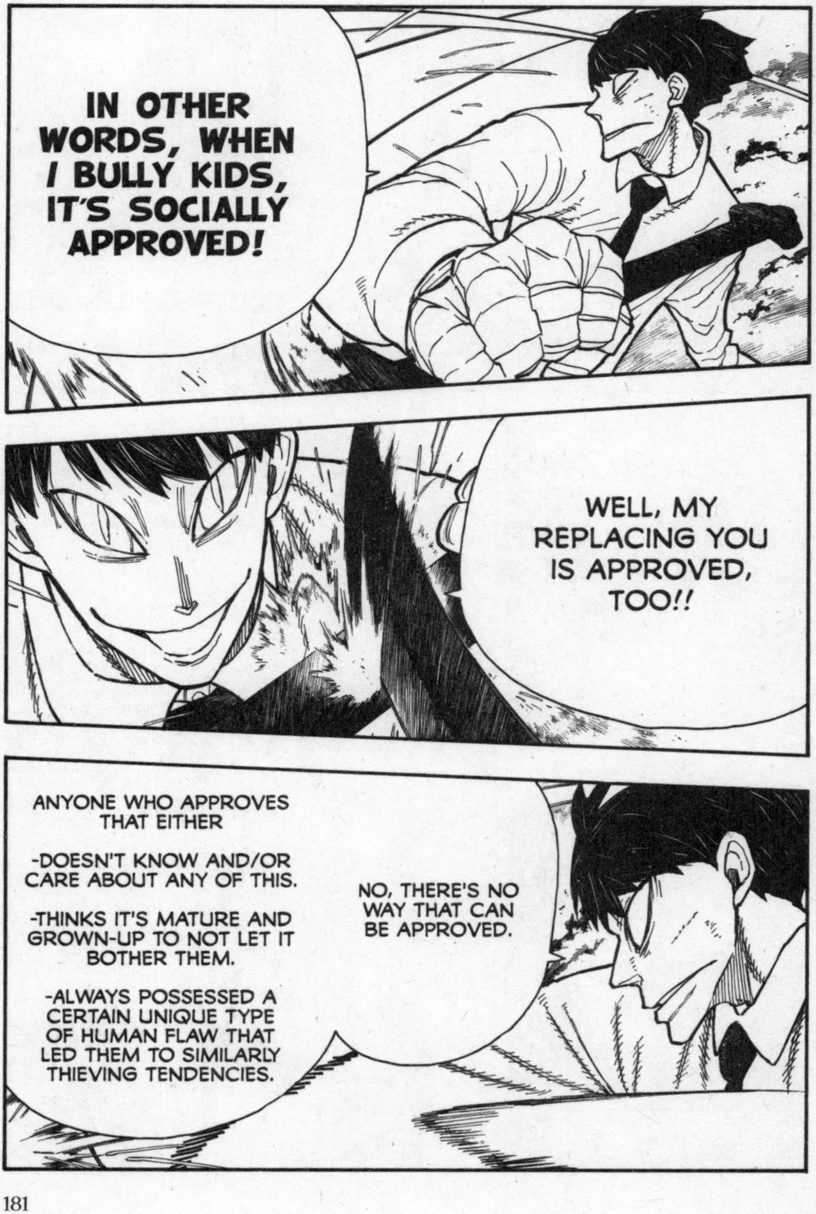
IN OTHER WORDS, WHEN I BULLY KIDS, IT'S SOCIALLY APPROVED!
WELL, MY REPLACING YOU IS APPROVED, TOO!!
NO, THERE'S NO WAY THAT CAN BE APPROVED.
ANYONE WHO APPROVES THAT EITHER
-DOESN'T KNOW AND/OR CARE ABOUT ANY OF THIS.
-THINKS IT'S MATURE AND GROWN-UP TO NOT LET IT BOTHER THEM.
-ALWAYS POSSESSED A CERTAIN UNIQUE TYPE OF HUMAN FLAW THAT LED THEM TO SIMILARLY THIEVING TENDENCIES.

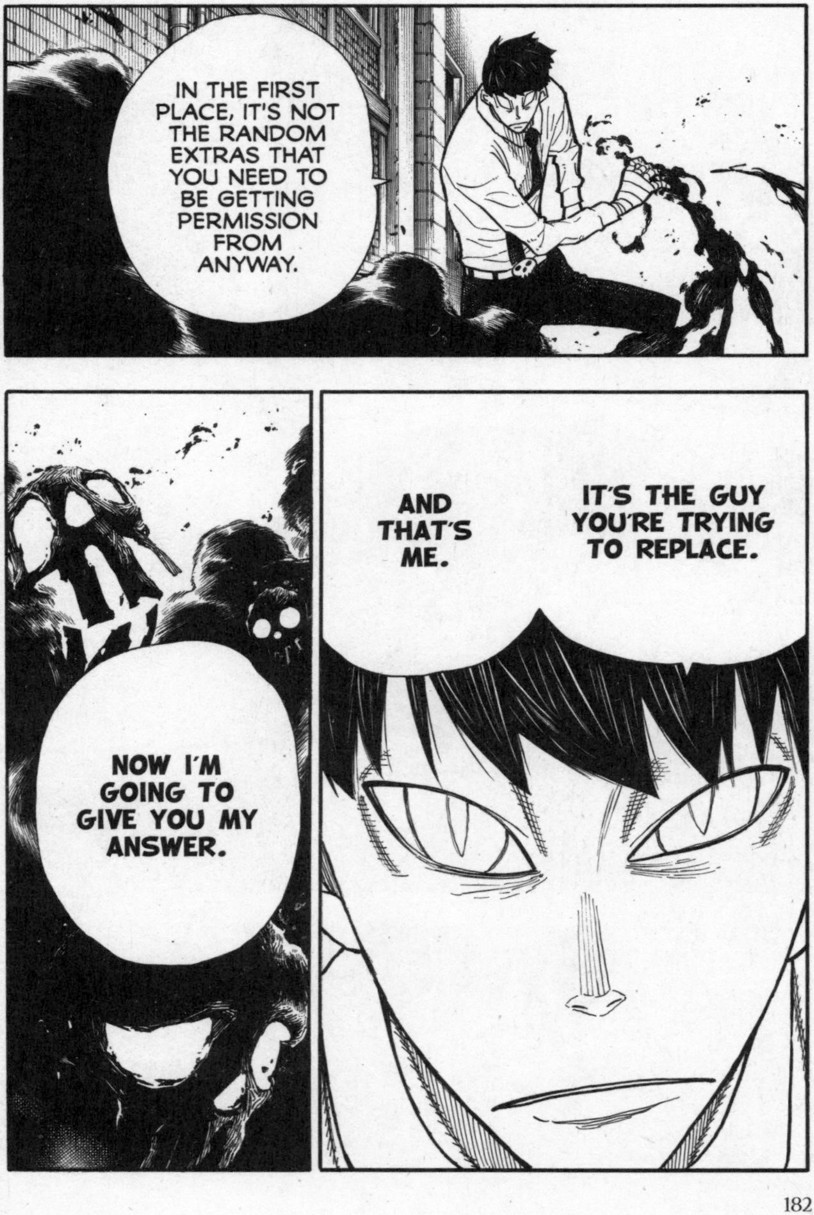
IN THE FIRST PLACE, IT'S NOT THE RANDOM EXTRAS THAT YOU NEED TO BE GETTING PERMISSION FROM ANYWAY.
IT'S THE GUY YOU'RE TRYING TO REPLACE.
AND THAT'S ME.
NOW I'M GOING TO GIVE YOU MY ANSWER.

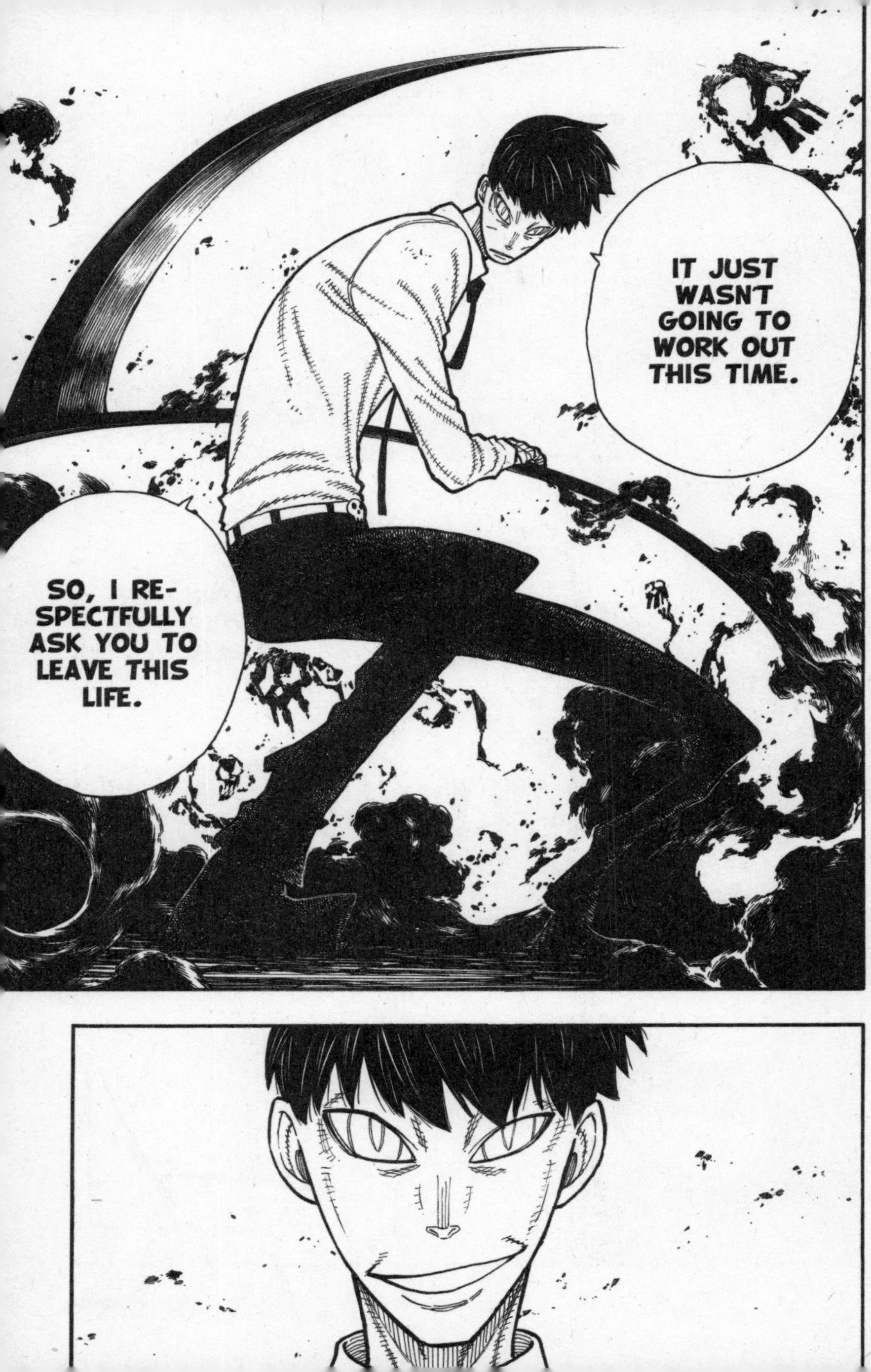
IT JUST WASN'T GOING TO WORK OUT THIS TIME.
SO, I RE-SPECTFULLY ASK YOU TO LEAVE THIS LIFE.

FIRE FORCE

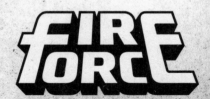

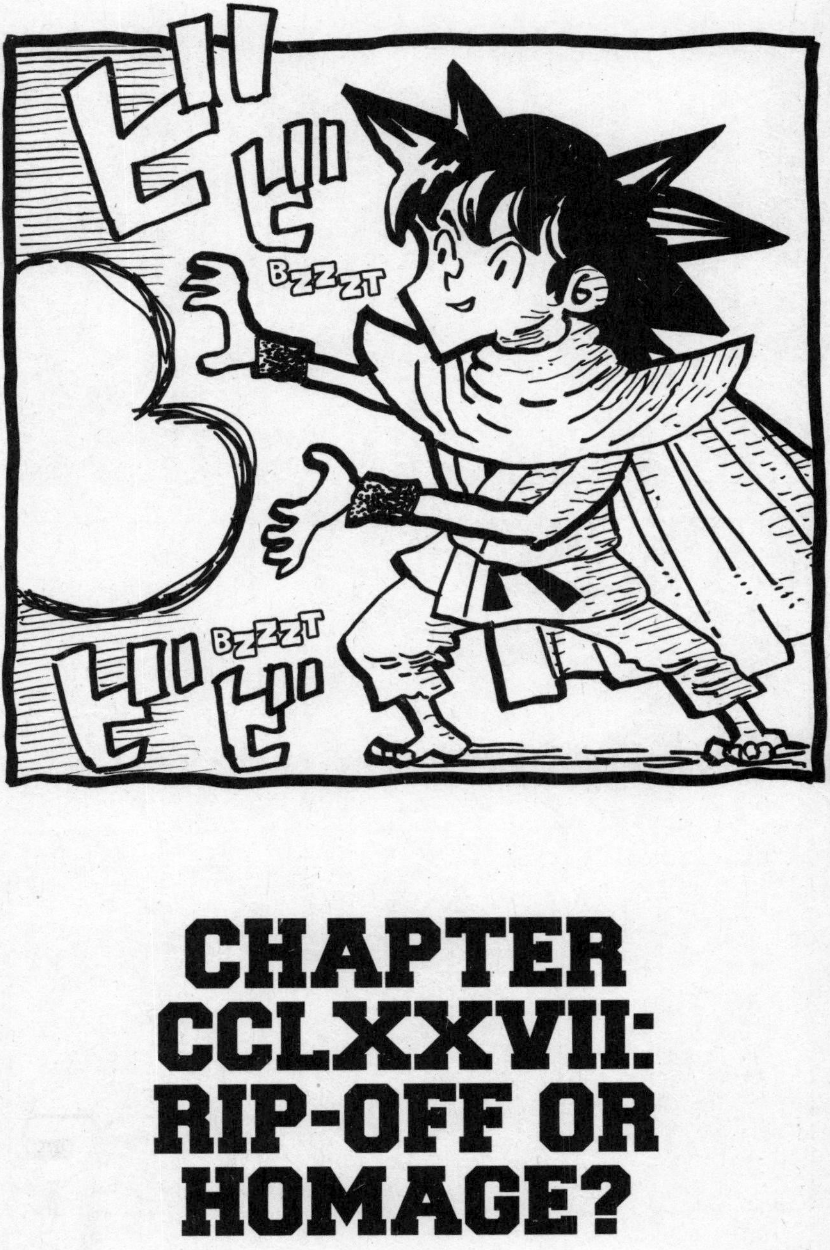
BZZZT
BZZZT

CHAPTER CCLXXVII: RIP-OFF OR HOMAGE?

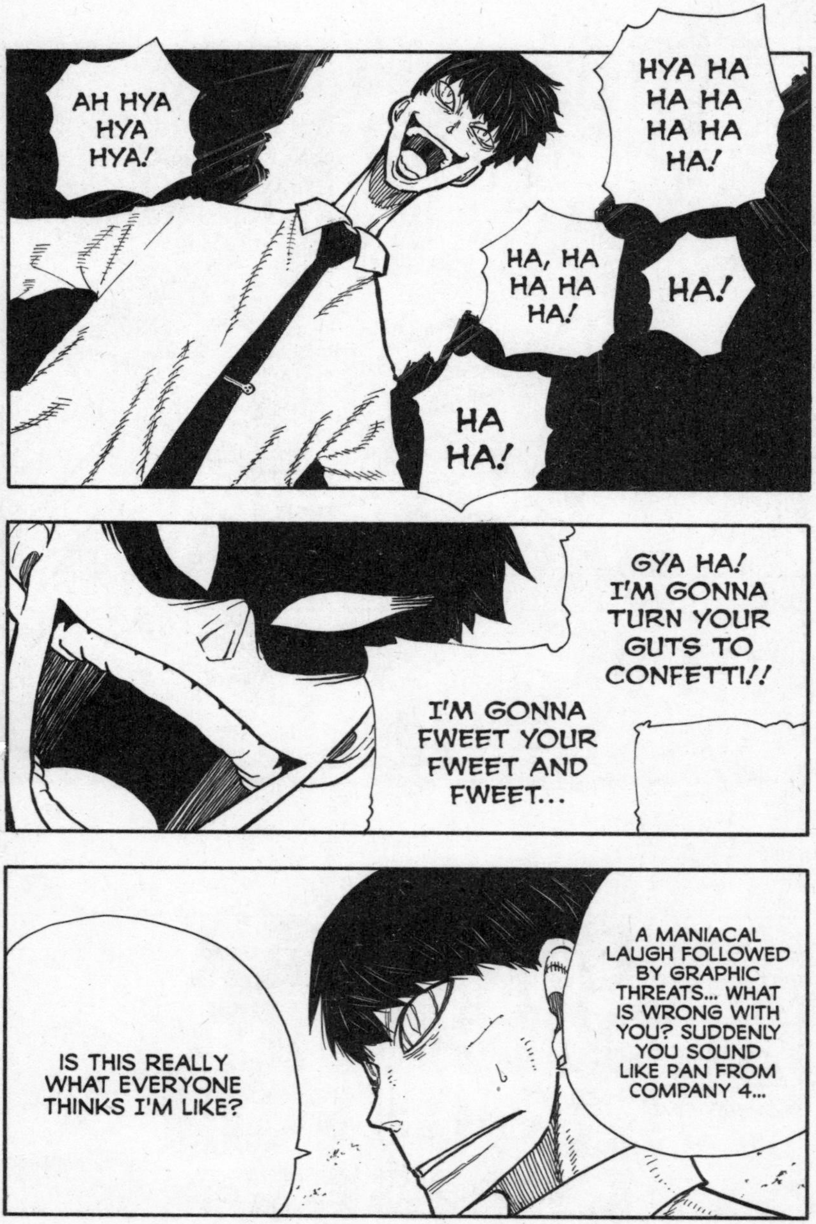

HYA HA HA HA HA HA HA!
AH HYA HYA HYA!
HA!
HA, HA HA HA HA!
HA HA!
GYA HA! I'M GONNA TURN YOUR GUTS TO CONFETTI!!
I'M GONNA FWEET YOUR FWEET AND FWEET...
A MANIACAL LAUGH FOLLOWED BY GRAPHIC THREATS... WHAT IS WRONG WITH YOU? SUDDENLY YOU SOUND LIKE PAN FROM COMPANY 4...
IS THIS REALLY WHAT EVERYONE THINKS I'M LIKE?

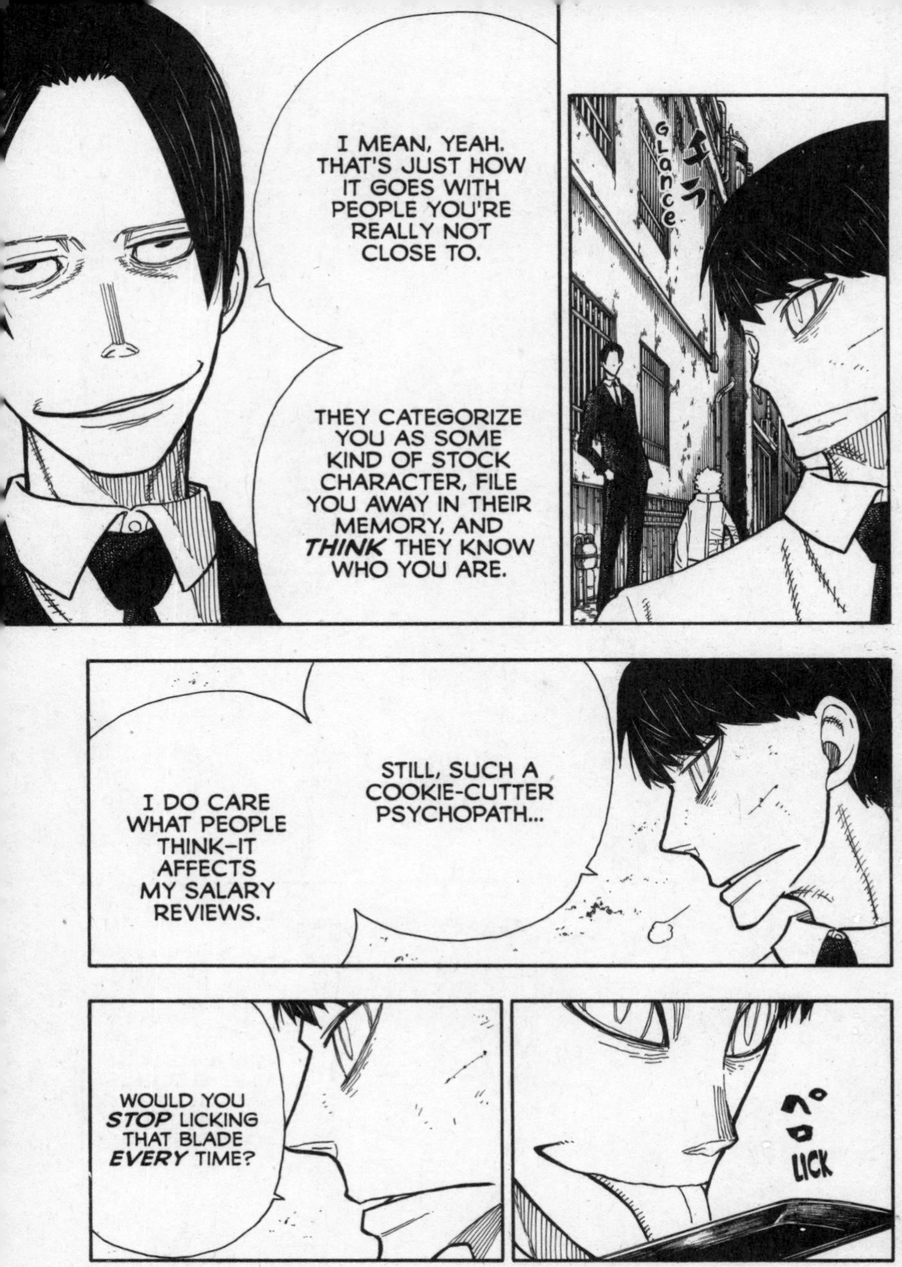
チラ
GLANCE
I MEAN, YEAH. THAT'S JUST HOW IT GOES WITH PEOPLE YOU'RE REALLY NOT CLOSE TO.
THEY CATEGORIZE YOU AS SOME KIND OF STOCK CHARACTER, FILE YOU AWAY IN THEIR MEMORY, AND *THINK* THEY KNOW WHO YOU ARE.
STILL, SUCH A COOKIE-CUTTER PSYCHOPATH...
I DO CARE WHAT PEOPLE THINK—IT AFFECTS MY SALARY REVIEWS.
ペロ
LICK
WOULD YOU *STOP* LICKING THAT BLADE *EVERY* TIME?

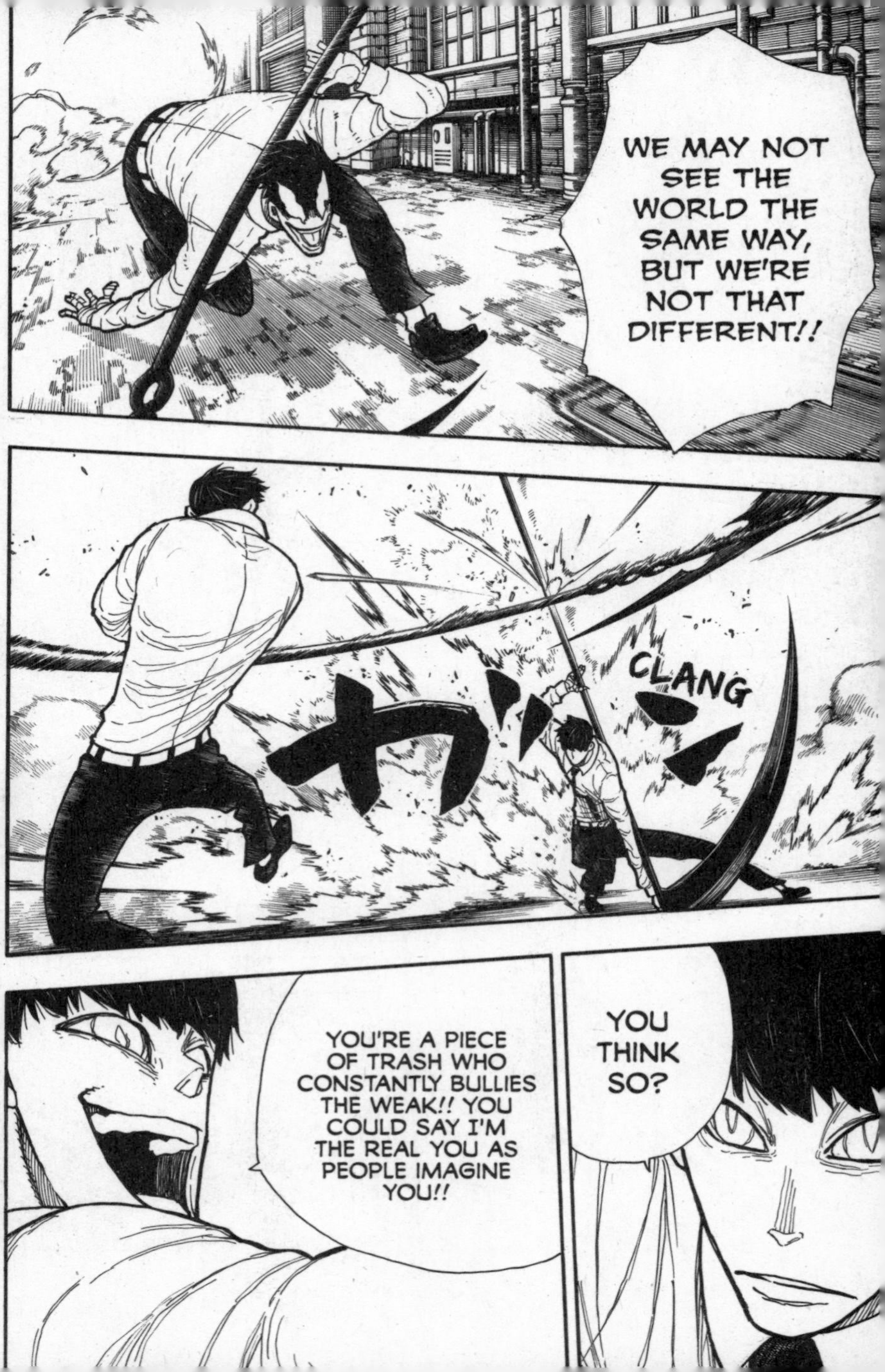
WE MAY NOT SEE THE WORLD THE SAME WAY, BUT WE'RE NOT THAT DIFFERENT!!
CLANG
YOU THINK SO?
YOU'RE A PIECE OF TRASH WHO CONSTANTLY BULLIES THE WEAK!! YOU COULD SAY I'M THE REAL YOU AS PEOPLE IMAGINE YOU!!

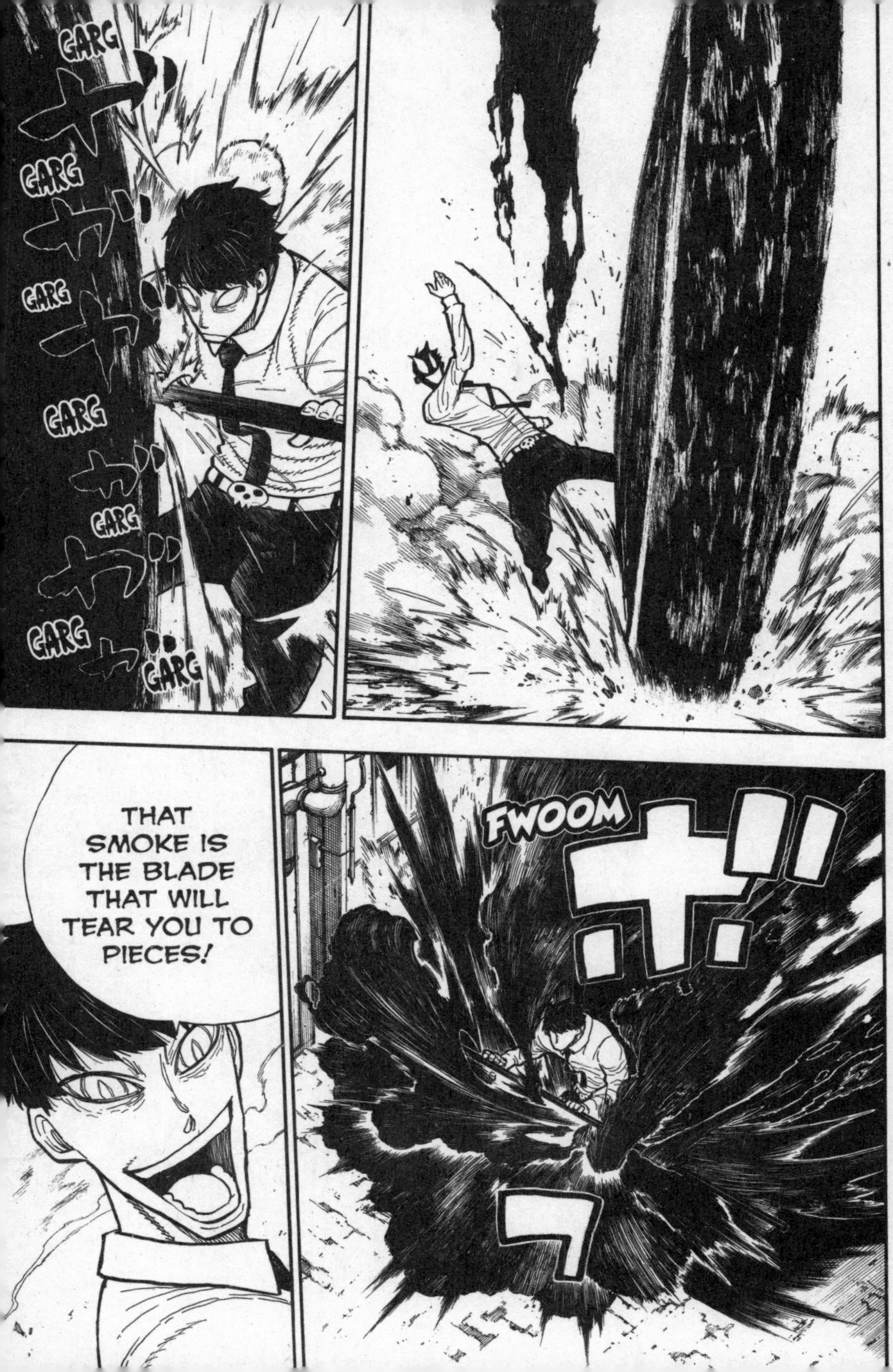
GARG
GARG
GARG
GARG
GARG
GARG
GARG
FWOOM
THAT SMOKE IS THE BLADE THAT WILL TEAR YOU TO PIECES!

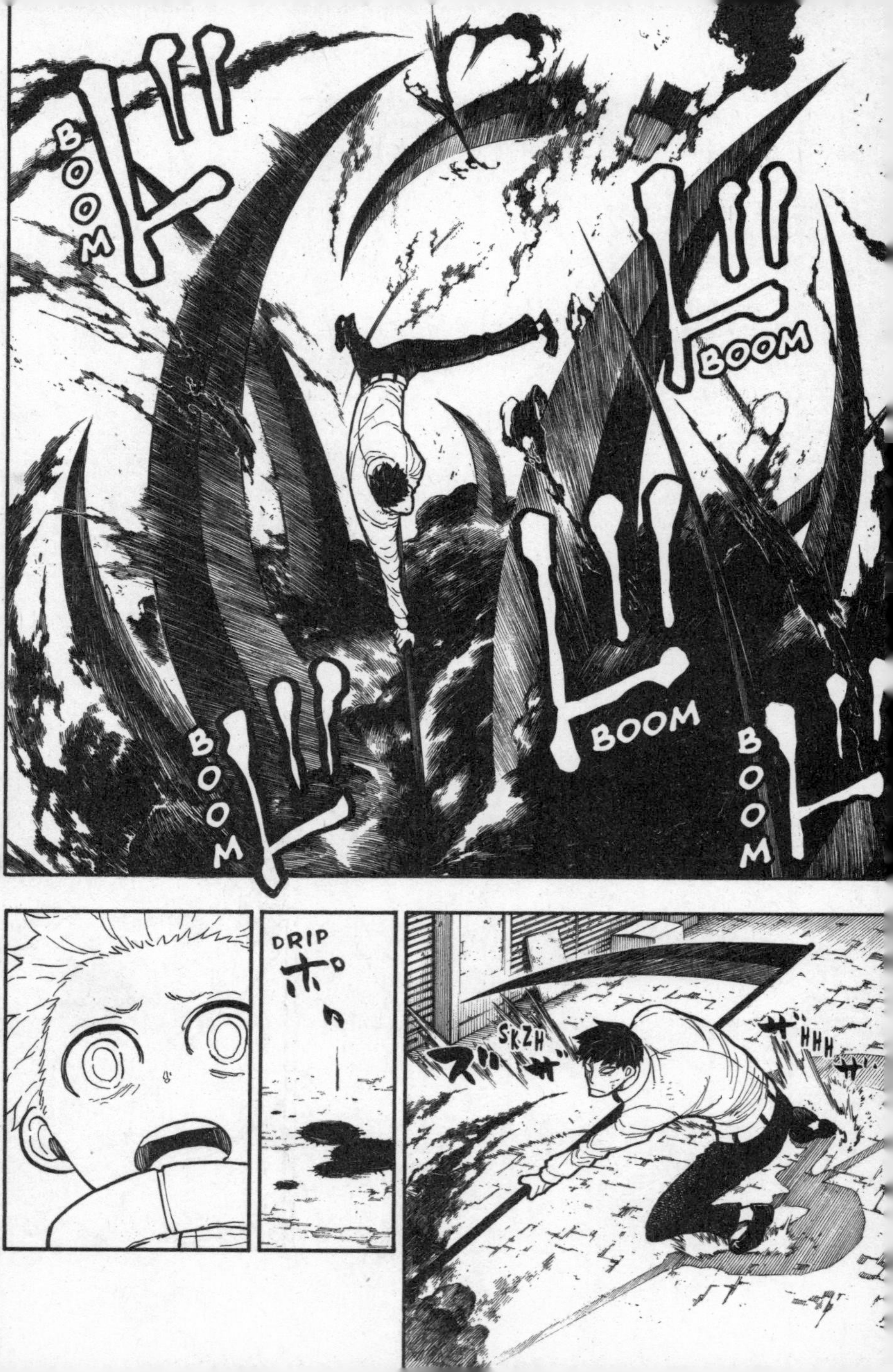
BOOM
BOOM
BOOM
BOOM
BOOM
SKZH
HHH
DRIP

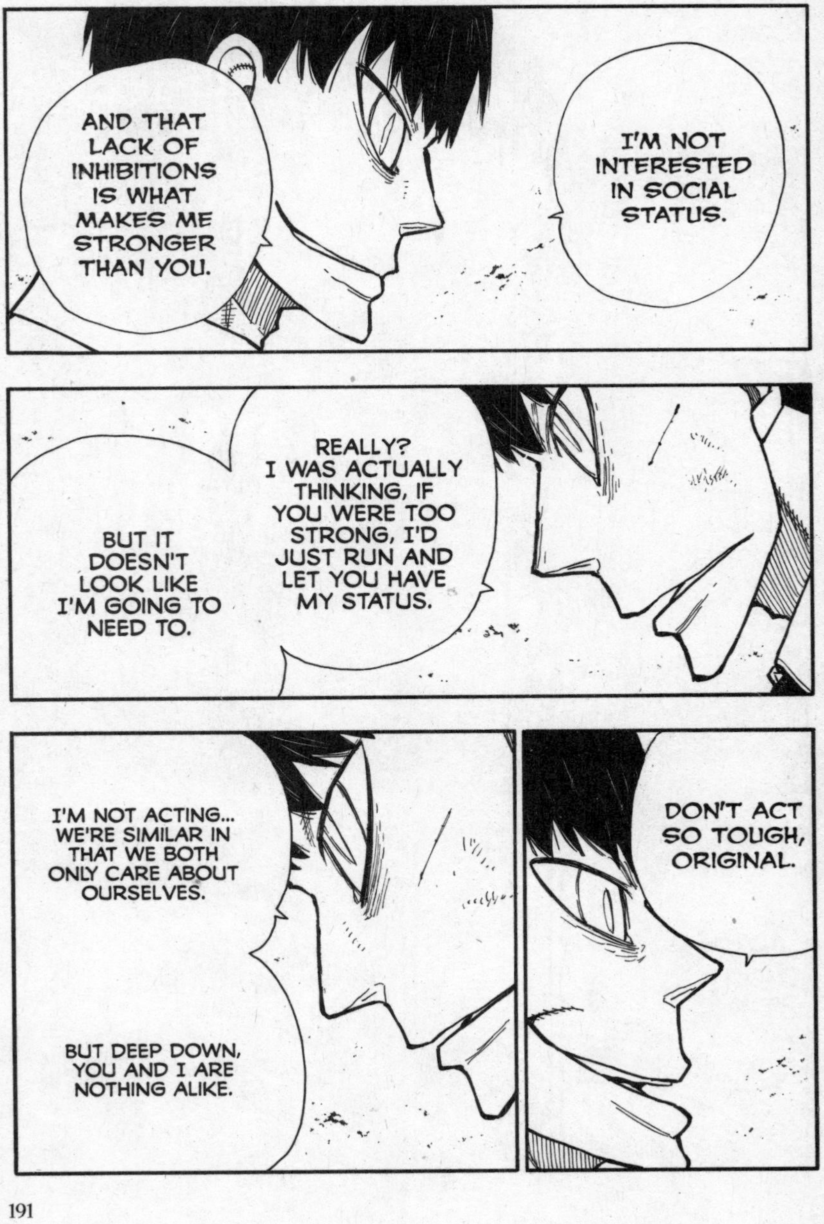
I'M NOT INTERESTED IN SOCIAL STATUS.
AND THAT LACK OF INHIBITIONS IS WHAT MAKES ME STRONGER THAN YOU.
REALLY? I WAS ACTUALLY THINKING, IF YOU WERE TOO STRONG, I'D JUST RUN AND LET YOU HAVE MY STATUS.
BUT IT DOESN'T LOOK LIKE I'M GOING TO NEED TO.
DON'T ACT SO TOUGH, ORIGINAL.
I'M NOT ACTING... WE'RE SIMILAR IN THAT WE BOTH ONLY CARE ABOUT OURSELVES.
BUT DEEP DOWN, YOU AND I ARE NOTHING ALIKE.

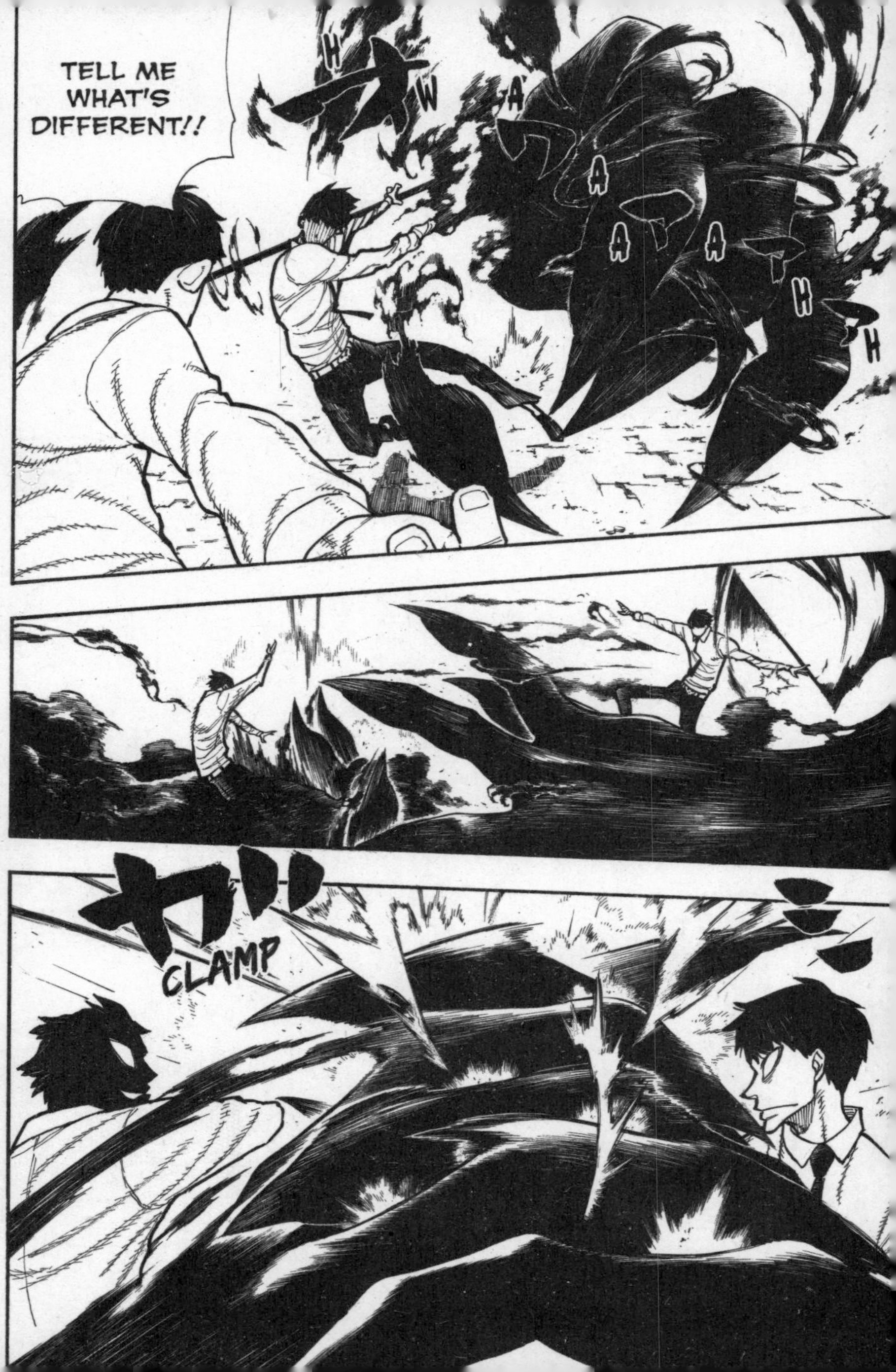
TELL ME WHAT'S DIFFERENT!!
HWAAAAAHH
CLAMP

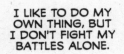

I LIKE TO DO MY OWN THING, BUT I DON'T FIGHT MY BATTLES ALONE.

!!

AND YOU'RE SAYING THAT MAKES YOU STRONGER THAN ME?!

CHOMP

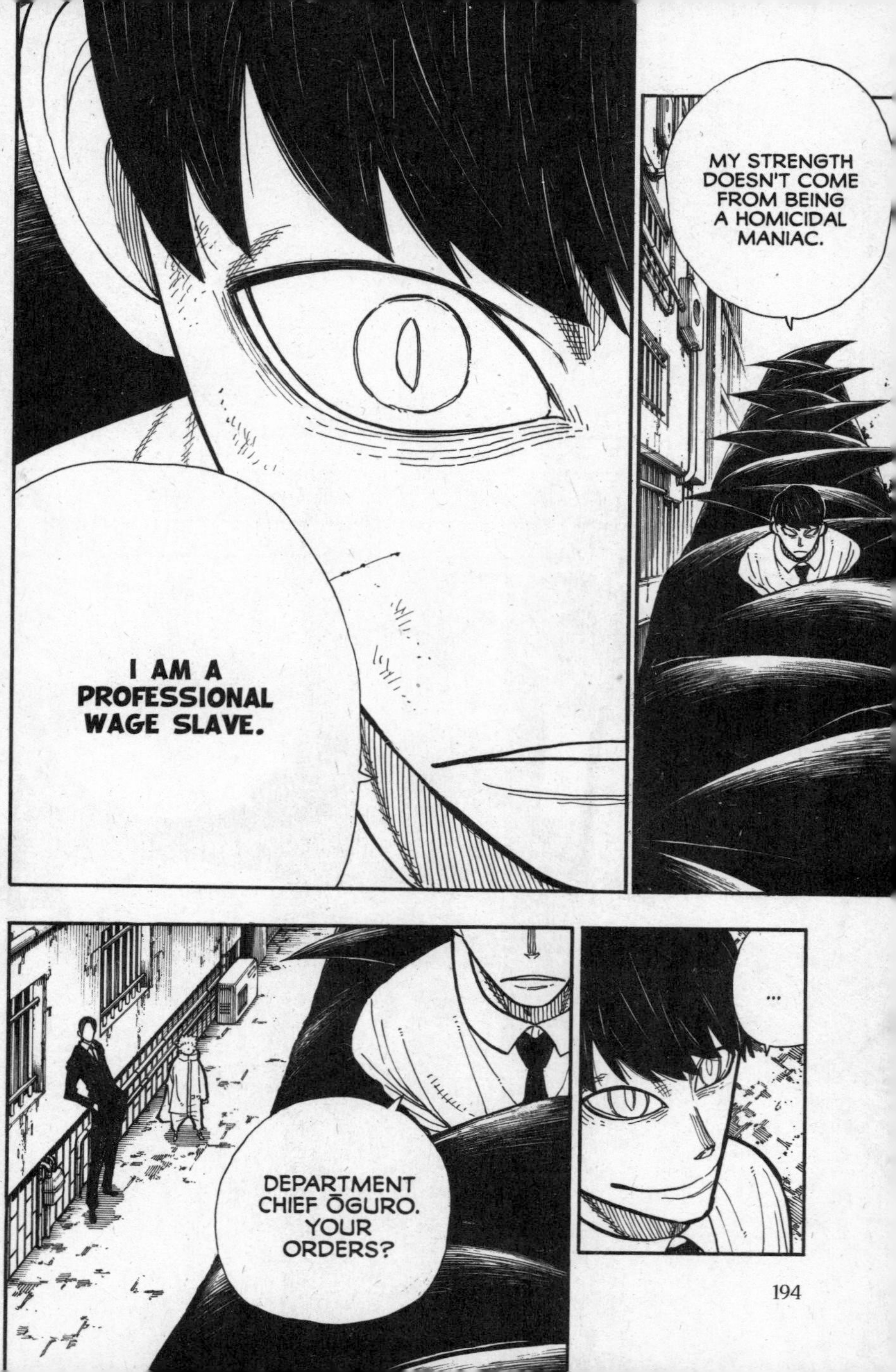
MY STRENGTH DOESN'T COME FROM BEING A HOMICIDAL MANIAC.
I AM A PROFESSIONAL WAGE SLAVE.
...
DEPARTMENT CHIEF ŌGURO. YOUR ORDERS?

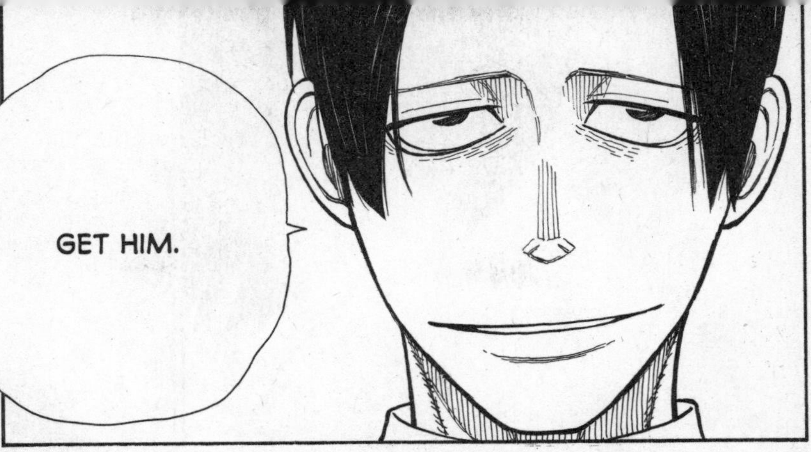
GET HIM.
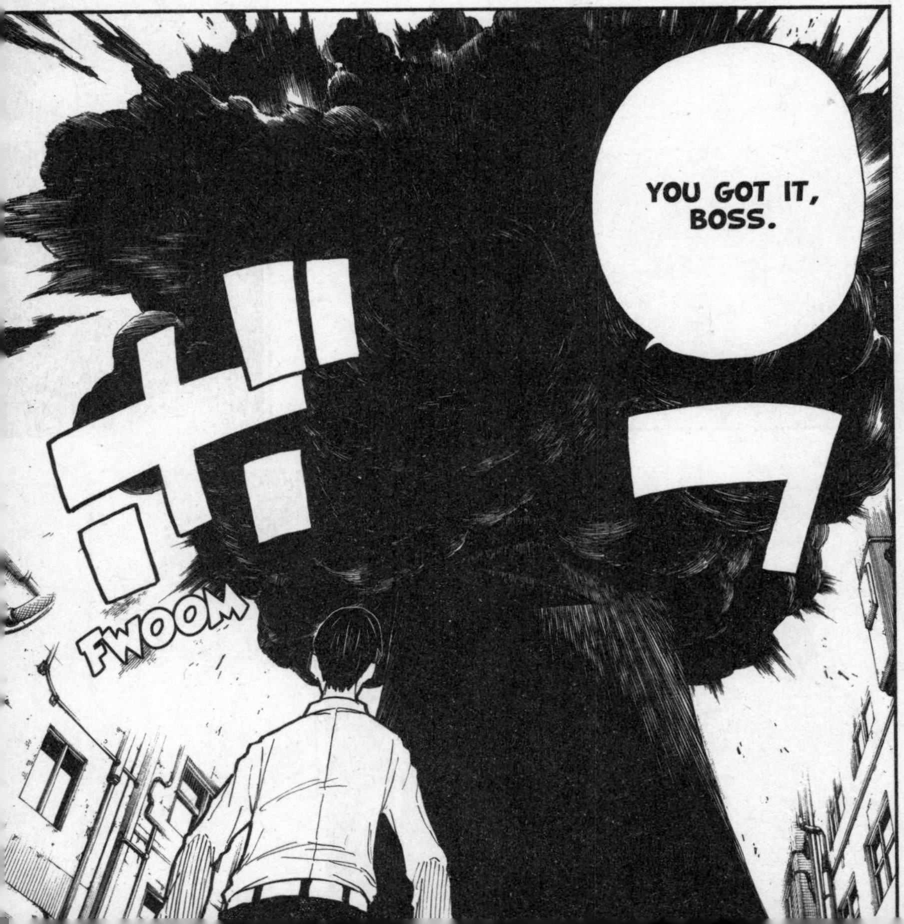
YOU GOT IT, BOSS.
FWOOM

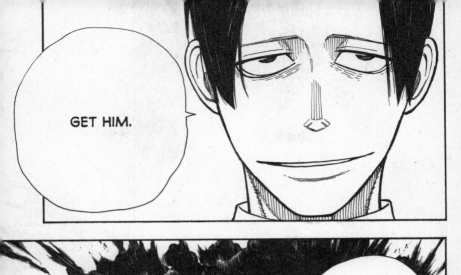

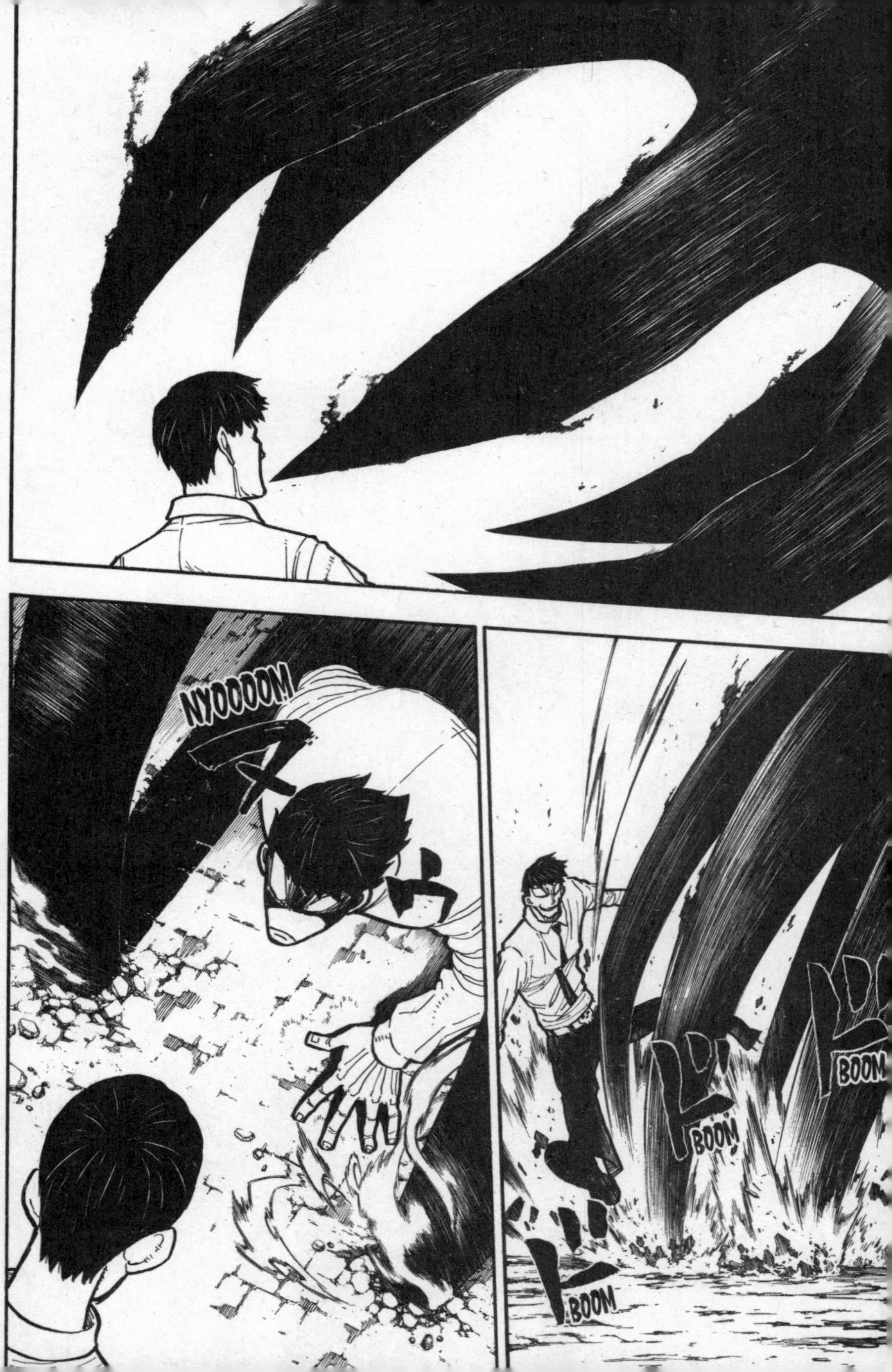
BOOM
BOOM
BOOM
NYOOOOM

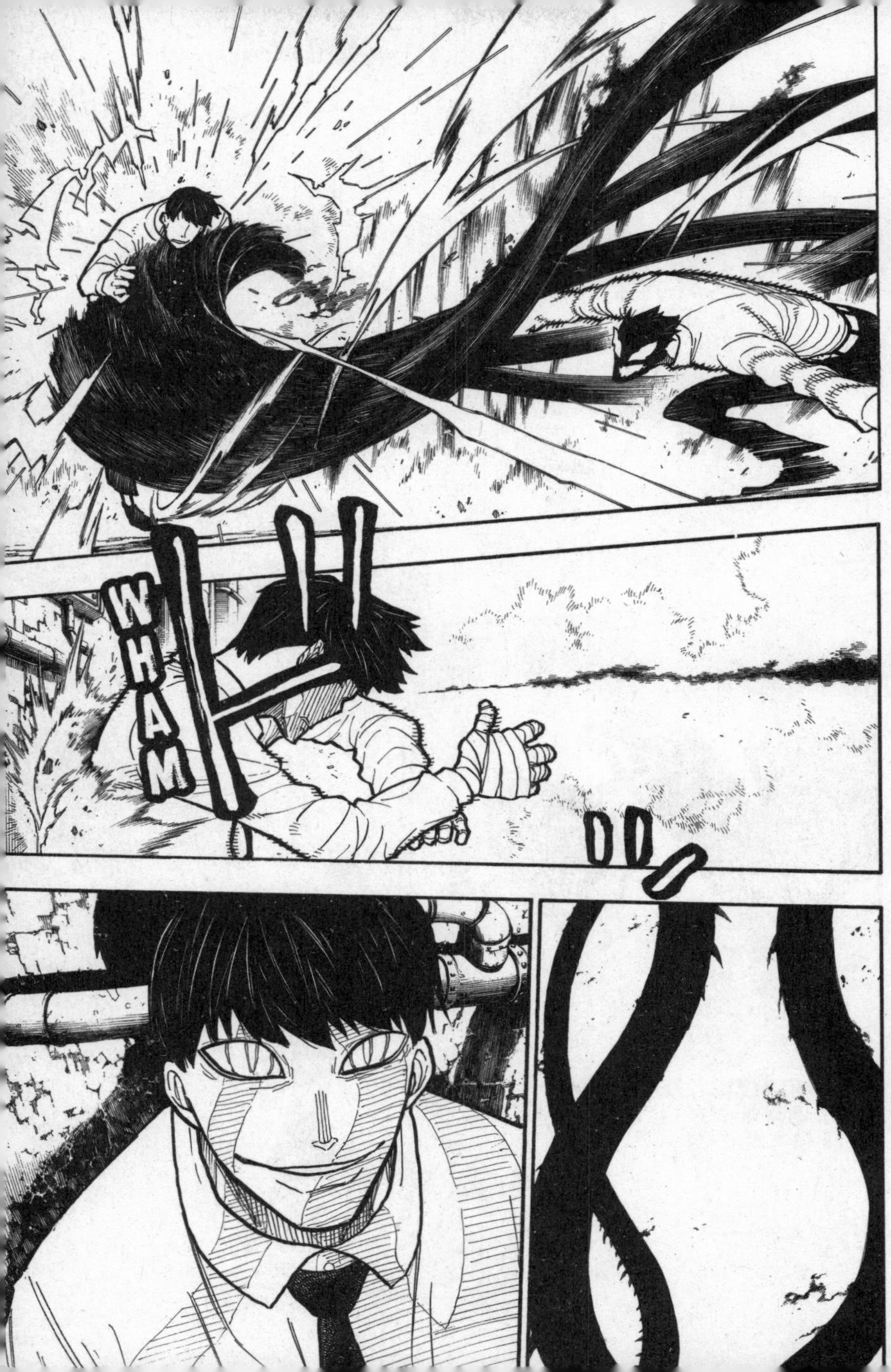
WHAM

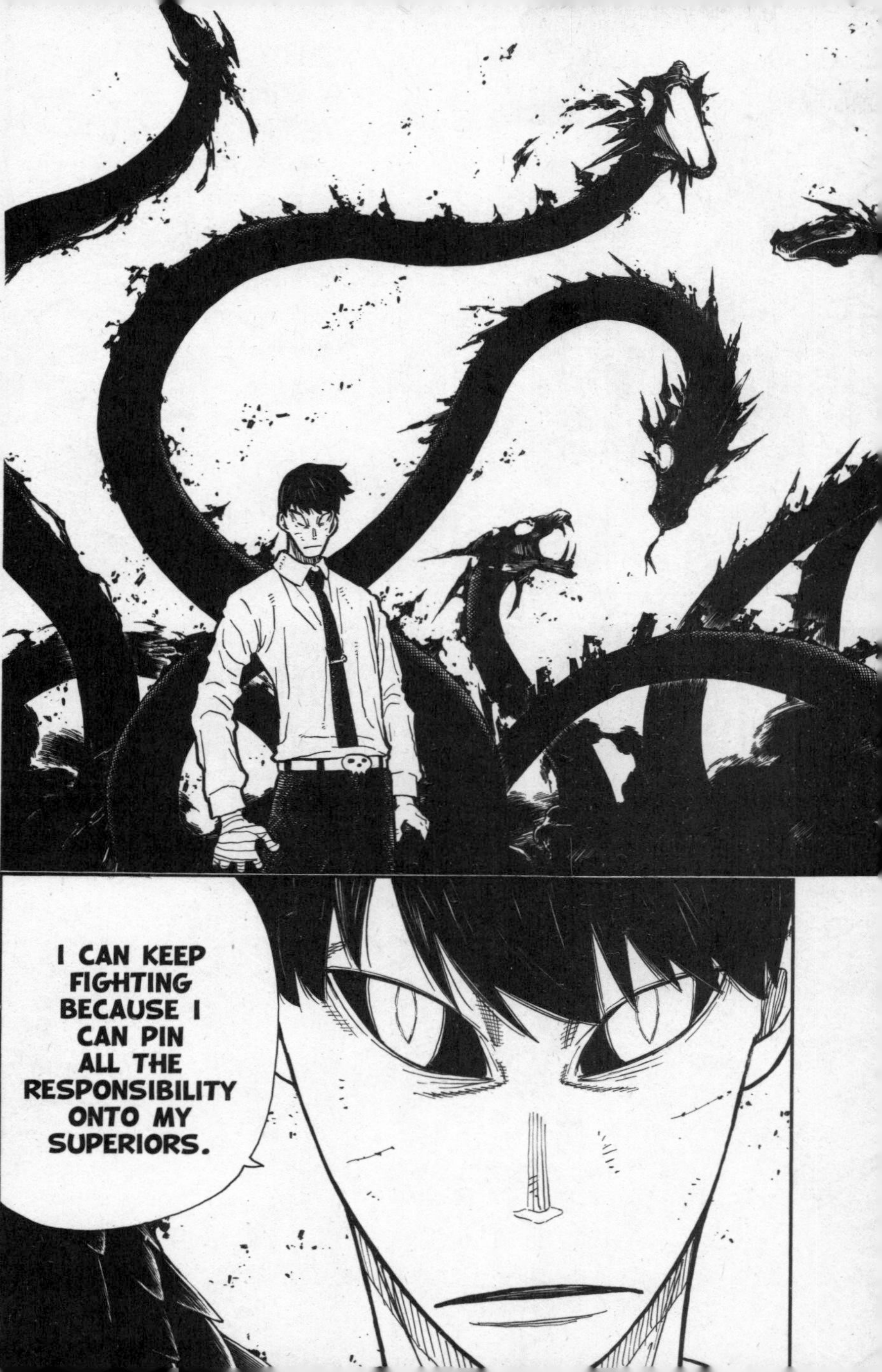
I CAN KEEP FIGHTING BECAUSE I CAN PIN ALL THE RESPONSIBILITY ONTO MY SUPERIORS.

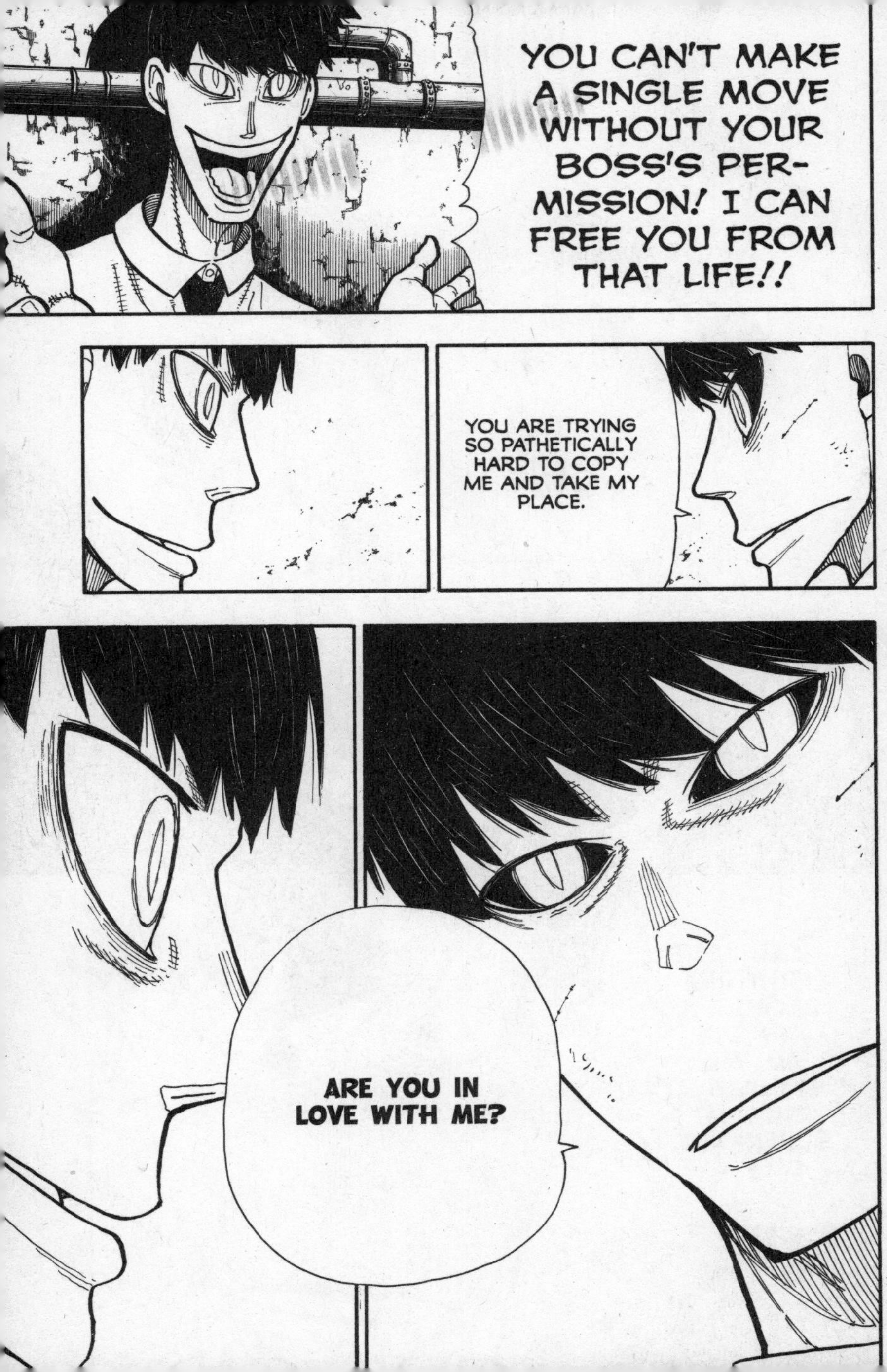
YOU CAN'T MAKE A SINGLE MOVE WITHOUT YOUR BOSS'S PER-MISSION! I CAN FREE YOU FROM THAT LIFE!!
YOU ARE TRYING SO PATHETICALLY HARD TO COPY ME AND TAKE MY PLACE.
ARE YOU IN LOVE WITH ME?

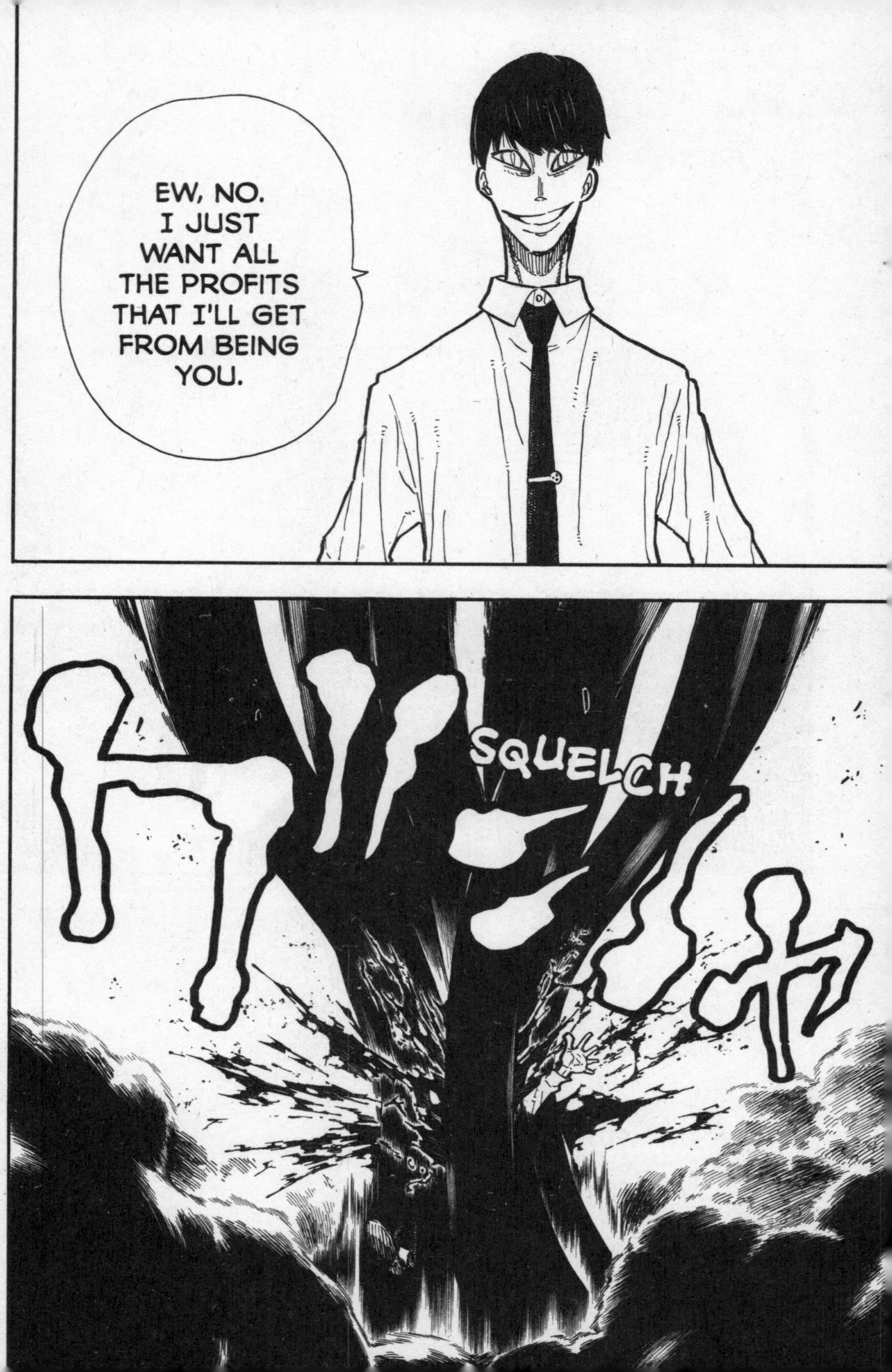
EW, NO. I JUST WANT ALL THE PROFITS THAT I'LL GET FROM BEING YOU.
SQUELCH

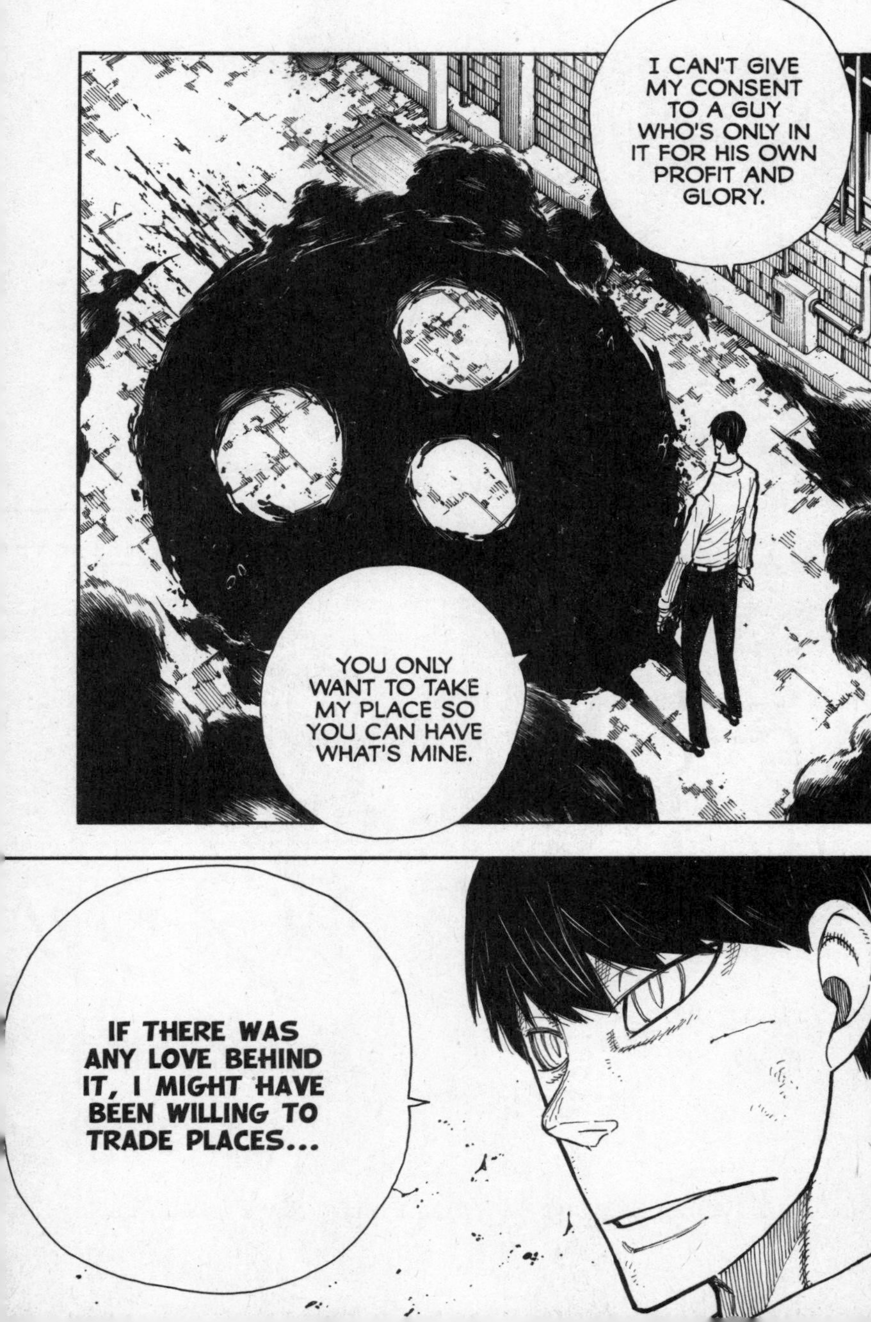
I CAN'T GIVE MY CONSENT TO A GUY WHO'S ONLY IN IT FOR HIS OWN PROFIT AND GLORY.
YOU ONLY WANT TO TAKE MY PLACE SO YOU CAN HAVE WHAT'S MINE.
IF THERE WAS ANY LOVE BEHIND IT, I MIGHT HAVE BEEN WILLING TO TRADE PLACES...

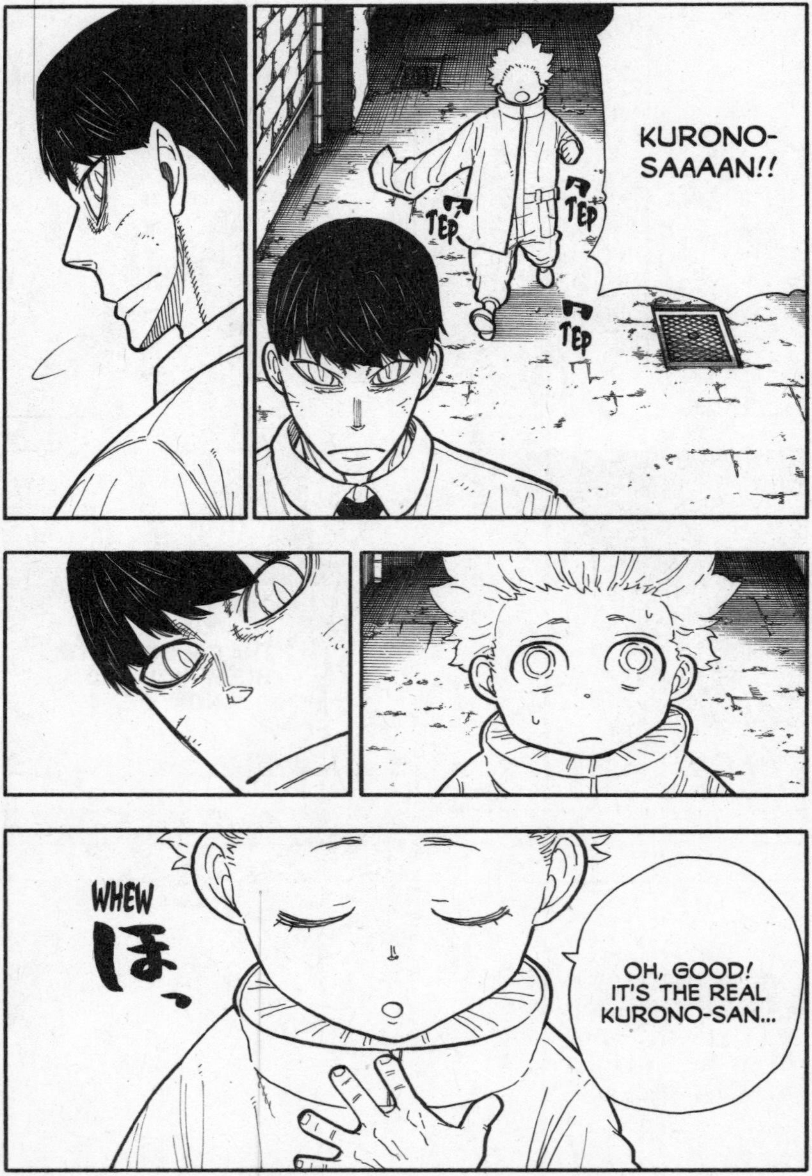
KURONO-
SAAAAN!!
TEP
TEP
TEP
OH, GOOD!
IT'S THE REAL
KURONO-SAN...
WHEW
ほっ

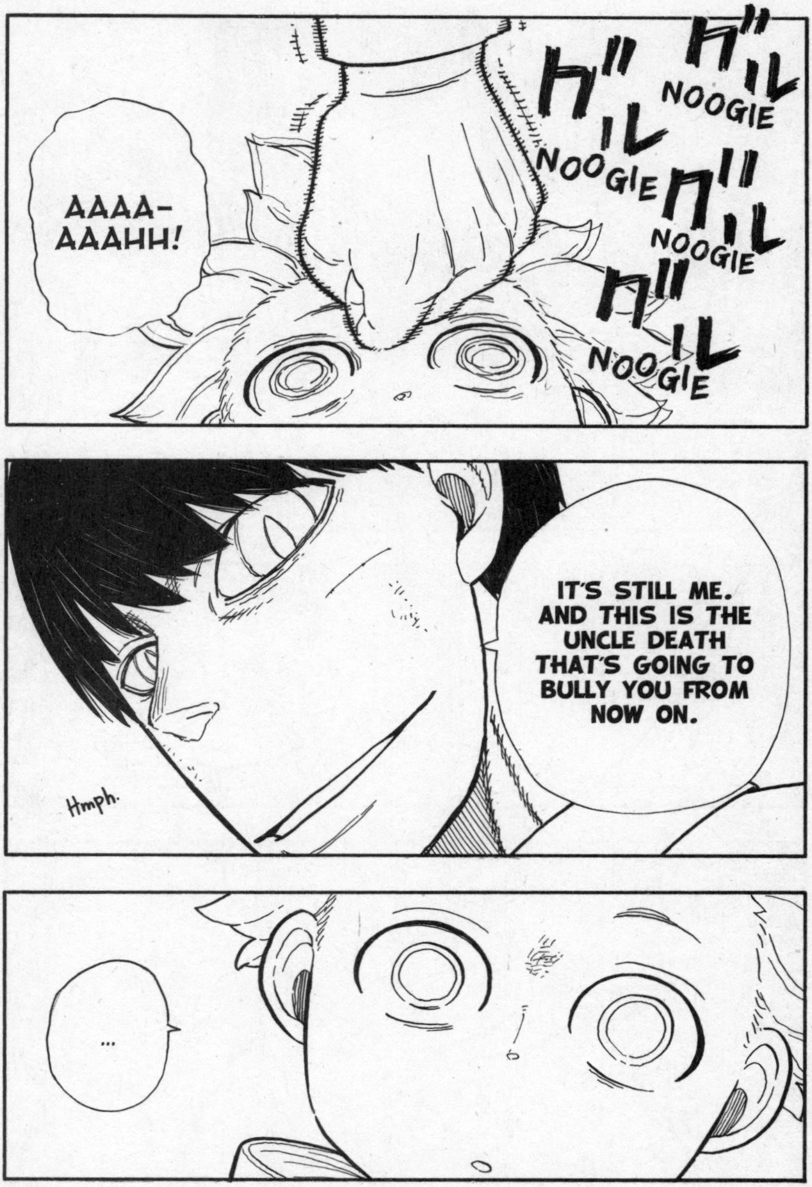
ガル
NOOGIE
ガル
NOOGIE
ガル
NOOGIE
ガル
NOOGIE
AAAA-AAAHH!
IT'S STILL ME. AND THIS IS THE UNCLE DEATH THAT'S GOING TO BULLY YOU FROM NOW ON.
Hmph.
...

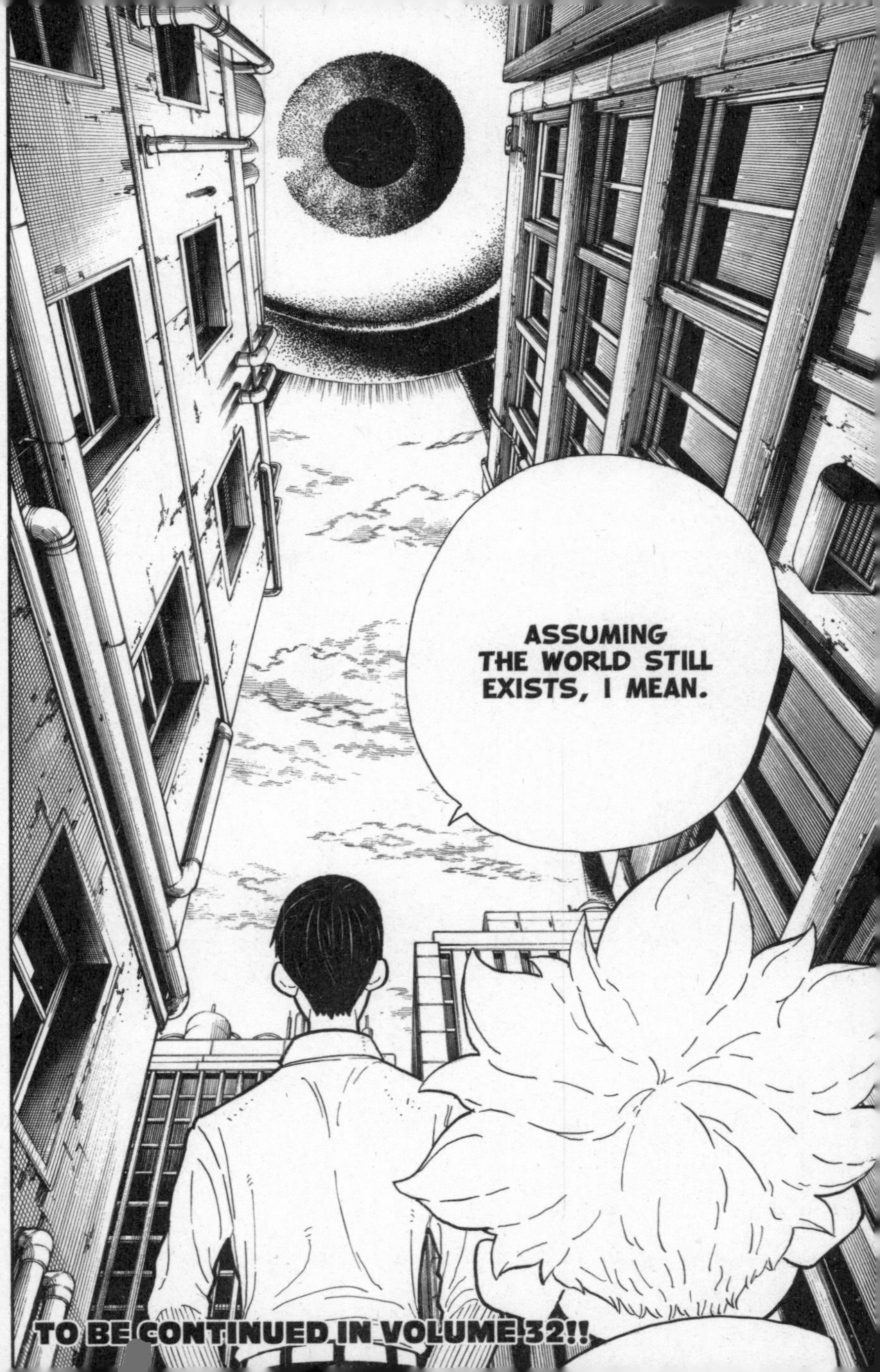
ASSUMING THE WORLD STILL EXISTS, I MEAN.
TO BE CONTINUED IN VOLUME 32!!

AFTERWORD MANGA: ATSUSHIYA

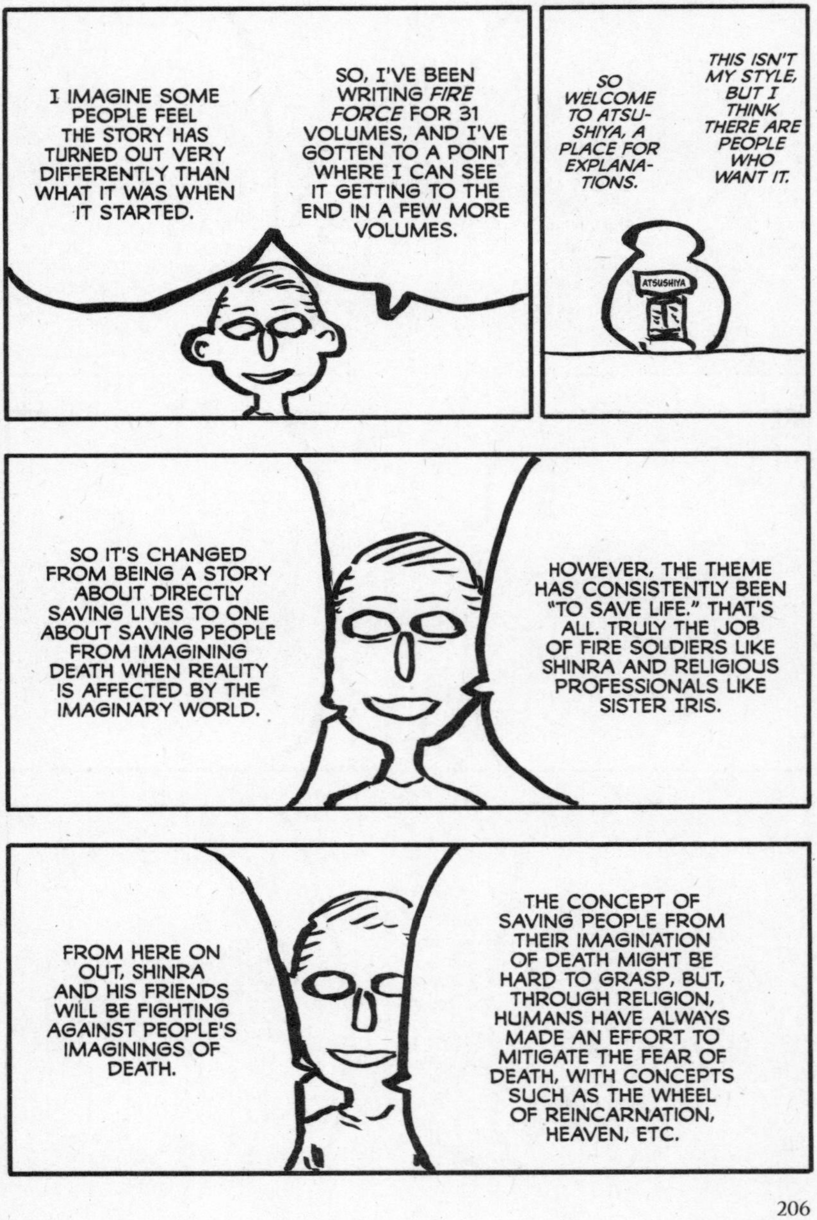
THIS ISN'T MY STYLE, BUT I THINK THERE ARE PEOPLE WHO WANT IT.
SO WELCOME TO ATSUSHIYA, A PLACE FOR EXPLANATIONS.
ATSUSHIYA
SO, I'VE BEEN WRITING *FIRE FORCE* FOR 31 VOLUMES, AND I'VE GOTTEN TO A POINT WHERE I CAN SEE IT GETTING TO THE END IN A FEW MORE VOLUMES.
I IMAGINE SOME PEOPLE FEEL THE STORY HAS TURNED OUT VERY DIFFERENTLY THAN WHAT IT WAS WHEN IT STARTED.
HOWEVER, THE THEME HAS CONSISTENTLY BEEN "TO SAVE LIFE." THAT'S ALL. TRULY THE JOB OF FIRE SOLDIERS LIKE SHINRA AND RELIGIOUS PROFESSIONALS LIKE SISTER IRIS.
SO IT'S CHANGED FROM BEING A STORY ABOUT DIRECTLY SAVING LIVES TO ONE ABOUT SAVING PEOPLE FROM IMAGINING DEATH WHEN REALITY IS AFFECTED BY THE IMAGINARY WORLD.
THE CONCEPT OF SAVING PEOPLE FROM THEIR IMAGINATION OF DEATH MIGHT BE HARD TO GRASP, BUT, THROUGH RELIGION, HUMANS HAVE ALWAYS MADE AN EFFORT TO MITIGATE THE FEAR OF DEATH, WITH CONCEPTS SUCH AS THE WHEEL OF REINCARNATION, HEAVEN, ETC.
FROM HERE ON OUT, SHINRA AND HIS FRIENDS WILL BE FIGHTING AGAINST PEOPLE'S IMAGININGS OF DEATH.

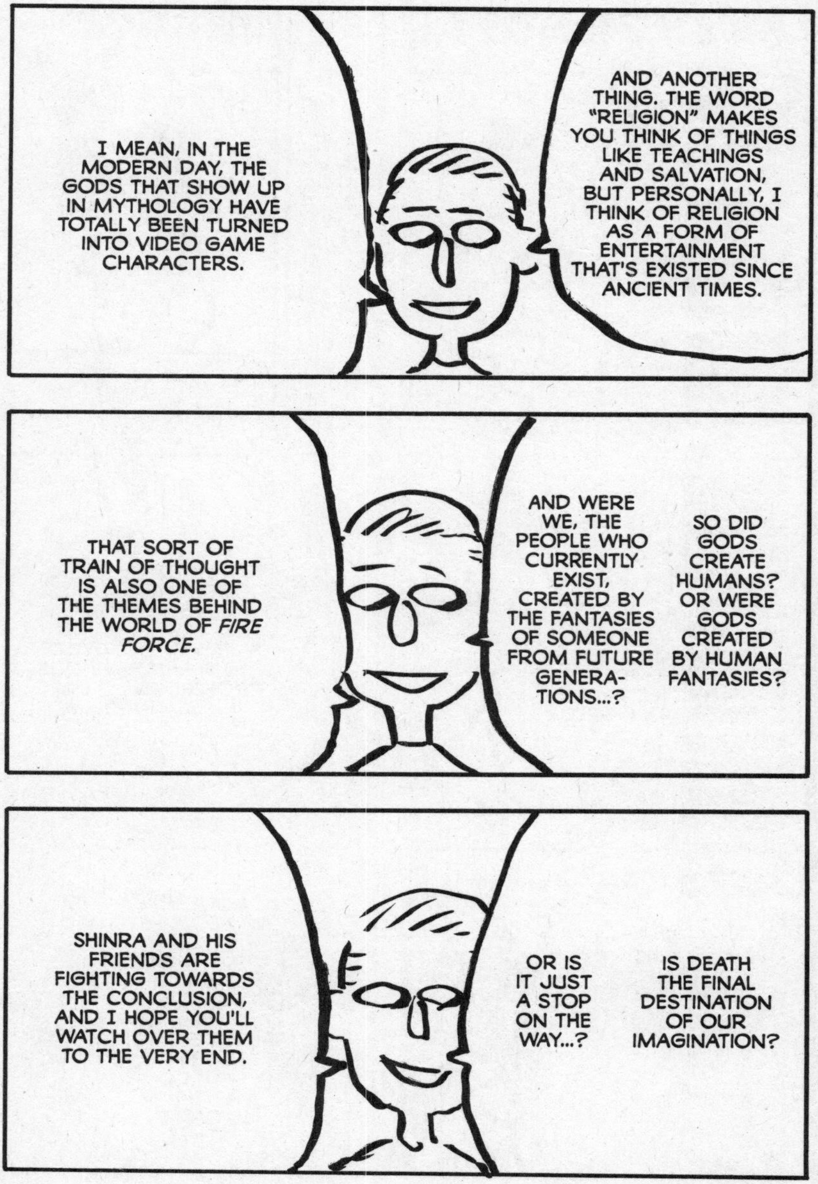

AND ANOTHER THING. THE WORD "RELIGION" MAKES YOU THINK OF THINGS LIKE TEACHINGS AND SALVATION, BUT PERSONALLY, I THINK OF RELIGION AS A FORM OF ENTERTAINMENT THAT'S EXISTED SINCE ANCIENT TIMES.
I MEAN, IN THE MODERN DAY, THE GODS THAT SHOW UP IN MYTHOLOGY HAVE TOTALLY BEEN TURNED INTO VIDEO GAME CHARACTERS.
SO DID GODS CREATE HUMANS? OR WERE GODS CREATED BY HUMAN FANTASIES?
AND WERE WE, THE PEOPLE WHO CURRENTLY EXIST, CREATED BY THE FANTASIES OF SOMEONE FROM FUTURE GENERA-TIONS...?
THAT SORT OF TRAIN OF THOUGHT IS ALSO ONE OF THE THEMES BEHIND THE WORLD OF *FIRE FORCE*.
IS DEATH THE FINAL DESTINATION OF OUR IMAGINATION?
OR IS IT JUST A STOP ON THE WAY...?
SHINRA AND HIS FRIENDS ARE FIGHTING TOWARDS THE CONCLUSION, AND I HOPE YOU'LL WATCH OVER THEM TO THE VERY END.

ARTHUR BOYLE

DRAGON

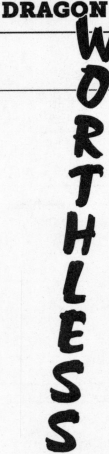

AFFILIATION: SPECIAL FIRE FORCE COMPANY 8
RANK: SECOND CLASS FIRE SOLDIER
ABILITY: THIRD GENERATION PYROKINETIC
Emits a blade of flame from the hilt of his sword

Height	174cm [5'8.5'']
Weight	64kg [141lbs.]
Age	17 years
Birthday	July 10
Sign	Cancer
Bloodtype	A
Nickname	Stupid
Self-Proclaimed	Knight King
Favorite Foods	Court Cuisine (has never had any) The ramen Captain Obi buys him
Least Favorite Food	Horse meat sashimi
Favorite Music	Court Music (has never heard any)
Favorite Animal	Horse
Favorite Color	White, Blue
Favorite Type of Girl	A girl who looks good in glass slippers and a tiara
Who He Respects	King Arthur
Who He Hates	No one
Who He's Afraid Of	No one
Hobbies	Building model castles
Daily Routine	Sword practice
Dream	To be the Knight King
Shoe Size	26cm [9]
Eyesight	1.5 [20/12.5]
Favorite Subject	Physical Education
Least Favorite Subject	Everything taught in the classroom

WORTHLESS!

Translation Notes:

Moon shot, page 113

In a more literal translation, Faerie says that, with this *tsukiotoshi,* they will remember despair. *Tsukiotoshi* is a Japanese word referring to pushing someone such that they will then fall, such as pushing them out a window or off a cliff—in this case, he would be shoving them into the depths of despair. But in this case, it also literally means dropping (*otoshi*) the moon (*tsuki*).

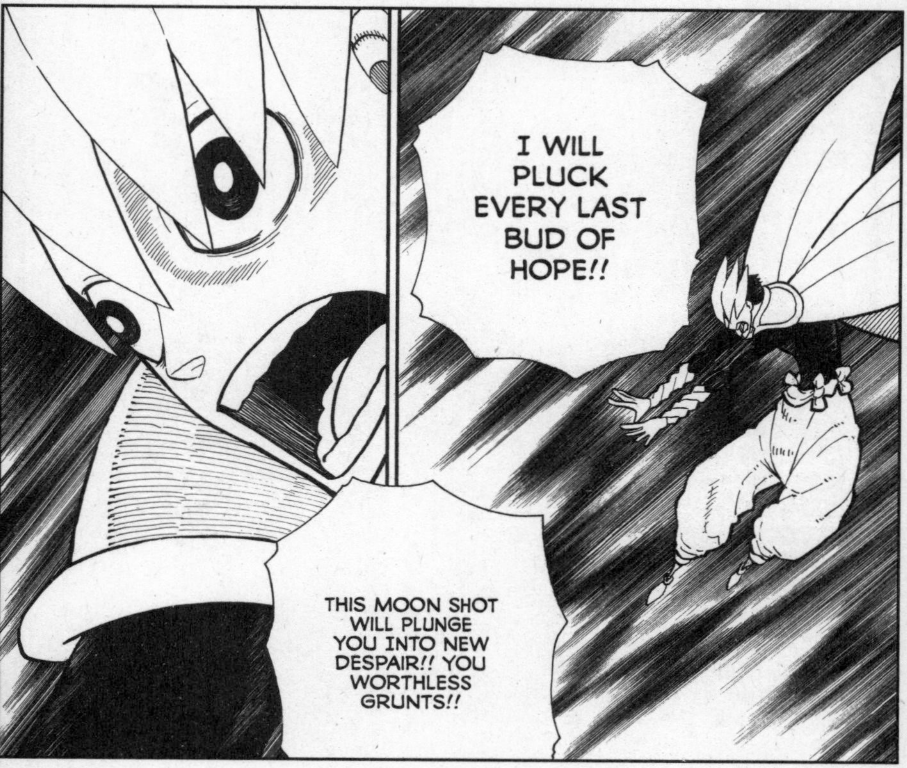
I WILL PLUCK EVERY LAST BUD OF HOPE!!
THIS MOON SHOT WILL PLUNGE YOU INTO NEW DESPAIR!! YOU WORTHLESS GRUNTS!!

Young characters and steampunk setting, like *Howl's Moving Castle* and *Battle Angel Alita*

Beyond the Clouds © 2018 Nicke / Ki-oon

A boy with a talent for machines and a mysterious girl whose wings he's fixed will take you beyond the clouds! In the tradition of the high-flying, resonant adventure stories of Studio Ghibli comes a gorgeous tale about the longing of young hearts for adventure and friendship!

A SMART, NEW ROMANTIC COMEDY FOR FANS OF *SHORTCAKE CAKE* AND *TERRACE HOUSE*!

KC
KODANSHA
COMICS

A romance manga starring high school girl Meeko, who learns to live on her own in a boarding house whose living room is home to the odd (but handsome) Matsunaga-san. She begins to adjust to her new life away from her parents, but Meeko soon learns that no matter how far away from home she is, she's still a young girl at heart — especially when she finds herself falling for Matsunaga-san.

1 Perfect World

Rie Aruga

A TOUCHING
NEW SERIES
ABOUT LOVE AND
COPING WITH
DISABILITY

An office party reunites Tsugumi with her high school crush Itsuki. He's realized his dream of becoming an architect, but along the way, he experienced a spinal injury that put him in a wheelchair. Now Tsugumi's rekindled feelings will butt up against prejudices she never considered — and Itsuki will have to decide if he's ready to let someone into his heart...

"Depicts with great delicacy and courage the difficulties some with disabilities experience getting involved in romantic relationships... Rie Aruga refuses to romanticize, pushing her heroine to face the reality of disability. She invites her readers to the same tasks of empathy, knowledge and recognition."
—Slate.fr

"An important entry [in manga romance]... The emotional core of both plot and characters indicates thoughtfulness... [Aruga's] research is readily apparent in the text and artwork, making this feel like a real story."
—Anime News Network

The boys are back, in 400-page hardcovers that are as pretty and badass as they are!

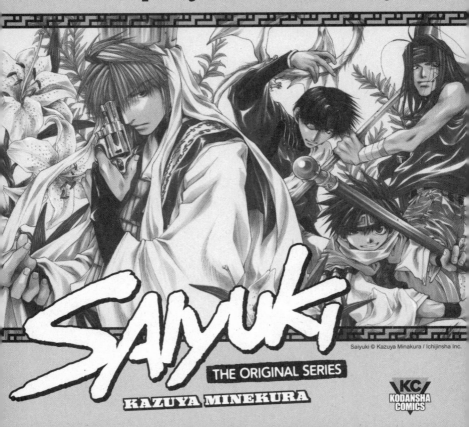

Saiyuki © Kazuya Minekura / Ichijinsha Inc.

SAIYUKI
THE ORIGINAL SERIES
KAZUYA MINEKURA

KC KODANSHA COMICS

"AN EDGY COMIC LOOK AT AN ANCIENT CHINESE TALE." —YALSA

Genjo Sanzo is a Buddhist priest in the city of Togenkyo, which is being ravaged by yokai spirits that have fallen out of balance with the natural order. His superiors send him on a journey far to the west to discover why this is happening and how to stop it. His companions are three yokai with human souls. But this is no day trip — the four will encounter many discoveries and horrors on the way.

FEATURES NEW TRANSLATION, COLOR PAGES, AND BEAUTIFUL WRAPAROUND COVER ART!

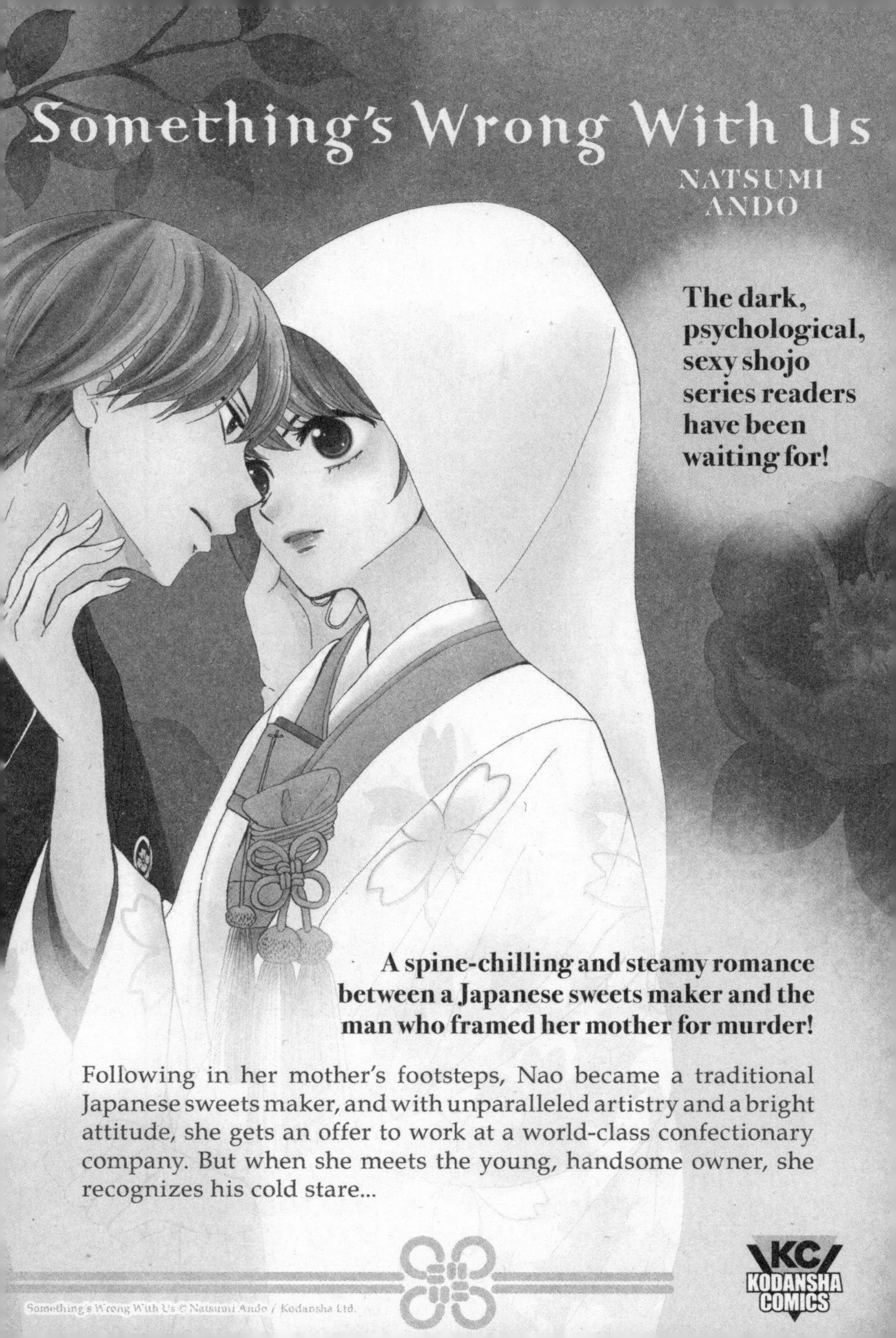
Something's Wrong With Us
NATSUMI ANDO
The dark, psychological, sexy shojo series readers have been waiting for!
A spine-chilling and steamy romance between a Japanese sweets maker and the man who framed her mother for murder!
Following in her mother's footsteps, Nao became a traditional Japanese sweets maker, and with unparalleled artistry and a bright attitude, she gets an offer to work at a world-class confectionary company. But when she meets the young, handsome owner, she recognizes his cold stare...
KC KODANSHA COMICS
Something's Wrong With Us © Natsumi Ando / Kodansha Ltd.

The adorable new odd-couple cat comedy manga from the creator of the beloved *Chi's Sweet Home*, in full color!

Praise for Chi's Sweet Home

"Nearly impossible to turn away... a true all-ages title that anyone, young or old, cat lover or not, will enjoy. The stories will bring a smile to your face and warm your heart."

—School Library Journal

Sue & Tai-chan
Konami Kanata

Sue is an aging housecat who's looking forward to living out her life in peace... but her plans change when the mischievous black tomcat Tai-chan enters the picture! Hey! Sue never signed up to be a catsitter! *Sue & Tai-chan* is the latest from the reigning meow-narch of cute kitty comics, Konami Kanata.

KC
KODANSHA
COMICS

THE SWEET SCENT OF LOVE IS IN THE AIR! FOR FANS OF OFFBEAT ROMANCES LIKE *WOTAKOI*

Sweat and Soap © Kintetsu Yamada / Kodansha Ltd.

In an office romance, there's a fine line between sexy and awkward... and that line is where Asako — a woman who sweats copiously — meets Koutarou — a perfume developer who can't get enough of Asako's, er, scent. Don't miss a romcom manga like no other!

CUTE ANIMALS AND LIFE LESSONS, PERFECT FOR ASPIRING PET VETS OF ALL AGES!

For an 11-year-old, Yuzu has a lot on her plate. When her mom gets sick and has to be hospitalized, Yuzu goes to live with her uncle who runs the local veterinary clinic. Yuzu's always been scared of animals, but she tries to help out. Through all the tough moments in her life, Yuzu realizes that she can help make things all right with a little help from her animal pals, peers, and kind grown-ups.

Every new patient is a furry friend in the making!

Chobits © CLAMP·ShigatsuTsuitachi CO.,LTD./Kodansha Ltd.

Poor college student Hideki is down on his luck. All he wants is a
good job, a girlfriend, and his very own "persocom"—the latest
and greatest in humanoid computer technology. Hideki's luck
changes one night when he finds Chi—a persocom thrown out
in a pile of trash. But Hideki soon discovers that there's much
more to his cute new persocom than meets the eye.

THE WORLD OF CLAMP!

Cardcaptor Sakura
Collector's Edition

Cardcaptor Sakura:
Clear Card

Magic Knight Rayearth
25th Anniversary Box Set

Chobits

TSUBASA Omnibus

TSUBASA WoRLD CHRoNiCLE

xxxHOLiC Omnibus

xxxHOLiC Rei

CLOVER Collector's Edition

Kodansha Comics welcomes you to explore the expansive world of CLAMP, the all-female artist collective that has produced some of the most acclaimed manga of the century. Our growing catalog includes icons like *Cardcaptor Sakura* and *Magic Knight Rayearth*, each crafted with CLAMP's one-of-a-kind style and characters!

The art-deco cyberpunk classic from the creators of *xxxHOLiC* and *Cardcaptor Sakura!*

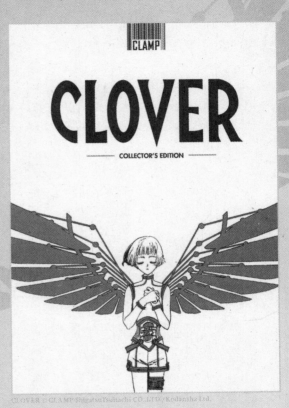

CLOVER © CLAMP ShigatsuTsuitachi CO.,LTD./Kodansha Ltd.

Su was born into a bleak future, where the government keeps tight control over children with magical powers—codenamed "Clovers." With Su being the only "four-leaf" Clover in the world, she has been kept isolated nearly her whole life. Can ex-military agent Kazuhiko deliver her to the happiness she seeks? Experience the complete series in this hardcover edition, which also includes over twenty pages of ravishing color art!

KC
KODANSHA
COMICS

MAGIC ● KNIGHT
RAYEARTH
25TH ANNIVERSARY EDITION
CLAMP

A BELOVED CLASSIC MAKES ITS STUNNING RETURN IN THIS GORGEOUS, LIMITED EDITION BOX SET!

This tale of three Tokyo teenagers who cross through a magical portal and become the champions of another world is a modern manga classic. The box set includes three volumes of manga covering the entire first series of *Magic Knight Rayearth*, plus the series's super-rare full-color art book companion, all printed at a larger size than ever before on premium paper, featuring a newly-revised translation and lettering, and exquisite foil-stamped covers. A strictly limited edition, this will be gone in a flash!